A·N·N·U·A·L E·D·I·T·I·O·N·S

Organizational Behavior

01/02

Second Edition

EDITOR

Fred H. Maidment

Dr. Fred Maidment received a bachelor's degree from New York University in 1970 and a master's degree from Bernard M. Baruch College of the City University of New York. In 1983 he received a doctorate from the University of South Carolina. His research interests include training and development in industry. He resides in Kansas City, Missouri, with his wife and children.

McGraw-Hill/Dushkin
530 Old Whitfield Street, Guilford, Connecticut 06437

Visit us on the Internet
http://www.dushkin.com

Credits

1. Introduction To Organizational Behavior
Unit photo—McGraw-Hill/Dushkin photo by Cheryl Greenleaf.
2. Individual Behavior
Unit photo—© 2000 by PhotoDisc, Inc.
3. Social and Group Process
Unit photo—Courtesy of IBM Microelectronics/Tom Way.
4. Organizational Systems
Unit photo—Courtesy of IBM Microelectronics/Tom Way.
5. Organizational Change and Development
Unit photo—© Blair Seitz/Photo Researchers.

Copyright

Cataloging in Publication Data
Main entry under title: Annual Editions: Organizational Behavior. 2001/2002.
    1. Business enterprises. 2. Employee motivation. 3. Business ethics. I. Maidment, Fred., comp.
II. Title: Organizational behavior.
ISBN 0–07–243312–4   658'.16   ISSN 1525–3600

Second Edition

Cover image © 2001 by PhotoDisc, Inc.

Printed in the United States of America   1234567890BAHBAH54321   Printed on Recycled Paper

To the Reader

In publishing ANNUAL EDITIONS we recognize the enormous role played by the magazines, newspapers, and journals of the public press in providing current, first-rate educational information in a broad spectrum of interest areas. Many of these articles are appropriate for students, researchers, and professionals seeking accurate, current material to help bridge the gap between principles and theories and the real world. These articles, however, become more useful for study when those of lasting value are carefully collected, organized, indexed, and reproduced in a low-cost format, which provides easy and permanent access when the material is needed. That is the role played by ANNUAL EDITIONS.

New to ANNUAL EDITIONS is the inclusion of related World Wide Web sites. These sites have been selected by our editorial staff to represent some of the best resources found on the World Wide Web today. Through our carefully developed topic guide, we have linked these Web resources to the articles covered in this ANNUAL EDITIONS reader. We think that you will find this volume useful, and we hope that you will take a moment to visit us on the Web at *http://www.dushkin.com* to tell us what you think.

This is the second edition of *Annual Editions: Organizational Behavior*. This book is a compilation of some of the most current research and articles in the field of organizational behavior. Articles have been selected from a wide variety of sources including: *The Harvard Business Review, Organizational Dynamics, The Academy of Management Journal,* and *Business Horizons.* We think you will find this collection to be a useful source of current educational materials in organizational behavior.

Annual Editions: Organizational Behavior contains a number of features designed to make it a useful tool for people interested in organizational behavior. These include a *topic guide* for locating articles on specific subjects, a *table of contents* with abstracts that summarize each article, and *World Wide Web* sites that can be used to further explore topics that are addressed in the essays. These sites are cross-referenced by number in the topic guide. The volume is organized into five units, each dealing with specific interrelated topics in organizational behavior. The overviews at the beginning of each section provide the reader with the necessary background information that allows the reader to place the selections in the context of the book. Also, at the end of each section are short exercises for use in the instructional setting, which are designed to illustrate selected topics from the section.

This is the second edition of *Annual Editions: Organizational Behavior,* and we hope that it will be a part of a long line of books addressing the most current developments in the field. This collection, we believe, provides the reader with the most current selection of readings available on the subject. Please take a few minutes to complete the article rating form in the back of the volume. Anything can be improved, and your comments will be important to the process of improving *Annual Editions: Organizational Behavior.*

Fred Maidment

Editor

Contents

UNIT 1

Introduction to Organizational Behavior

Four articles in this section review
the organizational paradigms and
development of industry. Also
considered are the relations of
the individual in the workplace.

UNIT 2

Individual Behavior

In this section, seven selections examine diversity in the workforce, organizational policies, ethical issues, motivation, and mentoring programs.

The concepts in bold italics are developed in the article. For further expansion please refer to the Topic Guide and the Index.

UNIT 3

Social and Group Process

Seven articles discuss how groups interact with regard to networking, establishing relationships, communication, negotiation, and team dynamics.

The concepts in bold italics are developed in the article. For further expansion please refer to the Topic Guide and the Index.

UNIT 4

Organizational Systems

Eight articles in this section examine the dynamics of organizational designs, external influences on the organization, training, the impact of women on the workplace, the significance of human resources, and the importance of commitment.

The concepts in bold italics are developed in the article. For further expansion please refer to the Topic Guide and the Index.

UNIT 5

Organizational Change and Development

In this section, three selections
examine the importance of
developing a learning organization, merger integration,
and the importance of
stress management.

The concepts in bold italics are developed in the article. For further expansion please refer to the Topic Guide and the Index.

1

This topic guide suggests how the selections and World Wide Web sites found in the next section of this book relate to topics of traditional concern to organizational behavior students and professionals. It is useful for locating interrelated articles and Web sites for reading and research. The guide is arranged alphabetically according to topic.

The relevant Web sites, which are numbered and annotated on pages 4 and 5, are easily identified by the Web icon (◉) under the topic articles. By linking the articles and the Web sites by topic, this ANNUAL EDITIONS reader becomes a powerful learning and research tool.

TOPIC AREA	TREATED IN	TOPIC AREA	TREATED IN
Communication	2. New Frontier 4. Toxic Handler 5. Cultural Diversity 6. Individual and Organizational Accountabilities 8. Beauty of the Organizational Beast 10. Guide Lines 12. Networks Within Networks 13. Identifying Who Matters 14. Passing the Word 15. Leadership A to Z 17. Interest Alignment 18. Team Structure and Performance 21. Creating a Hybrid Organizational Form from Parental Blueprints 22. Telework 23. Knowledge Transfer 25. Managing Social Capital 26. Effects of Leadership Style 27. Building Teams Across Borders 28. Less Stress, More Productivity 29. Desperately Seeking Synergy ◉ *1, 2, 5, 6, 7, 16, 17, 18, 19, 20, 21*		7. Walking the Tightrope 10. Motivation: The Value of a Work Ethic 10. Guide Lines 11. Managing Oneself 19. Structure-Driven Strategy 24. Future That Has Already Happened 22. Telework 23. Knowledge Transfer 24. What Do CEO's Want From HR? 28. Less Stress, More Productivity ◉ *1, 2, 3, 4, 5, 6, 8, 9, 10, 11, 12, 14, 15, 19, 21, 23, 24, 25, 27*
Diversity	1. Shifting Paradigms 2. New Frontier 3. Employer Sanctions 5. Cultural Diversity 6. Individual and Organizational Accountabilities 12. Networks Within Networks 13. Identifying Who Matters 17. Interest Alignment 24. Future That Has Already Happened 22. Telework 25. Managing Social Capital 26. Effects of Leadership Style 27. Building Teams Across Borders 29. Desperately Seeking Synergy ◉ *2, 4, 9, 10, 11, 12, 14, 15, 30*	**Leadership**	1. Shifting Paradigms 2. New Frontier 4. Toxic Handler 7. Walking the Tightrope 13. Identifying Who Matters 15. Leadership A to Z 16. Manager as Political Leader 18. Team Structure and Performance 19. Structure-Driven Strategy 20. Future That Has Already Happened 21. Creating a Hybrid Organizational Form From Parental Blueprints 23. Knowledge Transfer 24. What Do CEO's Want From HR? 25. Managing Social Capital 27. Building Teams Across Borders 29. Desperately Seeking Synergy ◉ *5, 6, 17, 19, 26, 27, 28, 29*
Group Behavior	1. Shifting Paradigm 2. New Frontier 4. Toxic Handler 5. Cultural Diversity 6. Individual and Organizational Accountabilities 7. Walking the Tightrope 8. Beauty of the Organizational Beast 12. Networks Within Networks 13. Identifying Who Matters 14. Passing the Word 16. Mananger as Political Leader 17. Interest Alignment 18. Team Structure and Performance 21. Creating a Hybrid Organizational Form From Parental Blueprints 25. Managing Social Capital 26. Effects of Leadership Style and Followers' Cultural Orientation 27. Building Teams Across Borders 29. Desperately Seeking Synergy ◉ *1, 2, 5, 6, 9, 16, 17, 18, 19, 20, 21*	**Morale**	1. Shifting Paradigms 2. New Frontier 3. Employer Sanctions 4. Toxic Handlers 6. Individual and Organizational Accountability 7. Walking the Tightrope 8. Beauty of the Organizational Beast 9. Motivation: The Value of a Work Ethic 14. Passing the Word 18. Team Structure and Performance 20. Future That Has Already Happened 22. Telework 25. Managing Social Capital 26. Effects of Leadership Style 27. Building Teams Across Borders 28. Less Stress, More Productivity 29. Desperately Seeking Synergy ◉ *1, 2, 5, 6, 9, 19, 23, 24, 25, 30*
Human Resources	1. Shifting Paradigms 2. New Frontier 3. Employer Sanctions 6. Individual and Organizational Accountabilities	**Organizational Development and Change**	1. Shifting Paradigms 2. New Frontier 5. Cultural Diversity 6. Individual and Organizational Accountabilities 7. Walking the Tightrope 8. Beauty of the Organizational Beast 10. Guide Lines 11. Managing Oneself 12. Networks Within Networks 13. Identifying Who Matters 16. Manager as Political Leader 18. Team Structure and Performance

TOPIC AREA	TREATED IN	TOPIC AREA	TREATED IN
	19. Structure-Driven Strategy	**Trust**	1. Shifting Paradigms
	20. Future That Has Already Happened		2. New Frontier
	21. Creating a Hybrid Organizational Form From Parental Blueprints		3. Employer Sanctions
	22. Telework		4. Toxic Handler
	23. Knowledge Transfer		6. Individual and Organizational Accountabilities
	24. What Do CEO's Want From HR?		7. Walking the Tightrope
	25. Managing Social Capital		10. Guide Lines
	26. Effects of Leadership Style		12. Networks Within Networks
	27. Building Teams Across Borders		14. Passing the Word
	29. Desperately Seeking Synergy		15. Leadership A to Z
	4, 5, 6, 8, 9, 10, 11, 12, 14, 15, 16, 17, 18, 19, 20, 22, 26, 27, 28, 29, 30		16. Manager as Political Leader
			17. Interest Alignment
Politics	3. Employer Sanctions		18. Team Structure and Performance
	4. Toxic Handler		22. Telework
	5. Cultural Diversity		25. Managing Social Capital
	6. Individual and Organizational Accountabilities		26. Effects of Leadership Style
	7. Walking the Tightrope		27. Building Teams Across Borders
	8. Beauty of the Organizational Beast		28. Less Stress, More Productivity
	10. Guide Lines		29. Desperately Seeking Synergy
	11. Managing Oneself		*1, 2, 6, 7, 9, 16, 17, 18, 19, 20, 21, 26, 27, 28, 29, 30*
	12. Networks Within Networks		
	13. Identifying Who Matters	**Values and Ethics**	2. New Frontier
	14. Passing the Word		3. Employer Sanctions
	16. Manager as Political Leader		4. Toxic Handler
	17. Interest Alignment		6. Individual and Organizational Accountabilities
	18. Team Structure and Performance		7. Walking the Tightrope
	22. Telework		8. Beauty of the Organizational Beast
	25. Managing Social Capital		9. Motivation: The Value of a Work Ethic
	26. Effects of Leadership Style		10. Guide Lines
	27. Building Teams Across Borders		11. Managing Oneself
	29. Desperately Seeking Synergy		13. Identifying Who Matters
	5, 6, 7, 13, 16, 17, 18, 19, 23, 24, 25		14. Passing the Word
			15. Leadership A to Z
Teams	1. Shifting Paradigms		16. Manager as Political Leader
	2. New Frontier		22. Telework
	6. Individual and Organizational Accountabilities		25. Managing Social Capital
	8. Beauty of the Organizational Beast		29. Desperately Seeking Synergy
	10. Guide Lines		*6, 7, 9, 10, 11, 12, 14, 15*
	11. Managing Oneself		
	12. Networks Within Networks		
	13. Identifying Who Matters		
	16. Manager as Political Leader		
	17. Interest Alignment		
	18. Team Structure and Performance		
	21. Creating a Hybrid Organizational Form From Parental Blueprints		
	23. Knowledge Transfer		
	26. Effects of Leadership Style		
	27. Building Teams Across Borders		
	29. Desperately Seeking Synergy		
	1, 2, 4, 6, 16, 17, 18, 19, 20, 21, 26, 27, 28, 29		

● AE: Organizational Behavior

The following World Wide Web sites have been carefully researched and selected to support the articles found in this reader. If you are interested in learning more about specific topics found in this book, these Web sites are a good place to start. The sites are cross-referenced by number and appear in the topic guide on the previous two pages. Also, you can link to these Web sites through our DUSHKIN ONLINE support site at *http://www.dushkin.com/online/*.

The following sites were available at the time of publication. Visit our Web site—we update DUSHKIN ONLINE regularly to reflect any changes.

General Sources

1. American Psychological Association
http://www.apa.org/books/homepage.html
Search this site to find references and discussion of important workplace issues for the 1990s and beyond, including restructuring and revitalization of businesses.

2. Human Resource Professional's Gateway to the Internet
http://www.hrisolutions.com/index2.html
Eric Wilson's site is rich with information about human resources management and links easily to additional Web sources.

3. HVL HR Internet Resources
http://www.hvl.net/hr_res.htm
This site covers topics that range from Benefits, to Salary Information, to Recruiting and Training.

4. Voice of the Shuttle
http://vos.ucsb.edu/shuttle/commerce.html
Information on many subjects includes Restructuring, Reengineering, Downsizing, Flattening; Outsourcing; Human Resources Management; Labor Relations; Learning Organizations; The Team Concept; and Diversity Management.

Introduction to Organizational Behavior

5. Center for Organizational Theory (COT)
http://socrates.berkeley.edu/~iir/cot/cot.html
COT was founded in 1995 at the Institute of Industrial Relations at the University of California, Berkeley. Its major research project centers on the demography of corporations and industries and organizational processes. Programs, publications and Web sites are available at this site.

6. Industrial-Organizational Psychology Resource Center
http://www.cs.ius.indiana.edu/LZ/PMCCARTH/web_docs/homepage.htm
Dr. Patrick McCarthy's site is for new students and experienced professionals alike. Both will find many valuable resources here, including documents and information on numerous industrial-organizational psychology topics of interest.

7. Monograph: Trust Within the Organization
http://www.psc-cfp.gc.ca/prcb/mono1-e.htm
This interesting monograph from the Public Service Commission of Canada concludes that trust is an essential element of effective change management and, ultimately, organizational success.

8. Society for Human Resource Management (SHRM) HR Links
http://www.shrm.org/hrlinks/
Here is a very complete collection of links that includes topics such as Diversity, Flexible Work Arrangements, International HR, and Management Practices. From this starting point, explore other aspects of SHRM also.

Individual Behavior

9. American Civil Liberties Union (ACLU)
http://www.aclu.org/issues/worker/campaign.html
The ACLU provides this interesting page on workplace rights in "Campaign for Fairness in the Workplace." Briefing papers on workplace issues cover issues of lifestyle discrimination, workplace drug testing, and electronic monitoring.

10. Career Magazine: Diversity Works in the Workplace
http://www.careermag.com/newsarts/diversity/fed.html
This keynote address by David Clark of Federated Department Stores offers seven indicators of an employer's genuine commitment to diversity.

11. Diversity in the Workforce
http://www.consciouschoice.com/issues/cc083/workdiv.html
This article by Lisa Stewart appeared in the magazine *Conscious Choice* and provides interesting reading on the issue of diversity in the workplace.

12. Diversity in Workforce Produces Bottom Line Benefits
http://www.villagelife.org/news/archives/diversity.html
Melissa Lauber's short article following the $176 million discrimination settlement with Texaco is presented here. Related Web sites are also available at this site.

13. Knowledge Management and Organizational Learning
http://www.brint.com/OrgLrng.htm
BRINT, the BizTech Network, provides this exhaustive site that covers definitions, discussions, and data mining, and it presents unlimited resources on organizational learning and learning organizations and out-of-box thinking.

14. Report on Workforce Diversity
http://www.fs.fed.us/land/fire/difference.htm
At this site, an update and revitalization of Fire and Aviation Management's efforts to improve workforce diversity is available. The report offers key recommendations for revitalizing the human resource specialist's position that can be adapted by other companies.

15. Workforce Diversity Plan for ORNL
http://www.ornl.gov/HR_ORNL/WFD/plan_pub.htm
Oak Ridge National Laboratory's (ORNL) report concerns diversity leadership in order to achieve mission success "in a rapidly changing scientific business and political environ-

ment through the unique strengths of our employees, community, and business partners."

Social and Group Process

16. IIR Library Site Map
http://socrates.berkeley.edu/~iir/sitemap.html
This site map of the Institute of Industrial Relations at the University of California, Berkeley, points out research planned by the Center for Culture, Organization, and Politics, the Center for Organization and Human Resource Effectiveness, and the Center for Work, Technology, and Society.

17. Journal of Organizational Behavior: Aims and Scope
http://www.interscience.wiley.com/jpages/ 0894-3796/aims.html
The Journal of Organizational Behavior reports on the growing research in organization behavior fields throughout the world. Topics include motivation, work performance, job design, quality of work life, training, leadership, and many more.

18. Teams, Teambuilding, and Teamwork
http://www.organizedchange.com/teamhome.htm
Here is a source for articles on teams that are accessible on the Internet. Titles include "Improving Cross-Functional Teamwork" and "Nailing Jelly to a Tree: Self-Directed Work Teams," among many others.

Organizational Systems

19. Center for Organization and Human Resource Effectiveeess
http://socrates.berkeley.edu/~iir/cohre/cohre.html
From this COHRE page navigate to Brief Policy Papers, Research in Progress, and a Virtual Library. The Center is dedicated to "anticipating and creating new responses to a continuously changing business environment."

20. Global Business Network (GBN)
http://www.gbn.org
Committed to perceiving the present in order to anticipate the future and better manage strategic responses, the GBN's activities and services are designed to think collaboratively about the business environment. GBN originates scenario planning and offers help with the process online.

21. Human Resources—Corporate Culture
http://www.auxillium.com/culture.htm
This site offers a short paper on corporate culture. It includes the Hofstede Cultural Orientation Model, which classifies cultures based on where they fall on five continuums.

Organizational Change and Development

22. Job Stress Network: Researchers Link Job Strain, Hypertension
http://www.workhealth.org/news/nwprahn98.html
Among the interesting research pieces available at this site is this one on stress by John Martin of America's Health Network.

23. APA HelpCenter: Get the Facts: Psychology at Work: Stress in the Workplace
http://helping.apa.org/work/stress5.html
This selection is adapted from *The Stress Solution* by Lyle Miller and Alma Dell Smith, and it is offered by the American Psychological Association.

24. Canadian Institute of Stress
http://www.stresscanada.org/wman.html
In this selection, which focuses on "corporate vitality," you are invited to evaluate "How Fit for Change" any particular workforce is when compared to 100 North American workplaces. Learn about change management programs here.

25. Employer-Employee.com: Preventing and Curing Employee Burnout
http://www.employer-employee.com/Burnout.html
This article offers suggestions for how to tell whether an employee problem is burnout and, if so, how to deal with it.

26. Organisation and Management Theory
http://www.nbs.ntu.ac.uk/staff/lyerj/list/hromt.htm
This part of Ray Lye's list of Human Resource Management Resources on the Internet includes links to Learning Organisation, Research at Harvard Business School, Human Change by Design, Learning and Change, and Organisations.

27. Organizational Behavior Resources
http://www.graceland.edu/~dungan/org-be/ resources_org-be.html
Andy Dungan keeps this Internet list on organizational behavior and human resource management research resources at Graceland College. Links include organizational behavior sources, an essay on corporate culture, material on organizational development, and a site on quality management principles.

28. Organized Change Consultancy
http://www.organizedchange.com/framesetindex.htm
This selection from an international consulting and training firm includes a useful miniquiz for evaluating companies, many articles, and a topical index.

29. Researching Organisational Change and Learning
http://www.nova.edu/ssss/QR/QR2-4/rhodes.html
Carl Rhodes's paper offers a qualitative narrative approach to organizational change and learning.

30. Studies in Cultures, Organizations, and Societies
http://www.ucalgary.ca/~cancomm/studies.html
A scholarly forum for critical debate on the culture and symbolism of everyday life in organizations can be accessed here.

We highly recommend that you review our Web site for expanded information and our other product lines. We are continually updating and adding links to our Web site in order to offer you the most usable and useful information that will support and expand the value of your Annual Editions. You can reach us at: *http://www.dushkin. com/annualeditions/*.

Unit Selections

1. **Shifting Paradigms: From Newton to Chaos,** Toby J. Tetenbaum
2. **The New Frontier: Transformation of Management for the New Millennium,** Michael A. Hitt
3. **Employer Sanctions Against Immigrant Workers,** Muzaffar Chishti
4. **The Toxic Handler: Organizational Hero—and Casualty,** Peter Frost and Sandra Robinson

Key Points to Consider

❖ How do you see the environment changing for organizations and their employees? What do you think their response will be to that change?

❖ How do you think employer/employee relations will change in the future?

 **Links**   **www.dushkin.com/online/**

5. **Center for Organizational Theory (COT)**
   http://socrates.berkeley.edu/~iir/cot/cot.html
6. **Industrial-Organizational Psychology Resource Center**
   http://www.cs.ius.indiana.edu/LZ/PMCCARTH/web_docs/homepage.htm
7. **Monograph: Trust Within the Organization**
   http://www.psc-cfp.gc.ca/prcb/mono1-e.htm
8. **Society for Human Resource Management (SHRM) HR Links**
   http://www.shrm.org/hrlinks/

These sites are annotated on pages 4 and 5.

Organizations are made up of people—not machines, balance sheets, or buildings. For an organization to be successful in today's highly competitive global environment, it must rely on its people.

For most organizations, competitive advantage is not found in technology. Indeed, most organizations in any given industry are operating with essentially the same technology as the others. Competitive advantage founded on technology is often transitory at best and deceptive at worst, especially as the pace of technological change quickens and today's cutting edge technology becomes tomorrow's obsolete equipment.

Organizations themselves must recognize that they are bound to change over time, if for no other reason than the fact that their personnel will change over time. It bears repeating that a corporation is a collection of individuals with different and varied talents, all seeking to achieve success in their daily lives, which includes their role in the company.

The only thing that is certain for any organization, today, is that things are changing. In the past, most organizations and people viewed the world in a sort of linear context, which meant that certain events depended on certain other events in order for them to happen. This linear view of the world can be traced back to one of the first modern scientists, Isaac Newton, who developed the intellectual basis for most of the world's scientific and intellectual development over the past 400 years. However, that linear approach to the world, as is the case with Newtonian physics, no longer necessarily applies. Just as Newton's physics was replaced by that of Albert Einstein's because it was inadequate to explain what scientists were observing in the real world, so the linear explanation of reality is about to be replaced. It is no accident that a recent business best-seller by Tom Peters was entitled *Thriving on Chaos* (Park Avenue Press, 1999). The old idea of "if X, then Y" is obsolete. Now the new paradigm amounts to "if X, then who knows what will follow," which Toby Tetenbaum discusses in "Shifting Paradigms: From Newton to Chaos."

The question in organizational behavior is how to deal with these rapid and unpredictable changes in the organization, and, of course, in society as a whole. Personal, internal values and ethics are the only true source of guidance in an environment marked by chaos. There is no great guiding beacon of light that can be used to navigate the world of work, no lighthouse of knowledge or techniques that can magically transform chaos into order. "The New Frontier: Transformation of Management for the New Millennium" (see article 2) will be determined by people who are true to themselves and their own set of values if they want to have an impact on their organizations.

This change, this chaos in the organizational environment, has led to a great deal of change on the part of employees who are simply responding to and trying to make some sense out of what is essentially a chaotic world. The old rules are gone. People simply do not work for an organization for 40 years and get a gold watch at the end of their working lives. Employees are no longer loyal to the organization in the old sense because the organization is no longer loyal to them. In the current environment, employees are trying to develop and prepare themselves for what is likely to happen next. They will remain loyal if they perceive that it is in their interest to remain with the organization. Otherwise, they will move on.

Perhaps the single greatest loss for organizations in their relations with their employees has been trust. During the era of downsizing, rightsizing, reengineering, and RIFs (reduction in force), trust has been lost in many organizations. When whole departments and divisions are simply eliminated in a maniacal frenzy of cost cutting, the employees, both those discharged and those retained, can only conclude that their individual efforts, successes, accomplishments, and concerns are of little or no consequence to the organization. The only thing that the company cares about is the short-term bottom line. Trust is thrown to the winds, and employees are left to fend for themselves.

As the twenty-first century begins, the American economy has the lowest unemployment in over 20 years, and the lowest unemployment rate among industrialized nations. Jobs are plentiful and often go begging because there are not enough qualified people to fill them. Wages are up and unemployment is down, but many employees are in a bad mood. Griping, lawsuits, and even violence are increasing because there is a gap between what organizations say and what they do. Many organizations may "talk the talk" but seem unable to "walk the walk" when the time comes. These unfulfilled expectations and promises on the part of the organization create an atmosphere of distrust. Putting the right spin on something has become more important than dealing with it in a straightforward manner. Firings become "reengineering," and layoffs, "rightsizing." Black becomes white in an almost Orwellian attempt at what amounts to "doublespeak." Machiavelli said that "people do not want the truth, they want to be comforted." But if you are not going to tell them the truth, do not make it so obvious. People quickly see through phonies.

Some employees find themselves placed in the position of having to act as a buffer between seemingly irrational acts on the part of management and the rest of the organization. The "Toxic Handler" (see article 4) plays an important role in the organization, but often pays a high price for his or her efforts. Most organizations need these people, but they are often abused and a consequence of their actions is often burnout.

People have learned that all is not as it seems and that organizations will quickly turn on people. Some organizations will even abuse the intent of the law to try to control their employees, as discussed in "Employer Sanctions Against Immigrant Workers." People have become cynical because they have been treated with disrespect and an obvious attitude that they, as individuals, do not matter. Is it any wonder that they have become distrustful, cynical, and angry?

But, like many situations, things are neither as dark or light as they seem. While the unspoken contract between employers and employees may have forever been torn, a new relationship is developing, based upon the expectation that people will move on and that organizations will change. The degree and amount of uncertainty has, indeed, increased, but so have the opportunities available to employees and employers. Both parties are developing an understanding that the future will be based on what the opportunities are, not on what has happened in the past.

Employees and their organizations must learn to be more flexible and responsive to a changing and chaotic environment that guarantees nothing, but will handsomely reward those willing and able to take advantage of the opportunities presented to them.

Introduction to Organizational Behavior

Shifting Paradigms:
From Newton to Chaos

Chaos theory shows us a world far more complex and unpredictable than Newton's physics can explain. Can we apply the theory to organizations?

Toby J. Tetenbaum

Chaos often breeds life,
When order breeds havoc.

—Henry Brooks Adams

Chaos theory and its spin-off, complexity theory, argue that relationships in complex systems, like organizations, are non-linear, made up of interconnections and branching choices that produce unintended consequences and render the universe unpredictable. Can this theory, now widely discussed in the scientific community, provide a new, more accurate lens for viewing organizations? Or is it something useful for physicists, with no application to management?

Various commentators have suggested that this new paradigm can be useful in dealing with current and future change in organizations. Using this lens, however, presents an unprecedented challenge for change agents in all types of organizations. The new realities differ dramatically from the past.

THE TRADITIONAL WORLD OF NEWTON

Newtonian science, the underpinning of civilization from the 1700s to the present, is rooted in physics and mathematics—rule-bound disciplines that require data "up front"

in order to operate. The core of the paradigm, the laws of motion, suggests that the world is a well-behaved machine. It offers the promise of a law-abiding and predictable universe, a belief strengthened by the notion that relationships between cause and effect are simple, clear, and linear. The "if X . . . , then Y" view of the world prevailed for two centuries, delighting scientists whose ultimate goal was to predict and control.

When we entered the industrial era, the lens of Newtonian science led us to look at organizational success in terms of maintaining a stable system. If nature or crisis upset this state, the leader's role was to reestablish equilibrium. Not to do so constituted failure. With stability as the sign of success, the paradigm implied that order should be imposed from above (leading to top-down, command-and-control leadership) and structures should be designed to support the decision makers (leading to bureaucracies and hierarchies). The reigning organizational model, scientific management, was wholly consistent with ensuring regularity, predictability, and efficiency.

When the future is viewed as predictable, organizations do well to send their top leaders off on a retreat where they can envision a future state and develop a long-range plan for realizing that vision. The leaders have various planning models at their disposal, some of which have been used effectively for years;

 Originally from *Organizational Dynamics,* Spring 1998, pp. 21-33. © 1998 by Elsevier Science. Reprinted with permission.

however, it may well be that their success has been more serendipitous than purposeful, a function of relatively quiescent times. But as the speed of change increases and as the complexities of life and of the workplace expand, the assumptions underlying models such as these, as well as traditional views of organizations and their leadership, will no longer tolerate violation. They rely too heavily on a belief in linearity and predictability.

Toby J. Tetenbaum founded Toby Tetenbaum and Associates, a consulting firm specializing in organizational behavior. Her clients include Exxon, Ciba-Geigy, Automatic Data Processing (ADP), United Water Resources, Conde Nast Publications, The New York Times Broadcasting Company, Guardian Insurance, Fidelity Investments, Fuji, TIAA-CREF, Merrill Lynch, and many colleges and universities.

Dr. Tetenbaum has designed and implemented programs and interventions in areas of management development, strategic planning, developing corporate culture, and managing change. She has created and implemented program evaluations and conducted qualitative research studies in organizations. She has also conducted workshops and seminars in various areas of organizational behavior, including leadership, interpersonal communication, managing and changing behavior, group dynamics and team building, and managing conflict.

Dr. Tetenbaum received her doctorate from New York University in educational psychology with a specialization in social psychology and research methodologies. Her post-doctoral studies at Harvard University focused on the interface between organizational behavior and management. A licensed psychologist, she has been a professor at Fordham University for 20 years where she initiated and directs the human resource education masters degree program. She has conducted research and published extensively in national and international journals.

THE NEW, NONLINEAR WORLD OF WORK

The shift from an industrial to information age has altered the nature of the workplace, the worker, and the work. Industrial era workers were located primarily in urban factories where they engaged in routine work, often on an assembly line. They worked a specific shift, punched a time clock, and performed tasks under close supervision. A "good" worker was one who was reliable and passive, capable of modest manual dexterity.

In contrast, thanks to modern technology, information era workers can be located anywhere and can conduct much of their work anytime. A telecommuter can be with his or her children after school and make up the work in the evening after the children are in bed. The prized worker is one who learns quickly and continuously, who works collaboratively, and who is comfortable in an environment of experimentation and risk. The new knowledge workers perform their work largely without supervision, and those who are engaged in collaborative efforts do so as members of self-managed teams.

It would seem obvious that these two worlds cannot operate effectively under the same set of guiding principles.

Characteristics of the 21st Century

As we enter the new millennium, the differences with the past are exacerbated by the context in which organizations operate. Organizations must now contend with six primary characteristics:

1 **Technology.** The infomedia industries (computers, communications, and consumer electronics) are capitalized at $3 trillion. It is not surprising, therefore, that whereas there were only 50,000 computers 20 years ago, that many are now installed daily. In 1994, 2.2 million people were on the World Wide Web. One year later, there were 6.6 million. Almost 20 million people own cellular phones and/or carry pagers. The new technologies increase efficiency, productivity, speed of production, and consumer power.

2 **Globalization.** Today everyone is interconnected in the flow of information, money, or goods. Between 1987 and 1992, the market value of U.S. investment abroad rose 35 percent to $776 billion. In 1994 alone, Americans bought $663 billion overseas. Foreign investment in the U.S. more than doubled between 1987 and 1992 to $692 billion. It is clear that our interdependencies are increasing.

3 **Competition.** Globalization and technology have led businesses to compete fiercely for market share. American icons such as the Eastman Kodak Company are finding their market share eroding on their home front. Japanese-owned Fuji, with newly built plants on American soil, has continually grabbed business from Kodak in both color film and photographic paper. The once proud auto industry has suffered as well. In 1950, America had 76 percent of the world's motor vehicle production. In 1995, our share had fallen to 25 percent.

4 **Change.** Today's changes are discontinuous and happening at a geometric rate. Organizations must be sufficiently agile to be instantly reconfigurable to meet new demands. The disequilibrium created is unprecedented in our history.

5 **Speed.** In 1946, the first computer, ENIAC, was capable of calculating 5,000 basic arithmetic operations per second, which was thought to be astounding. Today's 486 microprocessor, already being eclipsed by the Pentium chip, is capable of handling 54 million instructions per second. This incredible increase in technological speed is matched in business (product life cycles are measured in months not years) and in people's lives (most of us feel we are running as fast as we can merely to stay in place).

6 **Complexity and Paradox.** All of these factors contribute to the complex nature of our current existence, a situation reflected in the eruption of paradoxes that confront us. (See Exhibit 1 for examples of current organizational paradoxes.) Charles Handy predicts that paradoxes will be ubiquitous in the new millennium and will present a significant challenge to managers. As Gareth Morgan notes:

The management of organizations, of society, and of personal life ultimately involves the management of contradiction. . . .The choice that individuals and societies ultimately have before them is thus really a choice about the kind of contradiction that is to shape the pattern of daily life.

The conflicting choices or conditions that are the essence of paradox make most people uncomfortable, enveloping them in the ambiguity that attends the perceived need to choose between seeming bipolar opposites. It is human nature to prefer, to seek out, and even to expect certainty. Paradoxes threaten that world order. A common way to handle this unpleasant state is to "fix" on one polarity and to see the world as "either/or" rather than to reconcile the two polarities with "both/and" thinking.

Nowhere is this more prevalent than in managers' choice of order to the exclusion of disorder. While this option served them well in the 20th century industrial era, continuation of that practice will be a disservice in the 21st century. Tom Peters captured the essence of the situation a decade ago when he observed that we'd spent the past 40 years teaching people to create order out of chaos, but would have to spend the next 10 years teaching people to create chaos out of order. In fact, we have spent so much time teaching our organizations to be systematized and orderly that now they can't respond to the fast-changing environment.

CHAOS: THE NEW PARADIGM

Tom Peters did not use the term "chaos" gratuitously. He was on the cutting edge of a new order. The Newtonian vision of an orderly universe no longer exists.

The new world is full of unintended consequences and counterintuitive outcomes. In such a world, the map to the future cannot be drawn in advance. We cannot know enough to set forth a meaningful vision or to plan productively. In fact, engaging in such activities in the belief that we can predict the future and, to a degree, control it, is probably both illusory and dangerous, in that it allows a false and potentially debilitating sense of security.

The focus of chaos is the web of feedback loops present in every system. In some systems, the feedback loops are linear; in others, nonlinear. Business organizations, because they are made up of people and, hence, are highly complex, are nonlinear feedback systems. Feedback loops can be negative, pro-

EXHIBIT 1

PARADOXES FOR LEADERS AND ORGANIZATIONS IN THE 21ST CENTURY

Long-term and short-term	Independence and interdependence
Plan and experiment	People and productivity
Revenue growth and cost containment	Empowerment and accountability
Lower costs and increase quality	People skills and technical skills
Centralize and decentralize	Conflict and consensus
Product and process	Compete and cooperate
Creativity and efficiency	Stability and change
Core competency and diversification	Incremental and quantum
Specialist and generalist	Predictability and unpredictability
Entrepreneur and team player	Simplicity and complexity
Lead and follow	Intention and chance
Manager and leader	Regularity and irregularity
Take charge and everyone's a leader	Order and disorder

ducing stable equilibrium, or positive, producing unstable equilibrium. At their border, these two contradictory forces, operating simultaneously, pull the system in opposite directions. Scientists have discovered that, at this border area, where chaos lies, feedback autonomously flips between positive and negative, generating patterns that are neither stable nor unstable, but rather a paradoxical combination of both.

Chaos as Order

For the non-scientist, the term "chaos" conjures up images of a birthday party for 20 four-year-olds, or an airport terminal when runways have closed down in a blizzard, or a shopping mall on Christmas Eve. These images lead us to see chaos as synonymous with confusion, disarray, and pandemonium.

Scientists have learned that chaos is none of these. Rather, chaos describes a complex, unpredictable, and orderly disorder in which patterns of behavior unfold in *irregular but similar* forms. Consider, for example the regular irregularity of snowflakes: an always-recognizable six-sided figure, but each snowflake unique.

Similarly, every human is different, but we know one when we see one. Ralph Stacey calls this "bounded equilibrium" and Dee Hock, futurist and founder of Visa, calls it "chaordic," a combination of chaos plus order. As Hock puts it, "In chaordic systems, order emerges. Structure evolves. Life is a recognizable pattern within infinite diversity."

Chaos as a Self-Organizing Entity

Hock's words "emerges" and "evolves" are highly significant and at the core of chaos theory. In fact, they are what make chaos theory so intriguing: While irregular and unpredictable, the patterns that emerge from chaos have a "hidden" recognizable form. Chaos is actually constrained by the rules that govern it. If we can identify the rules, we can forecast the conditions under which the chaotic behavior will occur.

Waldrop describes research conducted by Craig Reynolds in 1987 in a nuclear physics lab in Los Alamos, New Mexico. Reynolds simulated bird-flocking behavior, having bird-like objects called "boids" fly together in a flock following only three rules: (1) fly in the direction of other objects, (2) try to match velocity with neighboring boids, and (3) avoid bumping into things. He found that the boids, forced to break apart to avoid an obstacle, soon regrouped into a new formation even though nothing about their programming told them to display this collective behavior. This demonstrates the essence of chaos theory; namely, that simple agents obeying simple rules can interact to create elaborate and unexpected behaviors.

Geographical economic development provides a real life example of this paradox of rules and randomness. How did Silicon Valley come into being? Its existence can be attributed largely to the intersection of distinguished research centers at Stanford and the University of California at Berkeley and the availability of skilled labor. While Silicon Valley is unique, other high-tech economic areas have emerged in Austin, Texas, the Triangle Research Center of North Carolina, and Route 128 outside Boston. Their emergence shares a commonality with Silicon Valley; namely, that they, too, arose in areas providing excellent educational institutions and skilled labor. Thus, while these centers differ from one another, clear patterns can be detected: The availability of advanced technology attracts electronics manufacturers which, in turn, attracts component suppliers and support companies.

The "rules" or common features in these patterns of geographical economic development would seem to suggest that they can be deliberately created, yet when governments attempt to artificially create these geographic concentrations, they often fail. One reason for this is that chaos is self-organizing. No individual was in charge of creating a high-tech industry. Silicon Valley "emerged." It is a prime example of how spontaneous self-organizing systems produce extraordinary outcomes out of chaos.

The global marketplace is another self-organizing system. No one is in charge of the market, yet considerable coherence emerges from millions of independent, but connected, decisions. The Internet is yet another example. No one is in charge of this mammoth entity, which is still in the process of evolving.

Margaret Wheatley explains the self-organizing concept in simple terms: "Life seeks order in a disorderly way . . . mess upon mess until something workable emerges." Whereas a Newtonian view of the world imposes structure on an organization from above, the biological model, represented by chaos theory, views the organization as a living, self-organizing system; complex and self-adaptive. It suggests that if you set a group of people in motion, each one following the right set of three or four simple rules, then, like the "boids" in Reynolds' study, they will spontaneously self-organize into something complex and unexpected.

Self-Organization and Emergent Change in Companies

Visa is an example of a self-organizing company. It has grown 10,000% since 1970 and is a trillion dollar business serving over half a billion people. It consists of 20,000 financial institutions operating in more than 200 countries and territories and has a staff of about 3,000 in 21 offices on four continents.

Despite its size and growth, you don't know where it's located, how it's operated, or who owns it. That's because Visa is decentralized, non-hierarchical, evolving, self-organizing, and self-regulating. Founded by Dee Hock, it is a chaordic system conceived as an organization solely on the basis of purpose and principle. Its structure evolved from them. Hock is a prime proponent of chaordic organizations and argues that the way organizations should develop is to imagine the world as it ought to be and behave accordingly.

Chaos theory is potentially threatening to organizations, particularly to those that are large and traditional, owing to the risk involved in the concept of self-organization. The concept has a prime audience, however, in the newer, smaller entrepreneurial companies whose workforces are made up of 20- and 30-year-olds who have little investment in traditional ways of doing things.

One such organization is Sony's PlayStation, a unit that had virtually no sales just three years ago. This year, PlayStation will generate worldwide revenues of more than $5 billion on gross retail sales of $9 billion. Almost everyone on the management team at PlayStation is in their 30s. Their entire day is spent managing the paradoxes of chaos and order as they juggle creativity and experimentation along with control and efficiency. In an industry that must push the envelope to survive, they live in a constant stream of tensions: balancing work with play, creativity with competition, complacency with outrageousness. The tempo in the industry is so rapid that people are assigned to new teams in readiness for a new project before they even know what that project will be. Teams are kept in constant motion, which is the essence of managing in chaos.

Motorola provides an example of a large American business that did not deliberately set out to apply the chaordic model to its organizational change (as Visa did), yet engaged in emergent change. The illustration is instructive regarding the problems change agents will face in managing the transition from the Newtonian to the Chaotic model of change in well-established organizations.

In 1983, Motorola's CEO, Bob Galvin, recognized that, despite experiencing 15 percent growth, the company faced a serious threat from foreign competition. At the biennial meeting of the company's top officers, rather than issue a directive, Galvin threw out a seemingly spontaneous challenge: renew the organization.

The officers, accustomed to specific, well-defined statements of need, goals, and plans, waited for Galvin to flesh out his ideas. When he didn't, they were baffled. Largely because they were unsure of what Galvin was proposing, they were unable to respond in their usual manner of efficiently carrying out their leader's wishes. They dealt with their confusion and anxiety by denying the need for change.

Throughout that year and into the next, managers struggled without a road map. Galvin's follow-up memo to the biennial meeting did not spell out specific actions to be taken or results to be achieved. Even a document produced late in 1984 by a Policy Committee (which included Galvin) raised more questions than it gave answers. Through it all, Galvin refused to provide a silver bullet solution.

Finally, when senior managers were asked to identify projects in their own business units and to report back on their plans and their results, progress was made. At long last, managers stopped agonizing over what Galvin wanted and began to act, to experiment, to accelerate the development and work of teams and projects. Suddenly, product development took less time and money than before. Galvin's challenge . . . indistinct and radical, providing neither vision nor means nor ends . . . produced emergent change.

BUILDING A CHAORDIC ORGANIZATION

Few companies have the temerity to embrace the emergent paradigm to the degree that Visa and Motorola have. Rather than immerse the entire organization in the messiness attending a full acceptance of chaos theory, they are proceeding cautiously, building a *readiness* to engage in the new order, designing and erecting one or more dimensions of a culture of chaos.

1 Knowledge and Information Sharing. Knowledge is one of the primary preconditions for emergent change. Companies that want to prepare themselves to become chaordic organizations must rely on the collective intelligence of their people to create a desired future. Knowledge and information sharing go hand-in-glove. The traditional practice of hoarding knowledge in order to enhance one's personal power is not only unacceptable in the new order, it will backfire. In the chaordic organization, power accrues to those who become a source of knowledge by sharing what they know. The concept of collective intelligence presupposes system-wide sharing of information so internal barriers, such as those that prevent cross-functional learning, must be eradicated. Hewlett-Packard deals with this issue by having an award called "Not Invented Here." It is an honor bestowed on a division that implements the most ideas from other divisions in the company.

One company that understands the importance of the knowledge element of emergent change is Buckman Laboratories International, a specialty chemicals company in Memphis, Tennessee. Buckman, the CEO of this privately held company, developed a global knowledge transfer network, called K'Netix, which makes a steady flow of information accessible to everyone in the company worldwide. Answers to problems or questions can come from anyone anywhere in the world, including Buckman himself. To ensure knowledge reciprocity and sharing of information, the company offers incentives and rewards to its best knowledge sharers.

2 Innovation and Creativity. Along with knowledge and information, emergent change requires innovation and creativity. These characteristics require an organizational culture in which rules are meant to be broken and assumptions are continually being tested. They call for an environment that supports experimentation, risk-taking, and failure, and views trial-and-error as a viable process.

Companies are beginning to acknowledge that many of their successes attributed to brilliant foresight were, in fact, the result of trying lots of different things and keeping what worked. 3M, for example, began as a mining company and its evolution into the tape business was totally serendipitous. The derivation of 3M's Post-it Notes is a classic tale of accidental success. Similarly, Johnson & Johnson did not deliberately set out to enter the baby-powder market. As the story goes, a director of research sent a packet of talc to a physician who complained that patients were developing a skin irritation from the company's plaster. The director began sending talc with various products and soon customers began to buy the talc separately. Today, 44 percent of the company's revenues come from baby powder.

3 Teamwork and Project Orientation. Knowledge growth, information sharing, creativity, and innovation thrive best in small groups where people can interact freely. A few people with new ideas and creative thoughts is not sufficient for institutional learning unless they are encouraged to interact with others.

Therefore, to prepare the organization for emergent change, companies need to delayer and decentralize, to organize work around tasks performed in teams and project task forces, and then ensure that these teams and project groupings are flexible enough to form, change, and dissolve, as needed. High-tech companies are always shifting jobs to areas that have higher potential payoffs. Their work groups need to be sufficiently agile to continually reorganize. Intel, for example, uses temporary teams drawn from a range of disciplines, constantly forming around specific business issues or projects. It's a task-oriented company where the organization is more like a web of teams and projects than a clearly defined vertical hierarchy.

Another example is 3M, a company synonymous with innovation. One way that the company achieves its goal of having 15 percent of its revenue come from new products is by providing its managers with the latitude to move from one business unit or laboratory to another without bureaucratic obstruction. Project groups, operating with little constraint

from the formal organization, come together to accomplish a task and disband when their work is completed. There's lots of self-organization and self-design without the need for formal coordination. Similarly, 3M researchers who cannot get funding for their ideas within their own center or lab are encouraged to search out other centers and labs.

The flexibility of work arrangements, the emphasis on ideas rather than structures, and the clear signal that it is better to share ideas rather than reinvent them, frees people to focus on their imagination and creativity, thus making 3M one of the most successful companies in the world and one that is close to being a chaordic organization.

4 Diversity. The secret to productive and creative project groupings is diversity. Homogeneous groups tend to produce homogeneous ideas. Executives talking with other executives rarely produces a diversity of opinion. To achieve a high level of creative thought, it is necessary to bring together diverse groups of people: people with different levels of expertise (including representatives of non-business disciplines), employees at all levels of the organization (representing a variety of ages, experiences, and backgrounds), people outside of the organization (customers, suppliers), and, above all, people representing a broad spectrum of ideas.

At Skandia, the Swedish financial services company, CEO Leif Edvinsson wanted to reach the future faster, so he created Skandia Future Centers with five elite Future Teams. These are based on a model he calls "3G": a mix of three generations ranging from their 20s to 60s as well as a variety of functional roles, organizational experiences, and cultural backgrounds. Edvinsson believes discussions among diverse groups advance learning faster than traditional groups.

For original thinking, the diverse mix should include the company's mavericks. Every company has them, but they often must struggle against company orthodoxy. Having their ideas dismissed out of hand leaves them so frustrated that they either stop participating or leave the company altogether. Arie De Geuss, reporting on a study of companies that survived one hundred years or more, found that one of the four traits they held in common was a tolerance of new ideas. Clearly, companies that crossed a century's worth of changes could not control their world; therefore, they learned to tolerate ideas and activities at the margin.

Honoring the contributions of everyone, including mavericks, requires a high tolerance for conflict. Levi-Strauss and Company is an example of an organization that believes people need to be allowed to challenge ideas, no matter where they originate. To foster dissension, the company hangs whiteboards in the halls and encourages people to anonymously contribute their criticisms of what is wrong with the company's plans. Managers hang bulletin boards at meetings for people who prefer to post anonymous comments rather than make them publicly.

At 3M, new recruits actually take a course with their supervisors on risk-taking in which they are explicitly taught to be willing to defy their supervisors. They are told stories of victories won despite the boss's opposition. Chaordic organizations are, by definition, conflictual, but the very tension that produces conflict also produces genuinely creative, fruitful ideas.

5 **Strong Core Values.** To enable individuals and small groups to pursue the learning and innovation that leads to self-organizing behavior, they must be allowed autonomy. But autonomy cannot be allowed to dissolve into anarchy. There must be some grounding entity that unites the independent participants and their efforts.

Traditionally, that entity was managerial control. In chaordic organizations, it is core values or, as was noted earlier, what Dee Hock refers to as purpose and principle. Collins and Porras, in their study of visionary companies, describe values as a bonding glue that keep a fluid organization from evolving beyond recognition. Values allow for coordination without control and for experimentation and adaptation without lawlessness. A value system creates a sense of purpose; the organization knows what it is about and can invest focused attention despite seemingly random behavior.

Boeing's ideology, for example, revolves around its commitment to push the envelope of technology and to take risks and accept challenges to do this. 3M's values center on innovation and the desire to solve real human problems with truly original ideas. At Sony, the focus is on being a pioneer in doing the impossible and experiencing the joy that comes from advancing and applying technol-ogy. Despite the complexity and chaotic nature of the environment and the messy state of the emergent change, it is the company's core ideology or values that can provide its direction and purpose.

THE ROLE OF THE MANAGER

Precisely how chaos and complexity theories will shape the work world isn't clear, nor are there many examples of emergent change to guide those responsible for managing on the edge of chaos. Nevertheless, five essential ingredients of the 21st century manager's role are apparent.

1 **Manage the Transition.** The most important role managers have *at this time* is to lead people through the transition from the industrial era to the information era, from the world of Newton to the world of Chaos. William Bridges defines transition as "the *psychological* process people go through to come to terms with the new situation" [italics added].

That process begins with letting go of the past and coming to terms with what is being lost. Today's workers are being asked to trade their comfortable, safe, stable, and predictable work world for one that is unstable, unpredictable, and highly ambiguous. Traditional workers are accustomed to carrying out decisions made by higher authorities, being told the end result and how to get there, and relying on tried-and-true knowledge and skills that have served them well in the past.

With the new order, however, they are being called upon to identify and solve problems, make decisions, experiment, generate perpetual novelty, and continually learn new skills and behaviors.

Their world has turned topsy-turvy. Managers need to help people understand the reasons behind these dramatic changes and generate a sense of urgency about the need to move forward in a different manner. To do this, they must be specific regarding the attitudinal and behavioral changes that are necessary, communicate consistently and often, expect and accept people's negative reactions, and reward their positive efforts.

2 **Build Resilience.** As the speed, volume, and complexity of change accelerate, workers, mental and physical stamina are worn down. Reeling from multiple downsizings, organizational restructurings, mergers and acquisitions, and programmatic initiatives over the past two decades, many of them feel incapable of gearing up for yet another assault on their energies. Feeling out of control, they have reached what Alvin Toffler termed "future shock." But much as they long for "the good 'ol days," they are destined to be disappointed. Chaos theory and emergent change tell us that ability to adapt and to absorb *even more change* is what lies ahead. Therefore, an important role for managers is to help people increase their resilience; that is, their capacity to bounce back no matter how intense the speed or complexity of the changes.

Daryl Conner argues that major change occurs when people have significant disruption in their expectations. When people can anticipate and prepare for the change, they respond better, in part, because they feel more in control. Negative reactions and dysfunctional responses come from being surprised, feeling unprepared and out of control.

Reaction to change is largely a function of perception and managers can build resilience by helping people adjust their expectations. Managers need to help workers understand the new realities; namely, that there is no going back, that change is the order of the day, and that we may never feel "in control" again. They need to explain the nature of chaos and emergent change, emphasizing the lack of predictability and stability along with the principle of "order in disorder."

But at the same time, managers need to ensure that people have the skills they need so they can feel equipped to meet the challenges ahead. Never before has training been so important to the workforce and to organizations. Motorola, with one of the best training programs in the country, pushes employees to continually redefine themselves and how they do their jobs, requiring each employee to attend a minimum of 40 hours of training annually. Motorola University, begun in 1987, delivered 123,000 hours of training by 1991 with 6,800 people participating in courses. One estimate is that 300 to 400 companies now have their own versions of corporate universities or learning centers.

3 **Destabilize the System.** In the industrial era, we viewed a successful organization as one that operates as close to equilibrium as possible. But a model that places stability at its core serves to restrict managers to strategies of repetition and imitation. As such, it is dysfunctional for a world that has become increasingly complex and competitive and in which organizations literally live or die on the basis of their ability to innovate.

Therefore, managers need to assume the important role of creating an environment that elicits, supports, and nurtures creativity by deliberately upsetting the status quo, escalating some changes while damping others, and seeking a chaordic state or a state of bounded instability.

One way to destabilize the system is to keep it in a state of tension. Tension is a necessary ingredient of creativity, but it will take particular skill on the part of managers to keep the tension level at a point where it generates dynamic imagination without exceeding people's ability to handle the stress engendered.

Another way to destabilize the system is to deliberately seek disconfirmation of our beliefs. A secret of success in the new order, according to Intel's CEO, Andrew Grove, is to continually try to prove yourself wrong, to challenge your thinking, to find flaws in your own mental models, to continually experiment and test every possible alternative.

To voluntarily annihilate one's ideas, however, is not as ego-satisfying as having them confirmed, so managers need to maintain constant vigil to ensure that the process of disconfirmation becomes a natural, acceptable mode of problem solving. They can do this by modeling an openness to the testing of their own ideas, by rewarding those who raise tough questions, and by playing devil's advocate when consensus is achieved too readily and without debate.

4 **Manage Order and Disorder, the Present and the Future.** The self-organizing principle of chaos theory might lead one to conclude that managers are superfluous. On the contrary, they have a critical role in providing the balance between the need for order and the imperative to change. They are responsible for seeing to it that the organization engages in enough innovation to keep it competitive yet enough stability to prevent its dissolving into total disarray.

This paradox, which is really a constellation of paradoxes consisting of regularity and irregularity, simplicity and complexity, predictability and unpredictability, and stability and instability, calls for tremendous agility on the part of managers. In the old order, with its either/or thinking, managers merely pursued one end of each continuum, but today, with both/and thinking required, they will have to juggle both ends.

One approach to the conundrum is to apply order, regularity, predictability, and stability to the daily business and disorder, irregularity, unpredictability, and instability to future change. Ken Blanchard suggests having people in the organization on two teams: a Present Team, focused on today, and a Future Team, focused on tomorrow.

Further, Blanchard argues that people are naturally suited to one or the other. He points to Michael Eisner, CEO of Disney, as a natural visionary, and the late Frank Wells, Disney's former President and COO, as a natural implementor. Where Eisner preferred to innovate, Wells preferred to redesign systems to support the new directions Eisner charted. By allowing managers to function in a capacity suited to their preferred mode of operation, Blanchard's model might well provide a means for easing the anxiety and tension that the paradox creates for many workers. Both the organization and the workers get their needs met.

5 **Create and Maintain a Learning Organization.** Learning is the *sine qua non* of an information/knowledge age and central to the self-organizing activities from which new systems emerge. Thus, a major role of managers in chaordic organizations will be to create the means by which everyone can be involved in continuous learning.

This should not be difficult since there is always potential for learning in the everyday problems and opportunities workers confront. Learning and doing are synchronous so workers can learn in real time, but only if learning is made an explicit organizational value and only if there is time put aside for reflection on what worked, what didn't, and why. When learning is an accidental byproduct of activity rather than a central core process, it is neither sustainable nor does it get integrated into the business.

To create and maintain a genuine learning organization, managers need to establish an environment supportive of and conducive to learning. If experimentation, risk-taking, and trial-and-error modes of problem solving are to compete with the overused rational, ana-

lytic modes, then the culture must tolerate failure, refrain from placing blame, and reinforce nontraditional thinking. If truly innovative ideas are a primary goal, then the culture must tolerate conflict, people "pushing back," public testing of one another's assumptions, and healthy debate around diverse ideas. If the organization wants to capitalize on its collective human capital, then the culture must tolerate a messy structure in which project groups form, reconstitute themselves, or disband as needed.

These five roles, critical for managers to enact if their companies are to enter the 21st century as chaordic organizations capable of engaging in emergent change, call for leaders who, themselves, understand and accept the assumptions of chaos and complexity theories. These invaluable agents of future change seek neither stability nor predictability, developing a comfort level that tolerates disequilibrium. They know that messiness and ambiguity are part of the process of self-organization and self-emergence and that, rather than attempt to manage it through command-and-control, their role is to support it through allocation of resources and the design of an appropriate culture. They recognize the futility of attempting to draw a map of the future in advance, appreciating the fact that, when the waters are uncharted, their destination can only be discovered through the actual process in real time; that the map can only get drawn as they go along.

To be a successful manager in the 21st century and to enact the five roles enumerated above calls for a new mental model of manager, one suited to a world of chaos. Those who retain their Newtonian world view will find themselves leading their organizations into oblivion.

IS CHAOS THE NEXT ORGANIZATIONAL PARADIGM?

Let's return to the question posed at the beginning of this article. Can chaos theory provide us with useful methods and metaphors for understanding the world of work? Does it lend itself to the self-organization of people in companies? Is there utility to chaos and complexity theory which could add to, or even supplant, the Newtonian order? Or is chaos theory the current darling of scientists with no application to organizations or management?

So far, complexity theory has been applied successfully to operational problems. At both GM and Deere & Co., complexity-based computer systems were used to develop programs for manufacturing. These models solved operational problems better than previously used linear techniques, saving the companies time and money.

To date, chaos and complexity theories have not been applied to human systems, although self-directed teams represent a small version of self-organization. The recent shift to team- and project-based processes in many organizations demonstrates the fact that groups of workers will, if given the chance, find ways to accomplish a task.

Top consulting firms, including Coopers and Lybrand, McKinsey, and Ernst & Young, sent people to the Sante Fe Institute (SFI), the heart of exploration into chaos theory, to find ways to use chaos and complexity theories in their consulting practice. While direct application has not yet occurred, Ernst & Young was so taken with the possibilities of this new paradigm that the firm ran a three-day symposium, "Embracing Complexity," and mailed 15,000 copies of Kaufman's *At Home in the Universe* to its clients.

The next steps in the application of chaos theory, and its off-shoot complexity theory, involve developing lifelike simulations followed by testing the theory in real time on actual human problems. Chaos theory may not be a viable model for understanding organizations as yet, but it is an intriguing way to think about the world.

SELECTED BIBLIOGRAPHY

For current data and thought-provoking forecasting data, see *The Futurist* and *Outlook '97* published by the World Future Society.

For more on the role of paradoxes and their ubiquity in the coming years, see C. Handy, *The Age of Paradox* (Cambridge, MA: Harvard Business School Press, 1994) and R. Farson, *Management of the Absurd: Paradoxes of Leadership* (New York: Simon & Schuster, 1994).

Some of the clearest writing on chaos and complexity theories can be found in S. Kaufman, *At Home in the Universe* (New York: Oxford University Press, 1995); Kevin Kelly's *Out of Control: The Rise of Biological Civilization* (Reading, MA: Addison-Wesley, 1994); and M. Waldrop, *Complexity* (New York: Simon & Schuster, 1993).

Books that provide an understanding of chaos theory and its application to organizations and management include: R. Stacey, *Managing the Unknowable: Strategic Boundaries Between Order and Chaos in Organizations* (San Francisco, CA: Jossey-Bass, 1992); M. Wheatley, *Leadership as Science: Learning About Organizations from an Orderly Universe* (San Francisco, CA: Berrett-Koehler, 1994); and M. Wheatley and M. Kellner-Rogers, *A Simpler Way* (San Francisco, CA: Berrett-Koehler, 1996).

One of the best sources of information about cutting-edge companies functioning on the border of chaos is *Fast Company* magazine. A brief history of the origins of Visa and a biography of its founder, Dee Hock, for example, can be found in the October-November 1996 issue. Buchman Laboratories was described in the June-July 1996 issue and Sony's PlayStation in the August-September 1997 issue.

The quote from William Bridges is taken from *Managing Transitions: Making the Most of Change* (Reading, MA: Addison-Wesley, 1991).

The New Frontier:

Transformation of Management for the New Millennium

Managers must become agile and flexible to help their firms develop and sustain an advantage in the competitive landscape of the new millennium. They will need to harness the powers of information technology and human capital with nonlinear thinking in the global marketplace of the 21st century.

MICHAEL A. HITT

Entry into the new millennium is shaping up as one of the most exciting and perhaps most challenging events in our history. The decade of the 1990s has presented us with unprecedented change. For example, we entered the 1990s with use of the Internet largely limited to scientific exchange and some government communications. We end the 1990s with almost one billion people globally communicating and conducting business on the Internet. As we enter the 21st century, we have seen elimination of industry boundaries, major technological advances, the opening of previously closed global markets, and intense global competition.

These changes and the environment faced in the new millennium require a new managerial mind-set. Standard management thinking and practice were developed at a time when most firms operated in a relatively stable environment. However, the environment of the new millennium represents a new frontier. This new frontier provides a distinctive, exciting, and challenging time for organizations. It is a time of technological revolution and a global market economy. Strategic discontinuities occur along with rapidly paced and broad-scope evolutionary change. These different sets of changes have produced a metamorphosis of the economic and competitive landscapes.

THE COMPETITIVE LANDSCAPE OF THE NEW MILLENNIUM

The competitive landscape of the new millennium will be characterized by substantial and discontinuous change. It will be

Michael A. Hitt is a Distinguished Professor of Management and holder of the Paul M. and Rosalie Robertson Chair of Business Administration at Texas A&M University. He received his Ph.D. from the University of Colorado after serving in a managerial capacity for Samsonite Corporation. Dr. Hitt is the author or co-author of over 150 publications, including 14 books. His recent books include *Strategic Management: Competitiveness and Globalization, Managing Strategically in an Interconnected World, New Managerial Mindsets: Organizational Transformation and Strategy Implementation,* and *Dynamic Strategic Resources: Development, Diffusion and Integration.* He has a forthcoming book on mergers and acquisitions to be published by Oxford University Press. He is the former editor of the *Academy of Management Journal* and past president of the Academy of Management. Currently, he serves on the board of the Strategic Management Society. He has served as a consultant to a number of organizations including IBM, Motorola, Citibank, Aerospatiate, GTE, and CEMEX. He received the award for outstanding academic contributions to competitiveness from the American Society for Competitiveness in 1996 and received an honorary doctorate from the Universidad Carlos III de Madrid in 1999.

From *Organizational Dynamics,* Winter 2000, pp. 7-17. © 2000 by Elsevier Science. Reprinted by permission.

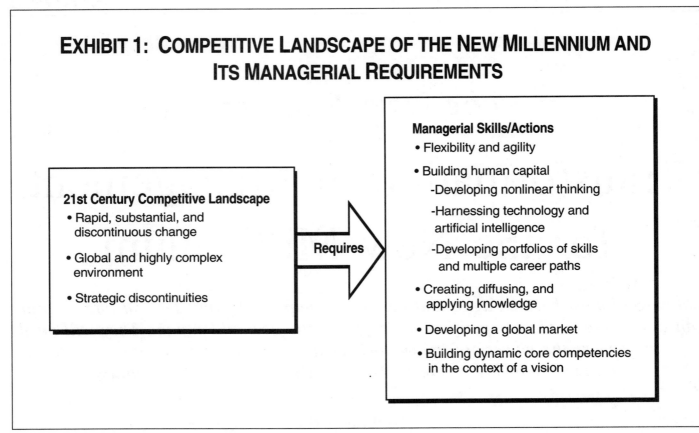

EXHIBIT 1: COMPETITIVE LANDSCAPE OF THE NEW MILLENNIUM AND ITS MANAGERIAL REQUIREMENTS

21st Century Competitive Landscape
- Rapid, substantial, and discontinuous change
- Global and highly complex environment
- Strategic discontinuities

Requires

Managerial Skills/Actions
- Flexibility and agility
- Building human capital
  - Developing nonlinear thinking
  - Harnessing technology and artificial intelligence
  - Developing portfolios of skills and multiple career paths
- Creating, diffusing, and applying knowledge
- Developing a global market
- Building dynamic core competencies in the context of a vision

rugged and large. Multiple strategic discontinuities will occur and the changes will be rapid. In other words, the periods of stability will be short. The substantial change in and the size and complexity of this landscape produce significant uncertainty. The global competitive landscape can be affected by political decisions such as the war in Kosovo and the accidental bombing of the Chinese Embassy in Belgrade. For example, bombing the Chinese Embassy heightened international tensions and could create a longer-term strategic discontinuity in the economic activity between NATO countries, particularly the United States and China. Other strategic discontinuities may occur in particular industries because of the advent of new technology or competitors' strategic decisions that take advantage of new technology. An example is the retail book industry, which experienced a strategic discontinuity with the entrepreneurial development of Amazon.com. Prior to the entry of Amazon.com into the retail book market, Barnes & Noble dominated the industry with the development of its new superstores. The concept for Amazon.com—retailing books over the Internet—came from outside the industry and used the available technology to reach current and new customers interested in acquiring books and other items that could be sold over the Internet.

The analogy of a soccer match can help explain the complexity of this new landscape. Typically, in a soccer match, two teams play each other for a defined period of time at a previously agreed-on date and time. They play on a field of known proportions that is level and with a prescribed set of rules that are enforced by referees. Winners and losers are eas-

ily identified at the end of the match. The coach of a soccer team develops a strategy utilizing the talents and capabilities of team members and based on the strengths and weaknesses of the opponent. It is a complex and oftentimes stressful job.

In contrast, the manager of a business often must prepare to compete against 20, 30, or more other businesses simultaneously. The firm must compete in multiple markets and often in multiple countries, each of which has its own rules and "referees" (e.g., government officials). Therefore, if a firm operates in markets across 20 different countries, there may be 20 separate sets of rules to which it must conform. Furthermore, while financial records provide data on the performance of a firm, there are multiple measures, some of them less tangible and ambiguous, by which to measure a firm's success, or lack thereof, in any particular market relative to other competitors. Also, the field on which a business must compete is no longer stable or level. It encounters many changes, often within short periods of time. The landscape is rugged with many hills, mountains, and valleys. And the changes in the landscape may occur with little or no warning. A firm may be a market leader and sitting on the "mountaintop." Yet within a very short period of time, that same firm may be down in a "valley" and behind many of its competitors because of a change in its landscape, even though the firm did not change its strategy or competitive actions.

This environment is exceedingly complex and in a constant state of transformation. The competitive landscape of the new millennium and the managerial requirements to be effective within it are depicted in Exhibit 1.

Drivers of the New Landscape

This competitive landscape has two primary drivers: the technological revolution and increasing globalization. The technological revolution is characterized by an increasing rate of technological change and diffusion, greater knowledge intensity, and the importance of knowledge to competitive advantage. Globalization is characterized by the liberalization of developing economies and emerging markets, new economic alliances and rules, and the growing interdependencies of national economies, along with worldwide economic development. In addition to these substantial changes, the drivers produce a landscape of multiple hypercompetitive markets, placing increasing importance on innovation and continuous learning and emphasizing price, quality, and satisfaction of customer needs. Therefore, these two environmental factors together are largely reshaping the competitive landscape for the new millennium.

GETTING A NEW PERSPECTIVE

One of the best ways to develop an understanding of this competitive landscape and the changes it creates is to think about our past and look to our future. Recall 1985, 15 years in our past. Two of the hottest high-technology companies were IBM and Apple Computer. These companies were competing fiercely to become the top manufacturer and marketer of personal computers and software. Today, both firms exist but they are no longer the market leaders in personal computers and general software development. Dell Computer is now the largest manufacturer and marketer of personal computers, and it is being challenged by other competitors such as Compaq. Microsoft is the leading software firm but it is also being challenged in the legal system by other software developers and in competitive markets. For example, a young new venture firm, Red Hat, distributes the Linux operating system that is 50 percent faster than Microsoft's Windows NT. Both Dell and Microsoft were in existence in 1985 but were small and insignificant companies at that time.

Looking to the future, who will be the market leaders in these related and interdependent industries in the year 2015? Will Dell and Microsoft still be at the forefront or will others like Gateway and Oracle be in the lead? Will totally new firms not now in existence be the market leaders in the year 2015? We can predict that these industries and most others will be markedly different in the year 2015 from what they are in 2000.

THE IMPERMANENCE OF SUCCESS

Mitsubishi

To understand the substantial changes occurring in the marketplace and the effects they have let us examine the Japanese Keiretsu Mitsubishi. In 1989, Mitsubishi "flexed considerable muscle." For example, it acquired 51 percent of what was considered an American icon, New York's Rockefeller Center. Mitsubishi Motors achieved 27 percent annual sales growth in the U.S. auto market. Demand for Mitsubishi's big-screen televisions sets exceeded their supply. Academics in Japan were referring to the "Mitsubishification" of global markets. In short, Mitsubishi's economic power was feared in the United States and Western Europe, in particular. However, as happens with many firms, substantial economic success often leads to an ingrained conservatism that produces inertia and an unwillingness to change, even in fast-changing global markets.

Because of this inertia and a shifting competitive landscape, Mitsubishi is now in serious trouble. Mitsubishi Electric lost approximately $330 million in 1999. Likewise, Mitsubishi Chemical Corporation and Mitsubishi Materials Corporation each experienced losses exceeding $200 million in 1999. Mitsubishi Motors is in such bad shape that it is now searching for a foreign partner. Thirteen of Mitsubishi's core members have a combined total debt of $132 billion but only $58 billion in shareholders' equity. The importance and economic effect of Mitsubishi's performance is shown by the fact that its top 30 companies produce approximately $400 billion in annual sales, which represents about 8 percent of Japan's total annual output. Thus, Mitsubishi's performance has a significant effect on the Japanese economy.

Levi Strauss

Levi Strauss experienced a similar transformation but its fall was more rapid. It had a brand name, Levi's, that was well known and highly regarded in most markets throughout the world. Levi's jeans were known as high-quality products and sold well in global markets. The stock price of Levi Strauss increased from $2.53 per share in 1985 to $265.00 per share in 1996, almost a 10,500 percent increase. However, in 1997, Levi Strauss closed 29 manufacturing plants and laid off over 16,000 employees. Its problems continued to worsen and sales declined by 13 percent to less than $6 billion in 1998. In short, Levi Strauss experienced substantial competition from such firms as Tommy Hilfiger and Gap. Both firms offered multiple varieties of jeans to satisfy consumer needs and desires while Levi Strauss maintained a largely stable product line (single brand). In contrast to Levi's problems, Gap's annual sales increased from approximately 57 billion in 1995 to over $40 billion in 1998. Levi Strauss announced the hiring of a new CEO from PepsiCo in 1999, hoping that he will be able to transform the firm back into a market leader again. His task is substantial.

GLOBALIZATION

Markets are fast becoming borderless or global. We can no longer evaluate many markets as national or domestic. For example, the auto market is rapidly becoming global. This is evidenced by the recent merger that created DaimlerChrysler and the acquisition of Nissan by Peugeot. In recent years, BMW acquired Britain's Landrover, and Ford Motor Company has had an interest in Mazda for a number of years. There have been strategic alliances between U.S. and Japanese automakers as well as U.S. and Korean automakers. Mercedes-Benz vehicles are now manufactured in the United States and many automakers sell their products in local markets all over the world.

Firms are trying to become stateless in order to transform themselves into global businesses. Among the competitive pressures on firms to become more international are increasing domestic competition and increasing multipoint competition. As markets become more open (as shown by free trade agreements across nations) more foreign firms are likely to enter domestic markets, thereby increasing the amount of competition. Furthermore, because firms are operating in global markets, competitors may not respond to competitive moves in a domestic economy but may act against the firm in another international market. The increasing amount and types of competition place pressure on firms to move into international markets in order to maintain their competitiveness in all markets in which they operate.

The growing interdependence across national economies is exemplified by the effects of the Asian crisis (sometimes referred to as the Asian flu) on global economic growth. In 1998, global economic growth was reduced by 25 percent because of the economic problems in Asia. Furthermore, the interdependence is growing as world financial markets become more integrated. The increasing power of these integrated markets was noted in an editorial by Robert Altman, a former U.S. Deputy Secretary of the Treasury, that was published on December 20, 1998 in the *Houston Chronicle:*

> The integrated world financial markets have become relatively seamless, but global financial markets have emerged as a powerful force, more powerful than nuclear weapons. . . . Earthquakes and erupting volcanoes compare with the financial and economic events in 1998.

Altman argues that these integrated financial markets can even topple governments, citing the changes in Indonesia. Financial market integration, the interdependence of national economies, the development of borderless markets and stateless corporations, and the increasing competitive pressures suggest that globalization has changed the boundaries and nature of strategy, competition, and competitive advantage.

TECHNOLOGY

Technological change and diffusion of that new technology are moving at an incredible pace. The development and diffusion of new technology increase the importance of innovation for firms if they are to be competitive. David de Pury, former co-chair of the board for Asea Brown Boveri claimed that "innovate or die is the first rule of international industrial competition." Likewise, the continuous technology development and change have produced decreasing product life cycles. In a recent presentation, Andrew Grove, chairman and former CEO of Intel, explained the introduction of new products at his company. In January 1998, Intel introduced a new sophisticated product in which it had invested considerable develop-

ment funds. However, he said that by December of that same year Intel would introduce a new product that would cannibalize its existing product. As a result, the life span of the new product introduced in January was effectively 11 months. This allows a company little time to recoup tremendous investments in research and development (R&D) and expenditures to commercialize the product. The result is substantial challenges for management.

Technological change both facilitates and increases knowledge intensity. The acquisition/development of knowledge and its application within organizations have become key components of competitive advantage. The critical function of knowledge to competitive advantage has placed increasing importance on the use of knowledge workers. In turn, growing knowledge intensity has greatly increased the importance of and emphasis on organizational learning. In the editor's introduction to the 1996 winter special issue of the *Strategic Management Journal,* Dan Schendel states:

> The process by which knowledge is created and utilized in organizations may be the key inimitable resource managers need to appreciate if not understand.

One of the most significant technologies inherent in the technological revolution is information and communications technology. This technology is used in almost all businesses, large and small, and is an integral part of many systems (e.g., manufacturing systems, inventory systems, communications systems). Information technology facilitates globalization because it allows ready access to employees all over the world at a nominal cost. Its integration into manufacturing technology is allowing the development of mass customization processes in many product lines ranging from clothing to bicycles to automobiles. It is also helping firms increase their productivity. In 1994, Navistar, an engine producer, employed 900 people at its Indianapolis plant that produced 175 engines per day (5.2 employees per engine). In 1999, that same plant, after making significant capital investments in new technology, manufactured 1,400 engines per day with 1,900 employees (1.3 employees per engine). Information systems also help coordinate and share the firm's collective knowledge across its major operations. Of course, this technology is fueling the rapid development of electronic commerce exemplified by Amazon.com.

E-commerce Revolution

E-commerce by U.S. companies exceeded $100 billion in 1998. Business-to-business transactions represented the largest segment of e-commerce, with $43 billion in revenue. Business-to-business e-commerce is expected to grow to more than $1.3 trillion by 2003. Online transactions not only increase firms' revenues, they also reduce costs. For example, Giga Information Group predicts that corporations will save $1.25 trillion by 2002 doing business over the Internet. This amount approximates France's annual gross domestic product.

While business-to-business transactions represent the largest single segment of e-commerce, many firms are marketing their products directly to the consumer through their Web pages. General Motors' new e-business unit, e-GM, has developed a "Web car"—at the Web site consumers can custom order their personal automobile, with projected delivery within 10 days.

At one time, many predicted that purely Internet-based retailers (e-tailers) would win the competitive battle over established retail chains. They had a cost advantage because of lower property and inventory costs, lower taxes, and lower printing and postage expenses. However, the large established retail chains have "brand recognition," and with their physical presence they can offer integrated shopping combining the Internet, retail stores, catalogues and telephone. Currently, multichannel retailers account for 62 percent of e-commerce retail sales. An example is Wal-Mart. It has market power with established suppliers and orders of large quantities; it uses its low-cost advantage in e-commerce competition.

The e-commerce revolution is becoming a global phenomenon. For example, Disco SA, a supermarket chain in Argentina, recently launched online shopping for its customers. Disco targeted nontraditional customers by offering telephone sales and online shopping. It has gained 3 million pesos of sales per month from this group. Over 70 percent of these customers had shopped elsewhere prior to Disco's new telephone and online services. The new customers are important to Disco because their average purchase is 100 pesos, whereas Disco's average purchase from a customer visiting one of its retail stores is 14 pesos.

The e-commerce revolution is changing other high-tech industries. For example, it is shifting the emphasis from personal computers to servers connected to the Internet. This change alone may have dramatic effects on PC manufacturers, semiconductor chip makers, and software development companies. Micho Kaku, the Henry Semat Professor of Theoretical Physics at New York University, predicts that by the year 2020 computer chips will be cheaper than bubble gum wrappers and PCs will be in museums.

Artificial Intelligence

While we often attribute intelligence to sophisticated machines, Stephen Hawking, a famous physicist, suggests that present computers are less complex than the brain of an earthworm. Micho Kaku states it another way. Computers can see and hear but they don't understand what they see and hear. They have no "common sense or vision." However, both Hawking and Gordon Moore, former chairman of Intel Corporation, argue that artificial intelligence will rapidly develop to the point that computers' "thinking capabilities" will equal or be greater that of human beings. Raymond Kurzweil, president of Kurzweil Technologies, predicts that the raw computing power of the human brain will be in machines by 2019 or perhaps sooner. By 2030, computer systems will have the power of 1,000 human brains. Thus, the technology will exist but the managerial challenge will be learning how to harness and most effectively use this "artificial" intellectual power.

The landscape of the new millennium, the new frontier, has created the need for new management thinking and practices.

Some of the more critical changes are explained in the next section.

MANAGEMENT IN THE NEW MILLENNIUM

As we enter this new business frontier, new forms of managerial thinking along with new organizational structures will be required. Thus, the new frontier demands new managerial mind-sets that are global in orientation and allow strategic flexibility. Managers must be able to think globally but also to react quickly and operate in a continuous state of change. This means that organizations will be in a constant state of transformation, leaving managers to operate in a fluid environment of ambiguity and uncertainty.

Because of the dynamic nature of the landscape expected in the new millennium, every aspect of a firm's operation and long-term health should be continuously reexamined. Managers must be able to balance both stable and fluid states of the organization. Thus, executives must ensure that their firms achieve strategic flexibility—the capability of the firm to proact or respond quickly to changing competitive conditions and thus build or maintain a competitive advantage.

One of the key factors in achieving strategic flexibility is highly developed human capital. This requires systematic and substantial investment in the development of employee skills. In fact, given the significant change in a firm's competitive environment and the difficulty of predicting the types and amounts of change, firms must build a portfolio of skills in their employee base. The portfolio of skills will allow firms to respond more flexibly to changes in their environment. Additionally, to deal with strategic discontinuities and to be able to proact effectively in a dynamic and discontinuous environment, firms must help develop their employees' capability for nonlinear thinking—"thinking outside the box." Clearly, had Barnes & Noble's executives been thinking outside the box, they might have developed Barnes&Noble.com prior to the implementation of Amazon.com. If they had done so, they likely would have forestalled the competitive intrusion by Amazon.com and built a stronger and more dominant position in the retail book market.

The development of nonlinear thinking will become more critical as artificial intelligence becomes more advanced. Managers will require advanced human capital to harness and effectively apply newly developed artificial intelligence along with other new technologies.

Also, because of the dynamic nature of most firms' environments and technological changes such as the development and application of artificial intelligence, firms must develop a mind-set of career flexibility among their employees. It may not be uncommon for individuals to have three to five or more different career paths during their work lives. Of course, as employees develop portfolios of skills, they will be better prepared to change career paths when needed.

To develop the firm's human capital in these ways will require a process of continuous learning. Furthermore, for a firm to take full advantage of the new knowledge created, this knowledge must be diffused throughout the organization. It is not uncommon for new knowledge to be created in one part of the organization (e.g., a particular subsidiary) but never be transferred to other parts of the company. Therefore, firms must take active steps to identify new knowledge and to transfer it to other units in the organization where it can be used effectively. For example, some firms have instituted special work units to identify successful practices that are developed in all major units of the organization, to evaluate those practices, and to ensure that knowledge of the practices that can be used effectively in other units is transferred to them.

A continuous learning organization that widely diffuses knowledge created within its boundaries is likely to develop an innovative culture. An innovative culture ensures continuous development of innovative ideas, practices, and products or services, while innovation itself is a critical component of competitiveness in international markets.

Contributing to a globalized mind-set and to an innovative culture is a multinational culture. Here, we refer to the development of multicultural work teams. These teams produce a diversity of thought and approaches, thereby contributing to a more innovative culture. Furthermore, the multicultural nature of the units, to include top management teams, will help the firm develop a global mind-set. Asea Brown Boveri (ABB) has developed a global mindset by creating multicultural management teams in all its major business units and in its top management team as well. In so doing, it has become a highly successful global corporation.

Managing multicultural organizations that are strategically flexible will require the use of sophisticated network and information technologies. Networking within and outside the organization may be critical to operating effectively and efficiently and to building competitive advantages. External networking can be created through the use of strategic alliances, a highly popular strategy in today's business environment. Equally important is the development and exercise of excellent strategic leadership. No longer can these large complex firms be led effectively by "a lone ranger." Rather, effective strategic leaders must build a top management team. Insightful top executives recognize that it is impossible for them to have all the answers. As such, they must depend on other knowledgeable and experienced executives as a part of a top management team. A wise philosopher once said that "none of us is as smart as all of us." Even more vivid is the statement by Italian author Lucianao De Crescenzo that "we are all angels with only one wing, we can only fly while embracing each other."

The top management team must develop a vision for the firm and help implement that vision. The vision, however, must allow for continual organizational change and transformation. The team must effectively exploit the firm's core competencies while continually developing those competencies or changing them when required by the external environment.

The new type of leadership has the appropriate managerial mind-set that allows the creation of strategic flexibility and develops human capital to have the skill sets appropriate to

respond to a dynamic environment. The need for flexibility and changing core competencies is exemplified by IBM's history. In 1986, IBM was ranked as the number one corporation in America using *Fortune*'s reputation rankings. However, in 1995, *Fortune* ranked IBM number 281 among the U.S. top corporations. IBM had suffered billions of dollars in net losses and had to lay off tens of thousands of employees. Why did this occur? IBM still had its primary core competence, which was the manufacture, marketing, and servicing of large mainframe computers. While IBM still performed this function exceptionally well, it was a competence that became less valuable as the technology and environment changed. Thus, IBM developed core rigidities that it found difficult to overcome and its performance suffered as a result.

After experiencing major losses, IBM implemented a number of changes. First, it hired a new CEO, Louis Gerstner, an outsider to IBM and the computer industry, to help the firm develop a new strategy and the managers to develop a new mind-set. Gerstner focused the company's efforts on networkcentric computing and brought IBM back from the precipice. Today, IBM is considered a power in computer services and a major player in e-commerce. Thus, by developing new core competencies, IBM has regained its agility and market prowess, albeit in different areas than before.

CONCLUSIONS AND IMPLICATIONS

Management in the new millennium must build an organization that is constantly being transformed. It must develop and respond continuously to new technologies, new markets, new businesses, and new people in the form of employees and customers. The arguments described here suggest the following managerial implications:

- Managers must be agile and make their strategies and their firms flexible.
- More than ever before success is dependent on human capital. Managers and knowledge workers must think in new ways, build portfolios of skills, and harness and utilize new technology and artificial intelligence.
- Managers must emphasize the creation of knowledge, diffuse it throughout the organization, and ensure that it is utilized.
- Managers must embrace a new and global mind-set.
- Dynamic core competencies should be developed in the context of a vision for the firm.

Perhaps the implications are best summarized by Heinrich von Pierer, president and CEO of Siemens AG:

As we move into what will be a century of unprecedented challenges, successful leaders will rely even more intensely on strengths that have become crucial in recent years—speed of decisions, flexibility, capable delegation, teamwork, the ability to build for the long-term while meeting short-term needs— and vision. Increasingly, networked and globalized thinking will be essential for coping with the accelerating pace of change.

Successful strategies will be built on internal capabilities. While the new competitive landscape in the new millennium will be dynamic and challenging, successful strategies will be determined by what executives do inside their companies. In the early 1990s, a number of executives were praised for returning their firms to profitability through large layoffs and the sale of substantial amounts of assets. This will not be the case in the 21st century. Turnover among top executives has increased significantly in the last few years signifying growing managerial challenges. The new frontier requires knowledge, flexibility, and vision. Managers will build human capital and effectively utilize its fruits to sustain a competitive advantage. The watchword in the new millennium is continuous transformation through the creation and application of new knowledge.

≈≈≈

SELECTED BIBLIOGRAPHY

Useful sources of explanation and more detailed information on the new frontier and competitive landscape in the new millennium can be found in the following: R. A. Bettis and M. A. Hitt, "The New Competitive Landscape," *Strategic Management Journal,* 1995, 16 (Special Issue), 7–19; M. A. Hitt, B. W. Keats and S. M. DeMarie, "Navigating in the New Competitive Landscape: Building Strategic Flexibility and Competitive Advantage in the 21st Century," *Academy of Management Executive,* 1998, 12(4), 22–42.

Insight about the 21st century landscape and navigation within it may be obtained in "21 Rules for the 21st Century," *Fast Company,* September 1999; "21 Ideas for the 21st Century," *Business Week,* August 30, 1999, 78–167.

For a thorough examination of the effects of globalization, the following sources are useful: S. M. Leong and C. T. Tan, "Managing across Borders: An Empirical Test of the Bartlett and Ghoshal (1989) Organizational Typology," *Journal of International Business Studies,* 1993, 24, 449–464; T. W. Malnight, "The Transition from the Centralized to Network-Based MNC Structures: An Evolutionary Perspective," *Journal of International Business Studies,* 1996, 27, 43–63; W. G. Sanders and M. A. Carpenter, "Internationalization and Firm Governance: The Roles of CEO Compensation, Top Team Composition, and Board Structure," *Academy of Management Journal,* 1998, 41, 158–178.

Excellent sources of the effects of technology and importance of organizational learning and knowledge include A. C. Boynton, "Achieving Dynamic Stability through Information Technology," *California Management Review,* 1993, 35, 58–77; W. M. Cohen and D. A. Levinthal, "Absorptive Capacity: A New Perspective on Learning and Innovation," *Administrative Science Quarterly,* 1990, 35, 128–152; S. Kotha, "Mass Customization: Implementing the Emerging Paradigm for Competitive Advantage," *Strategic Management Journal,* 1995, 16 (Special Issue), 21–42; D. Lei, M. A. Hitt and R. Bettis, "Dynamic Core Competencies through Meta-Learning and Strategic Context," *Journal of Management,* 1996, 22, 547–567.

Discussions of managerial characteristics and mind-sets relevant to the new millennium can be found in W. Bennis, "Cultivating Creative Genius," *Industry Week,* August 18, 1997, 84–88; M. T. Dacin, M. A. Hitt and E. Levitas, "Selecting Partners for Successful International Alliances: Examination of U.S. and Korean Firms," *Journal of World Business,* 1997, 32, 3–16; R. D. Ireland and M. A. Hitt, "Achieving and Maintaining Strategic Competitiveness in the 21st Century: The Role of Strategic Leadership," *Academy of Management Executive,* 1999, 13(1), 43–57; D. Leonard-Barton, *Wellsprings of Knowledge* (Boston: Harvard Business School Press, 1995); W. H. Miller, "Leadership at a Crossroads," *Industry Week,* August 19, 1996, 43–57; R. D. Nixon, M. A. Hitt and J. E. Ricart i Costa, "New Managerial Mindsets and Strategic Change in the New Frontier," in M. A. Hitt, J. E. Ricart i Costa and R. D. Nixon (Eds.), *New Managerial Mindsets: Organizational Transformation and Strategy Implementation* (New York: John Wiley & Sons, 1998), 1–12.

Employer Sanctions Against Immigrant Workers

Muzaffar Chishti

The employer-sanctions law has neither helped reduce undocumented immigration nor improved wages and working conditions of U.S. workers, but has become a tool to suppress workers' rights to organize.

AFTER decades of steady decline, union membership made an impressive gain last year. Effective and well-run organizing campaigns have received public attention, even admiration. What is less recognized is that some of the finest recent campaigns involve immigrant workers. Campaigns organizing home-care workers in California, demolition workers in New York, laundry workers in the Carolinas, hotel workers in Minnesota, meat packers in Nebraska, and apple pickers in Washington are only some examples of this unprecedented trend in the labor movement. Unions and immigrants have embraced each other in a big way.

Some fundamental changes in our society are responsible for this remarkable shift. Immigration has reached historic heights. New immigrants not only are settling in traditional urban centers, but are spreading, in significant numbers, all across the country. More than a quarter of the new entrants to the labor market are foreign-born—a figure expected to reach one-third in a few short years. This shift has been most dramatic in the low-wage sector. Despite earlier predictions to the contrary, jobs in the low-wage sector have grown in the 1990s. Globalization and the restructuring of the economy have resulted in a decline in the manufacturing sector and a huge gain in the service sector. (As academics like Saskia Sassen have reminded us, Wall Street yuppies create a demand for low-wage workers to cater to their diverse services needs!) This development has coincided with another

dramatic economic development of the last two decades: the real-wage decline in the low-wage occupations. It is not surprising, therefore, that, given choices, native-born workers are not drawn to these occupations. Immigrant representation in the low-wage market has thus shown a phenomenal increase. Research suggests that in some high-immigrant areas of the country, immigrant representation in the low-wage labor market is as high as 75 percent.

Thus, unions organizing in the low-wage sector today are, inevitably, organizing immigrant workers. Some of the biggest campaigns by Service Employees International Union (SEIU), Union of Needletrades, Industrial and Textile Employees (UNITE), Hotel Employees and Restaurant Employees (HERE), United Food and Commercial Workers (UFCW), and the Teamsters have involved immigrant workers. And immigrants have consistently demonstrated their commitment and desire to support and join unions. For immigrants in a new country, the need to belong is a compelling one.

While the unions have brought renewed vigor and commitment to organizing immigrant workers, they have found it to be a daunting task. Compounding the usual challenges of organizing in a hostile anti-union environment is the curious working of U.S. immigration laws. Central to the difficulty of organizing immigrant workers today is the immigration law provision popularly referred to as "employer sanctions."

Enacted in 1986 as part of the Immigration Reform and Control Act (IRCA), the employer-sanctions law makes it unlawful for an employer to *knowingly* hire or continue to hire a person unauthorized to work in the United States ("undocumented worker"). Prior to 1986, it was illegal for an undocumented worker to

MUZAFFAR CHISTI *is a lawyer and the director of the immigration project at the Union of Needletrades, Industrial, and Textile Employees (UNITE).*

From *Working* USA, Vol. 3, No. 6, March/April 2000, pp. 71-76. © 2000 M.E. Sharpe, Inc. Reprinted by permission from M.E. Sharpe, Inc., Armonk, NY 10504.

work, but there was no federal law that barred employers from hiring them.

The law provides for civil and criminal penalties for its violation. Employees are required to attest and employers are required to verify that employees are eligible to work in the United States. Procedurally, this requirement is satisfied by completing an Immigration and Naturalization Service (INS) Form I-9 at or around the time of hire. The completion of the 1-9 form establishes both the identity and the work authorization of an employee.

The employer-sanctions law was, from its very inception, a controversial piece of legislation. Immigrant defense advocates maintained that it would result in discriminatory employment practices toward ethnic minorities. (Three successive reports by the General Accounting Office have found that the law has led to widespread discrimination against Hispanic and Asian American workers.) Its proponents, on the other hand, argued that employment is the magnet for illegal immigration, and thus the point of hire was the critical place to address illegal immigration. Congress finally enacted the law because of its promise to reduce illegal immigration and consequently improve the wages and working conditions of U.S. workers.

Thirteen years of experience have proved, unfortunately, that the law has neither helped to reduce illegal immigration nor improved wages and working conditions of U.S. workers. Instead, it has, ironically, become a highly useful tool in the hands of unscrupulous employers in their ability to suppress workers' rights, especially the right to organize. Thus, a law whose intent was to penalize errant employers has become a potent weapon for employers to penalize workers.

The key to understanding this irony is the convenient loophole in the employer-sanctions statute itself. The law does not penalize employment of undocumented workers; it only penalizes an employer who "knowingly" employs an undocumented worker. Employers, Congress agreed, cannot be expected to be document experts. Thus, their legal obligation is satisfied if they are presented with any document that is acceptable for purposes of I-9 verification and which "on its face" appears valid. Consequently, the strict obligation of an employer is not to guarantee that undocumented workers are not hired, but only to verify that the documents presented to them for I-9 purposes appear to be valid. Not until the employer has "knowledge" that a worker is undocumented is he subject to the penalties of the law.

In the real world—especially in the real world of a tight labor market in the low-wage sector—many workers are undocumented. To meet their I-9 requirements, employers frequently hire them by accepting whatever documents appear valid in meeting the requirement. This arrangement works fine as long as the interests of the employer and the workers coincide. However, when workers decide to assert any of their workplace rights, the employer conveniently acquires the "knowledge" of their unlawful status and terminates them. This may happen when a worker complains to the Wage and Hour Division of the Department of Labor about a violation of the minimum wage law, or to the Occupational Safety and Health Administration (OSHA) for safety violations, or to the Equal Employment Opportunity Commission (EEOC) for Title VII charges, or simply votes for the union in an organizing campaign.

To be sure, employers did terminate workers in the middle of organizing campaigns in pre-IRCA days. However, the National Labor Relations Board (NLRB) and the courts have historically maintained that such terminations were unfair labor practices. IRCA has not changed that: All labor protection laws continue to apply to all workers, without regard to their status. What has changed is what in legal parlance are called "remedies." Prior to IRCA, if the NLRB or the courts found that an unfair labor practice had occurred, the remedy would be simple: reinstatement. After the enactment of IRCA, even when the courts or the NLRB find a labor practice unfair, the employee cannot be reinstated if the employer invokes the sanctions law as a defense against such a reinstatement. And, obviously, no court or administrative body can force an employer to violate a provision of the federal immigration law.

Thus, in a curious working of the immigration law, employers have found themselves with the best of all options: They can employ undocumented workers without any real fear of sanctions as long as the workers are compliant. When the workers become "inconvenient," they can be discharged with no threat of retribution. This is an ideal outcome for a sweatshop employer.

From the workers' rights perspective, this is clearly the worst of all outcomes. Undocumented workers are the most vulnerable in our society. Collective bargaining provides them the promise of some minimum protection. But when an undocumented worker finds himself terminated and without redress for the mere act of supporting a union, it sends a powerful message to other undocumented workers. They are left with little choice but to labor in exploitative conditions in silence. Holding the undocumented workforce hostage in such a manner inevitably undermines the ability of the entire workforce (immigrant and U.S-born) to seek collective bargaining rights. This results in depressing wages and working conditions for all workers. The sanctions law has, therefore, achieved the exact opposite of what its authors and supporters intended. It is a classic example of a law that offers only costs and no benefits. It is time to repeal it.

THE TOXIC HANDLER

ORGANIZATIONAL HERO—AND CASUALTY

When companies cause emotional pain through nasty bosses, layoffs, and change, a certain breed of "healing" manager steps in to keep the gears moving. They are toxic handlers—unsung corporate heroes who save the day, but often pay a high price.

BY PETER FROST AND SANDRA ROBINSON

AS A SENIOR PROJECT MANAGER at a public utility company, Michael had thrived in his job for nearly a decade. His team of 24 engineers worked quickly and effectively together and was often the source of creative ideas that helped the rest of the organization. All that changed, however, when the utility's board brought in a hard-charging CEO and made Michael one of his direct reports. "He walked all over people," Michael recalls. "He made fun of them; he intimidated them. He criticized work for no reason, and he changed his plans daily. Another project manager was hospitalized with ulcers and took early retirement. People throughout the organization felt scared and betrayed. Everyone was running around and whispering, and the copy machine was going nonstop with résumés. No one was working. People could barely function."

Rather than watch the organization come to a standstill, Michael stepped between the new CEO and his colleagues. He allowed people to vent their frustrations to him behind

---

Peter Frost is the Edgar F. Kaiser Professor of Organizational Behavior at the University of British Columbia's School of Commerce and Business Administration in Vancouver, Canada, and an editor of Organizational Reality: Reports from the Firing Line *(Addison-Wesley, 1997).* **Sandra Robinson** *is an associate professor of organizational behavior at the same school.*

closed doors and even cry or shout. At meetings, when the CEO picked on coworkers, Michael stood up for them—and often ended up taking verbal beatings. He also played the role of the CEO's front man, translating his seemingly irrational directives so that people could put them into action. "He's not such a bad guy," was Michael's common refrain. "Underneath it all, he wants the best for the company."

Michael kept at it for three years, until the board fired the CEO. By then, however, Michael was considering leaving not just the company but his profession. "I didn't know if I could take the heat in a large organization anymore," he says. "In the end, I stayed with the company, but I took a year off from being a manager and just worked with the team. I had to recharge."

Take the heat—that's how Michael describes his role of absorbing and softening the emotional pain of his organization. It was a critical role, too. After the bad-tempered CEO was gone, members of Michael's team told the board that they had kept at their work largely because of Michael's soothing words, compassionate listening, and protection.

Michael is what we call a *toxic handler,* a manager who voluntarily shoulders the sadness, frustration, bitterness, and anger that are endemic to organizational life. Although toxic handlers may be found at every level in organizations, many work near the top—they run the marketing or new-product development department, for instance, or oversee several cross-functional teams. Virtually all of them carry a full load of "regular" work, and do so very well. In fact, it is often their superior performance that affords them the job security to play the role of toxic handler in the first place.

Toxic handlers are not new. They are probably as old as organizations, for organizations have always generated distress, just as they have always generated feelings of joy and fulfillment. Strong emotions are part of life; they are part of business. And yet there has never been a systematic study of the role toxic handlers play in business organizations. For the past two years, they have been at the center of our research: we have interviewed and observed about 70 executives who are either toxic handlers themselves or have managed people in the role. Our goal has been to understand what toxic handlers do, why they do it, and how organizations can support them.

Research on topics such as organizational pain is sometimes derided for being soft or unrealistic or even for being "politically correct." "Those people," the criticism goes, "don't understand how real organizations work. Companies can't be bothered with making everyone feel warm and

fuzzy. There's a bottom line to worry about." But our study did not start with an assumption that organizations, per se, are responsible for their employees' personal happiness. Rather, we were motivated to study toxic handlers because of their strategic importance in today's business environment.

Toxic handlers voluntarily shoulder the sadness and the anger that are endemic to organizational life.

In our current market-based and knowledge-driven world, success is a function of great ideas, which, of course, spring from intelligent, energized, and emotionally involved people. But great ideas dry up when people are hurting or when they are focused on organizational dysfunction. It is toxic handlers who frequently step in and absorb others' pain so that high-quality work continues to get done. For that reason alone, understanding toxic handlers is essential: to miss their contribution, or to underestimate it, is to neglect a powerful source of organizational effectiveness.

The contribution of toxic handlers merits attention for another critical reason. Organizations must recognize the toxic handlers in their midst so that their important work can be supported before a crisis strikes. Because although toxic handlers save organizations from self-destructing, they often pay a steep price—professionally, psychologically, and sometimes physically. Some toxic handlers experience burnout; others suffer from far worse, such as ulcers and heart attacks.

What Toxic Handlers Do

To illustrate the varied tasks toxic handlers take on, consider Alexandra, a vice president at a large financial institution in New York. Technically speaking, Alexandra was responsible for commercial and small-business accounts, but in reality she spent at least half of her time counseling coworkers. For instance, she frequently played peacemaker between the bank's large administrative staff and its constant stream of new M.B.A.'s.

"They always came in acting like they owned the world. Let's just say they tended to be pretty arrogant and heavy-handed with the secretaries and clerical workers," Alexandra recalls. "They offended them so much that they couldn't concentrate on their work. So first I had to explain to the staff that these young professionals were really good people inside, just seriously lacking in interpersonal skills. Then I had to pull the new M.B.A.'s into my office and help them understand that being a boss didn't mean bossing people around. And I had to do that without getting their backs up, otherwise they would have panicked, and that would have killed productivity. It was incredibly delicate stuff.

Success is a function of great ideas. But great ideas dry up when people are hurting or focused on organizational dysfunction.

"I also spent hours on end talking other managers through their fears and insecurities around our possible merger with another bank," Alexandra says. "It was in the newspaper regularly, and people would come running to my office. Everyone was terrified they were going to get fired. One by one, I would calm everybody down so they could get back to their real jobs."

In general, then, toxic handlers alleviate organizational pain in five ways:

They listen empathetically. When staff members burst into his office on fire with anger and frustration, Michael, the project manager in our first example, almost always pointed them toward a chair while he closed the door. At that point, he would let them cool down without interruption. "I didn't say much," Michael recalls. "But I would look them in the eye and do a lot of nodding." Toxic handlers are experts at such nonjudgmental, compassionate listening.

They suggest solutions. Toxic handlers don't just listen, however, they also solve problems. Alexandra actively counseled staff members on how to speak with M.B.A.'s to avoid confrontations, and she similarly schooled M.B.A.'s in office etiquette. She often advised secretaries, for instance, to meet with the M.B.A.'s early in their tenures to lay out explicit ground rules for communication.

They work behind the scenes to prevent pain. When toxic handlers see a surefire case of organizational pain on the horizon, they typically leap into action to douse it. Consider the case of a talented employee who had lost her self-confidence working for a difficult boss and was bound to be transferred, against her wishes, to another department. Working without the knowledge of the unhappy employee, a toxic handler in the organization negotiated for weeks to move the woman to a department known for its upbeat boss and interesting work. The toxic handler commented later, "The whole thing had to be done very tactfully and with political sensitivity, including getting buy-in from the HR department, or the woman would have been labeled a whiner and a loser, and I would have been accused by her boss of meddling. In the end, everyone won." The woman, interestingly, never learned the story behind her transfer.

They carry the confidences of others. Toxic handlers can be like priests. In hearing and keeping secrets well, they allow their coworkers to walk away less troubled. Alexandra let her colleagues off-load their fears about the bank's merger onto her, and they returned to their jobs renewed. Similarly, Alan, a human resources manager at an insurance company, frequently listened to anguished colleagues who were preparing to fire someone. On one occasion, the CEO confided to him that a major layoff was in the works. Later, Alan found out he was the only one in the organization who knew beforehand. The CEO told him, "I had to proceed with the layoff decision, regardless of how much I might have felt for those let go. Sharing the news with you gave me some comfort."

They reframe difficult messages. Like Michael, who occasionally served as the abusive CEO's front man, toxic handlers act as diplomats and organizational translators. Alexandra heard staff members screaming about obnoxious new M.B.A.'s, but she delivered the message in language they could accept. "A company is like a small town," she often began, "where a bad reputation is hard to lose."

Another toxic handler was told by his boss, "Tell those idiots out there to get their act together and finish the job by Friday or else they're all doomed." The manager pulled his staff together and put the directive as such: "The boss needs us to complete this task by Friday, so let's put our heads together and see what we need to do to meet this deadline." By taking the sting out, the toxic handler allowed his staff to focus on the challenge of the directive without seeing it as an attack on their capabilities. The pain was managed, and the job got done.

Filling a Need

Toxic handlers are not new, but our research strongly suggests that two trends in recent years have intensified the need for them. Foremost among them is the growing prevalence of change initiatives. Pursuing the mantra that nonstop change is not just good, it's downright essential, many executives have spent the past decade reengineering, restructuring, and reinventing their organizations. In many cases, such transformations have created enormous shareholder value. Invariably, they have also caused confusion, fear, and anguish among employees.

Downsizing is the other trend that has increased the need for toxic handlers. Whenever a company lays off employees, the people left behind feel a backwash of guilt and fear. As the question "Who will be next?" swirls around the organization, toxic handlers step in to soothe nerves and redirect people's energies back to work.

Although change and downsizing have increased in recent years, some types of organizational pain have always been—and will always be—with us. For instance, every organization experiences bursts of incidental distress: a beloved manager dies in a plane crash, a major division faces an unexpected broadside from an upstart competitor, or senior managers simply do something unwise. Take the case of Rick, a human resources manager who was asked to implement a new policy of promotions based on performance rather than seniority. At first, the policy was strongly supported by the CEO and his team, but when it went into action, old colleagues lobbied them hard, and they quickly backed down. Younger employees who supported the new policy felt betrayed, and they clamored for the CEO and his team to stand firm. Rick was caught in the middle of this managerial muddle and, for several weeks, he heard fervent outpourings from both sides. His toxic-handling role ended two months later when the CEO announced that he would abandon the revamped policy. Not everyone was happy, but as the confusion dissipated, so, too, did the worst of the organizational pain.

By contrast, some organizational pain is chronic: the organizations themselves are toxic, systematically generating distress through policies and practices. The most common of these are unreasonable stretch goals or performance targets, but toxicity is also created by unrelenting internal competition—toxic organizations love "horse races." Moreover, organizations that are chronically toxic are usually characterized by cultures of blame and dishonesty. No one takes responsibility for mistakes. In fact, people work assiduously to cover them up.

The final reason that toxic handlers exist is because the business world has toxic bosses. People like the CEO in our first story create organizational pain through insensitivity or vindictive behavior. Other toxic bosses cause pain because they are unwilling to take on the responsibilities of leadership, leaving subordinates hanging, confused, or paralyzed—or all three. Still others are toxic because of their extraordinarily high need for control, looking over the shoulders of people who have a job to do. Finally, some toxic bosses are unethical, creating conditions that compromise their colleagues and subordinates.

Toxic bosses very often work in tandem with a toxic handler. That's not surprising, since toxic bosses without handlers can be found out and then may face censure or even be fired. (It is worth noting that many toxic bosses are highly adept at managing their own bosses.) In one case we studied, a toxic boss had brought his chief lieutenant—his toxic handler—with him from one job to another for 15 years. The toxic handler routinely filtered the toxic boss's anger and prevented chaos. After meetings filled with belligerent tirades, for instance, the toxic handler would walk from office to office, explaining the boss's "real" opinions and assuring people he was not an angry as he seemed. And so the organizations they worked for continued to function. (To understand why toxic handlers do it, see the insert "More Than a Job.")

The Toll of Toxic Handling

Managing organizational pain is vital to the health of the enterprise—but at great cost to the health of the toxic handlers themselves. The negative repercussions of toxic handling are particularly high when the role is played for too long or when there is no letup in the stream of emotional problems to which they are exposed, as is the case in companies with chronic toxicity.

The most common toll of toxic handling—whatever its cause—is burnout, both psychological and professional. Remember that Michael, the project manager described at the opening of this article, took a year off from project management to recover. But toxic handling can also take a physical toll. Most professional pain managers—be they counselors or psychiatrists—have been trained to recognize the physical warning signs of too much stress, such as stiff necks, nausea, and headaches. But toxic handlers are amateurs. Unlike workers at a real radioactive site, they do not have clothing, equipment, or procedures to protect them. They toil in danger zones completely exposed.

Dave Marsing is a case in point. In 1990, Marsing was assigned to turn around one of Intel's microprocessor fabrication plants near Albuquer-

More Than a Job

The seemingly thankless task of fronting for a toxic boss begs the question, Why do toxic handlers do it? That is, why do some people take on the emotional pain of their organizations? After all, few are openly rewarded for it. As a former senior vice president in the banking industry who was a toxic handler tells us, "You have to get your reward for doing this kind of work within yourself because you rarely get recognition from the corporation."

In some cases, toxic handlers emerge as a result of their position in the organization, usually as a manager in the human resources department. But more often, toxic handlers are pulled into the role—bit by bit—by their colleagues, who turn to them because they are trustworthy, calm, kind, and nonjudgmental.

Of course, it is possible to say "I'm sorry, I don't have the time" to needy coworkers. But the people who become toxic handlers are predisposed to say yes. Many have done so their entire lives—playing toxic handler at home and in school. These individuals often have a high tolerance for pain themselves, plus a surplus of empathy. Moreover, they read every situation for its emotionality—that is, they quickly notice when people are in pain and feel compelled to make the situation right. Indeed, if some toxic handlers had not gone into business, they would probably have become counselors or therapists.

A skeptic might suppose that toxic handlers must be emotionally unbalanced themselves, suffering from the "savior complex" that afflicts some social workers or from an unhealthy desire to be needed. Some might accuse them of being bleeding hearts, who feel sorry for everyone they meet. And still others might see in toxic handlers—in particular, those who work with toxic bosses—a tendency toward enabling or codependent behavior. As anyone who has studied alcoholism or drug addiction knows, both types of relationships are very unhealthy.

But in our research, we did not encounter toxic handlers of the ilk described above. Instead, we found professional managers who happened to be highly attuned to the human aspects of their organizations. And as one manager who has observed toxic handlers in his organization notes: "These people are usually relentless in their drive to accomplish organizational targets and rarely lose focus on business issues. Managing emotional pain is one of their means." We would suggest it is also a calling.

que, New Mexico. The situation he inherited was dire: the plant's yield rates were bad and getting worse. The company's senior managers were pressing very hard for a quick solution to the problem. Employees were in pain, too, saying unrealistic pressure from above had them anxious and frustrated. "I was trying to be a human bridge between all the parts of the company and cope with all the emotions," Marsing recalls. "On the outside, I was soothing everybody, and work was getting back on track. But on the inside, I was in turmoil. I couldn't sleep, couldn't eat." Two months after Marsing arrived on the job, he suffered a near-fatal heart attack. He was 36 years old. (Currently the vice president of Intel's technology and manufacturing group and general manager of assembly and test manufacturing, Marsing says, "The heart attack was the result of a hereditary condition that got pushed over the edge from the stress.")

Savannah is another toxic handler who became physically ill after playing the role for several months. Like Rick in our earlier example, Savannah led a team assigned to implement a new program that based promotion on performance rather than seniority. Resistance was enormous, but in this case, the program went through. In the process, however, Savannah's team was brutalized by many members of the organization. "It was a case of 'kill the messenger,'" Savannah says. "All the anger and bitterness that people felt for top management were directed at us."

As a toxic handler, Savannah worked hard to protect her team from the worst of the attacks. A senior manager who opposed the new policy, for instance, sent a scathing and personally insulting letter to one team member. Savannah intercepted it and sent back a memo that instructed him to send all future correspondence directly to her. Another senior manager who was opposed to the policy tried to punish Savannah's team by moving it to smaller, less attractive office space. Savannah deflected the move, and her team stayed put, but, she recalls, "I was as stressed as I ever have been in my life. At work, I would be strong for my team, but at home, I cried a lot. I slept away from my husband, although I didn't actually sleep very much, and often felt terribly depressed. The worst, though, were the panic attacks, which would come on so suddenly. My heart would pound, and I would lose my breath."

Dave Marsing and Savannah are not unusual. Many managers in our research told us of bouts of depression, severe heart palpitations, chronic sleeplessness, and cases of pneumonia.

These anecdotal cases are consistent with scientific evidence of a strong link between stress and illness. That link was first documented in the 1950s by Dr. Hans Selye, the renowned Canadian medical researcher who found that overwhelming stress leads to a breakdown of the protective mechanisms in the body—in other words, that stress compromises the body's immune system. In 1993, Bruce McEwen and Eliot Stellar reviewed two decades of research on the connection between stress and disease. Their analysis, published in the *Archives of Internal Medicine,* concluded that stress can compromise the immune system so severely that it raises blood pressure, weakens resistance to viral infections, increases the risk of heart attacks, and hastens the spread of cancer. Incidentally, the report says, stress puts intense pressure on the biological areas most susceptible to attack. Thus, if Harry's cardiovascular system is prone to weakness, his response to stress might be a heart attack. If Carmen's intestinal system is her weak spot, then stress for her may show up in chronic stomach ailments.

A study published in the *Journal of Advancement in Medicine* in 1995 demonstrated just how long the effects of stress can last. Researchers asked groups of healthy volunteers to focus on two emotions: either anger or compassion. Measures were then taken of a key immune system antibody, secretory immunoglobulin A—called IgA—which helps the body resist invading bacteria and viruses.

The researchers found that when the volunteers spent just five minutes remembering an experience that made them feel angry or frustrated, their IgA levels increased briefly then dropped substantially and stayed low for five hours. When volunteers focused on feelings of care and compassion, IgA levels rose and remained at a high level for six hours. What this study suggests is that simply remembering an emotion can have a strong impact on a person's health. Consider the implications for toxic handlers. When they go home and remember the events of their day, they certainly experience a drop in their IgA levels that lasts for hours, since the act of remembering surely lasts longer than five minutes at a time.

In addition to having an effect on the toxic handlers' immune systems, the stress triggered by negative emotions can influence neural pathways in the brain. As people think repeatedly about what makes them angry, stronger and stronger circuits are built in their brains. That increases the level of emotional distress until a neural architecture is built that supports those feelings. They become easier pathways to activate and run. They become our hot buttons.

Thus, the situation for toxic handlers—who shoulder the stress of others in addition to their own—would seem to be all the more dangerous. "Caregivers are human, too," says Dr. Michael Myers, a psychiatrist and clinical professor at the University of British Columbia. "As a specialist in physical health, I treat many physicians each year for clinical depression. Those in administrative medicine tell me how hard it is to cope with the problems of their staff doctors and other health professionals. The administrators have lost their ability to keep their armor in place."

Organizations must recognize the toxic handlers in their midst so that their important work can be supported before a crisis strikes.

Handling Toxic Handlers

The toll of managing organizational pain cannot be ignored: either organizations should better support toxic handlers in their role or they should make them unnecessary in the first place through practices that systematically manage and diffuse organizational pain. Our focus here will be on support because our years of experience studying organizational behavior, in addition to the prevalence of toxic handlers in our research, suggests that toxic handlers will be with us as long as organizations give rise to strong emotions. In other words, forever.

Acknowledge the dynamic. The first step in supporting toxic handlers is for executives to acknowledge, simply, that toxic handlers exist and that they play a critical role. Of course, in reality, there is nothing simple about such a public admission. A culture of toughness infuses many organizations, and a high value is often placed on technical competence. Emotional competence is irrelevant; it doesn't show up on the bottom line, or so the thinking goes. And even if executives agree that someone has to manage pain, they still consider the job to be the corporate version of society's "women's work"—the stuff of daily life that must be done but is thankless. In most families, for instance, women answer the cries of babies in the night and care for elderly and infirm relatives. Women make Thanksgiving dinner, clean up afterward, and then smooth out the argument between a pair of uncles who drank too much. People rarely acknowledge these efforts. Similarly, it would be quite a departure from business life as we know it for executives to show gratitude to those who practice emotional caretaking at work.

One other aspect of corporate life makes organizational pain a difficult, even dangerous, topic to bring to the table. Middle and senior managers are usually expected to tough it out during hard times. As one manager in our study recalls, "After a particularly bitter strike that churned up a lot of agony and anger, the company provided counseling for the workers. There was nothing for any managers. We were expected to suck in our emotions, stay quiet, and cope alone." Indeed, managers at the company felt, perhaps rightly, that to talk about their feelings would have hurt their careers.

Organizations must realize that effective pain management can—and does—contribute to the bottom line.

And yet, despite the strong corporate ethic not to discuss organizational pain—let alone thank toxic handlers—we think that when executives do so, the effects are likely to be immediate and positive. Take the case of a team leader at a media company who had played the toxic-handling role during a brutal six-month merger process in which many employees lost their jobs. The team leader had managed to hit all of her financial goals during the upheaval, and she expected that would be the main focus of her performance review. It was. But if her boss had also focused on how the woman saved the emotional health of the merger's survivors, we are confident that her response would have been relief and pride, and perhaps renewed energy.

Raising consciousness about the toxic handler role requires that a forum be established in the company to talk about the topic. It needs, for instance, to get onto the agenda of management meetings or retreats, and it needs a champion to ensure that it gets sufficient time and attention in these settings. Of course, it is unrealistic to expect that toxic handling and its consequences will be discussed openly when its source is a toxic boss. The toxic boss needs to learn about the dynamic in a more neutral setting, such as a conference of senior managers from several organizations. (This could only happen in the best-case scenario, however, because toxic bosses often lack a high enough degree of self-awareness to apply the discussion to themselves.)

Ultimately, a critical ingredient of any successful consciousness-raising about toxic handling is the recognition that effective pain management can—and does—contribute to the bottom line. No company can afford to let talented employees burn out. Nor can it afford to have a reputation as an unfriendly or unhappy place to work. Many good people simply won't join. It is essential, then, to make the business case for recognizing the work of toxic handlers. Otherwise, that role will stay in the closet, where most people are comfortable with it.

Arrange for toxic handlers to share their experiences. Executives can minimize the toll on toxic handlers by bringing them together or by arranging for them to meet periodically with professionals who are trained to help them decompress and rejuvenate. Of course, this presumes that toxic handlers know who they are or can be readily identified. Thus the process of raising consciousness can be a very important precondition to setting up the necessary support for toxic handlers.

It is possible for handlers themselves to take the lead in making this happen. At one company we studied, toxic handlers spontaneously formed their own support group. The company was going through a period of rapid downsizing, and the burden of assuaging widespread sadness, fear, and anger fell largely to five managers. After a month of going it alone, the group members started to meet for dinner once a week to "let off steam," as one manager puts it. Another recalls, "One of the worst parts of the downsizing was that there was no quick bang of departures, just a slow, painful bleed. We were helping individuals to leave the organization on a nonstop basis. We were the ones who helped the managers prepare for the termination discussions and supported the employees when they received the news. Needless to say, it was a heavy emotional burden. The only way we got through it was to support one another. It was like a bereavement group, to tell you the truth—the thing that helped the most was just knowing I wasn't alone."

Executives shouldn't count on support groups forming on their own, however, especially since most toxic handlers pride themselves on a high tolerance for personal pain. As one CEO in our study notes, "These folks don't know when to ask for help; they're too busy giving it. And it would kill them to let others down by breaking down themselves." Better, then, to suggest that the organization's toxic handlers meet with one another, and even arrange such meetings. And better yet to bring in experts who can guide toxic handlers through conversations that allow them to see, understand, and appreciate the pressures of what they do. Experts can also help toxic handlers tell if they are dangerously close to burning out or presenting worrisome physical symptoms.

That's what happened to one manager in our study who had been a toxic handler for two years during a company restructuring. The manager tells us, "It took a therapist to help me to recognize that I was taking it into my gut. I was ignoring all the signs my body was sending me. I was taking things very personally. The therapist allowed me to hear myself in denial."

Finally, a professional can help some toxic handlers learn how to say no. One manager in our research tells us, "I learned that it was possible to say 'no' with options." Until that point, the manager had had a lot of trouble turning away people who needed to vent their emotions and, as a result, he was drowning under the workload of his real job and his toxic-handling role. "I learned that 'no' doesn't mean 'I don't care,' and it doesn't mean 'not ever.' It can mean, 'No I can't help you, but let me find someone who can.'" That insight, the manager says, made work manageable again.

Reassign the toxic handler to a safe zone. Even when other actions, such as counseling, can help toxic handlers deal with stress, it also makes sense to move them out of the stressful situation. These moves need not be long term. One company, for instance, sent a toxic handler who was showing signs of burnout to a two-week conference in Florida. The conference was work related—there were at least three hours of meetings a day—but also included heavy doses of rest and relaxation. It was, in essence, a bit of a forced vacation. There needs to be a high level of trust, openness, and cultural support in the organization for this solution to work. Otherwise, there is a distinct risk that toxic handlers will feel threatened by such an assignment and think they have done something wrong and that their career is in jeopardy.

Research conducted in 1995 confirms the healing power of taking breaks. André Delbecq of the Leavey School of Business at Santa Clara University and Frank Friedlander of the Fielding Institute in Santa Barbara, California, studied the habits and routines of 166 business leaders in the computer and health care industries who were known to be happy, healthy, and well balanced. All of the participants in the study worked in companies undergoing rapid change, and inasmuch, managed considerable organizational pain. The researchers found that while the leaders' habits and routines varied widely, they frequently took short (two- to five-day) vacations, typically with their families. "The breaks allowed the leaders to step back, regain a fresh perspective on themselves and their situations," Delbecq observed, "Each time, they returned to work like new people."

In extreme cases of organizational distress, however, a short break is not enough to restore a toxic handler, and organizations should consider reassigning them to parts of the company that are less in the throes of emotional distress. Naturally, most toxic handlers will resist. They value what they do and understand its importance to the organization's well-being. Thus, it is important that the decision to relocate toxic handlers be thoroughly discussed with them. But when executives sense that a manager is overloaded by the role, they must act despite the toxic handler's objections. Later, when the spell is broken, the toxic handlers may come to see the wisdom of such an intervention and may even appreciate the spirit in which it was done.

Can an organization systematically manage the pain it generates—making toxic handlers unnecessary?

Model "healthy" toxic handling. If managing organizational pain is an open topic, then managers can feel comfortable demonstrating how to do it right. Following his heart attack, Dave Marsing made it a point to show other managers how to stay calm at work, even under intense pressure. "I try, to the greatest extent possible, to maintain a level of calmness in the face of frantic issues," he says. "I try to be as objective as possible in discussions, and if I'm in a face-to-face meeting with someone who has a short fuse, I'll sit right next to that person to make sure the fuse is never lit. I do that by being calm, even overly calm. When things get heated, I even change my voice. I will consciously take a deeper breath, or two deep breaths, in front of everybody to get them to calm down a little bit and talk about the specifics, about solutions."

Marsing also encourages his staff to keep their work and personal lives in balance. "When I coach the people who report to me, who manage very large sites around the company, I tell them how important it is to spend more time with their families, to spend more time exercising, to get some help to assist them to work through administrative things, rather than putting in extraordinarily long, tense days." Indeed, Marsing believes that teaching toxic handlers how to stay healthy in what is inherently an unhealthy role is one of his most important jobs as an executive.

Making Toxic Handlers Obsolete

Can an organization systematically manage the emotional pain that it generates—making toxic handlers entirely unnecessary? It's unlikely, but our research has found several practices that remove from individuals the burden of alleviating emotional pain. Consider the practice of public grieving. In some organizations, executives create opportunities for employees to participate in rituals that, frankly, resemble funerals. For instance, when a Canadian company was acquired and folded into a former competitor from France, managers from the acquired business invited employees to church-like ceremony where the company was eulogized by executives and hourly workers alike. Afterward, people went outside and, one by one, threw their old business cards into a coffin-shaped hole in the ground, which was then covered by dirt as a dirge played on a bagpipe. The event may sound ridiculous, but it did serve a healing purpose. Employees said later that they had buried their old company and were ready to embrace the new one.

The effectiveness of public grieving perhaps explains why Stanley Harris of Lawrence Technological University in Southfield, Michigan, and Robert Sutton of Stanford University's Department of Industrial Engineering, who studied dying organizations in the United States in the 1980s, were struck by "the prevalence of parties, picnics, and other social occasions during the final phases of organizational death. People had the opportunity to express sadness, anger, grief, perhaps in some cases even relief, during these ritualized ceremonies. Often people cried."

Another way companies can systematically manage organizational pain is to outsource the task. For instance, companies often hire consultants to steer or galvanize change initiatives. Some of these change experts are—by dint of experience—capable toxic handlers. If the toxic-handling role is explicitly given to them, then it won't as easily fall to in-house managers.

The following example from our research illustrates how outside consultants can effectively play the toxic-handling role during a change program. Two consultants from Deloitte Consulting worked closely with the client for three months. One of them, Heather McKay, remembers: "We got to know many of the company's key stakeholders, and in effect became the psychiatrists for the project. Because we provided an environment of anonymity, many people opened up with us to share their fears and reservations.

"I think our role as informal toxic handlers was helpful to employees in a couple of ways. We gave a number of individuals in the organization an outlet to release the pain they were carrying around with them rather than just transferring it amongst themselves. We also were in a position to stand back from the pain and help them to identify ways to reduce it. This is easier when you are not suffering from the pain yourself."

In the final analysis, then, bringing in external consultants to act as surrogate toxic handlers may make a great deal of sense. They can often be more objective than insiders, and they can also provide more pointed feedback than managers who have to face their colleagues daily. One caveat, however: for external consultants to be effective toxic handlers, they must be trusted and credible. One Australian manager who attempted to hire external consultants to deal with a toxic situation in his company quickly found resistance because employees felt the outsiders didn't understand the painful situation well enough to help resolve it. "People in pain won't go to outsiders unless they believe the consultant really know how things are in the company," he says.

Finally, companies can systematically manage organizational pain by providing employees with stress training. Such training could decrease the demand for toxic handlers—people would be able to deal with their emotions on their own—and also help toxic handlers understand how to help themselves. Several stress-training programs exist. For example, one used by both Motorola and Hewlett-Packard during strategic change projects was developed by HeartMath in Boulder Creek, California. The program uses several techniques, such as Freeze-Frame, which teaches employees to recognize a stressful feeling, then freeze it—that is, take a time-out and breathe more slowly and deeply. Freeze-Frame concludes with steps based on the biomedical notion of improving balance in the autonomic nervous system, brain, and heart that help employees handle stress differently from their usual reflex reaction. Instead of impulsively jumping in to take over another person's pain, for example, employees are taught to catch their breath, collect their thoughts, connect with their emotions, and then ask the other person to analyze his or her own unhappiness. Returning a problem to its sender may seem like a minor change, but for toxic handlers, it is a radical departure from standard operating procedure.

Programs like those offered by HeartMath come at a price; they can run to $7,000 a day for up to 20 people. But they may well be worth the costs saved through greater retention and productivity.

In Good Company

When we began our research on managing emotional pain, we expected quite a bit of resistance—even denial—from senior executives. We did indeed find some of that. But much more often, we found executives who were aware that their organizations spawned anger, sadness, fear, and confusion as a matter of course. And we found scores of people who managed those feelings as toxic handlers themselves or watched with gratitude and concern as others did. In many cases, our interviews about toxic handling were highly charged. Some cried as they recalled its demands; others felt anger. A few spoke of remorse.

Mainly, our research unearthed feelings of relief. Executives and middle managers alike indicated that this was the first time they had been able to talk about organizational pain. We are sure that it is neither possible, nor even desirable, to remove all pain in organizations. Emotional pain comes not only from downsizing, bad bosses, and change. It also accompanies the commitment and passion of individuals striving for excellence. Nevertheless, managing the pain of others, whatever its source, is hard work. It needs to be given the attention and support it deserves for everyone's benefit—the health of employees is a key element in the long-term competitiveness of companies and of our society. People who have felt alone in managing organizational pain, or in caring for people who do, should know that they are in good company.

Unit 2

Key Points to Consider

❖ Why do you think that diversity is important in the workplace?

❖ Why is motivation such an important factor to organizations and their employees?

❖ Why is learning and self-management a key to success in modern organizations?

DUSHKIN ONLINE Links — www.dushkin.com/online/

These sites are annotated on pages 4 and 5.

Organizations are made up of individuals who are all different. In the United States, the history of the country can be traced to these differences. As new groups emigrated to North America, their differences seemed large, but as these various groups settled in, those differences became less important. The United States traces its beginnings to the first English settlers in Massachusetts and Virginia. But soon other groups followed from Scotland and Ireland. While today we may view these differences between Scots and English as nonexistent, in the 1600s there were very real. There were differences of religion (Catholic vs. Anglican vs. Presbyterian vs. Puritan), language (English vs. Gaelic), and there were historical animosities that have run deep in the British Isles. Indeed, the Irish question, as the British government so delicately puts it, has still not been fully resolved and there is a separatist movement in Scotland to this day.

In America different groups, based on religion, ethnic background, and national origin, as well as other criteria, have generally been accepted after what may sometimes seem a rather long period of time. Some groups have taken longer than others (at the beginning of the twentieth century, it was not uncommon to end an employment notice with "NINA" for "No Irish Need Apply") and other groups are still waiting to fully participate in American society, notably Native Americans and African Americans. But America, while it may not have been the melting pot that historians called it a 100 years ago, could certainly be compared to a tossed salad. The origins of people may still be identifiable by their surname, religion, or skin tone, but they continue to work with each other to create the most productive society in the world. Diversity in the United States is a strength that other countries will find difficult to copy. Americans, indeed all people, need to strive to take better advantage of all peoples' talents, as discussed in "Cultural Diversity and the Dynamism of History," as well as in "Individual and Organizational Accountabilities: Reducing Stereotypes and Prejudices Within the Workplace."

For an organization to be truly successful in the next century, it is going to have to have to take advantage of the diversity that American society offers. No organization can hope to effectively compete in modern society by deliberately favoring one group over another. An organization must actively engage in building on the diversity of its workforce; one that includes all races, religions, and genders. Equal opportunity is about taking and accepting people for who they are, not what they are. Only by taking advantage of the talents of all of the available personnel in an organization can a company hope to be successful and maintain a competitive advantage in the economy. This is why diversity matters, not because it is politically correct or socially acceptable or even legally required, but because it is the only course of action that make sense for any organization trying to be successful in the marketplace.

Organizations are made up of people, and while the organizations may be credited with certain actions, those actions are actually taken by people. There are many guiding principles that people use when performing certain actions and tasks. Some are external to the individual and involve the policies of the organization, but others are internal and involve the values and ethics of the individual. People who are required to do things in an organization may find themselves out of balance with their own values

and ethics. With the possible exception of the founder, president and/or chairman of the board, people work for companies, and it is unlikely that their values and ethics will exactly correspond to the values and ethics of the organization. This is called dissonance. There are various levels of dissonance caused by situations that are illegal, unethical, and just plain unfair. As John Kennedy said, "Life is unfair." But, how much is the individual willing to tolerate within an organization and how close to home does that have to be before it begins to really bother him or her? Managers often find themselves in an ethical or perhaps even legal dilemma, "Walking the Tightrope, Balancing Risks and Gains" (see article 7). The question then becomes, how much can an individual tolerate?

Much has been written about motivation, but relatively little is understood. One thing is certain, however, and that is that there is very little that motivated people cannot accomplish, and there is relatively little that unmotivated people will accomplish. Alexander the Great conquered the known civilized world with 5,000 Greek warriors and Cortez with fewer than 200 Spanish conquistadors conquered the Aztecs of Mexico. (The conquistadors were probably more afraid of Cortez than they were of the Aztecs. Cortez burned his ships at Vera Cruz, so there was no retreat. It was conquer or die.) Peter Drucker, the well-known management guru, has written that "most things, I have learned, are accomplished by a monomaniac with a mission." While organizations may find if difficult to instill internal motivation in their employees, the advice in the article "Motivation: The Value of a Work Ethic" should not be underestimated. Organizations can develop reward systems that will help encourage external motivation in employees to accomplish organizational goals. But it must be remembered that there will be a trade-off between the benefits of the reward to the individual and the cost of that reward as well as its benefit to the organization.

In this rapidly changing world, the only thing that people and organizations can really do to protect themselves is to continue to learn, adapt, and change to meet the continuing changes in the environment. American society is based on the idea that people can learn and change their behavior based upon what they have learned. In the United States, millions of people are involved in the education system and hundreds of billions of dollars are spent on education in K–12 schools, colleges and universities, and corporations. American companies spend approximately $100 billion a year on educating and training their employees in a formal setting, to say nothing of the informal training and education that goes on. American society is based upon the idea that people can change their behavior; that they can learn and grow and become something better than they may be today. Without this learning and growth the society cannot and will not change because the society is made up of people. For the society to grow, change, and develop, the people who make up that society must do the same.

Today, people must take responsibility for themselves and their actions as well as their careers. While organizations may help, Peter Drucker, in his essay, "Managing Oneself," contends that it is ultimately the responsibility of the individual. People who do not assume this responsibility are, in fact, leaving their fate up to someone else.

Individual Behavior

Cultural Diversity and the Dynamism of History

By Sasaki Takeshi

Introduction

With the multipolarisation in international political structures since the end of the Cold War era, grave forms of friction and conflict have been on the rise in the international arena. It is clear that international relationships are going to become even more interdependent in the 21st century as a result of economic globalization and the information revolution. It is also clear that the destructiveness of science and technology (not only that of conventional weapons), arguably an agent of international conflict, is going to grow rapidly. The international disputes that erupt will thus result in an unimaginable amount of damage to the economic and military sectors. Consequently, containing outbreaks of international conflict can be no less than a matter of dire urgency in the 21st century. The same is also true regarding conflicts within a single nation that occur in extreme form or have a high probability of becoming extreme, and that exert a significant impact on international stability.

These kinds of conflicts are often deeply rooted in the intolerant attitudes shown by one of the disputing parties towards heterogeneity in terms of culture and religion held by the other party. Though it may seem that countless conflicts throughout history were directly caused by cultural and religious differences, this is not really the case nowadays. The majority of such disputes begin as conflicts of interest in the political or economic spheres. The emotional response to these conflicts, then, is often expressed in the form of cultural or religious intolerance. This does not necessarily mean, however, that the importance of the role played by cultural and religious intolerance in the escalation of conflicts is going to decline.

The immune systems of advanced animal species are equipped at the DNA level to perform the function of distinguishing between the body and elements that are foreign to the body, and to expel those foreign elements. If we assume that the origin of the kind of intolerance discussed above is thus deeply rooted in our physiological make-up, then efforts to contain intolerance would run counter to our instincts and result in serious difficulties. Even if that were the case, however, the human race has no choice but to conquer these difficulties in order to overcome the challenges of the 21st century.

Since intolerance is often attributed to ignorance or misunderstanding of the other parties, the logical conclusion is that an effective means of combating it is to provide accurate information to disputing parties about their opponents. Without a doubt, the increasing exchange of information has yielded a degree of mutual understanding, greater in this century than in the 19th century, and greater in the latter half of this century than in the first half. Nonetheless, it would be optimistic to expect intolerance to be alleviated in proportion to the rapid increase in the amount of information that is being shared as a result of advances in the information revolution.

"Clearly Francis Fukuyama and Samuel P. Huntington view Islam as the greatest challenger to Western values in the post-Communist world. However, they do not attempt to theoretically analyse the reasons that the various ideological parts of the Islamic faith pose a threat to Western values."[1]

The lack of use of information on Islam in spite of its plentiful availability is a typical example of the tendency toward a phenomenon referred to in classical psychological terms as the selective absorption of information. In other words, information of little interest to the individual is ignored or discarded.

"Alexis de Tocqueville, who visited the United States in the 1830s wrote: 'So, of all countries in the world, America is the one in which the precepts of Descartes are least studied and best followed.' Even now, the United States is a country in which transcendental thought is strong, and a country that believes in a single justice, does not doubt progress in the modern sense, and has a strong Cartesian tendency. Until very recently, the Soviet Union, which raised the banner for another concept of modern progress, was a worthy opponent, but now neither Japan nor the European countries can challenge the force of this belief in progress."[2]

"The civic morality emphasised by Thomas Jefferson was inextricably intertwined with the concept of freedom. For example, what Sir Isaiah Berlin called 'negative freedom,' or the freedom to do anything you want to do including making judgments about politics and religion without the intervention of any other person, even given the existence of an omnipotent God, may be self-evident

This article first appeared in *Journal of Japanese Trade and Industry*, January/February 2000, pp. 10-16, published by Japan Economic Foundation (JEF), and is reprinted here with the agreement of the author and JEF.

in the context of Anglo-Saxon values. Without even mentioning Englishmen John Locke and John Stewart Mill, when we consider these things, which were born of thinkers like Benjamin Constant de Rebecque and de Tocqueville from France, a country which experienced the bloodshed of the French Revolution, it may be said that a keen sense of 'the scope of a minimal inviolate personal freedom' has been cultivated in the modern Western world, drawing upon the Christian tradition. Regardless of the propriety of that assessment, it at least explains the origins of the concern over human rights that is a feature of contemporary U.S. diplomacy. However, sometimes in the world of Islam, freedoms and rights are not thought of in this way. Islam, which recognises the equality of all people before God, is wholly different from Anglo-Saxon democracy, but does not rule out the possibility for its own 'theocratic democracy.' Because Islam is a belief system about the authority of the sacred laws of God, it cannot unconditionally approve of the right of people to freely choose their own belief systems and to live without being bound by religious prohibitions, such as condemnation of Islamic doctrine."[3] Also, "even in the new millennium it would be unthinkable for Muslims to try to implement the kind of separation of church and state that Europe carried out during the 16th and 17th centuries in an attempt to redefine the relationship between God and humankind and the relationships between people."[3]

"But the non-Western cultures and civilizations, with their long history, have at least a certain degree of consistency. This, however, will not be apparent through the spectacles of modern progressivism. What will be apparent will only be the logic of a 'state of deficiency,' which is to say that the observer is aware that something remains unobserved when seen through these spectacles. Of course, the spectacles of modern progressivism are excellent, but they cause a number of biases and oversights. In the first place, it is impossible for humanity to have absolutely clear spectacles. And if this is the case, there is no way to proceed but to compare and contrast what we see by wearing the various spectacles."[4] This is the case where the Islamic world is looking at the Western world, or the other way around.

"As long as the United States tries to sustain its progressive/transcendentalist tendency, there will be no means for the American people to orient their own intellectual position other than as either an intellectual conversion of the world or intellectual isolation. Thus there is a danger that the United States, in dealing with international questions, will rely on abstract concepts and reject other kinds of ideas."[2]

"It would be natural for the Muslim community to detest being instructed by Westerners priding themselves in justice and good faith even in the most excellent of democracies. This is because they have developed a sense of identity in which they share a common fate, for better or for worse, with despots who share the same language and belief system. The 16th century Moroccan legal scholar Al-Wansharessy aptly wrote that 'a Muslim tyrant is preferable to Christian justice'."[6]

"Is it because of this quality, which does not start with a single justice, that the United States became particularly irritated with the Japanese way of thinking? Japan is in no way a country that rejects change; it adapts to change. But the adaptive changes Japan makes do not follow previously determined principles. The so-called American revisionists always point this out as Japan's problem. Certainly, given the present rapidly changing international situation, there is a danger that the Japanese pattern of gradual adaptation will cause serious friction. At the same time, dealing with specific problems one by one, without rejecting them ideologically, may be Japan's strong point."[5]

"Considering the question more broadly, with reference to the United States and Japan, what is now most necessary to create an international society that incorporates various cultures and races? Until now, the usual answer has been that an abstract, universal framework is needed, which can accommodate the uniqueness of individual cultures. Even if such a framework could be developed, it would bring with it difficulties almost like those of a new 'super-religion'."[5]

"Until now, the overwhelming military and economic force of Western culture has blocked viewpoints (spectacles) other than those originating in the West. From now on, however, with the decline in the significance of military force and the spread of economic power, if humanity is to continue to exist, all cultural units (natio) will have to search for a way to coexist and understand each other. Non-Western countries will have to create societies unlike the West, and Westerners will have to accept the polymorphism of such a future world. It is erroneous to imagine that in a world with thousands, or rather tens of thousands, of years of history, all societies will gradually become identical. No doubt 'mutual understanding' is necessary [for dealing with a world that is not converging simply toward homogenisation], but simply repeating this mantra is insufficient. What is really necessary is to redefine what 'understanding' is, and to do this, [a] methodology must be created that demands tolerance for the wearing of spectacles other than those produced in the West. This will of course not be easy, but it constitutes perhaps the core of 'understanding'."[4]

"A new composition for the 21st century world will likely have to be drawn by setting aside the enforcement of unilateral value systems while suppressing the biases of various theories of civilization. There is much to learn from European philosophers, such as Giovanni Battista Vico, who taught people to understand other cultures, and Johann Gottfried Herder, who emphasised the fact that each civilised world has its own richly unique way of life. Even an attempt to take a critical look at the Muslim world requires that the observer should take the stance of trying to cross the barriers of time and space in order to understand that world's principles and beliefs. The observer certainly need not agree with those principles, but he or she will not be able to deny the importance of what Herder calls understanding through sympathy, insight, and 'emotional ingression' in an attempt to sophisticate imagination required to deal with heterogeneous ways of thinking."[7]

"The question of the polymorphism of liberalism of action has been debated for a long time. The first example was perhaps the argument of John Locke, who discussed freedom of religious action in British society after the Puritan revolution, advocating the need for 'toleration' between the various sects. In fact, freedom of belief is the argument that is easiest to draw directly from freedom of thought. But what Locke was talking about was something more than simply freedom of religious action. He was discussing something more than 'relativism' as regards religion. He affirmed that each religion is orthodox (not heretical), and that there should be 'charity, meekness, and good will in general towards all mankind, in other words, the presence of natural companionship, and that toleration stems therefrom.' Locke's concept of toleration was derived by believing in a commonality that transcends religious positions. This fact distinguishes Locke's concept of toleration from ordinary relativism. When the link provided by God at its core is lost, the philosophy of natural rights, which posits that human beings have an innate right to freedom, easily becomes a relativism with no interest in relationships with others. At present, liberalism is globally exposed to this danger. It is only 'natural companionship' among all mankind that has the capacity to save us from this danger and nothing is thus more important than mutual understanding that can cultivate this companionship. We cannot discover a just criterion for action that should be applied to the whole world."[8]

"In a sense, the assertion that human beings are the same, or should be the same, is dangerous because it can be too easily betrayed and tends to foster indifference or apathy. Our starting point should be to believe that human beings, or societies, are different but that they have some commensurability. The key to ensuring that liberal societies continue should be mutual tolerance that differentiates itself from relativism, commensurability that differentiates itself from sharing of common identity, and the creation of a set of rules that bases itself on this perception.

This is the substance of the 'understanding' for which I have consistently argued. There may be those who perceive that this may be minimal, or unreliable. But given the present conditions, even such an understanding is difficult to obtain. It is now necessary to start out from such a minimum understanding. Adam Smith, for example, sought in 'sympathy' the way to achieve this minimum understanding. In the terms of this book, this would mean to control the impatient predilection for a single justice and universal principle, and to make an effort to seek commensurable points by means of overlapping images of diversified individuals and societies."[8]

There are many cases in history where general cultural intolerance was deeply rooted in religious intolerance. Nonetheless, it is encouraging to see a certain epoch-making development in progress steadily though quietly which could be expected to find out a way out of the impasse with regard to this issue. That is to say, the Christian church has taken the initiative, based upon a decision made by the Second Vatican Council, to embark on dialogue with non-Christian religions, and interactions with adherents of Buddhism have been proceeding especially well. Ways of thinking that have given impetus to these interactions must have much in common with the ways of thinking discussed above.

1. Masayuki Yamauchi, Islam and the United States (Japanese Version), p. 321.
2. Yasusuke Murakami, An Anticlassical Political Economy (Japanese Version), p. 528. (An Anticlassical Political-Economic Analysis: A Vision for the Next Century, trans. Kozo Yamamura (Stanford: Stanford University Press, 1996).)
3. Yamauchi, p. 80–81.
4. Murakami, pp. 472–473.
5. Murakami, p. 529.
6. Yamauchi, p. 84. 6.
7. Yamauchi, pp. 57–58.
8. Murakami, pp. 506–508.

How should we approach today's diversity of culture and religion? How might we foster tolerance for diversity? Difficult questions, indeed. A meaningful discussion is impossible without first having a clear picture of the complex historical underpinnings of each one, and I believe it is necessary to treat specific phenomena with due caution when developing a general theory. For example, in recent years in Japan we have witnessed an increasing number of bizarre incidents involving cults such as *Aum Shinrikyo*, while at the same time arguments in favor of conserving Japanese culture—in all of its forms from corporate to traditional—are as popular as ever. It is reckless to attempt to discuss all these separate phenomena in the same breath. The social ecology of culture and religion is not a static thing, but changes day by day, and making sense of its constant metamorphosis of form and function is accordingly a never-ending task. In this essay, I will attempt to approach this problem with reference in particular to 20th century Japan.

I. The 20th Century and the Rise of Awareness of Diversity

One of the most salient features of the 20th century is the fact that history unfolded on a truly worldwide scale, that events in one part of the world came to affect those in other parts to such an extent that to discuss one's own society or history without making any reference to world events became meaningless. In former times, diversity was by and large accepted as a given, on the premise that regions and nations are by nature isolated and separate entities, but this world order changed for good in the 20th century. Of course, the occasional rise of empires sometimes destroys independence based on the premise of isolation and separation, as the history of the Mongol empire illustrates, but looking back through the ages, such examples are if anything exceptions in history. The 20th century was however different. In terms of their geographical spread, temporal scale, and depth of social penetration, events occurring in different regions of the world began to significantly impact the lives of people throughout the world. The main reason for this is the way in which stunning advances in science and technology brought about unprecedented changes in our daily lives and enabled a heretofore unimaginable telescoping of time and space.

Even Europe and the United States, who could justifiably regard themselves as the principal players in the recent history of the world, found that the way in which history increasingly tended to boomerang on them was troublesome at times. Imagine, then, the tremendous impact that technology and rapid change must have had on those regions and nations who were on the fringe of world events, and found themselves being dragged willy-nilly onto the world stage. Contact with the modern age put enormous pressures on their political and economic institutions, pressures which often resulted in their colonization. The culture of such nations was also affected deeply, the shock of contact often bringing about a crisis in identity. This emotional and intellectual stress was great not only for colonized regions, but also for countries such as Japan which appeared to be very successful in this historical challenge. Natsume Soseki (1867–1917), Japan's most famous Meiji-era literary figure, warned astutely that the impact of the modern era had left Japan emotionally scarred, and voiced his concern about the path that such a Japan would take. The reason for the enduring popularity of Russian literature in Japan was the often vivid depiction of battles for identity fought between supporters of the Slavic and western world views.

Moreover the emergence of a single stage for the enactment of history has had the effect of heightening awareness in the people of different regions or nations of their distinctiveness vis-a-vis the rest of the world. The more that a particular nation or region considers its role on the world stage, the more its people will be forced to ponder their own diversity and identity. And the more successful a nation is, the more it will be tempted to reject the role or rules assigned to it, and instead assert what it claims to be its "real self." Victory in the Russo-Japanese War led Japan to fall into just such a temptation, resulting in internal divisions that eventually led to the tragic political events of the 1930s. The most barbaric and simplistic form that the assertion of identity can take is racism or ethnic hatred, and sure enough the beginning of the 20th century witnessed a surge in racism which in time threatened to destroy human society. It is clear that a major theme in the history of the 20th century has been the tension between the forceful imperative for unification on the one hand and aggressive claims of distinctiveness on the other.

Japan too made strenuous efforts to play a major role on the world stage, sometimes eagerly pursuing a strategy of rapid westernization, at other times engaging in rapid nationalism, but whatever behavior it took becomes understandable to some extent against the backdrop of

world history in the 20th century. Thus, we see how China's defeat in the Opium War made a deep impression on Japan's leaders, triggering in them a deep fear of colonization by the Great Powers. It was such a fear that forced them to thoroughly rethink their system of government, which was built on an isolationist stance. The leaders of the preceding Edo period had used the premise of isolation to build a system that succeeded superbly in containing all social and political dynamism, as a result of which Japan enjoyed a period of unbroken peace lasting an unprecedented 200 years. But this system, which so brilliantly combined isolation from outside influences with internal stability (or stagnation, if you will), a system which in the final analysis was characterized by the naive complacency of its creators, was to crumble abruptly in the face of growing pressure from external events.

According to a recent report, Japan's economy grew more than that of any other country in the world during the 20th century. And yet, almost all of the foreigners who visited Japan in the last years of the Edo period and the beginning of the Meiji era had the same to say about the Japanese—that they were a lazy people. Nowhere in the reports of foreign observers was there any hint that the Japanese were capable of such dramatic success, which strongly suggests that the popular image of the Japanese as "tireless workaholics" is little more than myth, or at the very best, a product of recent history. The same can be said of the image of Japanese as a "warlike people"; to liken present-day Japanese to their counterparts of the 1930s is nothing more than simplistic demagoguery.

What we can say now with some certainty is that the social diversity of a particular group, nation or region is to a large extent "manufactured," a product of history closely connected with the concrete economic and political circumstances of the nation or region concerned.

There is in fact a large historical element to almost all social diversity, but in contrast to the past when the lower pace of change gave such identity the appearance of having "grown" naturally, the frenetic pace of change in the 20th century has made us more keenly aware of its "manufactured" nature. Taking 20th century Japan as an example, we find in the first half-century an inordinate emphasis on militarism, while life in Japan in the latter half-century has been dominated by economic endeavors. The success of the Japanese economy led in the 1980s to a great deal of theorizing about the apparent uniqueness of the Japanese economic system, but while this system looks on the surface to be deeply embedded in Japanese history and social mores, it is now common knowledge that its history goes back little further than fifty years. In fact, Japan's economic system before the 1920s, far from being dominated and controlled by bureaucrats, was much closer to an Anglo-Saxon model. Moreover the system, which until ten years ago was considered to be almost inseparable from Japanese national identity, has in recent years become the butt of criticism as a system that serves only to benefit the bureaucracy and other parties with vested interests. Japan's social system has frequently been explained as a manifestation of some unique Japanese character, but the fact is that this Japanese character is more often than not an artifice which has been "invented" to provide support for and justification of the social system. This way of thinking encourages an attitude of smugness which, when the system loses its muscle, serves only to deepen the sense of despondency and provoke the kind of identity crisis that we have been witnessing in Japan since the beginning of the 1990s.

In contrast to the above, it is possible to argue for the existence of cultural differences and distinctiveness which are much more independent of the prevailing economic and political system at any given juncture in history. The most obvious examples are moral values or religious beliefs that have become established over a long period of time, together with traditional customs that are often the products of those beliefs. Such cultural elements could perhaps be better described as having "grown" naturally as opposed to being "manufactured," and as such are far less likely to be affected by the twists and turns of history. These beliefs and values undoubtedly influence individual behavior and have important consequences for society over the long term. Japan is no exception in this respect, being regarded as possessing its own unique identity, but insofar as that identity is not closely connected to any particular religious belief system, it is highly elusive, giving rise to Japan's reputation for inscrutability. It is in fact this very elusiveness which has attracted the Japanese people's attention to their own character. Maruyama Masao, the world-renowned authority on the history of Japanese thought, identifies what he calls an *"basso ostinato* (ancient layer)" in Japanese consciousness, and argues that this *"basso ostinato"* has served to dampen or otherwise control the influence of foreign religious beliefs and ideologies on Japanese thought.

When the influence of this kind of cultural diversity and identity is limited to personal interests and everyday life, it rarely warrants discussion. When, however, a clear political or social function is attached to traditional beliefs and values, they can easily become confused with the historically "manufactured" elements mentioned earlier. For example a sudden threat from outside might result in an appeal to the power of tradition, leading to the use of social mores as a political weapon. Had Shinto not been used as a tool to promote national policies, it would likely never have become the subject of so much discussion. In short, religious beliefs and traditional customs have little political significance unless they are deliberately employed as a means of establishing a group identity, but once they are used in such a way, they have to pay the political consequences. Japan's Emperor system owes its survival in part to its isolation for much of its history from the political arena, but when the system was given a central role in politics with the Meiji Restoration, it was once more automatically exposed to political risks. One could say that for Japan the 20th century was characterized by the political exploitation of cultural resources, that it was a century of inexorable, politically motivated mythmaking. With its relative stability/stagnation threatened by outside pressures, Japan embarked on the path of deliberately politicizing its apolitical customs and social mores.

II. The Upsurge in Assertion of Cultural Identity in the Post–Cold War Era

It was Edmund Burke who argued famously that the French revolution was the first revolution to have been instigated by theoretical arguments, and by and large the 20th century inherited that current. People came to realize that theory and ideology, far from reflecting reality, had the power to "create" it. Ironically Marxism, an ideology which maintains among other claims that economic sub-structure will determine ideology, demonstrated a remarkable ability to change society and "create" a new reality. When ideology is combined with the power of the state, it has proved to be relatively easy to "create" a certain reality, and the Cold War was in fact a dangerous game played out under the premise that it was eminently possible to use ideology to "create" reality. And it proved possible to make not only the political and economic system, but also a nation's culture part of that reality. However, the "creation" of a reality by theory does not necessarily result in a reality possessing its own diversity and distinctiveness. On the contrary, such experiments invariably promote homogeneity and uniformity, and the Cold War made effective use of ideology to promote an enforced uniformity on an unprecedented world-wide scale.

Moreover both liberalism and socialism were hampered by the content of their ideologies when faced with such problems as ethnic differences. Liberalism is naturally tolerant of diversity, but being a basically individualistic ideology, displays a keen aversion to any debates which treat groups as a given reality. And socialism regards ethnic distinctiveness as a problem that needs to be overcome in the course of history, as a result of which it has tended to avoid dealing directly with the subject. Proponents of both of these ideologies seem to have adopted the attitude that with the defeat of fascism, ethnic distinctions basically became a "problem of the past." The Cold War managed through ideology and military power to keep a lid on problems of ethnic and cultural diversity. As a result, the end of the Cold War, far from bringing about a solution to such problems, succeeded only in exposing them once more to the light of day. Particularly in the former socialist nations where the economic and political systems had collapsed, appeals to ethnic affiliation proved to be highly effective in bringing people together, as a result of which the free expression of ethnicity came to be regarded as an almost inseparable element of democratic government. Moreover the upsurge in ethnicity had a snowball effect, stimulating similar feelings in one ethnic group after another, and to such an extent that independence movements and ethnic cleansing escalated in tandem, feeding into and off to each other, as we saw in the tragic events following the break-up of Yugoslavia.

The end of the Cold War had two major effects on the power of states. Firstly, since the Cold War had had the effect of freezing national boundaries by upholding the status quo in the name of international stability, the end of the Cold War meant that such constraints no longer operated. The effects of this were left most tragically in Africa, where without anyone attempting to mediate, one bloody ethnic dispute after another took place. (If any such disputes had occurred during the Cold War era, either the United States or Russia or their proxies would have stepped in to bring the area concerned under their sphere of influence.) Secondly, the end of the Cold War freed borders to market penetration, and accordingly heralded a rapid globalization of the market economy. Governments were forced to restructure their economies and adopt policies that were attuned to the so-called global standard, and affiliation to East or West was no longer of any relevance. Viewed in this light, it is no coincidence that the end of the Cold War also signaled an intensification in economic friction between Japan and the United States. Moreover, the emphasis of the global standard shifted from the opening up of markets to regulation of economic activity according to the rules of the financial market, and nations found their authority suddenly subordinated to the vagaries of the international money markets. The fact that government bonds came to be rated on international money markets pushed home the point that nations were now the object of regulation. As they began to lose political methods to manage their national economies in the face of invasive market forces, national governments witnessed concomitant erosion of the power they had managed to accumulate since the 1930s. Little by little, they have had to relinquish their authority to international organizations, to the market place, and even to local governments. The European Monetary Union can be viewed in this regard as an attempt at a new political union in response to the erosion of the power of nation states. At the same time, the way in which one Asian country after another succumbed to financial crisis in the 90s also serves to demonstrate how nations have been weakened by the globalization of markets.

Naturally, the weakening of state power erodes their abilities to suppress potentially troublesome elements such as cultures or religions, which as a result gain new opportunities of asserting themselves. Erosion of the economic autonomy of nations and the emergence of groups challenging their authority will escalate apace through a process of mutual amplification. Accordingly, we have witnessed a dramatic increase in the number of minorities clamoring for autonomy in recent years. Moreover, governments attempting to suppress such movements through military force are increasingly likely to become the targets of international censure in the name of upholding human rights. For example, policies such as ethnic cleansing in the successive wars which plagued the former Yugoslavia resulted in military intervention by Western nations, and intervention by the UN enabled East Timor to achieve independence. Such events suggest that the international environment is now ripe for pressing home claims for democratization and independence.

However, states in the present day are also undergoing a different kind of change. Both liberalism and socialism, differing though they do in their claims, are firmly grounded in modern-day secularism. Both ideologies agree on the point that the state should play a basically secular role, and differ only in what they see to be the extent of that role. However since the end of the Cold War, we have seen a growing number of examples where the common premise of political secularism is being called into question. The rise in Islamic, Hindu and other religious fundamentalism are typical examples. Contrary to the claims of minority groups, those fundamentalist movements are noteworthy for being grounded in universal religions. Secularism is based on the premise that a government should concern itself only with the outward behavior of people, and when a government starts to involve itself in deciding religious matters, it is bound to collide with peoples' notions of freedom. It is still difficult to judge whether religious fundamentalism is merely a self-defense repose to the spread of secularism, or whether it represents a viable new choice for the world. While it has been proven time and again that religion can be a tremendously powerful tool when exploited for political ends, it is equally true that fundamentalist movements tend to be limited in their influence by their very religiosity.

III. The Future for Cultural Diversity in the 21st Century

It would be reasonable to assume that in the 21st century too, any discussion about group, regional or national diversity would be fruitless without reference to the global context. The problem is: what should one select as the central axis around which world events unfold? Presently the most prominent candidate for such a role is global capitalism, which is not only eroding existing economic structures but also sending shock waves through the political structures of nations. I regard this as a very significant shift in the direction of history, one which may even represent a reversion.

In the 19th century the system of individual nations was based on the economic and social control exercised by the international market mechanism, but the Great Depression put an end to this system and heralded the start of the age of strong national governments. One could say that World War II and the emergence of welfare states were two sides of the same coin of strong government. Looking back on Japan's history, it financed its war with Russia by issuing government bonds on the world financial market (New York), and up until a certain date even displayed a readiness to implement domestic restructuring in order to maintain the gold standard. However when the world economic order gave way, the Japanese government realized that it need no longer be bound by the constraints of the international financial market, and could freely pursue its own policies. And compared with other countries, Japan appears to have managed to maintain a strong national government right to the end, but those days are now clearly numbered. The mechanism governing the direction of world history seems to be reverting once more to that of the 19th century.

As I hinted at earlier, global capitalism is not necessarily at odds with cultural and religious diversity or with groups asserting their distinctiveness. Particularly if these claims are basically apolitical, or if they serve to erode the authority of the nation state, there is no reason for global capitalism to be hostile to them. In fact we see in progress a joining of forces between global capitalism and movements in support of human rights and democracy which is making it increasingly difficult for states to resort to military suppression. As a result, governments find themselves obliged to accommodate such demands through such measures as decentralization of authority or adoption of a federal system. Of course it is not admirable to see that groups asserting their identity will join forces with a national government to target global capitalism as the enemy without going against democracy and human rights. However the weaker the concept of a national economy becomes, and the more the power of national governments to influence the economy decreases, the less likelihood there is of such an outcome. In the event of the break-up of a powerful nation, global capitalism has already proven itself eminently capable of "accommodating" the claims to cultural identity of the various groups. What one finds, in fact, is that those groups that have allied themselves

with a state in asserting their distinctiveness have tended to be hard hit when that state goes into decline, while those with no national affiliations have tended to flourish in such situations. In short, claims to distinctiveness are likely to be influenced differentially by the decline of nations, depending upon how closely they are affiliated to the nation concerned.

It cannot be denied that some of the Japanese equate the United States with the present global standard, and harbor more than a little mistrust and hostility towards U.S.-centered global capitalism. Such hostility is of course understandable. There is considerable nostalgia for the post-war *Belle Epoque,* and some people voice fears that Japan will lose its identity. Such arguments are however retrogressive, and smack of wishful thinking based on simplistic notions of Japanese exceptionalism. One has only to ponder the vast economic resources that Japan has squandered over the past ten years or so to realize that such arguments are indulgent. The kind of hostility and mistrust for global capitalism seen in present-day Japan is probably not particularly rare in other parts of the world, too. The immediate problem is that no amount of mistrust or hostility can do anything to replace the present global system, since, although a world of diversity awash with mistrust and hostility might be an ideal stage for "the clash of civilizations," it is not a particularly alluring prospect.

A number of important points remain to be addressed. Firstly, there is the problem of the sustainability of global capitalism. If any big structural distortions pushed the system to the limits of its powers to regulate itself, we could well see a repeat of the kind of situation faced by the world in the 1930s. Particularly over the last twenty years, the influence of the global financial market has grown considerably, and the speed and scope of market fluctuations is such that these risks are very real. Compared with the gold standard

days, the financial market has become more flexible, but there is a danger of that very flexibility being used to postpone dealing with problems and allowing contradictions to accumulate. In particular, regulation of the financial markets is presently largely dependent on the U.S. government, and world financial markets are in turn very much dependent on the U.S. market. This situation gives much cause for concern, since the U.S. government will always be tempted to put U.S. interests above those of global capitalism—and we shouldn't forget that the United States itself is vulnerable, burdened as it is with a huge current account deficit. If global capitalism, shouldering as it does the responsibility for global homogeneity, should ever cease to command trust on a worldwide scale, we will be beset with the dilemma of a veritable flood of assertions of self-determination without any means in place to deal with them.

The second remaining point concerns the tension between democracy and global capitalism. The two are not necessarily at odds, but neither are they natural bedfellows. This has become clear in recent years with the rise in unemployment and growing social unrest. Insofar as it positions itself as "government for the people," democratic government cannot afford to sit on the sidelines and allow the law of the jungle, the survival of the fittest, to take over. The rush of births in recent years of moderate left-wing governments can be taken as a sign that the relationship of tension between global capitalism and democratic government is reaching a certain equilibrium. The so-called "Third Way" does not necessarily represent a direct challenge to global capitalism, but by arguing for the need of a social sphere which is not at the mercy of global capitalism, and calling for the mobilization of "social capital" to create such a sphere, it clearly distances itself from a situation in which global capitalism dominates all aspects of human existence.

Where in the past socialism attempted to modify capitalism through political means, the Third Way is attempting to do the same through more purely social means. One can interpret this in a way as an appeal for respect for cultural diversity. In the past, Karl Polanyi has argued that it is only natural for society to oppose the millstone of capitalism, and it could be that such a movement has already begun.

What I expect to see in that direction is a trend towards using respect for diversity as a means of actively restricting the dynamism of capitalism. In other words, I foresee the creation of a new set of rules for global capitalism, the purpose of which would be to provide active support for cultural diversity from the stage of liberating it from the control and suppression of state authorities. If one also considers factors such as the need to protect the natural environment, global capitalism cannot continue singing the praises of freedom forever. A point of vital importance is that, while global capitalism is not necessarily at odds with cultural diversity, it could be a culture in itself, and moreover one which tends to force itself on its surroundings to the exclusion of other cultures. There is in fact a distinct possibility that a closer examination of its cultural aspects will lead to a heightening of tension between global capitalism and cultural diversity. Here it is important to note that this is not a problem that any single state would be capable of solving. The only way in which this problem can be tackled is to establish the rules for economic activities through international agreement, and then see that those rules are enforced. This requires democratic governments to expand their point of view from that of the single state to one encompassing the whole world, and if and when that happens, the way in which the emerging global democratic government handles the problem of diversity will certainly be the subject of careful attention. In our present position as democratic governments of single states, we are engaged in an unequal confrontation with global capitalism. The major theme of the 21st century may concern the relationship between global capitalism and global democracy, but the immediate problem is how long it will take for us to arrive at the doorstep of global democratic government.

Sasaki Takeshi is a dean in the Faculty of Law, the University of Tokyo, and is a member of the Prime Minister's Commission on Japan's Goals in the 21st Century.

Individual and Organizational Accountabilities

Reducing Stereotypes and Prejudice Within the Workplace

Bryan Gingrich

Within the workplace, inequalities due to differences in physical and mental abilities, gender and race are extensive. Members of subordinated groups (people of color, gays and lesbians, white women and so forth) who are also disabled often

People with disabilities are too often excluded from the work force *and, if they are employed, are regularly limited in their potential for upward mobility.*

encounter more prejudice and discrimination in the workplace than do their counterparts who do not have a physical or mental disability. Additionally, it has been argued that such individuals are not only "tracked into low-skill, low-pay, low-prestige jobs, but also they are often further marginalized by being disconnected from the informal social

Bryan Gingrich is director of training and assessments for the Memphis Diversity Institute.

Reprinted from *The Diversity Factor*, Winter 2000, pp. 14-20. © 2000 by Elsie Y. Cross Associates, Inc.

networks and productive mentoring experiences that can be crucial to occupational advancement."[1] The talents and skills of persons with disabilities and members of other subordinated groups often go unrecognized. Because others' perceptions of them as being poor risks, incompetent, having performance limitations, and adding increased liabilities are exaggerated, people with disabilities are too often excluded from the work force and, if they are employed, are regularly limited in their potential for upward mobility.[2]

The inequities experienced by persons with disabilities are often the products both of stereotypes and prejudices held and communicated by individuals within an organization, and the culture and climate of the organization itself—that is, institutionalized discrimination. Methods to eliminate these barriers and inequalities that do not focus on both individual and organizational transformations will fail to produce the desired result—the creation of an inclusive, dynamic, productive workplace. Yet, the approaches many organizations take to address these issues focus on individual change and ignore organizational-transformation requirements. Furthermore, too often the individual-change approaches are only addressed via cultural sensitivity or "diversity" training programs. Many of these programs lack a sound theoretical basis in the stereotyping and prejudice-reduction literature, are exclusionary in that persons with disabilities may not even be discussed, and neglect to discuss organizational transformation processes that are necessary if these barriers and inequalities are to be eliminated or even reduced.[3]

Research shows that a multi-method approach that includes change at the individual level as well as at the organizational and social-cultural level is most effective.[4] In this article I explore various methods of combating stereotyping, prejudice and discrimination in the work force that should be addressed and discussed in organizational diversity-awareness and skill-building educational programs. Implementing these various methodologies assists in developing an organizational culture in which valuing diversity and managing diversity inclusively is the preferred way of work and life.

Developing change agents: Individual transformations

Often when people are confronted or asked about their use of stereotypic information, they retreat, deny the use of

> ## *Research shows that a multi-method approach that includes change*
> *at the individual level as well as at the organizational and social-cultural level is most effective.*

such information, berate the questioner, or state, "I never stereotype." These responses exemplify a misunderstanding of stereotypes. Although people often report that they do not stereotype, stereotypic information is activated in our memory on a daily basis. In fact, research suggests that this activation may be automatic and, as one might assume, it is extremely difficult to stop an automatic process.[5] This automatic activation, coupled with findings suggesting that high- and low-prejudiced people are equally knowledgeable of cultural stereotypic information, leads one to believe that stereotypes may be an inevitable cognitive process.

Despite these findings, however, various cognitive methods can be used to reduce the effects of stereotypic information on our behaviors, judgments and decisions. Since behaviors, judgments and decisions based on stereotypes can affect the bottom line or lead to serious legal liabilities, loss of a consumer base, a tarnished public image, and poor retention of talented employees, addressing these issues is vital to an organization's success.

Of particular importance when discussing these methodologies is the need to address the accountability of *all* individuals within the organizational environment, including those who have a known physical or mental disability or are members of other subordinated groups. No one is exempt from the influence of stereotypes and prejudices, and all programs should be reflective of this fact.[6] Being born of a particular gender, race or ethnicity, or being born with or developing a physical or mental disability should not make

> ## *Each person represents a complete diversity package,*
> *and perceptions, interactions, marketing efforts, and learning opportunities must be reflective of such.*

one exempt from these learning opportunities. Nor does being a member of a particular group make one an expert in this area.

Furthermore, an important aspect of this inclusive approach is that we must not, in designing and delivering educational programs or in managing or working with individuals with disabilities, only identify these individuals according to their disability. People with disabilities represent a cross section of all other "diverse" population segments—racial, ethnic, socioeconomic status, gender, sexual orientation, religious, etc. Each person represents a complete diversity package, and perceptions, interactions, marketing efforts, and learning opportunities must be reflective of such.

With these caveats in mind, I propose that all individuals may act as change agents in developing an inclusive organizational culture. The important benefits of this approach include the following:

- It incorporates persons with disabilities into the change equation.
- It perceives individuals as a complete diversity package.
- It eliminates the perception that change is only needed in persons relying on or utilizing stereotypic information or acting upon their prejudices.
- It decreases the feeling of helplessness and victimization in targets.
- It assists in developing and maintaining momentum at the individual and organizational levels.
- It recognizes that developing competencies in diversity management are necessary.

How can stereotyping and prejudice be reduced or eliminated in the workplace? Many of the methods to be discussed here involve changing the way we think about others. People can change from more stereotypic responses to more person-based responses through attention and motivation. Given that much work within organizational environments is under time constraints, providing the necessary attention and motivation to reduce stereotypic thinking may be easier said than done. However, it is possible, and economically a more cost-effective approach than allowing stereotypic thinking and acting to fester into legal liabilities.

Challenging categorization and in-group inclusion

People have a strong tendency to categorize and place labels on everything, and categorization, much like stereotyping, is thought to be an automatic process.[7] Consider how often you may think of someone as disabled, a white man, a woman, or a black man. These categories activate the cultural stereotypic information that is associated with the labels, and consequently, can and usually do affect our judgments, decisions and behaviors.

One means of reducing the effects of categorization, then, would be to change the categories that we use when identifying or relating to others. That is, for example, instead of identifying a coworker as "disabled," we might identify her as a manager or an accomplished supervisor. Challenging the categories we use can help to reduce the impact of negative stereotypic information that is usually associated with the old label, while choosing a new label that emphasizes more of the positive qualities of the individual. Since in many circumstances members of subordinated groups, including individuals who have a physical or mental disability, may represent a small proportion of the total work force within an organization, recategorizing can represent a means to reduce the distinctiveness of their minority status. This may remove much of the negativity that is inherent with the old label, while also decreasing perceptions to incompetence.

In-group inclusion is, utilizing a phrase from renowned chef Emeril Lagasse, "kicking it up a notch": recategorizing taken to the next level. Instead of just modifying the categories used in identifying and relating to others, with in-group inclusion the new labels are those that also are used by the categorizers to define their own group memberships. For example, a categorizer who sees himself or herself as a mid-level

Including others in one's in-group is a means of reducing negative stereotyping and prejudices

since people generally view in-group members as "more diverse," more positive, and more similar to themselves.

manager will see the other person as a mid-level manager as opposed to as a person with a disability. Including others in one's in-group is a means of reducing negative stereotyping and prejudices since people generally view in-group members as "more diverse," more positive, and more similar to themselves.[8] This perception of increased diversity and similarity may also lead to more person-based perceptions, as opposed to category-based perceptions, consequently reducing the negative effects of labels.[9]

Communication and common goals

As a diversity-management consultant, one of the critical issues I often find within organizational environments is a poor communication system. Employees often do not feel that they are receiving vital information about the organization's operating successes and failures, and more importantly, the breakdown in communication has resulted in many employees not seeing where they fit into a place of value within the overall picture or the bottom line. Within many organizations, employees see themselves, and are perceived by others, according to their role or task (e.g., maintenance worker, secretary) instead of as a contributor working to realize the mission and vision of the organization. These communication barriers inhibit employees from perceiving their future successes and the future successes of the organization as connected. What is lacking is a communicated message of interdependence—a common goal if you will—that drives the organization's success.

According to the contact hypothesis and interdependence theory, people pay more attention to others and are more motivated to learn about others with whom they are cooperatively interdependent.[10] When people feel that their outcomes or successes are dependent upon their success in working with other individuals, the reliance on and influence of stereotypic information is decreased, and more effort is given to discounting stereotypic information and to getting to know the person behind the label.

Think of how often individuals with disabilities are excluded from team assignments, even those focused on the recruitment and retention of people with disabilities. Company outings or outdoor management-team-building exercises may not accommodate or include people with disabilities. Implementing a teamwork environment and encouraging communication within that framework can help to decrease stereotyping and prejudice and

refute the perception of a "conspiracy" that often results when others perceive two or more people who are members of subordinated groups communicating with one another. It will also foster the development of improved human relations and an organizational culture that embraces diversity as an asset as opposed to a liability. Interdependence, then, can lead to recognizing the talent within each person instead of relying on largely inaccurate and negative stereotypic information.

Walking the talk

Often people report that because they are low in prejudice and high in egalitarian views they don't stereotype and that stereotypes do not influence their judgments and behaviors—however, as stated earlier, this is easier said than done. Devine found that high- and low-prejudiced individuals are equally knowledgeable of cultural stereotypic information.[11] Although they may believe in this information to differing degrees, they share a common knowledge through social learning (e.g., the influence of parents, peers and other adults, the media, etc.). Because of this shared knowledge, both high- and low-prejudiced individuals are susceptible to the automatic activation and influence of stereotypic information. This paints a somewhat grim image of combating stereotyping and prejudice, because even though managers and employees may have the best of intentions, they may still treat people with disabilities in a stereotypic, non-inviting, and condescending fashion. There is, however, a means to assist individuals (and organizations) in walking their talk.

According to the dissociation model, when people realize the discrepancies between their ideal (should) and their actual (would) behavior, they are often motivated to reduce the discrepancy.[12] For example, individuals may state that they would feel uncomfortable having a manager who is disabled even though they also state that they know they should not feel uncomfortable. Or there are situations in which organizations hire

High- and low-prejudiced individuals are equally knowledgeable of cultural stereotypic information.

people with disabilities to appear in their marketing campaign, despite the fact that these talented individuals are not reflected in the executive or management ranks—or even in the work force in general. This discrepancy between ideal and actual behavior has been found to create feelings of discomfort, shame and embarrassment, and people may be motivated to reduce those feelings by altering their actual behavior.[13] Unfortunately, this has only been found to work with individuals who are low-prejudiced and who accept egalitarian views, and has not been found to be effective on individuals who may need it the most—that is, high-prejudiced individuals.

Having a diverse employee base does not mean that

the diversity is being managed inclusively, diversely, efficiently, wisely and ethically.

Within the workplace, diversity-education programs can increase awareness about these potential discrepancies and consequently motivate individuals to reduce them in favor of more egalitarian behaviors. Additionally, appreciating and acknowledging people's egalitarian and just behaviors can help to elicit those behaviors in the future, since people generally feel positive about themselves knowing that they are fair and just. Caution should be taken with this methodology, however, since informing individuals of their "should and would" discrepancies can be an uncomfortable experience and can lead to denial, dismissal or conflict.

Organizational accountabilities

Most organizations actively support equal-employment opportunities and affirmative action, and many have diversity councils. These efforts communicate a message of a fair and just environment; however, these philosophies, activities and programs are not enough to transform organizational environments to ones in which diversity is recognized as an asset as opposed to a liability. Having a diverse employee base does not mean that the diversity is being managed inclusively, diversely, efficiently, wisely and ethically. And effec-

tive diversity management is increasingly a business issue in most organizations.

We should not belittle the intelligence of the average consumer. In this highly active information age, consumers are aware of organizations that hire, promote, develop vendor relationships with, or have boards of directors that include people who look like them. Consumers are quickly becoming aware of which organizations are walking the talk, and which are not. Without taking a process approach as opposed to a project approach (e.g., food festivals), and without unequivocal and unambiguous management support, organizations cannot transform themselves into the kind of environments people want to support.

Although some barriers have been eliminated through the Americans with Disabilities Act and other legislation, barriers still exist and manifest themselves in organizational cultures and climates. Many of these barriers are based on stereotypic information held by employees, often those in management positions, about the lack of skills, abilities and intelligence of disabled individuals. These stereotypic perceptions inhibit hiring, promoting and utilizing individuals with disabilities. This is often exacerbated by people who are not disabled deciding for themselves what would assist an individual with disabilities within an organization, or what the cost of accommodation compared with the economic benefits of accommodation would be, without asking an individual employee with a disability for advice.

Sandy Mayhew, who has had multiple sclerosis for seven of the eighteen years she has worked as an internal consultant for a national organization, states that her own experience has shown her that organizations may not want to change, and that they are often erroneously concerned with the costs of accommodation, even though many of the requested changes (e.g., lessening the tension on doors) can be done at no cost. Mayhew believes that there are several things an organization should do to reflect and value diverse human capital. These include "not being afraid," "knowing that it is not going to be cost prohibitive," "not setting boundaries and making decisions before trying things out," and "not telling yourself why it [hiring people with disabilities] won't work." She states that increasing the diversity within the work force "makes the environment richer," and that "people can succeed if given the chance."

Mayhew acknowledges that a "change in human spirit" is often necessary to help people see beyond the labels and stereotypes and recognize that "there are some very intelligent individuals with disabilities who are not being given a chance." Her insight is reflective of the individual and organizational accountabilities that are necessary to promote the development of inclusive organizational environments.[14]

At the organizational level, there are many actions that should be taken, beyond awareness- and sensitivity-level training opportunities, to transform the organizational environment. These actions include going above and beyond vigorously enforcing anti-discrimination laws. And as previously stated, having a diverse employee base does not mean that all barriers have been eliminated and that all human potential is being recognized, respected, valued and utilized. As reflected in the contact hypothesis, mere contact between diverse individuals is not enough to transform the organizational culture and climate. According to Cook, several conditions must be met in order for contact between members of diverse groups to decrease derogatory out-group attitudes.[15] These conditions include equal status, interdependence, egalitarian norms, sanction by authority, and a high-acquaintance potential. Translated into organizational-environment lingo, there must be a group mentality, a common goal or mission, non-discriminatory policies and actions, recognition by top management of valuing diversity as an economic imperative, and an inclusive environment that fosters communication. This means that individuals with disabilities should be included in team-building activities, be recognized as sharing the same goals as other employees, have the opportunity to work in an environment that has eliminated all barriers, and have their talents and skills recognized and valued.

Many national school-reform efforts incorporate these basic conditions in restructuring classroom environments. These same conditions can also be used to assist in organizational-transformation processes at the corporate, for-profit levels. Nowhere in these conditions does it state that all activities or programs should be funneled through a human-resources department, that only certain dimensions of diversity should be acknowledged or discussed, that awareness courses are the panacea for all diversity-related problems, or that only reprimanded individuals should attend diversity-education learning opportunities.

These individual- and organizational-change methods are manageable means to an end. At the Memphis Diversity Institute, my colleagues and I use an eight-step process approach that incorporates both individual- and organizational-change methodologies; emphasizes education, leadership

and organizational assessments; stresses leadership and organizational accountabilities; and promotes pluralism as the preferred way of work and life. In short, we employ a multi-method, multi-dimensional approach that assists organizations in setting the standards of excellence within their respective industries.

Yet these ends cannot be accomplished without learning, and organizations will need to learn fast in order to attract and maintain diverse customers, diverse investors, diverse vendors, and talent that comes in diverse human packages. Failure to do so will set the stage for mediocrity, wasted talent, legal liabilities, and missed business opportunities. It is in an organization's best interest to take the necessary steps to develop and nurture individual and organizational norms of valuing diversity and promoting pluralism. Learning that valuing diversity is an economic imperative, learning about individual and organization accountabilities, and learning about factors impacting upon our organizations and communities are the first steps in building affirmative momentum and reducing stereotyping, prejudice and discrimination in the workplace. As Sandy Mayhew put it, "This is a relatively new world for me—I continue to learn." We must all continue to learn.

End Notes

1. J. L. Eberhardt and S. T. Fiske, "Motivating individuals to change: What is a target to do?" in C. N. Macrae, C. Stangor and M. Hewstone, eds., *Stereotypes and Stereotyping* (New York: Guilford Press, 1996), p. 397.
2. See J. R. Feagin and M. P. Sikes, *Living with Racism: The Black Middle-Class Experience* (Boston: Beacon Press, 1994).
3. Although these programs *may* have the correct intent, they may miss the desired effect due to the use of inexperienced leaders who lack facilitation skills and knowledge of the processes involved, choice of programs that are of insufficient length, adoption of a conflict-oriented approach, and failure to address organizational accountabilities.
4. See J. Duckitt, *The Social Psychology of Prejudice* (New York: Praeger, 1992).
5. See J. A. Bargh, "The four horsemen of automaticity: Awareness, intention, efficiency, and control in social cognition," in R. S. Wyer, Jr. and T. K. Srull, eds., *Handbook of Social Cognition*, 2nd edition (Hillsdale, NJ: Erlbaum, 1994), Volume 1, pp. 1–40. And P. G. Devine, "Stereotypes and prejudice: Their automatic and controlled components," *Journal of Personality and Social Psychology* (1989), Volume 56, pp. 5–18.
6. Segmented training programs should be avoided. Educational programs that discuss the multiple dimensions of diversity (e.g., age, gender, physical and mental abilities, race, ethnicity,

sexual orientation, religion, etc.) should be utilized and all individuals should be encouraged to attend.

7. See M. B. Brewer, "A dual process model of impression formation," in T. K. Srull and R. S. Wyer, Jr., eds. *Advances in Social Cognition* (Hillsdale, NJ: Erlbaum, 1988), Volume 1, pp. 1–36. And S. T. Fiske and S. L. Neuberg, "A continuum model of impression formation: From category-based to individuating processes as a function of information, motivation, and attention," in M. P. Zanna, ed., *Advances in Experimental Psychology* (San Diego: Academic Press, 1990), Volume 23, pp. 1–108.

8. See C. M. Judd and B. Park, "Out-group homogeneity: Judgments of variability at the individual and group levels," *Journal of Personality and Social Psychology* (1988), Volume 54, pp. 778–788.

9. See M. B. Brewer, "In-group bias in the minimal intergroup situation: A cognitive-motivational analysis," *Psychological Bulletin* (1979), Volume 86, pp. 307–324.

10. See S. L. Neuberg, "The goal of forming accurate impressions during social interactions: Attenuating the impact of negative expectancies," *Journal of Personality and Social Psychology* (1989), Volume 56, pp. 374–386.

11. Devine (1989).

12. See P. G. Devine, M. J. Monteith, J. R. Zuwerink and A. J. Elliott, "Prejudice with and without compunction," *Journal of Personality and Social Psychology* (1991), Volume 60, pp. 817–830.

13. See Devine et al. (1991).

14. Telephone interview, November 3, 1999.

15. S. W. Cook, "Interpersonal and attitudinal outcomes of cooperating interracial groups," *Journal of Research and Development Education* (1978), Volume 12, pp. 97–113.f

WALKING THE TIGHTROPE, BALANCING RISKS & GAINS

*In making judgment calls on ethics issues, HR needs
to balance the organization's fundamental values,
the needs of employees and the bottom line.*

BY LIN GRENSING-POPHAL

A former senior human resource executive for a health care organization in a Southern state tells of some outrageous activities connected with hiring minority workers to fill management positions. "This was a lily-white organization when I joined it," he says. "The only diversity was in the lower end jobs. I brought in two minority managers and, shortly thereafter, started receiving some pressure from the board along some stereotypical lines: 'We don't hire people like that. You're not from here. You don't understand.' They wanted me to fire them. I refused, and it ultimately cost me my job."

Another HR professional lost her job at two companies because, she says, she refused to sit back and do things she considered wrong. What kind of things? Allowing a pay inequity to persist between a male employee whose salary was more than double that of two female colleagues; testing new applicants for HIV and basing hiring decisions on the results; screening out female applicants in their 30s based on the boss's fear that they would miss a lot of work due to child-care issues. "I went through a period of really agonizing over the behavior I was seeing—things I didn't expect to encounter," she says. "It was very discouraging."

HR-related online bulletin boards, such as SHRM's HR Talk, are filled with similar examples of ethical dilemmas and judgments faced by HR professionals every day. Ethical issues spill over into the media and professional literature as well. Consider these two examples:

•A story appearing in newspapers around the country reported that a Catholic nurse in Erie, Pa., was fired for refusing to hand out birth control pills or condoms to single men and women. She wants her job back and feels it was unfair to be terminated because of her deeply held religious beliefs.

•The book *Dante's Dilemma: MBAs from Hell!*, by management consultant Larry Baytos, explores ethical dilemmas involving disparate treatment of minorities, executive compensation rip-offs, sexual harassment and other issues in a fictitious corporation. Baytos, former senior vice president of HR at Quaker Oats Co., says his book is based on real events.

ETHICAL, ILLEGAL OR JUST UNFAIR?

Terminating an employee solely based on race is illegal. So is refusing to consider applicants who are HIV-positive or who are females in their 30s. Many of the issues HR deals with have clear legal ramifications—there is a "right" answer and a "wrong" answer. Where, then, does ethics come in? The distinctions aren't always black and white, and the issues tend to line themselves up along a continuum. Baytos has developed a "scale of transgressions" that may help to clarify the distinctions between illegal, unethical and simply unfair. On one end of the continuum is "unfair." On other end is "illegal." In the middle, and much less well-defined, is "unethical."

An unfair incident might be a CEO receiving a huge pay increase after massive layoffs. "That certainly seems unfair, but it's not illegal, and it's hard to make a case that it's unethical by existing standards," Baytos says. An illegal incident might occur when an employer tells a search firm not to submit names of female applicants. He tells another story of a CEO who confided that he engaged in a large diversity study, using an outside consultant, simply to appease a minority board member. "The CEO had no real commitment to the process or to making any changes," he explains. "This was a real dilemma for the people involved in the study process. To me, that clearly would be an ethical issue—not a fairness one." An unethical situation, according to Baytos, might be a company that puts its employees' retirement security at risk by forcing the investment of the retirement funds in its own securities.

Even when dealing in the center of the spectrum—ethical issues—a distinction should be made between ethical dilemmas and ethical judgments, says Frank Navran. He is senior consultant with the Ethics Resource Center (ERC), a Washington, D.C.-based nonprofit organization which, he says, essentially invented ethics consulting.

"We find that there are fewer ethical dilemmas than there are ethical judgments," Navran explains. "A dilemma occurs when two or more values are in conflict. It's the classic example you get in Philosophy 101 of 'do you steal a loaf of bread to feed a starving child?' "

Here's a recent instance. An article in the *Washington Times* on March 10, 1993, related the story of Lt. David Quint, then a Navy public affairs officer. He was censured for "expressing his opposition to lifting the ban on homosexuals in the military." In this case and that of the Catholic nurse, neither side is "right." The people involved simply have different values, which conflict with those of the organization.

Ethical judgments are different in that the values do not conflict. An example might be an organization in which "fairness" is a shared value between the company and the HR manager. A situation occurs that requires a decision to be made. Both senior management and HR are committed to "fairness," yet they differ in their approach to the issue. "The difficulty occurs when both the employee and management look at the values of the organization and come to different conclusions as to what is the right way to act," Navran says.

THE BOTTOM LINE VS. THE FIRING LINE

As one online bulletin board participant commented, "It has been comforting to know that ethical issues are out there and I'm not alone. But, on the other hand, it's disheartening to know that they're so commonplace." Why are these issues so prevalent in the workplace?

"Maybe there's some ignorance initially, but mostly I think it's disregard," says a woman who is currently working in HR at a nonprofit and actively seeking employment elsewhere. "They're trying to get the HR person to find 'loopholes'— ways to skirt the law," she adds. "I think HR people are willing to find ways to meet the boss's expectations so long as they are ethical and legal. I don't think anybody has any problem with that. When they cross that line, it's difficult."

"High-tech companies and entrepreneurs are used to calculating risk," says the woman who lost two jobs because of value conflicts. "Some of these decisions like 'will we be sued?' are based more on a risk calculation than on principle. If the risk is small enough and the perceived benefit is great enough, I believe they'll take the risk." One of the values shared by every profit-making company is to "maximize the wealth of the shareholders." That's Finance 101. One value shared by virtually every HR manager is to be an advocate for employees. Those two values are, all too frequently, in conflict. It's important, Navran says, "not just for HR, but for every line and support department to understand what the values and culture of the organization demand of them so they're operating in ways that are congruent."

BALACING HR NEEDS AND ORGANIZATION NEEDS

Many HR professionals find themselves caught between a rock (upper management) and a hard place (disgruntled, poorly treated employees). When making decisions they want to do "what's right." But sometimes it's hard to know what that

SURVEY REINFORCES NEED TO DEVELOP WORKPLACE ETHICS GUIDELINES

Despite growth in the field of business ethics since 1980, ethical dilemmas in the workplace continue to challenge HR professionals, according to the *1997 SHRM/Ethics Research Center Business Ethics Survey*. The findings were based on responses from 747 HR professionals.

Overall survey results show that although an increasing number of organizations have developed written standards of ethical conduct, many still need to do more to integrate the standards into daily operations. Of the 73 percent in organizations with written ethical standards, 61 percent reported that their organizations do not provide training on the standards.

Here are a few telling findings on ethics challenges for HR:
• Almost half of the respondents (47 percent) said they had felt at least some pressure from other employees or managers to compromise their organization's standards of ethical business conduct in order to achieve business objectives.
• Those who felt some pressure to compromise their organization's ethical business standards cited three principal causes: overly aggressive financial or business objectives (50 percent), schedule demands (38 percent) and the need to help the organization survive (30 percent).
• Respondents tend to think their own ethical standards are more in line with those of subordinates' than with those of peers and senior management.

• 53 percent of survey respondents reported that, either occasionally or often, they observed conduct in the organization that they believed violated the law or the organization's ethical standards, and 79 percent of that group said they reported their observations to management or another appropriate person.

REACTIONS TO SPECIFIC ETHICAL DILEMMAS

When presented with hypothetical ethical situations at work, the HR professionals gave the following responses:
• 88 percent would report to their supervisor the accidental discovery of information related to a major downsizing initiative in the HR department.
• 83 percent would encourage a key employee, whose position would be difficult to fill, to notify the company of their plans to leave.
• 81 percent would further investigate a third-party report of an employee abusing legal substances on the job, such as prescription medicine, and 31 percent would further investigate a third-party report of an employee abusing illegal substances off the job.
• 34 percent would further investigate a third-party report that an employee is HIV-positive; an equal number would do nothing.

means. In fact, as Navran points out, often it's not even an issue of "what's right," but of balancing divergent perspectives and holding decisions up against the organization's stated values.

In one of the corporations he has consulted with, the benefits administration and medical departments were engaged in an ongoing struggle. "Members of the medical department saw themselves as the employees' advocates, and their concern was to protect the health of employees," Navran explains. "Those in the benefits department saw themselves as managing the company's health care benefits budget. There was a tension between the two departments in terms of how long to allow an employee to be away from work, for example, after a surgical procedure.

"The way these issues get resolved," he says, "is not by arguing the medical facts, but really by understanding the organization's core beliefs. If one of the organization's fundamental principles is to be compassionate and caring about employees, then the decision needs to be tested against the compassion and caring standard. The organization's values become a benchmark." In this instance, he says, "we have an obligation to be good to shareholders, so we have to manage our costs. We also have an obligation to employees. The struggle is, how do we balance those issues? If you remember to talk about the issues in terms of the fundamental principles you're working to-

ward, it helps you reach a balance that is palatable and appropriate."

Consultant Lynn Brailsford believes "it really does boil down to the issue of 'money vs. people' or 'bottom line vs. people.' It's short-term vs. long-term thinking. The tendency of most business managers is to really look at things in a quantifiable, bottom-line perspective." Brailsford is former vice president of training and development for Chase Manhattan, and now works with financial services companies, helping them to review their employment practices and come up with suggestions and recommendations for how to create more respectful environments.

HR managers, she says, often have a credibility problem. It stems from not taking a broader, more strategic, view of the issues they're dealing with and framing those issues in terms that upper management understands. Brailsford learned that lesson firsthand from her experience as president of a small company in New Jersey. "Senior management will look at these issues if you can quantify them—if you can say 'here are the costs,' or 'here's what will happen—let me quantify it for you.' It's taking the same language they're using and franing your positions in the same way, instead of constantly trying to harp on them from an HR point of view."

Baytos agrees. "There are other priorities that CEOs are wont to look at such as earnings per quarter, how analysts are looking at the company, and how the stock is going to do next year. You'd better be familiar with these priorities. If you're not at a high level in the organization, at least find a way to have access to that high level, or your voice will be lost."

WHEN YOU MUST AGREE TO DISAGREE

What if you are truly are taking a broad view of the issues you deal with? What if your recommendations are clearly aligned with the corporation's stated values and you still feel that you're beating your head against the wall?

Navran says that when he conducts focus groups of employees, one of the most frequent criticisms he hears is that management "doesn't walk the talk." What makes the HR manager's job especially difficult, he says, is when management sends mixed messages—"when the rhetoric says 'we really believe in caring for employees' and everyone knows what they really care about is the bottom line." What to do? Know yourself. Know your own values. And live by them.

David Quint is in the private sector today, working as an HR professional in the construction industry. He admits that his experience was a difficult one, but what helped, he says, was having a solid understanding of his own guiding principles and values. "If you have a foundation of character, when difficult issues come up you can address them as easily as possible. Decide ahead of time what hills you're going to die on," Quint advises. Clarifying your values, he says, "doesn't make it easy, but it does make it less difficult."

Quint's advice is echoed by the HR manager who refused to terminate minority employees without cause. His advice: "Don't back down."

Baytos agrees. "If it's something that you really feel strongly about, you have to be willing to put your career at risk. Unless the HR person is willing to take these risks they're really not part of the solution, they're just going along with the tide and riding it out."

"The real myth that needs busting is the myth of powerlessness," Navran says. "Too many HR managers tell me what they can't do as opposed to doing what they can. I would suggest to people that powerlessness is a convenient place to hide but, very often, it's a lie. We often have more power than we're willing to accept, because we

don't want to put ourselves at risk. We use the excuse of powerlessness so that we don't have to make the decision, whether or not we have the moral fortitude to do what's difficult."

WHEN IT'S TIME TO MOVE ON

Several HR professionals who expressed frustrations about ethical issues they face in their current positions are changing jobs. "Life's too short," says one HR professional who wants to make a job change. "It's just not worth it. You have to know when it's time to move on." Here they share some suggestions on how to screen prospective employers to determine if they're the right "ethical fit."

One job seeker comments, "I would ask questions of the person interviewing me to get a feel for how they have handled certain dilemmas. Listen to your intuition. If you get a feeling that something's not quite right, it probably isn't."

"It's tough to assess from the outside, but I think there may be some clues," says Baytos. "One clue to me is 'what has been the tenure of HR people at key levels?' Constant turnover at the top may indicate that anybody who tries to come forward with a strong HR agenda quickly meets a sudden death."

David Quint offers some suggestions on the types of questions to pose to prospective employers:

•Is this a new position? If not, why did the last person leave?

•What characteristics does a successful person have in your organization?

•And, perhaps most telling: Is there anything unusually demanding about this job that I should know about?

Quint encourages HR professionals to ask the tough questions. "They're either going to respect you for that—or they won't and they won't hire you. If that happens, you're really better off."

Lin Grensing-Pophal, SPHR, is a business journalist with HR consulting experience in employee communication, training and management issues. Her articles have previously appeared in HR News and other business and trade journals. She is the author of A Small Business Guide to Employee Selection and Motivating Today's Workforce: When the Carrot Can't Always Be Cash (Self-Counsel Press).

The BEAUTY of the Organizational BEAST

How to live with and renew the places we work.

By Geoffrey M. Bellman

Many of us are as intrigued with the potential of organizations as we are disturbed with their reality. We are drawn into relationships with these powerful creatures out of attraction and necessity. We try to join our personal purpose with organizational purpose, hoping for the best and making the most of an uneasy union—for better or for worse, for richer or for poorer, in sickness and in health.

We struggle to find our personal meaning within these structures, structures not built with our meaning in mind. We know these behemoths figure in the future of life on this planet, and that awesome knowledge feeds our savior fantasies and our slave fantasies at the same time. We are part of a highly educated workforce that, each day, walks into companies that haven't caught up with what we've learned about ourselves. We seek personal actualization in organizations put together for other purposes. We sense our schizophrenia as our minds and hearts proclaim the possibilities and as our actions in our work proclaim our fears and limitations.

We recognize how essential organizations are to what we've achieved so far, and we see the immense potential they represent. Our enterprises are mad and magnificent, wretched and wonderful, beauty and beast. Recall the fairy tale in which a father—in hopes of saving his life—gives his pure-hearted daughter, Belle, to the Beast. Belle, after her initial horror, chooses to look for the best in the beast and (I don't want to ruin the story for you, but . . .) gradually finds fulfillment where she first felt revulsion.

Belle's story is our own—at least, my own. In my 35 years of work with huge organizations, I've discovered that my best contributions and greatest fulfillment came from facing the corporate Beast and discovering the Beauty within. We can live with and appreciate the beauty *of* the beast—not "the beauty *and* the beast."

Reprinted from *Training & Development,* May 2000, pp. 67-73. © 2000 by ASTD, *www.astd.org.* Reprinted by permission. All rights reserved.

Beauty is in the eye . . .

Beautiful organizations *are* possible. Perhaps you've seen some in operation, such as when a work team spins off into a creative and productive session or when a faculty cooperates to bring new learning opportunities to students.

> There are millions of fleeting glimpses of organizational beauty. If we're to see beauty in our organizations, we need to know what it is and value it.

There are millions of fleeting glimpses of organizational beauty that suggest the possibilities in our future. If we're to see beauty in our organizations, we need to know what it is and value it. When we can imagine what we want, we're more able to create it. Our ideals help us interpret and shape our experience. Imagining beautiful future organizations isn't usually identified as a common corporate pastime, and discovering the beauty in these times presents a challenge. That leads to a truth for our work and our lives: Discover the beauty.

I offer these assertions about discovering the beauty:

- Pursue life.
- Commit to a compelling unknown.
- Face the future ready to learn.

Honoring those assertions has had the consequence of altering my approach to working in organizations. Those assertions caused me to look at my work differently, to see new opportunities, to take courageous action. Let's explore them and consider the provocative questions they generate.

Pursue life. The world is changed by passionate, committed people creating better lives for themselves, their families, and future generations. That is what political revolution, the women's movement, the civil rights movement, the reformation, the union movement, and educational reform have in common. The source of energy for those efforts was aspiration for a larger life, worth working toward.

The heart of renewal in our organizations is just as grand, though not as romanticized. We too are pursuing our lives in these organizations. We too are reaching for a future beyond what we've experienced. We too want the work world to be better for all who follow us.

Our organizations are not renewed by people inspired by their job descriptions. No, people reach into their hearts and mine their life aspirations to find the energy they need. That is where renewal energies brew; that is how organizations are enlivened over and over again into future generations.

When you encourage workers to reach for what they want from their lives, they may do it. Their reach may be in directions that have nothing to do with creating a better company and everything to do with creating better lives for themselves. That risk may be worth it—depending on our investment in our present organization, depending on whether we are workers, consultants, managers, customers, or stockholders. When we avoid the risk, we miss the creative and passionate energy that people release when they see the prospect of making their lives better. To avoid the risk is never to know what we might have done together to revitalize the organization.

We must choose our struggle—whether to struggle with the issues that come from helping people release their creative energies or the issues coming from asking people to live in their present, more predictable roles.

Here are some questions that might provoke a healthy exploration:

- What do key people in the organization aspire to in their lives?
- How do they currently realize life aspirations through their work?
- What is the organization reaching for that has the promise of fulfilling people's lives?
- What opportunities are there to engage people in these questions?

Commit to a compelling unknown. Imagine an organization renewal team that has been working together for six months. It's in the midst of yet another meeting to figure out how to put some visionary and risky recommendations before the entire plant of 800 people. One team member makes (what turns out to be) a pivotal statement: "I don't know if our proposal will be accepted. And I don't know whether it will work. What I do know is that we must

The Gist

- The way to discover the good in your organization is to pursue life, commit to a compelling unknown, and face the future ready to learn.
- If we can see beauty in our organizations, we're more likely to create more of it.
- Future survival and success require humility, openness, and a desire to learn.

propose it. This organization must do something, and this team has the opportunity to offer a new direction, even if we risk failing in the process."

She spoke for everyone present and speaks to this additional assertion: Important change reaches far beyond what we know. It contains these defining elements:

- We have not been there before.
- It feels new, mysterious, and compelling.
- It is full of life for the people involved.
- We don't know whether we'll be able to do it.
- We believe passionately in it.
- We're drawn forward by its possibilities.

Another story from the same organization a few months later, after the adoption of the renewal team's ideas: The general manager and the consultant (me) are having a celebratory drink after a successful three-day meeting involving 60 people from the plant. Together, that group had described the ambitious future they'd like to create. The general manager is excited about what the group has just accomplished. He begins to muse on what might happen next. And, engineer that he is, his musings become charts, and charts become timelines, which become decisions about what ought to done next.

My discomfort begins to grow. Though not wanting to dampen his enthusiasm, I finally burst out, "If we knew precisely where we were going, I wouldn't want to go there." He looked at me, confused and disappointed. But then, he wadded up the napkins and put them aside. "I get it," he said. "It's not my job to make our future entirely predictable; that's what we always do. It's my job to encourage this exploration and the discovery of what we might do next." He expressed what I was feeling.

Yes, there is a place for planning. But in the three-day group meeting, people discovered the aspirations that precede and bring life to plans. They became committed because they didn't know where they were going. If they went after an assured success because they'd been there before, they wouldn't be renewing their organization, just redecorating it.

Take these questions to the people you work with:

- Individually, what do you find compelling in what you're doing now?
- Individually, describe some projects you've participated in that were especially exciting. What made them that way?
- What would a renewal effort have to involve for you to commit to it strongly?
- What is the best outcome we hope to see from our work together?

Face the future ready to learn. Helping an organization move toward a future it has never experienced requires humility and openness. If you're committed to guiding people toward a new vision, you will be humbled frequently. If you're a person who needs to know "first and most," you probably will take advantage of the numerous opportunities to embarrass yourself. Lack of humility is a great block to progress.

Two personal examples, one of humiliation and one of humility: I was beginning work with a new client, a marketing company. From the start, I knew what it needed. How fortunate for them to have me! I knew that we could make changes around there faster because of my success elsewhere. You can imagine what that approach did for me, and that isn't the worst of it.

Because I "knew," I didn't have to ask. In fact, I couldn't ask. Because I was "experienced" and the client wasn't, I expected deference. Because I was "wise," I expected everyone to listen. My myopia cost the client and the project critical time. I wasn't open to learning. I took an aggressive stance and blamed the client when things went wrong. That was not fun work for me to do; it was less fun for the client. The company decided it didn't need to continue working with me.

Contrast that story with my experience on a project in my community: I helped conceive the project and joined five others in shaping its direc-

tion. Then, the six of us reached out to the larger community for support. As citizens began showing up. I became more aware of how much experience I had that was potentially useful to the project and to the newly involved people. I also became aware of how little they knew about doing this kind of work.

So far, I sound something like my earlier description but with a dash of tolerance, right? Nevertheless, something had shifted, and I approached this effort differently. I still knew what I knew, but I also knew that I needed to learn from them. I saw it as a special opportunity for me. Instead of using my time to brag about what I already knew, I tried to find out more about them and what we were doing together. I had special talents, and so did they. I made a point of delving into their experience, and they brought so much. We succeeded in creating the project together, each of us with an openness to what the future might hold and the readiness to influence it.

Approaching work with new eyes, the eyes of a novice, serves my work well. That is my repeated experience. My ego had made sure that I've learned this lesson over and over again.

Here are questions for you to take to work:

- How does this organization uphold the importance of learning?
- Where have we seen leaders valuing humility?
- What do we need to learn? What are our key unanswered questions?
- How might we show a readiness to learn in the midst of renewal?

Facing the beast

Many organizations are beastly creatures to live with. They've developed power, energy, and intelligence beyond what most of us ever imagined. Many of us pull away. We see their lack of humanity and heart, we see their primitive power, we stand back from their threat and unpredictability.

Our fears often turn to prejudice: We think we know what an organization is before we experience it. Like Belle, we sense that our lives are at risk. We must choose how we see the Beast before us. When I'm at my best, I make Belle's choice: I proceed with the belief that there's something to be appreciated, something worth working with. That's courageous and, I hope, not foolish. When we take such steps, we may be rewarded as Belle was–the prince, love, and life happily ever after. Or we may not be rewarded. We aren't guaranteed fairy tale endings.

There's no transporting ourselves to a new and more perfect organizational world; this is it. This is as perfect as it gets. Whatever we do to move ourselves or our organizations in the direction of our aspirations begins right here. That may not be the truth we want to hear, but it's a primary truth for work and life: Face the beast.

Here are some additional assertions; these are about the importance of starting where the organization is and respecting what it brings to this moment:

- Renewal takes root in the past.
- Change doesn't make sense.
- People spend years preparing not to change.

If you are in an old organization, you're working with people who have been there for years. They've learned a great deal about the life of the place; they *are* the life of the place. It may not be the life that you or they aspire to, but it is life nevertheless.

Renewal takes root in the past. Agricultural metaphors are particularly appropriate to organizations. Their fertile, earthy, organic substance tends to ground those of us working high up in glass towers. Today and tomorrow, we're rooted in yesterday.

The past is held by the people who've been there through it all and are proud of what they've done. They have been essential to what the organization has accomplished so far,

and they will be part of what happens next. People with organizational roots have aligned their habits and deepened their loyalties. It's easy for a new arrival to criticize these dedicated, stubborn workers.

Yet, the largest and most successful change efforts I've witnessed have had the support of the rooted population–not that it started out that way. No, it can take months or years of work with the people who have a history–frustrating, hard work because they're holding onto what they have spent years learning and succeeding in. It's a challenge to use the past in building the future, but any renewal effort that disrespects the ingrained history is in for trouble.

In mature organizations, the majority who invested for the long haul represent what the organization is re-

Why is it that change is attractive in the evenings and so unattractive in the mornings?

ally about, like it or not. These folks know (or assume that they know) where the company is going and determinedly take it there–whether or not management shares that direction. They're the corporate strategy in action, regardless of what the leaders espouse. The veterans know what's important to them and pursue it without talking about it. A newcomer may have difficulty getting them to discuss it, but their silence is not ignorance. They're investing in their security, their pension, and their future. They've decided, and they intend to stick with their decisions as the future unfolds.

Here lies the dilemma you face in each moment of an organization renewal effort: respecting what has

gone before while discovering what might happen next. Live in that dilemma. Don't put yourself on one side or the other, but keep the dilemma alive in yourself and in the people around you. The dilemma lives in the discussions held, the future imagined, and the past respected–assuring a deeper consideration of how to best renew the organization.

Here are some questions for that dynamic:

- What are the essential values and purposes that made us what we are, without which we would cease to be?
- Which of those are most important to our future?
- How are we supporting their continuation from our past into our future?
- Who can we learn from who know those values deeply?
- Who must we engage in our renewal work?

Change doesn't make sense. Listen in as some employees get their first training on a new work process: The trainer says, "You have been working here for about five years, and you've done a good job. But now the company has come up with a new way for you to approach your work. We're calling it ACCEL. It tells you better ways to do your job. After you learn ACCEL, you'll approach your work in brand new ways."

Imagine the employees' reaction, the looks on their faces. For five years, the company has been encouraging them to do their jobs in just the way they are doing them, until today. Thousands of times, they found reinforcement for thinking they knew how to do their jobs. Then ACCEL comes along. Should it be a surprise that they don't leap for joy? From where they sit, change doesn't make sense. What makes sense is continuing to refine what they've been doing, to get better and better at it.

The employees who resist ACCEL may, in their personal life, sign up for evening classes in Spanish or line dancing. Why is it that change is attractive in the evenings and so unattractive in the mornings? It's not about what makes sense; it's about who's motivated to change. When the ACCEL program was introduced, management was motivated to change, not the workers. For change to work smoothly, it must be chosen. When we force it on people, we live with the consequences.

Consider these questions:

- What makes sense to the people working here? How do they express that?
- What changes do they consider to be nonsense? How do they express that?
- How does the organization appreciate people's contribution, experience, service, and loyalty?
- How might we help employees feel good about themselves while participating in renewal?

People spend years preparing not to change. Imagine a department full of accountants who've been working quite successfully and separately for seven years. Imagine that you have a plan that would allow them to help each other get work done. It's a good plan. It would enrich their work, serve customers better, cost less, and make the accountants happier, more fulfilled.

Reality check: The accountants spent at least seven years preparing not to accept your plan. They've found that working alone is rewarding enough, and so they haven't quit. They've shown up for work for more than 1,800 days and done their jobs. They've created informal systems and social groups. They have norms for dealing with each other. They share jokes that relate to their work, their bosses, the company, and each other. They aren't exactly saying, "We want to keep doing what we've been doing the way we've been doing it." But showing up for years makes them more determined to do just that, not to do what you're proposing.

That's reality—not to be cursed but accepted. When you offer a great opportunity (read: change) and employees frown, that's your opportunity to say to yourself (brightly), "Well, of course! They've spent years moving and learning in a direction different from what I'm suggesting. And the department rewarded them for being predictable in doing the work as the department wanted it done."

And you could also say to yourself, "I'm not going to rail against them because they're stuck in old ways and can't see the brilliance of the future I offer. I'm going to stop and learn about what they've been doing for years and how they feel about it, because that's my starting point for engaging them in thinking about new ways of designing their work."

Yes, you could say all of that, but will you?

Here are some questions to open up that door:

- What are some habits you've established that have been valuable?
- What habits have you replaced? What caused you to change?
- What's your reaction when people suggest that you change what you've been doing for years?
- How could you reconsider your work habits to make sure they serve you well?

We are the same as the accountants. We also have our habits, and we need to go through the same considerations we're proposing to them.

What assertions would you make? What do you believe is necessary as organizations struggle to become better, more beautiful? The assertions rooted in the beastly past are every bit as essential to an organization renewal effort as are the more beautiful assertions offered at the beginning of the article.

It truly is a matter of discovering the beauty of the beast.

Geoffrey M. Bellman *is a consultant and author living in Seattle; gbellman @aol.com. His new book is* The Beauty of the Beast: Breathing New Life Into Organizations (*Berrett-Koehler, 2000*).

Motivation:
The Value of a Work Ethic

by J. Clifton Williams

The motivation challenge of an organization's leaders is extremely complex. Employees enter an organization with very different needs, personality traits, levels of formal education, skills, aptitudes, interests, and other attributes. They most certainly have different expectations of their employer and different views of what their employer has a right to expect of them. These differences provide leaders their greatest opportunity to become effective motivators and their greatest risk of failing the motivational challenge.

Employee Selection

Given the legal constraints surrounding personnel hires today, managers often give up trying to make professional selection decisions and decide primarily on the basis of intuition. That is not to say that intuition should play no part in the selection process. It is regrettable however when 75 years of research on personnel selection is ignored because managers are so afraid of discriminating illegally that they become totally non-discriminating.

In every position certain personal qualities correlate more highly with

Hire people who are self-motivated because of their self-expectations, and do everything possible to help them live up to both your expectations and theirs.

on-the-job effectiveness than do others, and the law allows for selecting on the basis of those characteristics. Some organizations select employees who have a high probability of being productive. Others play a guessing game and hire applicants who are likely to be mediocre performers at best.

Many employees who otherwise have the qualities needed to serve their employer well, lack the motiva-

tion to do so. Many are highly motivated but not highly motivated to do what their employer needs done. Some, for example, are past masters at keeping their jobs and getting raises without ever making an effort to solve problems, develop new skills, or seriously identify with the mission and goals of their employer.

The actions of leaders and the policies and practices of organizations can greatly influence employee motivation, but what employees bring to the employment situation may influence their motivation even more. Some more than fulfill their employer's highest expectations because it is their nature to do their best; others barely meet acceptable standards despite their employer's most cleverly contrived motivational efforts.

The Protestant Work Ethic

The so-called Protestant or Puritan work ethic was important in the theology of John Calvin. It is thought to have supported the industrial revolution by creating a large pool of highly motivated workers—workers who believed it was their duty to put their God-given talents to work. They responded to the usual work incen-

From *Baylor Business Review*, Spring 1998, pp. 13-14. © 1998 by Baylor Business Review. Reprinted by permission.

tives, but aside from those sources of motivation, they were productive because of their belief that it was the right thing to do.

Furthermore, the financial prosperity resulting from productive work, simple living, and saving part of their earnings was viewed as a sign of God's favor and evidence of their *elect* position. Similar beliefs about one's moral obligation to be productive are also present in other cultures. A Confucian work ethic, for instance, plays an important motivational role in Eastern cultures.

Modern studies of work motivation indicate that the Protestant work ethic is far from dead in the United States. Many Christians and others whose values have been influenced by Christianity still believe they have a moral obligation to be productive.

The point to remember is that employees who hold some version of the Protestant work ethic have a special faith-related motivation to work. If you are such a person, you know from experience that you don't need close supervision to keep you working and you are probably as effective when your pay is low as when it is high.

High Self-Expectations

Internal motivation need not be linked psychologically to religious values. Many people whose behavior is virtually identical to that of those with a strong Protestant work ethic have learned from their families or other subcultures a sense of "oughtness" about work. They feel good about themselves when they are productive and bad about themselves when they are not. When they perceive that the quantity and or quality of their work falls below their high self-imposed standards, they become anxious. They have a *need* to excel in their work as surely as they have a need for food and drink. A leader is indeed fortunate when a significant number of his or her direct reports possess this characteristic. One caveat is in order: these subordinates will have no respect for supervisors who lack such motivation.

High Organizational Expectations

Employees who are committed to a Protestant work ethic, or whose culture has conditioned them to make productivity a high priority, are motivated by deeply embedded *acquired* personality characteristics. Fortunately, employees who lack such motivation can often learn it.

Some leaders build high productivity expectations into the value systems of their organizational cultures. They expect a high sense of responsibility, high productivity, and high quality of output from all of their employees. These expectations are impressed upon new employees. The actions of pace setters demonstrate that the organization is serious about them and social pressures also reinforce them. Employees who don't fulfill those expectations soon find occasion to seek work elsewhere.

Conversely, in organizations with few pressures for high productivity, individual differences in productivity can be enormous. Some secretaries and clerks may produce two or three times as much as others. Employers' expectations can have quite an impact. Early in my career as a professor I had a typing and library assistant whose atrocious typing I tolerated only because she seemed to be a conscientious and good person. Was I surprised when she returned from a summer of working in the executive suite of a large corporation. Apparently at the end of her first day there, her supervisor carefully explained that she had the rest of the week to quit making typing mistakes and to increase her speed to that of the top secretaries in the office. She did exactly that! By the time she came back to work for me she had tripled her typing speed and rarely had to correct a mistake. It was a good learning experience for both of us.

Clif Williams is Distinguished Professor Emeritus of Management at Baylor University and also serves as an organizational consultant to the university.

How to mentoring

Many organisations now use mentoring as part of management development, but the relationship between mentor and mentee can be fraught with difficulties. **Alan Fowler** explains how to overcome them and introduce an effective mentoring programme

Guide lines

Although it is only since the early 1970s that mentoring became a formal component of many development programmes, the concept of experienced individuals handing down their wisdom to their young protégés is centuries old. The term comes from Greek mythology—Mentor being the friend to whom Ulysses entrusted the education of his son before he went off on his odyssey. Historically, the relationship between master and apprentice has strong mentoring characteristics.

In modern times, mentoring has been used outside the business environment. There are mentoring programmes in the social services to help disturbed young people, for instance, and other schemes that assist academic high-flyers in higher education. But its most common use is in management development.

Organisations wishing to introduce a mentoring scheme first need to consider its main objectives. They then have to decide whether mentors should be internal or external, how to select them, the level of support they need and the type of relationship required between the mentor, mentee and the mentee's manager.

It might seem that the objectives are obvious—to aid the development of inexperienced managers—but in reality priorities can differ considerably between organisations. The goal could be to contribute to a culture-change programme by helping to change mentees' behaviour. But it might also be to improve people's performance, develop their skills or improve their long-term career development. Or it could be to assist mentees in disadvantaged or under-represented groups to break into management roles.

These objectives affect the selection of the participants and the type of guidance offered. They will also influence the decision on whether to use mentors from inside or outside the organisation. If the emphasis is on helping mentees to attain the skills of existing high-performers or technical specialists, internal mentors may more readily provide the necessary expertise.

Alternatively, an emphasis on more general personal and career development may indicate the selection of a mentor from another organisation who can help to broaden the mentee's horizons. External mentors can be valuable when an organisation is trying to achieve a culture change. One example is the use of private-sector mentors for senior managers in public-sector organisations that are having to become more commercial. They can also be of particular help to mentees who are having difficulties that they are reluctant to discuss with anyone in their own organisation.

It is generally accepted that if mentors are to be internal, they should not be the mentees' line managers. The mentoring relationship differs from that between individuals and their line managers, and they should not be confused. It is not uncommon for mentees to need to discuss issues involving their line management relationships. This can't be done if the mentor is the manager. A common approach is for an internal mentor to be in a different function and to be one or two hierarchical levels above the mentee.

There are several criteria for selecting mentors. In addition to having specific, job-related skills, they need to be fully committed to the role—they should always be volunteers. Excellent communication skills are vital, but mentors must also be patient and avoid offering solutions too readily. The role is most effective when people are encouraged to form their own solutions. Mentors should recognise that they too can learn from the process and treat it as part of their own continuous development.

The selection of mentees will also be influenced by the scheme's aims. If it is designed to develop high-flyers, the results of appraisals or assessments may be needed for the initial selection. If it is aimed at under-represented groups such as women or ethnic minorities, this will largely dictate the preliminary selection. (Positive action of this kind is not in breach of equal opportunities legislation if it is specifically to correct a significant imbalance in the workforce. It is also necessary for the scheme to be categorised clearly as a training initiative.)

Another approach, sometimes used for graduate trainees or for skilled technical jobs, is for mentoring to be arranged for all staff involved in a particular activity. In this case, mentors may be selected from the same function.

Reciprocal recipe

For a mentoring relationship to be successful, both individuals need to possess certain personal qualities. Mentees must be honest, open-minded and willing to learn. They should also be prepared to consider their weaknesses and be able to develop a high level of self-aware-

From *People Management*, October 1998, pp. 48-50. © 1998 by Alan Fowler. Reprinted by permission.

ness. But they should not be reluctant to challenge their mentor's views.

While potential mentees may be strongly encouraged to embark on a mentoring relationship, there is little point in forcing this on someone who feels uncomfortable with it. As with mentors, they should be able to opt into—or out of—the scheme.

Matching mentor to mentee is critical, as the relationship is a personal one. It might be thought that the best match is one in which both parties have similar personalities, but experience has shown that this is not the case. Indeed, if the individuals are too similar, they may avoid discussing issues they both feel uncomfortable about, and the mentor may not be able to bring new insights to bear.

There must, of course, be mutual respect and confidence. Mentors have to be able to identify with their mentees, while mentees should feel that their mentors really have valuable know-how and experience that they can tap. But some of the most effective relationships can be between two people with very different personalities who can gain insights from each other's different perspectives.

In the matching process it may be necessary to consider the issues involved in mixed-sex mentoring. Mentoring by an older man of a younger woman needs particular care. There have been examples of outstandingly successful mentoring of this kind, in which women at a junior level are helped to break through the glass ceiling by highly respected senior male managers. In addition to the conventional mentoring role, his support can give her greater visibility and legitimacy within the organisation, which may be needed before her managerial potential is fully recognised.

But there can be problems beyond that of the possibility of unpleasant office gossip about the relationship. Male mentors need to have a constructive attitude towards the different attributes that women may bring to the management role. A male mentor who tries to turn his female mentee into "one of the boys" instead of helping her to develop her own qualities is doing neither her nor the organisation any favours.

The mentoring of a young male manager by a more senior woman may not only carry much less risk, it can also make a positive contribution towards breaking down the sexual stereotyping that in some organisations still influences male managers' attitudes. But in all mixed-sex mentoring there is a need for care about personal behaviour and the problems that can be generated by the relationship going beyond the purely professional—actual or perceived.

The eternal triangle

There is a tendency to think of mentoring as involving only two people, but successful arrangements also recognise the involvement of line managers. Problems are likely to arise if managers think that mentors are undermining their authority, perhaps if mentees are given advice that they see as conflicting with the needs of their department. They may also be suspicious that mentees are telling mentors about their shortcomings, and that these tales out of school will adversely affect their relationships with senior management. This is a particular risk when the mentor is more senior in the hierarchy than the manager, but the dangers are reduced by the organisation clearly defining the objectives of the mentoring programme and distinguishing the role of the mentor from that of the line manager.

Mentors should also never arrange for the mentee to be away from the workplace—for example, to accompany them to a meeting—without first seeking the consent of the line manager. It is essential for mentors to make it clear that a key aspect of the whole process is to assist, not undermine, the mentees' relationships with their line managers.

From a broader organisational viewpoint, too, the whole scheme needs to be monitored to ensure that it is not developing into an alternative power base.

The launch of any mentoring scheme should include training sessions for both mentors and mentees. Mentors need to understand the primary aim of the programme and the implications this has for the type of guidance they should offer. Some training in the principles of effective counselling is also appropriate.

Mentees require briefings on the objectives of the scheme and the nature of the mentoring relationship. It is important, for example, to avoid misunderstandings about the purpose of a relationship, and to explain that decisions about job changes and promotions will be made through the normal channels and do not lie with the mentor.

The fourth person in the mentoring relationship, of course, is the personnel and development professional. All he or she has to do is design the scheme, secure top management backing, administer the selection and matching process, provide the necessary training, deal with any individual problems that may arise and monitor the impact of the scheme.

Further reading

A selection of Alan Fowler's "how to" articles was published in two books launched at the IPD's national conference in Harrogate.

Get More—And More Results—From Your People and **Get More—And More Value—From Your People** are available, price £9.95 each, from Plymbridge Distributors (01752 202301).

Success in the knowledge economy comes to those who know themselves—their strengths, their values, and how they best perform.

MANAGING ONESELF

By Peter F. Drucker

History's great achievers—A Napoleon, a daVinci, a Mozart— have always managed themselves. That, in large measure, is what makes them great achievers. But they are rare exceptions, so unusual both in their talents and their accomplishments as to be considered outside the boundaries of ordinary human existence. Now, most of us, even those of us with modest endowments, will have to learn to manage ourselves. We will have to learn to develop ourselves. We will have to place ourselves where we can make the greatest contribution. And we will have to stay mentally alert and engaged during a 50-year working life, which means knowing how and when to change the work we do.

What Are My Strengths?

Most people think they know what they are good at. They are usually wrong. More often, people know what they are not good at—and even then more people are wrong than right. And yet, a person can perform only from strength. One cannot build performance on weaknesses, let alone on something one cannot do at all.

Throughout history, people had little need to know their strengths. A person was born into a position and a line of work: the peasant's son would also be a peasant; the artisan's daughter, an artisan's wife, and so on. But now people have choices. We need to know our strengths in order to know where we belong.

Peter F. Drucker is the Marie Rankin Clarke Professor of Social Science and Management at Claremont Graduate University in Claremont, California.

The only way to discover your strengths is through feedback analysis. Whenever you make a key decision or take a key action, write down what you expect will happen. Nine or 12 months later, compare the actual results with your expectations. I have been practicing this method for 15 to 20 years now, and every time I do it, I am surprised. The feedback analysis showed me, for instance—and to my great surprise—that I have an intuitive understanding of technical people, whether they are engineers or accountants or market researchers. It also showed me that I don't really resonate with generalists.

Feedback analysis is by no means new. It was invented sometime in the fourteenth century by an otherwise totally obscure German theologian and picked up quite independently, some 150 years later, by John Calvin and Ignatius Loyola, each of whom incorporated it into the practice of his followers. In fact, the steadfast focus on performance and results that this habit produces explains why the institutions these two men founded, the Calvinist church and the Jesuit order, came to dominate Europe within 30 years.

Practiced consistently, this simple method will show you within a fairly short period of time, maybe two or three years, where your strengths lie—and this is the most important thing to know. The method will show you what you are doing or failing to do that deprives you of the full benefits of your strengths. It will show you where you are not particularly competent. And finally, it will show you where you have no strengths and cannot perform.

Several implications for action follow from feedback analysis. First and foremost, concentrate on your strengths. Put yourself where your strengths can produce results.

Second, work on improving your strengths. Analysis will rapidly show where you need to improve skills or acquire new ones. It will also show the gaps in your knowledge—and those can usually be filled. Mathematicians are born, but everyone can learn trigonometry.

Third, discover where your intellectual arrogance is causing disabling ignorance and overcome it. Far too many people—especially people with great expertise in one area—are contemptuous of knowledge in other areas or believe that being bright is a substitute for knowledge. First-rate engineers, for instance, tend to take pride in not knowing anything about people. Human beings, they believe, are much too disorderly for the good engineering mind. Human resource professionals, by contrast, often pride themselves on their ignorance of elementary accounting or of quantitative methods altogether. But taking pride in such ignorance is self-defeating. Go to work on acquiring the skills and knowledge you need to fully realize your strengths.

It is equally essential to remedy your bad habits—the things you do or fail to do that inhibit your effectiveness and performance. Such habits will quickly show up in the feedback. For example, a planner may find that his beautiful plans fail because he does not follow through on them. Like so many brilliant people, he believes that ideas move mountains. But bulldozers move mountains; ideas show where the bulldozers should go to work. This planner will have to learn that the work does not stop when the plan is completed. He must find people to carry out the plan and explain it to them. He must adapt and change it as he puts it into action. And finally, he must decide when to stop pushing the plan.

At the same time, feedback will also reveal when the problem is a lack of manners. Manners are the lubricating oil of an organization. It is a law of nature that two moving bodies in contact with each other create friction. This is as true for human beings as it is for inanimate objects. Manners—simple things like saying "please" and "thank you" and knowing a person's name or asking after her family—enable two people to work together whether they like each other or not. Bright people, especially bright young people, often do not understand this. If analysis shows that someone's brilliant work fails again and again as soon as cooperation from others is required, it probably indicates a lack of courtesy—that is, a lack of manners.

Comparing your expectations with your results also indicates what not to do. We all have a vast number of areas in which we have no talent or skill and little chance of becoming even mediocre. In those areas a person—and especially a knowledge worker—should not take on work, jobs, and assignments. One should waste as little effort as possible on improving areas of low competence. It takes far more energy and work to improve from incompetence to mediocrity than it takes to improve from first-rate performance to excellence. And yet most people—especially most teachers and most organizations—concentrate on making incompetent performers into mediocre ones. Energy, resources, and time should go instead to making a competent person into a star performer.

How Do I Perform?

Amazingly few people know *how* they get things done. Indeed, most of us do not even know that different people work and perform differently. Too many people work in ways that are not their ways, and that almost guarantees nonperformance. For knowledge workers, How do I perform?

may be an even more important question than What are my strengths?

Like one's strengths, how one performs is unique. It is a matter of personality. Whether personality be a matter of nature or nurture, it surely is formed long before a person goes to work. And *how* a person performs is a given, just as *what* a person is good at or not good at is a given. A person's way of performing can be slightly modified, but it is unlikely to be completely changed—and certainly not easily. Just as people achieve results by doing what they are good at, they also achieve results by working in ways that they best perform. A few common personality traits usually determine how a person performs.

Am I a reader or a listener? The first thing to know is whether you are a reader or a listener. Far too few people even know that there are readers and listeners and that people are rarely both. Even fewer know which of the two they themselves are. But some examples will show how damaging such ignorance can be.

When Dwight Eisenhower was commander in chief of the Allied forces in Europe, he was the darling of the press. His press conferences were famous for their style—General Eisenhower showed total command of whatever question he was asked, and he was able to describe a situation and explain a policy in two or three beautifully polished and elegant sentences. Ten years later, the same journalists who had been his admirers held President Eisenhower in open contempt. He never addressed the questions, they complained, but rambled on endlessly about something else. And they constantly ridiculed him for butchering the King's English in incoherent and ungrammatical answers.

Eisenhower apparently did not know that he was a reader, not a listener. When he was commander in chief in Europe, his aides made sure that every question from the press was presented in writing at least half an hour before a conference was to begin. And then Eisenhower was in total command. When he became president, he succeeded two listeners, Franklin D. Roosevelt and Harry Truman. Both men knew themselves to be listeners and both enjoyed free-for-all press conferences. Eisenhower may have felt that he had to do what his two predecessors had done. As a result, he never even heard the questions journalists asked. And Eisenhower is not even an extreme case of a nonlistener.

A few years later, Lyndon Johnson destroyed his presidency, in large measure, by not knowing that he was a listener. His predecessor, John Kennedy, was a reader who had assembled a brilliant group of writers as his assistants, making sure that they wrote to him before discussing their memos in person. Johnson kept these people on

his staff—and they kept on writing. He never, apparently, understood one word of what they wrote. Yet as a senator, Johnson had been superb; for parliamentarians have to be, above all, listeners.

Few listeners can be made, or can make themselves, into competent readers—and vice versa. The listener who tries to be a reader will, therefore, suffer the fate of Lyndon Johnson, whereas the reader who tries to be a listener will suffer the fate of Dwight Eisenhower. They will not perform or achieve.

How do I learn? The second thing to know about how one performs is to know how one learns. Many first-class writers—Winston Churchill is but one example—do poorly in school. They tend to remember their schooling as pure torture. Yet few of their classmates remember it the same way. They may not have enjoyed the school very much, but the worst they suffered was boredom. The explanation is that writers do not, as a rule, learn by listening and reading. They learn by writing. Because schools do not allow them to learn this way, they get poor grades.

Schools everywhere are organized on the assumption that there is only one right way to learn and that it is the same way for everybody. But to be forced to learn the way a school teaches is sheer hell for students who learn differently. Indeed, there are probably half a dozen different ways to learn.

There are people, like Churchill, who learn by writing. Some people learn by taking copious notes. Beethoven, for example, left behind an enormous number of sketchbooks, yet he said he never actually looked at them when he composed. Asked why he kept them, he is reported to have replied, "If I don't write it down immediately, I forget it right away. If I put it into a sketchbook, I never forget it and I never have to look it up again." Some people learn by doing. Others learn by hearing themselves talk.

A chief executive I know who converted a small and mediocre family business into the leading company in its industry was one of those people who learn by talking. He was in the habit of calling his entire senior staff into his office once a week and then talking at them for two or three hours. He would raise policy issues and argue three different positions on each one. He rarely asked his associates for comments or questions; he simply needed an audience to hear himself talk. That's how he learned. And although he is a fairly extreme case, learning through talking is by no means an unusual method. Successful trial lawyers learn the same way, as do many medical diagnosticians (and so do I).

Of all the important pieces of self-knowledge, understanding how you learn is the easiest to acquire. When I ask people, "How do you learn?"

most of them know the answer. But when I ask, "Do you act on this knowledge?" few answer yes. And yet, acting on this knowledge is the key to performance; or rather, not acting on this knowledge condemns one to nonperformance.

How do I perform? and How do I learn? are the first questions to ask. But they are by no means the only ones. To manage yourself effectively, you also have to ask, Do I work well with people or am I a loner? And if you do work well with people, you then must ask, In what relationship?

Some people work best as subordinates. General George Patton, the great American military hero of World War II, is a prime example. Patton was America's top troop commander. Yet when he was proposed for an independent command, General George Marshall, the U.S. chief of staff—and probably the most successful picker of men in U.S. history—said, "Patton is the best subordinate the American army has ever produced, but he would be the worst commander."

Some people work best as team members. Others work best alone. Some are exceptionally talented as coaches and mentors; others are simply incompetent as mentors.

Another crucial question is, Do I produce results as a decision maker or as an adviser? A great many people perform best as advisers but cannot take the burden and pressure of making the decision. A good many other people, by contrast, need an adviser to force themselves to think; then they can make decisions and act on them with speed, self-confidence, and courage.

This is a reason, by the way, that the number two person in an organization often fails when promoted to the number one position. The top spot requires a decision maker. Strong decision makers often put somebody they trust into the number two spot as their adviser—and in that position the person is outstanding. But in the number one spot, the same person fails. He or she knows what the decision should be but cannot accept the responsibility of actually making it.

Other important questions to ask include, Do I perform well under stress or do I need a highly structured and predictable environment? Do I work best in a big organization or a small one? Few people work well in all kinds of environments. Again and again, I have seen people who were very successful in large organizations flounder miserably when they moved into smaller ones. And the reverse is equally true.

The conclusion bears repeating: do not try to change yourself—you are unlikely to succeed. But work hard to improve the way you perform. And try not to take on work you cannot perform or will only perform poorly.

What Are My Values?

To be able to manage yourself, you finally have to ask, What are my values? This is not a question of ethics. With respect to ethics, the rules are the same for everybody, and the test is a simple one. I call it the "mirror test."

In the early years of this century, the most highly respected diplomat of all the great powers was the German ambassador in London. He was clearly destined for great things—to become his country's foreign minister, at least, if not its federal chancellor. Yet in 1906 he abruptly resigned rather than preside over a dinner given by the diplomatic corps for Edward VII. The king was a notorious womanizer and made it clear what kind of dinner he wanted. The ambassador is reported to have said, "I refuse to see a pimp in the mirror in the morning when I shave."

That is the mirror test. Ethics requires that you ask yourself, What kind of person do I want to see in the mirror in the morning? What is ethical behavior in one kind of organization or situation is ethical behavior in another. But ethics are only part of a value system—especially of an organization's value system.

To work in an organization whose value system is unacceptable or incompatible with one's own condemns a person both to frustration and to nonperformance.

Consider the experience of a highly successful human resources executive whose company was acquired by a bigger organization. After the acquisition, she was promoted to do the kind of work she did best, which included selecting people for important positions. The executive deeply believed that a company should hire people for such positions from the outside only after exhausting all the inside possibilities. But her new company believed in first looking outside "to bring in fresh blood." There is something to be said for both approaches—in my experience, the proper one is to do some of both. They are, however, fundamentally incompatible—not as policies but as values. They bespeak different views of the relationship between organizations and people; different views of the responsibility of an organization to its people and their development; and different views of a person's most important contribution to an enterprise. After several years of frustration, the executive quit—at considerable financial loss. Her values and the values of the organization simply were not compatible.

Similarly, whether a pharmaceutical company tries to obtain results by making constant, small improvements or by achieving occasional, highly expensive, and risky "breakthroughs" is not primarily an economic question. The results of either strategy may be pretty much the same. At bottom, there is a conflict between a value system that sees the company's contribution in terms of helping physicians do better what they already do and a value system that is oriented toward making scientific discoveries. Whether a business should be run for short-term results or with a focus on the long term is likewise a question of values. Financial analysts believe that businesses can be run for both simultaneously. Successful businesspeople know better. To be sure, every company has to produce short-term results. But in any conflict between short-term results and long-term growth, each company will determine its own priority. This is not primarily a disagreement about economics. It is fundamentally a value conflict regarding the function of a business and the responsibility of management.

Value conflicts are not limited to business organizations. One of the fastest-growing pastoral churches in the United States measures success by the number of new parishioners. Its leadership believes that what matters is how many newcomers join the congregation. The Good Lord will then minister to their spiritual needs or at least to the needs of a sufficient percentage. Another pastoral, evangelical church believes that what matters is people's spiritual growth. The church eases out newcomers who join but do not enter into its spiritual life.

Again, this is not a matter of numbers. At first glance, it appears that the second church grows more slowly. But it retains a far larger proportion of newcomers than the first one does. Its growth, in other words, is more solid. This is also not a theological problem, or only secondarily so. It is a problem about values. In a public debate, one pastor argued, "Unless you first come to church, you will never find the gate to the Kingdom of Heaven."

"No," answered the other. "Until you first look for the gate to the Kingdom of Heaven, you don't belong in church."

Organizations, like people, have values. To be effective in an organization, a person's values must be compatible with the organization's values. They do not need to be the same, but they must be close enough to coexist. Otherwise, the person will not only be frustrated but also will not produce results.

A person's strengths and the way that person performs rarely conflict; the two are complementary. But there is sometimes a conflict between a person's values and his or her strengths. What one does well—even very well and successfully—may not fit with one's value system. In that case, the work may not appear to be worth devoting one's life to (or even a substantial portion thereof).

If I may, allow me to interject a personal note. Many years ago, I too had to decide between my values and what I was doing successfully. I was doing very well as a young investment banker in London in the mid-1930s, and the work clearly fit my strengths. Yet I did not see myself making a contribution as an asset manager. People, I realized, were what I valued, and I saw no point in being the richest man in the cemetery. I had no money and no other job prospects. Despite the continuing Depression, I quit—and it was the right thing to do. Values, in other words, are and should be the ultimate test.

Where Do I Belong?

A small number of people know very early where they belong. Mathematicians, musicians, and cooks, for instance, are usually mathematicians, musicians, and cooks by the time they are four or five years old. Physicians usually decide on their careers in their teens, if not earlier. But most people, especially highly gifted people, do not really know where they belong until they are well past their mid-twenties. By that time, however, they should know the answers to the three questions: What are my strengths? How do I perform? and, What are my values? And then they can and should decide where they belong.

Or rather, they should be able to decide where they do *not* belong. The person who has learned that he or she does not perform well in a big organization should have learned to say no to a position in one. The person who has learned that he or she is not a decision maker should have learned to say no to a decision-making assignment. A General Patton (who probably never learned this himself) should have learned to say no to an independent command.

Equally important, knowing the answer to these questions enables a person to say to an opportunity, an offer, or an assignment, "Yes, I will do that. But this is the way I should be doing it. This is the way it should be structured. This is the way the relationships should be. These are the kind of results you should expect from me, and in this time frame, because this is who I am."

Successful careers are not planned. They develop when people are prepared for opportunities because they know their strengths, their method of work, and their values. Knowing where one belongs can transform an ordinary person—hardworking and competent but otherwise mediocre—into an outstanding performer.

What Should I Contribute?

Throughout history, the great majority of people never had to ask the question, What should I contribute? They were told what to contribute, and their tasks were dictated either by the work itself—as it was for the peasant or artisan—or by a master or a mistress, as it was for domestic servants. And until very recently, it was taken for granted that most people were subordinates who did as they were told. Even in the 1950s and 1960s, the new knowledge workers (the so-called organization men) looked to their company's personnel department to plan their careers.

Then in the late 1960s, no one wanted to be told what to do any longer. Young men and women began to ask, What do I want to do? And what they heard was that the way to contribute was to "do your own thing." But this solution was as wrong as the organization men's had been. Very few of the people who believed that doing one's own thing would lead to contribution, self-fulfillment, and success achieved any of the three.

But still, there is no return to the old answer of doing what you are told or assigned to do. Knowledge workers in particular have to learn to ask a question that has not been asked before: What *should* my contribution be? To answer it, they must address three distinct elements: What does the situation require? Given my strengths, my way of performing, and my values, how can I make the greatest contribution to what needs to be done? And finally, What results have to be achieved to make a difference?

Consider the experience of a newly appointed hospital administrator. The hospital was big and prestigious, but it had been coasting on its reputation for 30 years. The new administrator decided that his contribution should be to establish a standard of excellence in one important area within two years. He chose to focus on the emergency room, which was big, visible, and sloppy. He decided that every patient who came into the ER had to be seen by a qualified nurse within 60 seconds. Within 12 months, the hospital's emergency room had become a model for all hospitals in the United States, and within another two years, the whole hospital had been transformed.

As this example suggests, it is rarely possible—or even particularly fruitful—to look too far ahead. A plan can usually cover no more than 18 months and still be reasonably clear and specific. So the question in most cases should be, Where and how can I achieve results that will make a difference within the next year and a half? The answer must balance several things. First, the results should be hard to achieve—they should require "stretching," to use the current buzzword. But also, they should be within reach. To aim at results that cannot be achieved—or that can be only under the most unlikely circumstances—is not being ambitious; it is

being foolish. Second, the results should be meaningful. They should make a difference. Finally, results should be visible and, if at all possible, measurable. From this will come a course of action: what to do, where and how to start, and what goals and deadlines to set.

Responsibility for Relationships

Very few people work by themselves and achieve results by themselves—a few great artists, a few great scientists, a few great athletes. Most people work with others and are effective with other people. That is true whether they are members of an organization or independently employed. Managing yourself requires taking responsibility for relationships. This has two parts.

The first is to accept the fact that other people are as much individuals as you yourself are. They perversely insist on behaving like human beings. This means that they too have their strengths; they too have their ways of getting things done; they too have their values. To be effective, therefore, you have to know the strengths, the performance modes, and the values of your coworkers.

That sounds obvious, but few people pay attention to it. Typical is the person who was trained to write reports in his or her first assignment because that boss was a reader. Even if the next boss is a listener, the person goes on writing reports that, invariably, produce no results. Invariably the boss will think the employee is stupid, incompetent, and lazy, and he or she will fail. But that could have been avoided if the employee had only looked at the new boss and analyzed how this boss performs.

Bosses are neither a title on the organization chart nor a "function." They are individuals and are entitled to do their work in the way they do it best. It is incumbent on the people who work with them to observe them, to find out how they work, and to adapt themselves to what makes their bosses most effective. This, in fact, is the secret of "managing" the boss.

The same holds true for all your coworkers. Each works his or her way, not your way. And each is entitled to work in his or her way. What matters is whether they perform and what their values are. As for how they perform—each is likely to do it differently. The first secret of effectiveness is to understand the people you work with and depend on so that you can make use of their strengths, their ways of working, and their values. Working relationships are as much based on the people as they are on the work.

The second part of relationship responsibility is taking responsibility for communication.

Whenever I, or any other consultant, start to work with an organization, the first thing I hear about are all the personality conflicts. Most of these arise from the fact that people do not know what other people are doing and how they do their work, or what contribution the other people are concentrating on and what results they expect. And the reason they do not know is that they have not asked and therefore have not been told.

This failure to ask reflects human stupidity less than it reflects human history. Until recently, it was unnecessary to tell any of these things to anybody. In the medieval city, everyone in a district plied the same trade. In the countryside, everyone in a valley planted the same crop as soon as the frost was out of the ground. Even those few people who did things that were not "common" worked alone, so they did not have to tell anyone what they were doing.

Today the great majority of people work with others who have different tasks and responsibilities. The marketing vice president may have come out of sales and know everything about sales, but she knows nothing about the things she has never done—pricing, advertising, packaging, and the like. So the people who do these things must make sure that the marketing vice president understands what they are trying to do, why they are trying to do it, how they are going to do it, and what results to expect.

If the marketing vice president does not understand what these high-grade knowledge specialists are doing, it is primarily their fault, not hers. They have not educated her. Conversely, it is the marketing vice president's responsibility to make sure that all of her coworkers understand how she looks at marketing: what her goals are, how she works, and what she expects of herself and of each one of them.

Even people who understand the importance of taking responsibility for relationships often do not communicate sufficiently with their associates. They are afraid of being thought presumptuous or inquisitive or stupid. They are wrong. Whenever someone goes to his or her associates and says, "This is what I am good at. This is how I work. These are my values. This is the contribution I plan to concentrate on and the results I should be expected to deliver," the response is always, "This is most helpful. But why didn't you tell me earlier?"

And one gets the same reaction—without exception, in my experience—if one continues by asking, "And what do I need to know about your strengths, how you perform, your values, and your proposed contribution?" In fact, knowledge workers should request this of everyone with whom they work, whether as subordinate, superior, colleague, or team member. And again, whenever this is done, the reaction is always, "Thanks for asking me. But why didn't you ask me earlier?"

Organizations are no longer built on force but on trust. The existence of trust between people does not necessarily mean that they like one another. It means that they understand one another. Taking responsibility for relationships is therefore an absolute necessity. It is a duty. Whether one is a member of the organization, a consultant to it, a supplier, or a distributor, one owes that responsibility to all one's coworkers: those whose work one depends on as well as those who depend on one's own work.

The Second Half of Your Life

When work for most people meant manual labor, there was no need to worry about the second half of your life. You simply kept on doing what you had always done. And if you were lucky enough to survive 40 years of hard work in the mill or on the railroad, you were quite happy to spend the rest of your life doing nothing. Today, however, most work is knowledge work, and knowledge workers are not "finished" after 40 years on the job, they are merely bored.

We hear a great deal of talk about the midlife crisis of the executive. It is mostly boredom. At 45, most executives have reached the peak of their business careers, and they know it. After 20 years of doing very much the same kind of work, they are very good at their jobs. But they are not learning or contributing or deriving challenge and satisfaction from the job. And yet they are still likely to face another 20 if not 25 years of work. That is why managing oneself increasingly leads one to begin a second career.

There are three ways to develop a second career. The first is actually to start one. Often this takes nothing more than moving from one kind of organization to another: the divisional controller in a large corporation, for instance, becomes the controller of a medium-sized hospital. But there are also growing numbers of people who move into different lines of work altogether: the business executive or government official who enters the ministry at 45, for instance; or the midlevel manager who leaves corporate life after 20 years to attend law school and become a small-town attorney.

We will see many more second careers undertaken by people who have achieved modest success in their first jobs. Such people have substantial skills, and they know how to work. They need a community—the house is empty with the children gone—and they need income as well. But above all, they need challenge.

The second way to prepare for the second half of your life is to develop a parallel career. Many people who are very successful in their first careers stay in the work they have been doing, either on a full-time or a part-time or consulting basis. But in addition, they create a parallel job, usually in a nonprofit organization, that takes another ten hours of work a week. They might take over the administration of their church, for instance, or the presidency of the local Girl Scouts Council. They might run the battered women's shelter, work as a children's librarian for the local public library, sit on the school board, and so on.

Finally, there are the social entrepreneurs. These are usually people who have been very successful in their first careers. They love their work, but it no longer challenges them. In many cases they keep on doing what they have been doing all along but spend less and less of their time on it. They also start another activity, usually a nonprofit. My friend Bob Buford, for example, built a very successful television company that he still runs. But he has also founded and built a successful nonprofit organization that works with Protestant churches, and he is building another to teach social entrepreneurs how to manage their own nonprofit ventures while still running their original businesses.

People who manage the second half of their lives may always be a minority. The majority may "retire on the job" and count the years until their actual retirement. But it is this minority, the men and women who see a long working-life expectancy as an opportunity both for themselves and for society, who will become leaders and models.

There is one prerequisite for managing the second half of your life: you must begin long before you enter it. When it first became clear 30 years ago that working-life expectancies were lengthening very fast, many observers (including myself) believed that retired people would increasingly become volunteers for nonprofit institutions. That has not happened. If one does not begin to volunteer before one is 40 or so, one will not volunteer once past 60.

Similarly, all the social entrepreneurs I know began to work in their chosen second enterprise long before they reached their peak in their original business. Consider the example of a successful lawyer, the legal counsel to a large corporation, who has started a venture to establish model schools in his state. He began to do volunteer legal work for the schools when he was around 35. He was elected to the school board at age 40. At age 50, when he had amassed a fortune, he started his own enterprise to build and to run model schools. He is, however, still working nearly full-time as the lead counsel in the company he helped found as a young lawyer.

There is another reason to develop a second major interest, and to develop it early. No one can expect to live very long without experiencing a serious setback in his or her life or work. There is the competent engineer who is passed over for promotion at age 45. There is the competent college professor who realizes at age 42 that she will never get a professorship at a big university, even though she may be fully qualified for it. There are tragedies in one's family life: the breakup of one's marriage or the loss of a child. At such times, a second major interest—not just a hobby—may make all the difference. The engineer, for example, now knows that he has not been very successful in his job. But in his outside activity—as church treasurer, for example—he is a success. One's family may break up, but in that outside activity there is still a community.

In a society in which success has become so terribly important, having options will become increasingly vital. Historically, there was no such thing as "success." The overwhelming majority of people did not expect anything but to stay in their "proper station," as an old English prayer has it. The only mobility was downward mobility.

In a knowledge society, however, we expect everyone to be a success. This is clearly an impossibility. For a great many people, there is at best an absence of failure. Wherever there is success, there has to be failure. And then it is vitally important for the individual, and equally for the individual's family, to have an area in which he or she can contribute, make a difference, and be *somebody*. That means finding a second area—whether in a second career, a parallel career, or a social venture—that offers an opportunity for being a leader, for being respected, for being a success.

The challenges of managing oneself may seem obvious, if not elementary. And the answers may seem self-evident to the point of appearing naïve. But managing oneself requires new and unprecedented things from the individual, and especially from the knowledge worker. In effect, managing oneself demands that each knowledge worker think and behave like a chief executive officer. Further, the shift from manual workers who do as they are told to knowledge workers who have to manage themselves profoundly challenges social structure. Every existing society, even the most individualistic one, takes two things for granted, if only subconsciously: that organizations outlive workers, and that most people stay put.

But today the opposite is true. Knowledge workers outlive organizations, and they are mobile. The need to manage oneself is therefore creating a revolution in human affairs.

Unit 3

Unit Selections

Key Points to Consider

❖ Do you think that group dynamics are important to the individual? Why or why not?

❖ How can informal communication be as important as formal communication?

❖ Discuss some of the ideas about leadership mentioned in the articles. Which ones do you agree with?

❖ Why are teams important to organizations?

 **Links** **www.dushkin.com/online/**

These sites are annotated on pages 4 and 5.

Human beings are social animals. Since before the dawn of recorded history they have lived in groups, whether in small bands of hunter-gathers, in a nuclear family, or in urban centers. Psychologists, sociologists, and anthropologists have recognized this for years. Indeed, two of the five steps in Abraham Maslow's hierarchy of needs involve the group: belongingness and status. Maslow recognized this when he devoted 40 percent of his hierarchy of human needs to these concerns. They occur in importance right after the physiological needs of food, clothing, shelter, and safety. In other words, after people are reasonably certain that they will have enough food to eat, will not die from exposure to the elements, and will not be killed by a saber-toothed tiger or their fellow man, they want to have someone to talk to. Once that has been achieved, issues of status within the group become important. Nobody wants to be the proverbial "low man on the totem pole." Status is important within the group because it helps to define who and what people are and how they relate to others. The higher an individual's status, the more power, the more prestige, and the more control that person has over his or her own fate. People live in groups because it is necessary for self protection, nurturing, propagation of the human race, and achievement. There are only a few things that individuals can accomplish strictly on their own. The help and assistance of others becomes necessary even in the accomplishment of simple tasks such as lifting a heavy object, and great accomplishments have become almost impossible without help. Leo Tolstoy wrote *War and Peace* on his own, but someone taught him how to read and write; Ludwig von Beethoven created some of the greatest music in the history of civilization, but he needed an orchestra to play it; and Albert Einstein developed the theory of relativity, but he had to stand on the shoulders of the giants who preceded him. Human beings need each other if they are going to fully achieve their potential. To be a hermit is to cut oneself off from the rest of the human race, and, for all intents and purposes, to die in terms of role, contribution, and legacy to the society.

Group dynamics, or the way groups work, has always been one of the major focuses of organizational behavior. People make up groups and, over time, will develop groups within larger groups, or cliques. How people interact within the cliques and how those cliques interact within particular networks or groups is the subject of "Networks Within Networks: Service Link Overlap, Organizational Cliques, and Network Effectiveness." Another aspect of the social and group process is how groups, especially informal groups, are formed. As children, this took place in the simple act of choosing sides on the playground. As adults, the motives become far more complex and the desired characteristics of fellow group members become far less obvious. This is especially true in the workplace as shown in the article "Identifying Who Matters: Mapping Key Players in Multiple Environments."

Communication is one of the chief activities that occurs in any group. One of the primary functions of any group is educating the members as to the expectations of the group. This is called the socialization process. Members become socialized when they become conversant with the group's rules, both written and unwritten. For groups to succeed and to continue, those norms must be adopted by new members. Often, the unwritten rules are more important to the individual's success in the group than the written ones, and violating those rules can result in the termination of the individual's membership. Communication is necessary for all aspects of the work environment. Even informal communication can be a key to the success of an individual, as Nancy Kirland and Lisa Hope Pelled demonstrate in "Passing the Word: Toward a Model of Gossip and Power in the Workplace."

Leadership may be the least understood aspect of human behavior. Leaders come in all shapes, sizes, colors, religions, and genders. They are not limited to any particular group or social status. Winston Churchill was a member of the English aristocracy, and his distant cousin, Franklin Roosevelt, was a member of the American upper class. Both were successful leaders and great orators who became symbols of their country's struggle against Adolf Hitler, who was also a great orator, who symbolized his country's struggle in World War II, and was a member of the Austrian middle class. Hitler wrote about his warped vision in *Mien Kampf,* and he was able to communicate it to the German people, who then adopted it as their own. Hitler possessed the qualities of great leadership in leading his evil crusade against mankind. Leadership requires more than just a high IQ, ability to communicate, and a vision. To be successful requires other skills, as discussed by James O'Toole in "Leadership A to Z," by Haidee Allerton.

Power is often the goal of individuals within an organization. The amount of power that a person has in an organization is often a direct indicator of the status of the individual in that organization. Power is essential for the individual to survive and prosper in the organization. One of the primary reasons for unionization in the United States has been an attempt on the part of the workers to equalize the power relationship between themselves and the corporation. A single worker, negotiating with General Motors or Ford, has very little power. But, if the entire workforce is negotiating for pay, benefits, and working conditions, then the balance of power has changed and the workers have more power at the bargaining table. A large organization, such as GM or Ford, will find it difficult to ignore the entire workforce if it wants to continue to produce cars.

In most organizations, individuals are placed in teams to work together to accomplish the goals of the organization. They must make decisions that are affected by a variety of factors, including the feedback that the team receives. These and other factors of teams are discussed in "Team Structure and Performance: Assessing the Mediating Role of Intrateam Process and the Moderating Role of Task Type."

Intergroup behavior is yet another aspect of the social and group process. How groups interact with each other is as important as how individuals act with each other inside the group. There are many factors that can play a role in this, including status, culture, and experience.

The group process is highly important to the success of any organization. Individuals can rarely succeed on their own and will almost always need the help of others to accomplish their goals. Successful social and group behaviors are the hallmarks of successful organizations that have been, are, and will be able to meet the coming challenges of the next millennium.

NETWORKS WITHIN NETWORKS: SERVICE LINK OVERLAP, ORGANIZATIONAL CLIQUES, AND NETWORK EFFECTIVENESS

KEITH G. PROVAN
University of Arizona

JULIANN G. SEBASTIN
University of Kentucky

This study explored the use of clique analysis for explaining network effectiveness. In data from networks of mental health agencies in three cities, effectiveness, measured as client outcomes, was negatively related to the integration of full networks. In contrast, effectiveness was positively related to integration among small cliques of agencies when these cliques had overlapping links through both reciprocated referrals and case coordination. The findings have implications for both theory and research, demonstrating the value of studying network clique structure and developing clique-based explanations of network behavior and outcomes.

Despite strong recent interest in the study of interorganizational networks (see, for example the special issue of the *Academy of Management Journal* published in April 1997), very little attention has been devoted by researchers to assessing the effectiveness of multifirm networks (as opposed to that of dyadic alliances and partnerships) or to explaining the network structural properties associated with effectiveness. Most of the research on networks in both profit and not-for-profit contexts has not addressed effectiveness explicitly, focusing instead on such issues as network formation, structure, and governance (Larson, 1992), or examining firm-level outcomes like power and influence (Marsden, 1990). Recent work has touted the presumed advantages of networks (Powell, 1990), but the lack of empirical evidence on why some networks might be more effective than others has limited the contribution of network scholars to both practice and the development of a network theory (Salancik, 1995).

For those studying networks of business firms, the lack of interest in network effectiveness is to some extent justified, since firms typically become network members to enhance their own individual performance. Nonetheless, there may be substantial network-level outcomes in the form of new product development, customers who are able to receive more comprehensive services, or the

This research was funded by a grant from the National Institute of Mental Health (R01-MH43783). We would like to thank Brint Milward and Michael Berren for their earlier contribution to the project. We would also like to express our appreciation to the three anonymous reviewers for their many helpful and insightful comments on previous versions.

generation of jobs in a region. In health and human services, agencies can and do join networks to lower operating costs and gain competitive advantage. However, network-level outcomes are especially salient because clients often have multiple needs, and many of the services typically provided in community-based settings are highly fragmented. This fragmentation is due in part to categorical funding streams that pay for one type of service but not another and in part to traditions of service organized around a single, narrowly defined problem or illness.

The prevailing assumption among researchers, planners, and practitioners in health care and human services about the dilemma of multiple client problems and service fragmentation across many providers has been that treatment outcomes will be enhanced when provider organizations form an integrated network of service delivery (Alter & Hage, 1993; Dill & Rochefort, 1989). Integration occurs when organizations that provide services to a particular client group work together to coordinate the services these clients need. Integration may be formal or informal and may involve a simple exchange of information about a client or a full-scale sharing of resources and programs. The presumed tie between the integration of services and client outcomes has been especially prevalent for noninstitutionalized clients with severe and chronic conditions, like mental illness, HIV, and drug abuse, and for the homeless, in part because of the breadth of likely services needed and in part because these clients are very likely to have difficulty navigating the intricacies of an unintegrated system on their own. Yet there has been scant empirical evidence that integrated networks are effective (Department of Health and Human Services, 1991).

The few studies that have examined the relationship between network structure and effectiveness have focused on networks as wholes (Lehman, Postrado, Roth, McNary, & Goldman, 1994; Provan & Milward, 1995). Although this approach seems intuitively obvious, concerns about network bounding (Doreian & Woodard, 1994; Laumann, Marsden, & Prensky, 1983)—about which organizations to include and which not to include in a study—can lead researchers to oversample, making findings and conclusions about the relationship between organizational integration and network outcomes somewhat misleading. Specifically, many organizations that might be included as network members may have little real impact on network outcomes. Network effectiveness may owe far less to integration across a network as a whole than to ties among a few organizations that provide the bulk of relationships and services to clients. Even in networks of for-profit business firms, network success is likely to be the result of effective interaction among small, overlapping subsets of firms, often linked through a lead firm (Lorenzoni & Ornati, 1988) or an administrative entity (Human & Provan, 1997), rather than the result of integration across the network as a whole.

Especially in health and human services, many organizations in a community may well be considered part of a broadly defined delivery system and connected to one another in a variety of ways. The reality of integrated services, however, is that outcomes for a particular clientele are likely to be more affected by the activities of a small group, or clique, of tightly connected providers than by the activities of the complete network. For instance, although homeless individuals may need many different services, their primary needs are for temporary shelter, food, physical health care, and perhaps mental health and substance abuse treatment. Even though the entire system of agencies that serves this population may not be highly integrated, client and network effectiveness may be quite high owing to close coordination among the small clique of agencies that provide these core services. The basic point applies to business firms as well: stronger cooperative ties can develop among small clusters of firms (Barley, Freeman, & Hybels, 1992), mutually dependent constellations of a few key firms (Lorenzoni & Ornati, 1988), and small-scale buyer-supplier networks (Larson, 1992) than can develop among the multiple firms that may compose a broadly defined network.

This study explored the relationship between network effectiveness and the structure of service integration within each of three health and human services networks. Since we measured effectiveness using client outcomes, we also assessed service integration at the client level, using referrals and case coordination rather than administrative-level links. The study is unique in that we attempted to explain network effectiveness, not by examining integration across full networks, but by examining the links, or interorganizational ties, among small subsets, or cliques, of provider agencies. We focused in particular on overlapping cliques whose members shared multiple ties with the members of one or more other cliques. A clique is a group of mutually connected actors within a larger network (Alba, 1982; Scott, 1991). Each member of a clique must be directly linked to every other member.

Because the approach was new, because the findings were from only three networks, and because much of the analysis was descriptive, this research was exploratory. The goal of the study was to examine and compare clique structure and overlap across the three networks, relate these findings to measures of network effectiveness, and discuss the implications for both network methods and the development of network theory.

METHODS

The study examined the mental health systems in Providence, Tucson, and Albuquerque, three U.S. cities that were selected in part because of their comparable size. Data were collected in 1991 and early 1992 from the individual health and human service agencies that composed the system at each site and from a sample of adult clients having severe and persistent mental illness and their families. The research was part of a larger study of the general relationship between system structure and client outcomes (Provan & Milward, 1995). The three cities displayed a range of effectiveness, measured in terms of client outcomes, from low, through medium, to high.[1]

At each site, we first identified the organizations that composed the full system of service delivery to adults with severe mental illness by meeting with key professionals and administrators involved with mental health services. These agencies were mostly small to midsized (under 100 employees), private, and not-for-profit, although some were large public agencies or their subunits in such areas as housing, vocational rehabilitation, and criminal justice. Once a full list of agencies had been developed for each site, questionnaires were sent out to the highest-level administrator at each agency who would be knowledgeable about services for adults with severe mental illness. The primary purpose of the questionnaire was to determine the interorganizational service links maintained by each agency with every other organization in the system.

The lead author and another researcher flew to each site and conducted personal interviews with administrators at each agency. The purpose of the interviews was to go over the questionnaire to ensure its full and accurate completion and to seek additional information about the agency and the system. Extensive follow-up procedures enabled us to collect nearly complete network data at each site. The number of organizations from which data were obtained and specific response rates were as follows: Providence ($N = 35$, 92%), Albuquerque ($N = 35$, 92%), and Tucson ($N = 32$, 97%).

The key survey data obtained from agencies concerned their ties to other organizations in the community through reciprocated referrals and case coordination for adults with severe mental illness. Clients who are able to move from one provider agency to another through intensive, service-level links like reciprocated referrals and case coordination enhance the prospect that their multiple problems will be addressed in a truly integrated fashion. Many of the agencies in the networks were also linked through board ties, information sharing, planning, and the like, but these administrative links need not involve clients. It was our intent to examine only those links that would involve the direct provision of client services and then to relate these to client-level outcomes.

Data were collected for both referrals sent and received, and those data were then combined into a single measure of reciprocated referrals. We used both reciprocated referrals and case coordination because both require considerable interorganizational involvement and

commitment to client outcomes. When referrals are reciprocated, it means that agencies develop an ongoing pattern of interaction with one another through the exchange of clients. Reciprocated referral flows are likely to generate considerable knowledge among the staffs of participating agencies concerning client needs and approaches to treatment. Simple nonreciprocated referrals reflect what Alter and Hage (1993: 97) discussed as sequential task integration and do not necessarily provide the level of coordination required to achieve favorable outcomes. With case coordination, case workers actively manage the treatment of clients across agencies to ensure that all needed services are obtained and client progress is monitored. In Alter and Hage's (1993) model, task integration through reciprocated referrals and case coordination is reciprocal and often collective, so the two highest levels of integration are achieved.

Since no interaction data were available from agency records, we confirmed links in two ways to ensure validity and reliability. First, whenever possible, at least two respondents per agency were asked to participate in completing the survey. Discrepancies were discussed and resolved at the time of the interviews. Second, only data on confirmed links were used in the actual data analysis (Marsden, 1990). Thus, for instance, we only considered agency A to have case coordination with agency B if each agency separately indicated that it had such a link with the other. For reciprocated referrals, not only did each type of referral link have to be confirmed, but agencies A and B had to exchange clients with each other through *both* referrals sent and referrals received. Confirmed data on each of the two types of referrals and the single measure of case coordination were dichotomously coded (0 = no link, 1 = a link) and organized into three separate matrixes, one for each type of link. A reciprocated referral matrix was then constructed from the two separate confirmed referral matrixes (referrals sent and referrals received). We then analyzed the two final matrixes, reflecting organizational link data on reciprocated referrals and case coordination, using UCINET IV (Borgatti, Everett, & Freeman, 1992) network analysis software and a plotting subroutine called Krackplot (Krackhardt, Lundberg, & O'Rourke, 1993).

Data on client outcomes were obtained from 5 percent samples of severely mentally ill clients and their families drawn in each city. This procedure resulted in samples of 64 clients in Tucson, 59 in Albuquerque, and 62 in Providence. Clients were selected randomly from a coded list provided by the core mental health agency at each site.[2] Each of these agencies was responsible for de-

---

[1]A fourth site, Akron, was part of the larger study but was not included in the present research because it had recently undergone a major system overhaul that appeared to have had a negative impact on outcomes.

[2]The process of random selection minimized the risk that a larger proportion of more (or less) severely ill clients would be sampled at any one site. Although it is possible that the overall level of illness at one site might have been higher than it was at the others, data we were able to collect at two sites on client functioning (based on the Global Assessment of Functioning Scale) gave no indication that this was the case.

TABLE 1

Factors Scores of Client Outcome Data for Each Site[a]

Perspective[b]	Tucson	Albuquerque	Providence
Client: Quality of life/ satisfaction	−.18	−.17	.43
Client: Psychiatric/ medical status	−.29	.05	.56
Family	−.10	.06	.26
Mean factor score	−.19	−.02	.42

[a]The numbers of clients sampled at each site were as follows: Tucson, 64; Albuquerque, 59; Providence, 62.

[b]Outcome scores in Providence were significantly higher ($p < .05$) for all three perspectives than they were in either Tucson or Albuquerque. Outcomes in Albuquerque were significantly higher ($p < .05$) for client psychiatric/medical status than in Tucson.

livering and coordinating care and services to all or most of the publicly funded adult clients with severe mental illness in their respective communities. Clients who were institutionalized or unstable at the time of data collection were not interviewed.

Clients and their families (when available) were interviewed by people trained by a clinical psychologist who was a member of the research team. The interviews were structured and involved recording five-point Likert-scale responses to questions concerning the clients' quality of life, adjustment, satisfaction with services, and psychopathology. We selected the interview items from several standard assessment instruments, most notably, the Colorado Client Assessment Record and the New York Functioning Scale, and modified them to fit the study. Other assessment instruments were considered, and many of the items we used were very similar to items from those instruments. However, other aspects of these alternative instruments were not appropriate for our work (too many questions, predominant focus on a less severely ill population, and so forth). In pretests conducted by Bootzin, Berren, Figueredo, and Sechrest (1989) as part of an earlier project, both methods and measures were found to be reliable and valid.

Once data were collected, results from all sites were pooled and factor analyses (with "varimax" rotation) were conducted on the items, first for the client data, then for families. The purpose of the factor analysis was to reduce the data, if possible, so that a single broad measure of effectiveness might be obtained. For the client data, this analysis produced two relatively distinct factors, one related to quality of life and one to psychiatric/medical status, collectively explaining 48 percent of the total variance in client scores. A single factor emerged from the family perspective data, reflecting both client

quality of life and psychiatric/medical status and accounting for 42 percent of total variance.

Factor scores were then calculated for each of the three factors, and these scores were then broken down by site (see Table 1). Despite some differences, the overall patterns of results within each system were similar. That is, the three factor scores for Tucson were the lowest of the four sites initially studied, the scores for Providence were consistently highest, and the scores for Albuquerque were generally in the middle. We then averaged the three factor scores generated for each site to produce a single mean factor score for that site, reflecting the overall effectiveness of each system regarding client outcomes. In terms of this final outcome figure, Providence was a particularly effective system (achieving a positive mean factor score), Tucson was an ineffective system (a negative score), and Albuquerque was in the middle (a neutral score). Outcome scores were found to be statistically unrelated to differences in client age, gender, race, and ethnicity.

ANALYSIS AND RESULTS

As a first step in the analysis, the overall level of integration at each site through each of the two types of links was computed and expressed as a percentage of the maximum possible number of links of each type at each site ($n[n - 1]$). These network density scores (Scott, 1991) based on dyadic links indicated that the most effective site, Providence, had the lowest network-wide integration measured as both reciprocated referrals (10.1%) and case coordination (6.1%), and that Tucson, the least effective site, had the highest scores (13.3% and 9.3%, respectively). Albuquerque, with moderate effectiveness, fell in the middle on integration, with density scores of 12.9 percent for referrals and 6.7 percent for case coordination. The differences across sites were statistically significant at the .05 level according to Pearson chi-square tests for both referrals ($\chi^2 = 6.57$) and case coordination ($\chi^2 = 9.04$). These results appear to shed considerable doubt on the generally held belief that integrated networks of service delivery are more effective than less integrated systems (Department of Health and Human Services, 1991; Dill & Rochefort, 1989). However, it was our belief that the underlying argument for service integration was not incorrect—only its implicit focus on dyadic, nonoverlapping links across an entire network.

Before we could begin the analysis of clique overlap, a key issue to resolve concerned the size of cliques. Since no research existed to guide a decision, we simply examined the data and based our decision on findings from the three networks. A major assumption of the research was that greater and more intensive integration within and across cliques would be more effective than less integration. Thus, the first phase of the clique analysis was simply to determine the largest clique size that could be compared across the three systems. Determining this involved generating a list of the cliques in each network, based first on reciprocated referral links and then on case coordination links.

Using UCINET software (Borgatti et al., 1992), we analyzed the agency data for each site to determine which agencies were directly connected to which others, first in groups/cliques of three agencies, then four, and so on until the data yielded no cliques of a given size at each site. Using this approach, we found that all three sites could be compared using a minimum set size of four or more agencies per clique. We found four-member cliques at all three sites for both types of links, although Albuquerque (for referrals only) and Tucson (for case coordination only) had some cliques of five agencies.

The results of the clique analysis are reported in Table 2. The analysis consisted of first calculating both the number of cliques with four or more agencies each network had and the total number of agencies in the network involved in one or more of these cliques. We then calculated the overlap across cliques and across types of service links. Each approach is explained below.

The top half of Table 2 is simply a count of the number of cliques and the agencies involved in cliques in each network, with no consideration of overlap. One obvious finding is that the most effective site, Providence had fewer cliques (especially reciprocated referral cliques) and fewer agencies involved in cliques than either Tucson or Albuquerque, despite roughly similar city sizes and similar numbers of agencies in the cities' networks. This finding suggests that the coordination of clients and their needs may be most effective when only a small number of closely connected subgroups of agencies are involved. The results are mixed and not especially

strong, however, and do not consider integration across cliques, or what we refer to as clique overlap.

Clique overlap was calculated in several ways. We first examined, for each network, the extent to which those agencies in a particular type of clique (either reciprocated referrals or case coordination) appeared in at least half the cliques of that type. It might be that a network would have eight case coordination cliques of four agencies each, for example, but each of these cliques might contain agencies that were members of few or none of the other seven case coordination cliques. Such low overlap would mean that the members of one clique would interact among themselves but not across cliques, thus depriving clients who might need the services of agencies in other cliques of the benefits of a strongly integrated service system. In contrast, in a system with high clique overlap, many clique members would also be members of other cliques, thus providing a highly integrated core of provider agencies spanning multiple cliques.

Findings for this part of the clique overlap analysis were not consistent across the sites, making interpretation difficult. Providence, the most effective system for client outcomes, had the highest clique overlap for reciprocated referrals (four, or 57.1 percent, of the seven agencies involved in the community's four referral cliques were members of at least half of those referral cliques). However, clique overlap in Tucson (27.3%), the least effective site, was more than twice as high as in Albuquerque (13.3%). Results for case coordination were even more puzzling, with Tucson having the highest level of clique overlap: 71.4 percent of clique members were involved in at least half the cliques, whereas the score was 50 percent for both the other two sites.

TABLE 2

Clique Characteristics and Client Outcomes: Minimum Set Size of Four[a]

Clique Characteristics	Tucson	Albuquerque	Providence
Number of cliques			
Reciprocated referrals	14 cliques	13 cliques	4 cliques
Case coordination	3 cliques	5 cliques	3 cliques
Number of agencies in cliques,			
Reciprocated referrals	11 agencies	15 agencies	7 agencies
Case coordination	7 agencies	8 agencies	6 agencies
Clique overlap[b]			
Reciprocated referrals	3/11 = 27.3%	2/15 = 13.3%	4/7 = 57.1%
Case coordination	5/7 = 71.4%	4/8 = 50%	3/6 = 50%
Service link overlap			
Multiplexity[c]	2/7 = 28.6%	6/8 = 75%	5/6 = 83.3%
Identical overlap[d]	0/3 = 0%	1/5 = 20%	2/3 = 66.7%

[a]Client outcomes were the lowest in Tucson and the highest in Providence, with Albuquerque in the middle.

[b]Clique overlap was the number of agencies in at least half the cliques of a particular type expressed as a percentage of the total number of agencies in that clique type.

[c]Service link overlap/multiplexity was the percentage of agencies in case coordination cliques that were also members of reciprocated referral cliques.

[d]Identical overlap was the percentage of case coordination cliques exactly matching reciprocated referral cliques.

FIGURE 1
Reciprocated Referral and Case Coordination Links in Providence

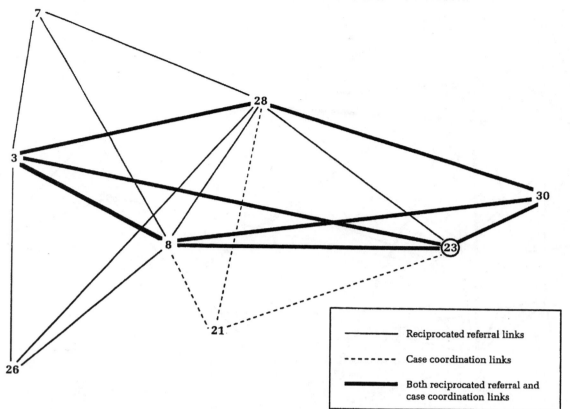

Reciprocated referral links

Case coordination links

Both reciprocated referral and case coordination links

Results become clearer, however, when we examined service link overlap, or multiplexity. Rather than focusing on the extent to which agencies in one clique were also members of other cliques of the same type (overlap across case coordination cliques, for instance), this second measure reflected overlap in service link type. That is, the focus was on examining the extent to which agencies in a case coordination clique were also members of a reciprocated referral clique. Systems with substantial service link overlap would have a core group of agencies that were heavily integrated and involved with one another in multiple ways that were critical for the overall well-being and satisfaction of their clients.

Table 2 indicates that the site with the best client outcomes, Providence, also had the highest level of service link overlap. Specifically, in Providence five of the six agencies (83.3%) involved in the city's three case coordination cliques were also members of reciprocated referral cliques. Tucson, the low-outcome site, had little overlap, with only two of seven (28.6%) members of case coordination cliques also belonging to reciprocated referral cliques. Albuquerque, with moderate client outcomes, was in-between, although its figures were quite close to those of Providence (six of eight, or 75 percent service link overlap).

An alternative way of computing service link overlap resulted in further evidence of the relationship between

network clique structure and client outcomes. For this measure, overlap in clique membership for the two types of service links had to be identical. Results indicated that in Providence, two of the three case coordination cliques consisted of exactly the same agencies as the reciprocated referral cliques. This pattern of identical overlap in cliques based on different types of links occurred only once in Albuquerque (20%), the site with moderate outcomes, and not at all in Tucson, the least effective site.[3]

The clique data for each site were displayed graphically as a final way of examining the findings regarding clique structure and overlap. Using the network-plotting subroutine Krackplot (Krackhardt et al., 1993) as a starting point, we developed plots of all clique members at each site. Figures 1, 2, and 3 present these plots. Included are all members of each reciprocated referral clique (thin solid lines) and each case coordination clique (dotted lines). Clique overlap, in which both types of links occur among clique members, is indicated by a thick solid line connecting each pair of agencies within a clique for which overlap exists.

The plots make it very clear that the overlap structures of cliques at each site are quite different. Link overlap among clique members in Providence (Figure 1) was sub-

---

[3]The analysis of service link overlap was also conducted for cliques having a minimum set size of three agencies. Results were consistent with those reported for cliques of four or more agencies, although the differences across sites were not as strong.

FIGURE 2
Reciprocated Referral and Case Coordination Links in Albuquerque

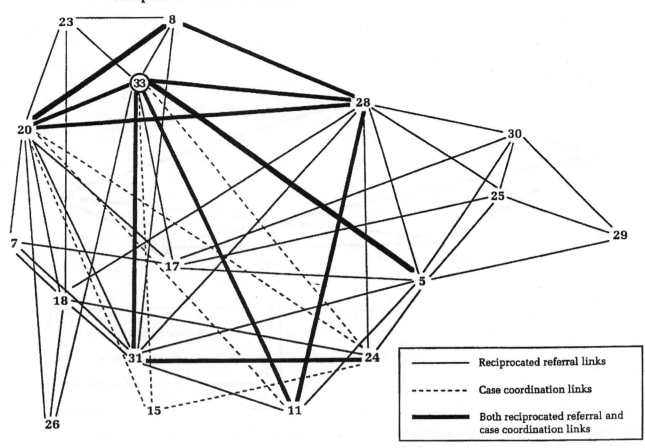

stantial, with five of the eight clique-member agencies included in both types of cliques (referrals and case coordination). Albuquerque (Figure 2) had many (seven) overlapping agencies, but most (ten) of the members of one type of clique did not overlap with the other type. Finally, although Tucson (Figure 3), the least effective site, had many agencies involved in cliques of each type, only two agencies (a single dyad, not a four-member clique) in one of the cliques shared both reciprocated referral and case coordination links. It is also interesting to note that the core mental health agency in Tucson (Figure 3, agency number 1, circled) had no reciprocated referral ties to any other agencies involved in the city's clique structure. This situation is in contrast to the situations in Providence and Albuquerque, where the core mental health agencies (Figure 1, agency 23, and Figure 2, agency 33, respectively) maintained both types of links to many of the other agencies involved in the cliques. Thus, overlap in service links across cliques appears to be important in a general way for explaining system effectiveness, but the specific composition of these overlapping cliques also seems to matter, particularly when the cliques involve agencies, like the core mental health agencies, that may be critical to overall network success.[4]

DISCUSSION AND CONCLUSIONS

The findings of this study offer preliminary evidence that network effectiveness can be explained by intensive integration through network cliques but that integration across a full network is likely to be a poor predictor of network effectiveness. Our data on systems of service delivery for severely mentally ill clients generally supported the idea that differences in client outcomes across

---

[4]Chi-square analyses revealed few or no statistically significant differences when we compared clique overlap across sites. Specifically, the Pearson chi-square statistic for overlap through referrals was 4.68 (p. 10), and it was 0.87 (n.s.) for overlap through case coordination. For the two measures of service link overlap, chi-squares were 5.04 (p. 10) for multiplexity and 3.61 (n.s.) for identical overlap. The weakness of these statistical results is not surprising, since there were relatively few cliques and only three networks. These small numbers represent a general problem for research on cliques, which will typically be few in number in all but the largest networks. In addition, since collecting reliable link and outcome data on multiple networks and getting high response rates is extremely time consuming and costly, most network studies will inevitably suffer from problems of small sample size. Since this research was exploratory, we based our interpretations on the magnitude of the differences in overlaps across sites, particularly for the two measures of service link overlap, and on the linear relationship between these clique overlap measures and effectiveness scores. The findings were supported by our clique plots shown in Figures 1–3.

FIGURE 3
Reciprocated Referral and Case Coordination Links in Tucson

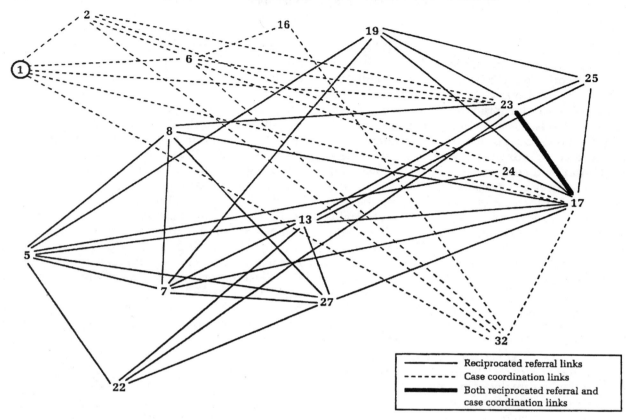

————————	Reciprocated referral links
- - - - - - - -	Case coordination links
▬▬▬▬▬	Both reciprocated referral and case coordination links

systems could be explained reasonably well by focusing on the overlap among cliques of provider agencies through both reciprocated referrals and case coordination.

Although it is risky to generalize about findings from a sample of only three networks in a single area of health and human services, the results of this exploratory study are suggestive for the study of networks in a number of ways. Most notably, the study points to the need to consider networks and network structure in a more microanalytic way than has been done previously. Integration across an entire network of organizations, whether in the health care, manufacturing, or service sectors, is difficult to achieve and is probably not a very efficient way of organizing. Nonetheless, one should not draw the conclusion that integration is undesirable. Rather, if networks are to perform well, especially regarding client outcomes, integration must occur, but at the clique, or subnetwork, level. To be most effective, clique integration must be intensive, involving multiple and overlapping links both within and across the organizations that compose the core of a network. When this sort of intensive, multiplex integration occurs, clique members learn a great deal about each other, minimizing their transaction costs and establishing working relationships built on norms of cooperation and trust (Larson, 1992; Uzzi, 1997). Other organiza-

tions that are more loosely linked to these cliques can also benefit, contributing to the effectiveness of the entire network.

The logic of clique integration is also likely to hold in networks outside of health and human services. For instance, R&D links in biotechnology networks (Barley et al., 1992; Powell, Koput, & Smith-Doerr, 1996) appear to be most prevalent among clusters or cliques of firms working on a common problem. When cliques overlap, the ideas developed in one cluster of firms can be built on by others, and learning can be disseminated effectively throughout a network, enhancing product development. Full-scale integration among the scores of firms that compose the complete network is neither needed nor desirable. Exactly what sizes and kinds of cliques and what types of clique overlap are needed to maximize effectiveness will depend on the unique characteristics of each type of network studied, including which activities are critical to achieving network-level outcomes.

The study also points to the need to examine and assess network effectiveness at the level of the client or customer. Both case coordination and reciprocated referrals are important mechanisms by which health and human service agencies can integrate their activities to have a direct impact on client outcomes. Unlike administrative links through governing boards or top managers involving financial, managerial, or planning issues, service links involve the professional staff members who actually serve clients daily (Bolland & Wilson, 1994). Thus, if integration among providers is to affect client outcomes, the impact is likely to be greatest when integrative efforts are through links that are meaningful to clients.

The findings also have implications for interorganizational and network theory. Salancik (1995) recently expressed the concern of many organization theorists that the study of networks has primarily been an exercise in analysis and methods. He suggested that "a network theory of organization should propose how structures of interactions enable coordinated interaction to achieve collective and individual interests" (Salancik, 1995: 348). This study introduces an alternative method for network analysis and, rather than simply demonstrating that this method can be utilized, it makes a contribution to building network theory by examining and explaining how one unique aspect of network structure, overlapping cliques, might promote the interests of network members and the clients they serve. The findings clearly build on Granovetter's (1973) theory of weak ties by demonstrating that, at least in certain contexts, strong, multiplex, reciprocal ties among small network subgroups can be particularly effective. This conclusion has significant implications for network governance, implying that network administrative organizations or lead firms might focus on building and maintaining intensive integration among cliques of key member firms, who will then have weaker ties to other members, rather than on attempting to loosely integrate entire networks.

There are clearly some shortcomings of the research. Most obvious is the small sample size, which is, unfortunately, a common problem when the unit of analysis is an organizational network. Other problems are perhaps less obvious. For instance, the clients we evaluated were served by the systems being studied, but we cannot be certain that the particular clients sampled were actually served by the specific agencies involved in the cliques, except for the core mental health agency in each system. It also may be that client outcomes, although related to clique overlap, could be better explained by other variables not considered here, like the mix of services within the cliques, commitment of key staff, or the use of certain treatment methods. Finally, despite our efforts to the contrary, it is certainly possible that the client outcome measures used, which were tied to individuals, did not accurately reflect network effectiveness at each site, especially in view of the difficulty in accurately assessing mental health care.

To summarize, the results of this study point to several suggestions for future research and theory development. First, network researchers should consider the role of strongly connected and overlapping cliques of organizations, rather than focusing solely on full network integration, particularly when attempting to explain network-level outcomes, or effectiveness. Second, it is

critical in such analyses to be certain that the types of interorganizational links used to construct cliques have relevance for the level at which network outcomes are being measured. Thus, for instance, it would probably be inappropriate to examine board interlocks and CEO friendship ties among cliques of manufacturing firms to explain network outcomes regarding the level of new product development achieved by the R&D staffs of these firms. For health and human service agencies like those studied here, client outcomes will be most affected by multiplex, overlapping links at the client level, rather than by broader, organization-level integration. Finally, it seems important to measure and analyze clique overlap using complementary linkage mechanisms, like the referral and case coordination links studied here. If clique overlap is to have an impact on effectiveness, it is likely to be through multiple links that build and reinforce competencies rather than through links that only contribute superficially to organizational outcomes. In general, research on networks should shift from a concern with firm-level outcomes to a concern with network effectiveness. At the same time, the analysis of networks needs to become more narrowly focused, especially when broad, poorly specified structural issues like integration are considered.

REFERENCES

Alba, R. D. 1982. Taking stock of network analysis: A decade's results. In S. B. Bacharach (Ed.), *Research in the sociology of organizations*, vol. 1: 39-74. Greenwich, CT: JAI Press.

Alter, C., & Hage, J. 1993. *Organizations working together.* Newbury Park, CA: Sage.

Barley, S., Freeman, J., & Hybels, R. 1992. Strategic alliances in commercial biotechnology. In N. Nohria & R. Eccles (Eds.), *Networks and organizations: Structure, form, and action:* 311-347. Boston: Harvard Business School Press.

Bolland, J. M., & Wilson, J. V. 1994. Three faces of integrative coordination: A model of interorganizational relations in community-based health and human services. *Health Services Research,* 29: 341-366.

Bootzin, R. R., Berren, M., Figueredo, A. J., & Sechrest, L. 1989. *Evaluation of the Arizona Pilot Project on capitation financing for the severely mentally ill.* Phoenix: Arizona Psychological Association.

Borgatti, S. P., Everett, M. G., & Freeman, L. C. 1992. *UCINET IV.* Columbia, SC: Analytic Technologies.

Department of Health and Human Services. 1991. *Services integration: A twenty year retrospective.* Washington, DC: Office of the Inspector General.

Dill, A., & Rochefort, D. A. 1989. Coordination, continuity, and centralized control: A policy perspective on service strategies for the chronic mentally ill. *Journal of Social Issues,* 45(3): 145-159.

Doreian, P., & Woodard, K. L. 1994. Defining and locating cores and boundaries of social networks. *Social Networks,* 16: 267-293.

Granovetter, M. S. 1973. The strength of weak ties. *American Journal of Sociology,* 78: 1360-1380.

Human, S. E., & Provan, K. G. 1997. An emergent theory of structure and outcomes in small-firm strategic manufacturing networks. *Academy of Management Journal,* 40: 368-403.

Krackhardt, D., Lundberg, M., & O'Rourke, L. 1993. Krackplot: A picture's worth a thousand words. *Connections,* 16(1 & 2): 37-47.

Larson, A. 1992. Network dyads in entrepreneurial settings: A study of the governance of exchange processes. *Administrative Science Quarterly,* 37: 76-104.

Laumann, E. O., Marsden, P. V., & Prensky, D. 1983. The boundary specification problem in network analysis. In R. S. Burt & M. J.

Minor (Eds.), *Applied network analysis: Structural methodology for empirical social research:* 18-34. Beverly Hills, CA: Sage.

Lehman, A. F., Postrado, L. T., Roth, D., McNary, S. W., & Goldman, H. H. 1994. Continuity of care and client outcomes in the Robert Wood Johnson Foundation program on chronic mental illness. *Milbank Memorial Quarterly,* 72: 105-122.

Lorenzoni, G., & Ornati, O. A. 1988. Constellations of firms and new ventures. *Journal of Business Venturing,* 3: 41-57.

Marsden, P. V. 1990. Network data and measurement. In W. R. Scott (Ed.), *Annual review of sociology,* vol. 16: 435-463. Palo Alto, CA: Annual Reviews.

Powell, W. W. 1990. Neither market nor hierarchy: Network forms of organization. In B. M. Staw & L. L. Cummings (Eds.), *Research in organizational behavior,* vol. 12: 295-236. Greenwich, CT: JAI Press.

Powell, W. W., Koput, K. W., & Smith-Doerr, L. 1996. Interorganizational collaboration and the locus of innovation: Networks of learning in biotechnology. *Administrative Science Quarterly,* 41: 116-145.

Provan, K. G., & Milward, H. B. 1995. A preliminary theory of interorganizational network effectiveness: A comparative study of four community mental health systems. *Administrative Science Quarterly,* 40: 1-33.

Salancik, G. R. 1995. Wanted: A good network theory of organization. *Administrative Science Quarterly,* 40: 345-349.

Scott, J. 1991. *Social network analysis: A handbook.* London: Sage.

Uzzi, B. 1997. Social structure and competition in interfirm networks: The paradox of embeddedness. *Administrative Science Quarterly,* 42: 35-67.

Keith G. Provan is a professor in the School of Public Administration and Policy, which is part of the College of Business and Public Administration at the University of Arizona. He also holds a joint appointment with the Department of Management and Policy. Professor Provan received his Ph.D. from the State University of New York at Buffalo. His primary research interests are in the areas of interorganizational and network relationships. Recent empirical work in these areas has focused on health care systems and small-firm manufacturing networks.

Juliann G. Sebastian is an associate professor and the assistant dean for advanced practice at the University of Kentucky College of Nursing. She received her Ph.D. in management from the University of Kentucky College of Business and Economics. Her research interests include understanding the structure and behavior of organizational systems such as health care under imperfect market conditions and, in particular, interorganizational dynamics within a network context.

Identifying Who Matters:

MAPPING KEY PLAYERS IN MULTIPLE ENVIRONMENTS

Jeffrey L. Cummings
Jonathan P. Doh

No company today can be competitive unless it simultaneously manages relationships in each critical realm of managerial operations. In particular, managing exclusively within a traditional economically driven view of corporate strategy is insufficient. Political, social, and technological contexts must also be reckoned with if the firm is to incorporate the range of institutions and actors—both public and private—that affect its operations.

A purely economic view of stakeholder mapping and value creation is insufficient for incorporating the range of stakeholder interactions and contexts. Despite the "intrinsic intimacy" that exists between different managerial contexts,[1] their delineation is important for three reasons. First, as Baron has suggested, the strategies pursued in response to each context may need to be customized to each different environment and its players.[2] Second, since there is a different set of processes through which value is created in each environment, firms need to develop different sets of managerial capabilities and resources to deal effectively in each context. Third, the players or stakeholders with whom the firm interacts in each context often differ and have different abilities to affect the firm. Within each of the managerial contexts, examination of the operant value-creation processes supports context-specific stakeholder mapping and identification. Such mapping can alert firms to players and policies that might otherwise be overlooked.

Stakeholder Mapping in the Market Context

Brandenburger and Nalebuff developed the "value net" framework through which a company can map stakeholders on the basis of their relative impact on an organization's value chain and value system.[3] This framework suggests that four groups of organizations or "players" interactively and interdependently define the "game" of business for a company. The term "players" is used to represent the different roles or positions that various economic stakeholders have in their interactions with the focal company's economic value-creation process. Although distinct from Porter's five-forces model, the value net framework may be considered complementary.[4] Whereas Porter looks at the forces that various players can exert upon the degree of rivalry among a group of firms, the firm-centric value net maps out these same players—and one additional one, which Brandenburger and Nalebuff call "complementors"—on the basis of their interdependence with the focal firm. In addition to the focal company, the four players in the value net are customers, suppliers, competitors, and complementors.

Within the market context, firms must understand which players are important and which relationships are most pronounced in order to develop comprehensive business and corporate strategies. In Figure 1, the market context is illustrated by the economic flows between and among players, where such flows are collectively defined as the *economic value-creation process*. The flows between the players and the focal company vary according to the role that each stakeholder adopts. The players along the horizontal axis are the company's customers and suppliers.[5] Analysis of the focal company's value chain and value system provides guidance in terms of identifying these traditional economic players. In addition to customers and suppliers, two other players have an impact upon the firm's ability to add value. These players, along the vertical axis of the framework, are the company's economic competitors and economic complementors. Briefly stated, economic competitors make it harder for the firm to obtain and retain customers and supplies, while economic complementors make it easier to do so.

Stakeholders may play different roles simultaneously and/or their roles may evolve over time. For example, American and Delta are supplier complementors

Reprinted from the *California Management Review,* Vol. 42, No. 2, Winter 2000, pp. 83-104. © 2000 by The Regents of the University of California. Reprinted by permission of The Regents.

FIGURE 1. Stakeholder Mapping and Valuation: Economic Environment

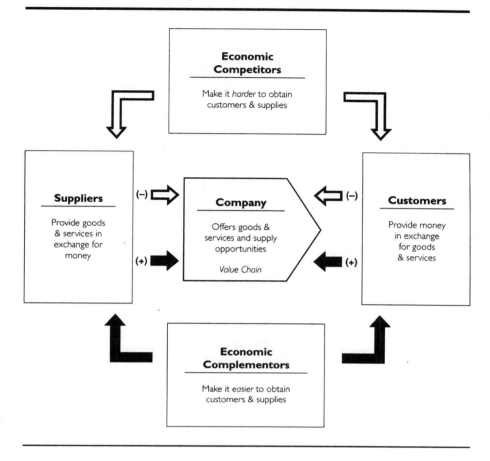

when it comes to procuring aircraft by combining their orders to allow aircraft manufacturers to reach minimum economic order sizes. At the same time, however, they are supplier competitors when it comes to obtaining pilots, flight attendants, and other employees. Moreover, while they are clearly customer competitors—the offerings of each make it harder for the other to obtain customers—on certain routes the presence of service by each allows a customer to reach his or her destination by flying a leg of the trip on each airline. This then makes them customer complementors.

Stakeholder theory has long recognized that stakeholders may occupy multiple roles. The value net framework provides managers with a tool to map those stakeholders (in all of their roles) that have the greatest impact on the firm's economic value-creation process. This then allows managers to develop micro- and macro-level strategies with respect to important economic players. For example, prior to its spin-off of Lucent Technologies, AT&T was a direct competitor with MCI and Sprint in one part of its business (long-distance service) and also a key supplier to them in

another part of its business (network equipment). This conflict—the fact that AT&T was serving as both competitor and supplier to its rivals—resulted in a decision to spin-off Lucent as a separate company so that it would be viewed solely as a supplier by other long-distance firms and not as a business unit of a rival. Previously, long-distance service providers were not sourcing equipment contracts from AT&T because of this rivalry. Once Lucent was organized as a separate, independent equipment company, it quickly gained position as one of the premier suppliers of network equipment to other domestic and international long-distance providers, as well as to local companies entering the newly deregulated U.S. long-distance market.

Another aspect of the value net is that players may frequently shift both their strategies and roles with respect to the focal company, adding a dynamic element to the framework. When suppliers, customers, and the focal company come together to create value for all involved, they generally operate on a cooperative basis. However, when the pie has to be divided up, the firms shift their strategies from cooperative to competitive.[6] Since

strategy and role shifts may prove detrimental to the focal company, the development of a clear picture of which players currently occupy which roles can enhance managers' ability to engineer these relationships. By developing stakeholder maps of existing and potential competitors and complementors, managers can better analyze alternative strategies and scenarios. Since "decision makers' perceptions and cognitions are phenomena that can be expected to influence industry evolution," the development of stakeholder maps requires integration of both empirical and perceptual data.[7]

Stakeholder Mapping in the Political/Social Context

In addition to the economic value-creation process that serves as the focus of the value net, there are also many players with whom an organization interacts on a non-economic basis—such as government regulators, special interest groups, and politicians. One approach to dealing with this added complexity is to distinguish between market and nonmarket environments.[8] Corporations pursue nonmarket strategies through specific legal, regulatory, and public affairs activities. The public affairs function within the firm is charged with effectively managing its political and social environments. As one component of firms' nonmarket strategies, public affairs activities can be distinct from, yet integrated with and related to, broader market-based strategic management activities.[9] For example, the Mexican cement manufacturer Cemex followed a politically savvy approach to gain a foothold in the U.S. by targeting areas where cement prices were higher and withdrawing from those where prices were lower, thereby reducing dumping margins and duties. This also allowed them to avoid politically charged confrontations in lower margin markets. Concurrently, Cemex was able to pursue lobbying and other political strategies in an attempt to modify the regulatory environment in a manner that would ultimately generate economic opportunities.

Activities that take place in the nonmarket environment represent the *political value-creation process*. Baron notes that while market and nonmarket environments may be "interpenetrating" or interdependent and that the strategies designed to deal with them must be integrated and coordinated, separating them for analysis purposes becomes very important.[10]

From a nonmarket perspective, corporations are not only economic instruments, but "social systems that have to perform acceptably in light of society's values. A corporation is never fully independent of society's values: it is subject to controls both in the form of generalized norms and in the form of laws which are enforced by popularly elected governments."[11] As such, companies might find their resources diverted from efficiency-enhancing activities to those that repair or enhance their social legitimacy. For example, Enron's experience in the Indian state of Maharashtra demonstrated a failure to properly identify and value non-economic stakeholders. After an election and change of government in the state, Enron was compelled to withdraw and then restructure an existing proposal to build an electricity generating facility. In the revised plan, Enron was forced to incorporate the views of local farmers, ecologists, and consumers as well as political representatives so as to regain the social legitimacy that had been eroded by its initial approach.

Firms can also purposefully expend resources to influence public policy in a manner that ultimately enhances their economic efficiency. MCI's effort in the 1970s to facilitate the breakup of AT&T demonstrates the efficacy of successful proactive politically directed strategies. Specifically, MCI's aggressive pursuit of a political/legal remedy to the anti-competitive effects of the AT&T monopoly resulted in a dramatic re-shaping of public policy and, ultimately, the market environment—not just for MCI, but for the entire telecommunications industry (see MCI Appendix).

Public policy involves two different, yet inextricably linked processes through which organizations interact.[12] The first is the process through which firms obtain corporate political advantage. As in the case of MCI, companies work toward the establishment of public policies that favor them by changing the size and structure of markets, thereby affecting the industry's basic competitive forces. To create advantages, companies seek to obtain information from key social actors about issues that might affect them and then influence public policy through political activities.

The second process involves the concept of social legitimacy. Companies seek to influence and respond to broad social actors and groups to preserve and enhance social legitimacy. They also seek to minimize the possibility of negative and disruptive reactions to corporate behavior, as Enron did after recognizing its failure to do so initially. This protective process is often referred to as social issues management or crisis management. Both the political advantage and the social legitimacy processes require

FIGURE 2. Stakeholder Mapping and Valuation: Political Environment

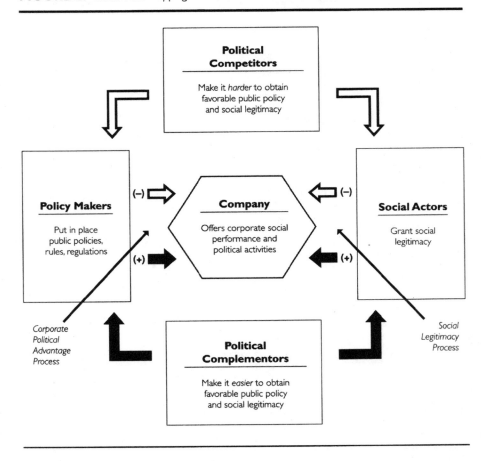

that companies obtain social issue information from key social actors through environmental scanning and conduct political activities by assembling and participating in ideological coalitions and constituencies among such actors.

The political value-creation process is the means by which companies pursue both political advantage and social legitimacy. A key reason for joining these two processes is that while the political pursuit of competitive advantage is possible, "a substantial increase in narrow self-interested activity, unconstrained by poorly operationalized social responsibility or ethical concerns, will call into question the legitimacy of the corporation."[13] In addition, while some public policy issues can have a significant impact on specific companies, and therefore might warrant a narrow corporate advantage approach, others are more broad-based and require the creation of large coalitions to respond to social legitimacy concerns. Moreover, the social legitimacy process, like the corporate political advantage process, "is essentially a political process ... a complex amalgam of power and influence that involves many actors pursuing different interests."[14] Hence,

companies often pursue strategies that focus simultaneously on gaining political advantage and on maintaining or enhancing social legitimacy. In terms of seeking corporate political advantage, the Chemical Manufacturer Association (CMA), for example, maintains an active lobbying program to ensure that changes in environmental laws and regulations are not excessively burdensome. Meanwhile, in terms of maintaining social legitimacy, CMA members have joined in promoting a "Responsible Care" initiative to assure the public that the industry is supportive of a responsible approach to environmental concerns.

In the political/social arena, the interactions among stakeholders exhibit many nuances. Figure 2 illustrates the contribution of stakeholder mapping to the political value-creation process. The flows in this process, as in the economic value-creation process, vary according to the roles that stakeholders adopt. The wide arrow representing the value chain of the economic context is replaced here with a two-way arrow to illustrate the interactive nature and the interdependencies in the political context. Social actors, for example, seek information about the quality of companies' efforts to be responsible institutions and judge the companies' standing based on their corporate social actions. In turn, social actors are also subject to the influence of the companies' political activities and attempt to influence public policy through political action. Regulators, who are also the focus of much political activity, are themselves politically active in trying to shape the political landscape to their own advantage, as public choice and agency perspectives have suggested. Moreover, they also try to influence both the flow of issues information and the social-legitimacy process.

Within the political/social context, the functional equivalent of the economic context's suppliers and customers are *policy makers* and *social actors*. Policy makers are the institutional stakeholders who put in place the rules, regulations, laws, and public policies that determine acceptable player behavior. Social actors are those institutional, organizational, and individual stakeholders who provide social issues information and social legitimacy for the corporate social actions of the firm. Unlike the economic environment in which only those stakeholders who transact business may play a role in affecting the economic value-creation process, in the political/social environment many different stakeholders are enfranchised to participate as social actors. The media, for instance, plays a role in the economic environment primarily through the market process: players exchange money or goods and services for the offerings of the media providers. In the political/social environment, however, the media, public interest groups, and others are always potential players. Social actors can work through traditional political avenues, or they can circumvent such processes and advocate their views directly to the public, media, or allied groups to create grassroots or other coalitions. It is for this reason that environmental scanning has received so much attention as a key activity in managing in this context.

In addition to policy makers and social actors, two other players affect the firm's ability to manage the political value-creation process. These players, along the vertical axis of the framework, are the company's *political competitors* and *political complementors*. The definitions of these political players directly parallel the definitions of the economic players described within the economic context. That is, political competitors make it harder for a company to gain political advantage or maintain social legitimacy, while political complementors make either or both easier. For example, in MCI's entry into Mexico, Telmex, with

its close governmental connections, was a political competitor. At the same time, AT&T and other foreign telecommunications firms were allied with MCI as complementors in its effort to force deregulation of Mexico's long distance market.

Multiple and Changing Roles, Linkages Between Contexts

Since players in the political context can occupy multiple and dynamically shifting roles, managers can benefit from learning which players are playing which roles so that appropriate constituency-building strategies can be developed to address key political or social legitimacy issues. It is important for managers to identify which players might have the greatest potential impact upon their firms' ability to maintain social legitimacy. One of the challenging aspects of this process is that there are few barriers to entry for social actors.

One link to the economic context involves efforts by the firm to enact regulations that favor it over customer or supplier competitors. American Airlines, for example, recently sought the enactment of an Open Skies Agreement between the U.S. and the U.K. in order to facilitate the integration of its domestic feeder and transatlantic routes with its partner, British Airways. US Air voiced opposition to the agreement, given that it would have the effect of diminishing US Air's market position relative to the integrated AA/BA share. However, while American and US Air compete in the political/social context on this issue, they recently initiated a partnership to code-share on some flights and integrate their frequent flyer programs, positioning the two political competitors as economic complementors in the economic context.

Another example of the integration of corporate strategies directed toward the market and political contexts is the recent decision by America OnLine and Netscape to pursue a business combination. This market-driven merger, designed to respond to the commanding presence of Microsoft in the software and browser markets, came about partly as a result of the public policy alliance these two firms staked out in the ongoing antitrust case against Microsoft. Such a move reflects a sophisticated mapping of commercial, political, and broader media and societal interests. Having decided to pursue a competitive public policy strategy, Netscape and AOL were forced to rethink their business relationships with Microsoft. Changing public and political sentiment further reinforced this change in direction.

In the political context firms pursue a very different set of players and relationships than those identified in the market context. To the extent that both political and economic player identifications prove necessary to support effective strategy making, the mapping of both sets of players becomes a critical managerial function. Had MCI focused solely on economic players, for instance, it is unlikely that the regulatory environment would have become so hospitable and thus eventually the market environment as well.

In addition to the political/social environment, there has recently been increasing attention directed toward the technological environment and the recognition that knowledge creation relies on how businesses relate to other participants in the knowledge economy, how well they capture value from knowledge assets, and how well they exploit infrastructures conducive to such knowledge creation.[15] For example, the performance of biotechnology companies is highly dependent upon the diffusion of innovations and knowledge from universities and other research organizations and individuals, and it requires more complicated and non-traditional models of learning.[16] Moreover, their performance also requires the transfer of best practices within and among multiple organizations as well as the adoption of technological standards and business models by knowledge workers and institutions. Since these seem to be qualitatively different processes than those found in economic or political contexts, the technological context similarly requires separate attention. Thus the value net should also be extended to the technological context.

Stakeholder Mapping in the Technological Context

Doing well in the market context requires companies to add economic value by effectively and efficiently transforming capital, goods, and labor inputs into product and service outputs. Doing well in the political/social context requires companies to build social legitimacy through their corporate social performance and to build corporate political advantage through their political activities. In the technological context, companies compete for ascendance in a technological system by persuading stakeholders to adopt their technology and related business model. Although these phenomena may be incorporated in some market-based models and frameworks, we differentiate the technological environment from the traditional market framework because many of the assumptions and constraints in a conventional economic model do not hold within the technological environment. For example, in the technological environment, first-mover, network externalities, standards setting, adoption and diffusion, tipping, and other imperfect market phenomena are often the principal determinants of competitive success or failure. In this environment, firms have relationships with stakeholders who can assist or impede the creation and diffusion of technology, and these processes are increasingly driven by factors not considered by traditional economic models. A company's wealth is increasingly intangible, residing in the expertise and knowledge of its members, and is dependent upon the acceptance of the firm's business model.[17]

In the personal computer industry, it is widely held that Microsoft Corporation's Windows has been accepted as the standard for PC operating systems. The acceptance of Windows as a standard does not mean that it is the best PC operating system. Rather, its acceptance means that technology adopters have developed a shared perspective that adoption of Windows makes sense, whether due to its quality or to the fact that is so widely diffused. The Qwerty keyboard provides another example of this quality/diffusion conundrum. This keyboard design has generally been viewed as substantially inferior to other ones, notably the Dvorak approach, in terms of enhancing typing efficiency.[18] Nonetheless, the Qwerty keyboard has never been replaced as the standard because of its extensive diffusion. In this way, the adopted technological standard is therefore the most valuable standard, regardless of whether it is the best technology or not.

Two different approaches to diffusion strategies can be seen in the battle for the browser market between Netscape and Microsoft. Netscape's strategy, rather than relying on diffusion of a common network or technological platform, instead was aimed at garnering support directly from consumers. As such, Intel and other potential complementors expressed frustration in working with Netscape, especially in contrast to Microsoft, which "lavished time, money, and support to companies, such as applications developers, that were aligned with its interests."[19] Given Microsoft's increasingly successful challenge to Netscape's dominance in the browser market, due in large part to Microsoft's dominance in operating systems and its ability to partner with other Web portals, Netscape attempted to use both a political strategy (opposing Microsoft in the

Justice Department's antitrust case) and, ultimately, a market- and technology-driven merger with AOL. That is, Netscape's counter to Microsoft's more effective diffusion strategy was to join with another successful diffuser, AOL.

Despite the widespread diffusion and standard status of a technology, at times a new technology will replace it. For example, in the early 1980s the application of microelectronics changed the telecommunications environment from one in which telephonic equipment was high-cost, undifferentiated, and technologically stagnant to one in which low-cost production and differentiation became the accepted norms. As Richard Rumelt has concluded, to create value in such a technological system, companies that had initially failed to participate in new technologies, such as AT&T, were forced to do so either at great cost or at risk of remaining outside the technology selection environment.[20] It is important to remain within such an environment because it ultimately dictates the standards that all industry participants, willingly or not, have to abide by to compete in the economic context. In this case, despite the widespread diffusion of rented rotary telephone and manual switching equipment, the new microelectronic technology took hold. Importantly, over time, a firm's failure to remain within such an appropriate standard-creating technology selection environment can leave it unable to play catch-up or to be locked out.[21]

The *business learning process* is the mechanism through which firms seek to gain ascendancy in their technological system and thereby achieve some form of technological advantage. This process requires a firm to diffuse its innovations widely enough to then allow its business model to be accepted. Also, it requires a firm to obtain a powerful enough coalition of key adopters to establish a de facto standard. Otherwise, a firm can simply embrace open standards and hope to enhance and maybe even lead them.[22]

A diffusion strategy that has been used in many high-tech industries is known as the Trojan horse or entrenchment strategy.[23] Through this strategy, a technology is all but given away to users to generate adoption and create desire for subsequent technologies. In the late 1980s, Nintendo pursued this diffusion strategy by offering its hardware at artificially low prices that allowed it to rapidly penetrate and gain adoption of its hardware as the standard in the home video game market. The company was later able to charge premium prices for its games and recoup its investment in the form of monopoly rents. AOL pursued a similar strategy in its online ser-

vice provider business. Lotus Corporation inadvertently benefited from the Trojan horse effect by having its software products proliferate through unauthorized copying—later, the company earned considerable margins by offering upgrades to this larger than expected installed base.

In such standard-setting strategies, companies seek to create standards of technology that differentially favor them. This is accomplished through the company's efforts to convey its business model and diffuse its technologies, ideally reaching enough adopters to set into effect the positive feedback cycles that lead to standards. Often, moreover, the interoperability of the given technology increases its value to users as their numbers increase. This then increases the pace and breadth of adoption as existing adopters seek to enhance their benefits. Once a winner appears imminent, a herd mentality, driven by the fear of lockout, further reinforces the leading approach.[24] As with the Qwerty keyboard, once a technology with interoperability benefits is learned by a threshold of adopters, the technology gains staying power from the so-called tyranny of the installed base to the extent that any change requires a significant new learning investment or a loss of benefits by adopters. Hence, the strategy here is to identify and aggressively pursue a broad base of end-users whose adoption might lead to acceptance of the firm's technology and related business model as a standard.

However, getting to this threshold of adopters is often beyond the individual firm's direct control. This is because a broad base of complementary goods and services is usually required for a technology to be adopted.[25] The VHS standard in videotapes, for example, won out over the arguably higher quality Beta standard due, in large part, to the fact that there was a much larger selection of VHS videotapes than Beta videotapes when videocassette recorders first became available. As such, in addition to diffusing its technology broadly, a firm must also seek out and support technologies for which complementary offerings are or will be extensively available. This explains the broad spectrum of marketing and business alliance strategies being pursued by many telecommunications companies today as they seek to gain thresholds of adopters for their mobile telephonic transmission approaches while simultaneously extending the range of complementary offerings.

A key adopter or sponsorship strategy is also available to firms seeking to gain ascendance in their technological systems.[26] Rather than pursuing end-user diffusion to gain adoption, rival groups Toshiba-Time Warner and Sony-Philips instead pursued a strategy of reaching a consensus on a DVD standard prior to manufacturing a single product. The combined firms' relative dominance virtually assured the acceptance of their standard. In the microprocessor field, Sun Microsystems and Philips have pursued joint production agreements allowing Sun's RISC chips to be more readily incorporated within a broader range of products than Sun was able to accomplish on its own. Standard competitor MIPS Computer Systems, similarly, has aggressively pursued licensing agreements with major manufacturers such as Siemens. In all of these cases, the game involves creating a dominant coalition of technological adopters who then collectively legitimize and thereby enforce the group's standard. By gaining key adopters who thus set the standards, the firms avoid the need to pursue broad dissemination strategies. The widespread use of technological alliances is consistent with this key adopter approach. Unfortunately, as demonstrated by David Yoffie's research on digital convergence and the above examples, rarely has the key adopter strategy worked.[27] Moreover, while attracting stakeholders into a company's business model is central to achieving technological advantage, the firm must also simultaneously learn from its environment to modify its technology and related business model. Only then can it maintain its advantage within its technological system.

Microsoft's efforts to provide seamless document viewing through its Web browser, Explorer, depends on its advantage of dominating the PC operating system business. By seeking to extend its technologies from its existing operating systems platforms, Microsoft is effectively seeking to forestall the adoption by its customers of other standards related to non-operating system software. If a JAVA-based Web browser was to reach a threshold of adopters, for example, Microsoft's hold on technological standards would be significantly weakened. As a result, Microsoft must continuously learn about potential alternative offerings and seek to incorporate essential innovations within its core offerings to prevent alternative standards from emerging. This means that a firm cannot pursue only a diffusion or a key adopter strategy to assure its ascendance in its technological ecosystem. Rather, since firms must continually pursue both strategies, it is essential that they systematically identify who to target and who can help or harm them in their efforts. Often, this requires

the firm to seek "creative combination" strategies that focus initially on products, services, and technologies that are complementary to the firm's installed base.[28] Moreover, this often requires the firm to be willing to cannibalize its own offerings in order to avoid technological lockout. Hence, a comprehensive mapping of the key players providing potentially complementary technological offerings can provide managers with an essential tool for identifying who to include and who to exclude from creative combination strategies.

As with the market and political/social processes, the business learning process is a representation of a complex system involving interdependent stakeholders, but it may be mapped simply according to the various roles stakeholders play, as illustrated in Figure 3.

Within the technological context, the focal company is the change agent in its technological system. It acts as the encoder of knowledge and the marketer of technology. The functional equivalent of the economic context's suppliers and customers are key adopters and end-user adopters. Key adopters are those stakeholders who exchange their knowl-

edge, ideas, and business platforms for the opportunity to encode their ideas or their own business models through the focal company's technology. They include major organizations or groups of professionals, technical experts, consultants, and researchers whose adoption of a technology translates into legitimization of the technology as a potential standard and eventually the widespread diffusion of it. End-user adopters are those stakeholders who adopt the focal company's business model for the use of the technology. They seek to benefit from what they perceive as increased capabilities and choices from the complementaries afforded to them through use of the technology. They might be individuals or institutions, and sales are not necessarily an indicator of adoption. Every new user of Netscape Navigator is an end-user adopter, regardless of whether or not they paid for it, as are all users of free downloadable software or shareware. End-user adopters are on the receiving end of firms' diffusion strategies, whereas key adopters are the targets of firms' legitimization efforts.

Technology competitors are those stakeholders that compete with the com-

FIGURE 3. Stakeholder Mapping and Valuation: Technological Environment

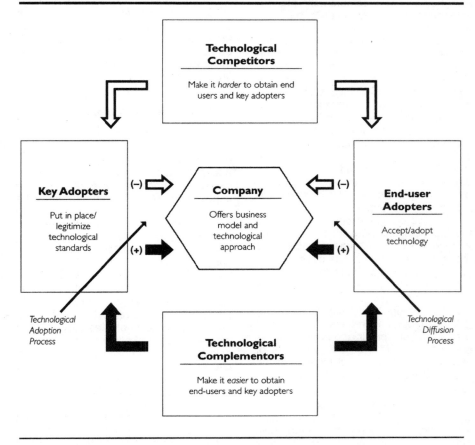

pany for key adopters and end-user adopters. Sun and MIPS exemplify the idea of technology competitors, as each offers a different standard with respect to microprocessors. Competition among earlier and later versions of technologies is also possible. This means that, in addition to competing with rival firms' technologies, at times a firm could be competing against its own earlier versions of its technology. The programming languages C and C++ are competing technologies since the value to adopters of the earlier technology drops when a later version is introduced, and the earlier version represents a competing technology to the later one if it already has a strong user base. This effect is most noticeable among end-user adopters of word-processing applications who refuse to adopt a later release, or who refuse to use a competing vendor's superior product. With respect to key adopters, since the business model represents the way knowledge will be actualized, key adopters have their choice of business models through which they encode their technologies. Any organization or institution offering alternative business models through which key adopters might seek to implement their ideas represent a potential technological competitor.

Technology complementors represent stakeholders who complement the development of the company's business model or the adoption of its technologies. By doing so, they make it easier for the focal firm to diffuse its technology or gain key adopters. While value accrues to the focal company through complementor technologies, such as hardware and software compatibility in the PC industry, the network advantages of complementors go beyond other companies offering compatible technology. Compatibility is the degree to which an innovation is perceived as consistent with the current norms, values, and beliefs of adopters as well as the perceived technical advantages of the innovation. In other words, innovation is affected by the technological network that supports adoption. However, the structure that matters to diffusion often goes far beyond the features of the technology itself. Participation in the network by end-users and key adopters is essential to value creation through compatibility. Each additional adopter increases the value of the innovation for all adopters. This occurs because of the reduced costs of learning, distribution and sales, and the growth of valuable installed base advantages.

The dual role of adopters as end-users and complementors is what allows for the possibility of reaching a threshold stage of diffusion and the creation of a

standard, the innovator's brass ring. Microsoft's MS-DOS benefited from such a threshold as the company's PC operating system became the standard in the late 1980s and early 1990s, as its Windows95 operating system benefits from its adoption as the standard today. Adopter compatibility effects can also be seen in the emerging business of online multi-player computer games. Some companies who normally charge about $50 for a computer game for individual use have begun giving away the online version to encourage players to learn their game and join others on multi-user Web sites. These companies recognize that the value to the adopter is not the product itself, but the inclusion in a community of gamers. If successful, the company may make money by charging adopters subscription or pay-per-use fees for access to the company's gaming network, or by selling them variations or later versions of the game.[29] Technology complementors, in this and similar cases, are other adopters. In fact, many of the emerging Web-based e-commerce start-ups are relying on key adopters and complementors to provide their entire revenue base. Several firms are, in effect, giving away goods such as computers in order to "hook" the consumer on other services and products. A comprehensive map of technological stakeholders, therefore, must include not only those firms that offer or should be targeted to offer complementary goods or services, but also those that possess an installed base to which the focal firm's offerings can be marketed.

Linkages among Contexts

The business learning process of the technological context interacts with the other processes identified in the market and political/social contexts. For example, new technological standards can be imposed upon an industry through the use of political lobbying that leads to governmental regulations that either define standards by default or that create economic incentives for the adoption of certain standards. On the other hand, once established as standards, technologies can receive favorable political support given their technological legitimacy. The owners of such technologies, assuming the technologies provide them with economies of scale or scope or significant switching costs, can also translate their standard status into monopoly profits. This is the essence of the Trojan horse diffusion strategy described earlier. Microsoft's distribution of its Explorer Internet browser software for free along with its Windows operating system is an example of how it used diffusion to drive

adoption, and then ultimately to obtain potential monopoly benefits. Of course, Microsoft's recent trouble with the U.S. Justice Department with respect to this strategy further demonstrates the interactions among the contexts. Had Microsoft developed a more comprehensive map of the political/social arena, and proactively pursued appropriate lobbying and other political activities, it is conceivable that it could have better managed both the public policy and the social legitimacy processes.

The three contexts are also linked by common role sets. In the economic context, supplier strategies are developed to minimize supplier power and maximize the firm's economic value creation through its value chain. In the political/social context, a set of political strategies is developed to deal with the suppliers of public policies rather than economic inputs. In the technological context, strategies are developed to obtain an essential "supply" of technological legitimacy by gaining key adopters. On the other end of this horizontal chain of player interactions, economic customers are vied for in terms of their dollars; social actors are vied for in terms of their social legitimacy; and technology adopters are vied for in terms of their acceptance and use of the firm's technologies. In terms of these "customers," the basic strategies involve marketing processes through which they are enticed to buy, accept, and use/adopt, respectively, the offerings of the company within each context. Finally, the competitors and complementors within each context play similar roles with respect to the operant value-creation processes. Customer competitors make it harder for the firm to get customers' dollars, social acceptance, and technological use; supplier competitors make it harder to get the suppliers' goods, public policies, and technological adoptions; complementors simply make each of these activities easier for the firm.

Conclusion

Market economics, by its very broad and diffuse character, enables businesses to manage and dominate economic, political, and technological decisions. Indeed, historical analysis of the rise of the modern industrial enterprise has found considerable support for the idea that there is an inextricable link between the evolution of industrial organizations, political institutions, and technology life cycles.[30] As such, it might be thought that analysis on one context could not be meaningfully separated from the others. However, as Baron has suggested, the development of coherent integrated strategies can benefit from the simultaneous but separate consideration of the different contexts relevant to decision making.[31]

This article presents a framework through which to identify stakeholders based on the form of their interaction within three of a focal company's value-creation contexts. Such an identification process for stakeholders, and the ability to view them according to their positions within the multidimensional model, enhances understanding of who a firm's key stakeholders are and improves the ability of managers to evaluate the relative importance of stakeholder sets within a given set of circumstances. Corporate strategies pursued in response to competitive threats or opportunities within each of the managerial contexts are likely to take different forms because the tools and resources, as well as the positions of the major stakeholders, can be distinct and unique to each dimension. The framework can improve the ability of managers to identify and evaluate the relevance and influence of stakeholders based upon the dimension in which interactions are occurring, the positions those stakeholders occupy within the dimension, and the type of interaction or exchange.

In the political/social environment, managers need to be in a position to identify and respond to important stakeholders and key actors who influence the broader business environment as well as have a direct bearing on the firm's competitive position within the industry. In the rapidly changing technological environment, firms must be able to go beyond traditional market-based approaches to take advantage of first-mover, technological adoption and diffusion, and complementor strategies. Microsoft's recent approaches to challenges in the political/social and technological environments demonstrate how one firm can successfully navigate one environment while misreading another. Until recently, Microsoft prided itself on having a minimal Washington, D.C., presence, arguing that public policies were not relevant to the company's main strategy and customer relationships. Following the recent series of antitrust suits initiated by the U.S. Justice Department, the company was caught off guard and in a relatively weak position to respond to these policy makers or to enlist public actors in the media and elsewhere who might be sympathetic to its views.

The framework is also complementary to the emerging saliency approach to stakeholder valuation in which the broad attributes of power, legitimacy, and urgency of different stakeholders are assessed to determine the extent to which

a given player matters.[32] The framework identifies players on the basis of an understanding of the different fundamental value-creation processes through which they interact with a focal company. A sophisticated assessment of a player's importance using the saliency method requires an understanding of the underlying value-creation process or processes through which the player interacts with the focal company. Without such an understanding, key value creators or destroyers might be ignored and their power, urgency and legitimacy misjudged.

In sum, the framework can help managers to better understand how current and potential stakeholders can affect the firm's value-creation processes. Since the underlying processes that lead to value creation in each context are different, managers can use the framework to identify potentially different stakeholders in each context. Thereby, the framework provides a means by which managers can organize their efforts to assess the importance of different stakeholders. Moreover, with recognition of the differences among the value-creation processes, managers can develop targeted as well as integrated strategies, and do so in both market and nonmarket environments. In addition, by including the notion of complementors within each of the contexts, the framework provides a basis from which to develop not only competitive strategies, but also cooperative strategies. Finally, as resources and capabilities change over time as industry, technological, and political life-cycles play themselves out, the framework can be used to map out evolutionary scenarios to inform strategic planning efforts.

APPENDIX
Multi-Environment Strategy at MCI

MCI Corporation has, throughout its relatively short history, exhibited an ability to navigate and pursue strategies tailored to its environmental and historical circumstance. Headquartered in Washington, D.C., MCI was the main agent in advocating the break-up of the AT&T monopoly in domestic long distance service. MCI's legal suit, and the U.S. Justice Department's case against AT&T, led to the 1982 court decision that mandated AT&T's divestiture from local telephone service and opened competition in the long distance market. In its early development, MCI partnered with consumer groups and other nonmarket stakeholders in order to press the view

that market conditions no longer justified the preservation of AT&T's monopoly. It also interacted with other players, both competitors (AT&T), complementors (consumer groups), suppliers (government and legal officials), and customers to obtain this outcome. Primarily as a result of their public policy strategy, and the subsequent marketing strategy and technology investment, MCI and the other long distance entrants steadily gained market share throughout the 1980s and 1990s.

During the 1990s, MCI began developing relationships and alliances that would strengthen its international position. During this period, MCI's strategy centered on developing relationships with complementors in the public, private, and technological environments. U.S. telecommunications companies have identified foreign markets as preferential areas for growth because of the lucrative rent streams associated with the high volume of U.S. out-bound calls. MCI felt that having control of end-to-end networks was important for internalizing connection fee revenue. Initially, MCI developed a partnership with British Telecommunications. While this partnership was the subject of antitrust concerns, MCI and BT were successful in convincing U.S. and British authorities that competition would not be adversely affected by the partnership. During this period, MCI developed relationships with and responded to challenges from a range of other players, including British Telecom (complementor), European government and legal officials (suppliers), European and North America telecom firms (competitors), and customers (see Figure 4). Later, after a brief bidding war, MCI merged with WorldCom Corporation, partly as a way to diversify product lines in the face of growing competition that resulted from the 1996 Telecom Act which deregulated local services and allowed regional Bell operating companies to enter the long distance market.

MCI's expansion in Latin America through joint ventures reflects some of the challenges related to integration of corporate strategy directed toward market and nonmarket environments. In Mexico, MCI was the first foreign long distance provider to enter the market after the Mexican government opened its market following the privatization of Telmex. Despite MCI's early entry, it faced formidable challenges from Telmex and its partners, Southwestern Bell and France Telecom, because of the regulatory protections and market power accorded the incumbent. In Brazil, MCI partnered with the incumbent long distance monopoly, Embratel, as part of the Telebras privatization, perhaps reflecting

FIGURE 4. Illustration of Mapping across Three Dimensions: MCI

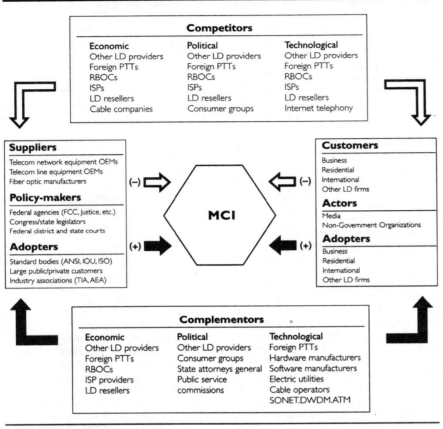

Abbreviations:

AEA: American Electronics Association	IOU: Investor Owned Utilities	PTTs: Post, Telephone and Telegraphs
ANSI: American National Standards Institute	ISPs: Internet Service Providers	RBOCs: Regional Bell Operating Companies
ATM: Asynchronous Transfer Mode	ISO: International Standards Organization	SONET: Synchronous Optical Networks
DWDM: Dense Wave Division Multiplexing	LD: Long Distance	TIA: Telecommunications Industry Association

an acknowledgment, based on the experience in Mexico, that first-mover positioning is critical in privatizing markets even when deregulation follows such privatization. Again, MCI identified the range of players active in the market and nonmarket environments in Latin American telecom reform and refined its approaches toward these stakeholders as its strategy developed.

MCI has also introduced innovative technology and marketing programs that have been adopted by other players in the industry. MCI's friends and family program in the early 1990s helped cement customers to the service in the face of lowering switching costs. More recently, MCI's 10–10–321 program and subsequent variations have responded to the demand for lower rates, regardless of the provider, and have helped the firm respond to competition, reflecting an awareness of changes in the domestic regulatory and market environments.

With the MCI-WorldCom merger, CEO Bernard Ebbers has aggressively

extended MCI's business offerings with the sell-off of low-margin businesses. In this effort, MCI WorldCom announced that it would sell its Systemhouse computer management business to EDS for $1.65 billion, while at the same time transferring in-house computing services to EDS in a deal worth $5–7 billion over ten years. In a third aspect of the agreement, EDS will purchase telephone and data communications services from MCI worth $6–8.5 billion. Such dealings illustrate the multiple and changing roles of one of MCI's key players—a player that is at the same time a competitor, a customer, and a supplier.

MCI WorldCom's proposed acquisition of Sprint represents yet another stage in the firm's development in response to changing environmental conditions. MCI has set a strategy to provide comprehensive "local-global-local" service, with call initiation and completion supported entirely by MCI's platform. The missing link in this infrastructure was the PCS network that Sprint had es-

tablished. Interestingly, MCI/Sprint might be forced to divest of some business segments—including Internet service provision in the U.S. and Sprint's "mirror" license for long distance in Brazil—just as AT&T was forced to divest of businesses in response to MCI's and the U.S. government's desire to prevent anticompetitive practices.

Throughout its history, MCI has assumed multiple roles that provide the basis for mapping its own strategic environment, identifying each of its principal stakeholders, and developing both competitive and cooperative strategies in response to its circumstances. These strategies have evolved over time as the strategic environment in which MCI has operated has changed, and MCI has both adapted to that environment as well as shaped it in a way to make it more favorable for the firm. As other firms begin to develop comprehensive stakeholder maps of their own multi-context landscapes, it remains to be seen whether MCI can continue its strategic leadership over the industry.

Sources

P. Beckett, "AT&T Venture Gets Fast Start in Mexican Race," *The Wall Street Journal,* December 16, 1996, p. A13.

Pat Blake, "Survival of the Fittest Network," *America's Network,* September 15, 1998, p. 520.

J. Friedland, "US Phone Giants Find Telmex Can Be a Bruising Competitor," *The Wall Street Journal,* October 23, 1998 (www.wsj.com).

Interview with MCI and CFE (Mexico) officials by author, 1998.

Annie Lindstrom, "Sonet Speed Limits," *America's Network,* May 15, 1998, p. 18.

"MCI WorldCom 1998 SEC 10K Filing," (http://www.sec.gov/Archives/edgar/data).

M. Mills, "MCI to Sell Unit to EDS; Area Jobs May Shift," *Washington Post,* February 12, 1999; Page E01.

Notes

1. Parsons and Smelser view the economic environment as a sub-system of society and argue that economic relationships are but special cases of social relationships. Rather than attempting to forge such a theoretical synthesis in this article, we instead adopt the view that the different contexts are related through the interdepencies of their different value-creation processes and their respective players. T. Parsons and N. Smelser, *Economy and Society* (Glencoe, IL: Free Press, 1956).

2. D. P. Baron, "Integrated Strategy: Market and Nonmarket Components," California Management Review, 37/2 (Winter 1995): 47–65. For an extended discussion of nonmarket environments and strategies, see D. P. Baron, Business and Its Environment (Englewood Cliffs, NJ: Prentice Hall, 1996).

3. A. M. Brandenburger and B. J. Nalebuff, Co-opetition (New York, NY: Doubleday, 1996).

4. Brandenburger and Nalebuff, op. cit.; M. E. Porter, Competitive Strategy: Techniques for Analyzing Industries and Companies (New York, NY: The Free Press, 1980).

5. We rotate the axes of the value net clockwise to facilitate integration of the value chain.

6. Brandenburger and Nalebuff, op. cit., p. 36.

7. R. K. Reger and A. S. Huff, "Strategic Groups: A Cognitive Perspective," Strategic Management Journal, 14 (1993): 103.

8. In this section, "nonmarket" refers to the political/social context as identified by Baron and others.

9. David P. Baron, Business and its Environment, 3rd edition (Upper Saddle River, NJ: Prentice Hall, 2000).

10. L. Preston and J. E. Post, Private Management and Public Policy (New York, NY: Prentice-Hall, 1975); Baron (1995), op cit.

11. A. Marcus, A. M. Kaufman, and D. R. Beam, eds., Business Strategy and Public Policy (New York, NY: Quorum Books, 1987), p. 8.

12. See D. Vogel, "The Study of Business and Politics," California Management Review, 38/3 (Spring 1996): 146–165.

13. J. Gale and R. A. Buchholz, "The Political Pursuit of Competitive Advantage: What Business Can Gain from Government," in A. Marcus, A. M. Kaufman, and D. R. Beam, eds., Business Strategy and Public Policy (New York, NY: Quorum Books, 1987), pp. 31–42.

14. Ibid.

15. D. J. Teece, "Capturing Value from Knowledge Assets: The New Economy, Markets for Know-how, and Intangible Assets," California Management Review, 40/3 (Spring 1998): 55–79.

16. A. H. Van de Ven, "Learning By Discovery During Innovation Development," International Journal of Technology Management, 11/7–8 (1996): 871–883.

17. L. Edvinsson and M. S. Malone, Intellectual Capital (New York, NY: Harper Collins, 1997); T. Stewart, Intellectual Capital: The New Wealth of Organizations (New York, NY: Doubleday, 1997); K. E. Sveiby, The New Organizational Wealth: Managing and Measuring Knowledge-Based Assets (San Francisco, CA: Berrett-Koehler Publishers, 1997); P. C. Grindley and D. J. Teece, "Managing Intellectual Capital: Licensing and Cross-Licensing in Semiconductors and Electronics," California Management Review, 39/2 (Winter 1997): 8–41; J. B. Quinn, J. J. Baruch, and K. A. Zien, Innovation Explosion: Using Intellect and Software to Revolutionize Growth Strategies (New York, NY: Free Press, 1997).

18. See S. Liebowitz and S. Margolis, "The Fable of the Keys," The Journal of Law and Economics, 33/1 (April 1990): 1–25. Although some of the relationships may hold for technological interactions within traditional industries, here we are primarily concerned with phenomenon related to high technology industries.

19. D. B. Yoffie and M. A. Cusumano, "Building a Company on Internet Time: Lessons from Netscape," California Management Review, 41/3 (Spring 1999): 8–28.

20. R. P. Rumelt, "Toward a Strategic Theory of the Firm," in R. Lamb, ed., The Competitive Challenge (Cambridge, MA: Ballinger, 1984), pp. 556–570.

21. For a comprehensive discussion of technological lockout, see M. A. Schilling, "Technology Lockout: An Integrative Model of the Economic and Strategic Factors Driving Technological Success and Failure," Academy of Management Review, 23/2 (April 1998): 267–284.

22. D. B. Yoffie, "Competing in the Age of Digital Convergence," California Management Review, 38/4 (Summer 1996): 31–51.

23. Schilling, op. cit.

24. The virtuous cycle is supported by researchers who have investigated similar patterns found in nature and in economics, such as patterns of increasing returns and complex adaptive systems, and have applied them to corporate innovation and entrepreneurship. See P. W. Anderson, K. J. Arrow, and David Pines, eds., The Economy as an Evolving Complex System (Redwood City, CA: Addison-Wesley, 1988); P. Anderson and M. Tushman, "Technological Discontinuities and Dominant Designs: A Cyclical Model of Technological Change," Administrative Science Quarterly, 35 (1990): 604–633; B. W. Arthur, "Increasing Returns and the New World of Business," Harvard Business Review, 74/4 (July/August 1996): 100–109; K. E. Boulding, Evolutionary Economics (Beverly Hills, CA: Sage, 1984); P. Hall, Innovation, Economics and Evolution: Theoretical Perspectives on Changing Technology in Economic Systems (New York, NY: Harvester Wheatsheaf, 1994); M. Rothschild, Bionomics: Economy as Ecosytem (New York, NY: Holt, 1990). A. DeGeus, The Living Company (Boston, MA: Harvard Business School Press, 1997); A. H. Van de Ven, "The Development of an Infrastructure for Entrepreneurship," Journal of Business Venturing, 8/3 (1993): 211–230. For a discussion of the herd mentality and lockout, see Yoffie, op. cit.; Schilling, op. cit.

25. Schilling, op. cit., pp. 274–276

26. Ibid.

27. Yoffie, op. cit.

28. Ibid.

29. M. Kull contributed to this section of the article.

30. See A.D. Chandler, Jr., Scale and Scope: The Dynamics of Industrial Capitalism (Cambridge, MA: Harvard University Press, 1990).

31. Baron (1995), op. cit.

32. Ibid.

PASSING THE WORD: TOWARD A MODEL OF GOSSIP AND POWER IN THE WORKPLACE

NANCY B. KURLAND
LISA HOPE PELLED
University of Southern California

Although gossip is widespread, seldom has it been a topic of management research. Here we build a conceptual model of workplace gossip and its effects on the power of employees who initiate it. After defining and distinguishing among different kinds of workplace gossip, we develop propositions about the effect of that gossip on gossipers' expert, referent, reward, and coercive power. We then suggest how moderators may shape those effects and discuss implications of the model.

As early as the Hawthorne Studies (Roethlisberger & Dickson, 1943), management scholars recognized the existence of the informal organization. Unlike the formal organization, which appears in organization charts and reflects prescribed patterns for officially sanctioned messages, the informal organization consists of spontaneous, emergent patterns that result from individuals' discretionary choices (Stohl, 1995: 65). This informal network, also called the *grapevine* (e.g., Baird, 1977; Daniels, Spiker, & Papa, 1997), has received considerable attention in the years since its discovery (e.g., Davis, 1953; Katz & Kahn, 1978; Krackhardt & Hanson, 1993; Podolny & Baron, 1997). Still, there is a need for closer examination of its specific components—for example, rumor, "catching up," and gossip (Goldsmith & Baxter, 1996). Accordingly, in this article we explore one such component: workplace gossip.

Although psychologists (e.g., Fine & Rosnow, 1978), sociologists (e.g., Eder & Enke, 1991), and anthropologists (e.g., Dunbar, 1996) have examined the nature and role of gossip in larger society, scholars have yet to develop a conceptual model of workplace gossip—or even agree on its definition—despite Noon and Delbridge's (1993) call for research on the topic. Thus, it is important to begin redressing this gap. In this article we draw on writings from multiple disciplines to offer a definition and theoretical model of workplace gossip and its consequences.

Models of general communication typically have been of two kinds. The first, most common kind is the linear model (e.g., Berlo, 1960; Osgood, Suci, & Tannenbaum, 1957; Shannon & Weaver, 1949), in which the researcher treats communication as a "left-to-right, one-way" process (Rogers & Kincaid, 1981: 33). Key components of linear models are the source (person who initiates communication), message (content of the communication), channel (transmission medium), and receiver (person receiving the message; Ruch, 1989). Communication is viewed as a process by which a message is transferred from an active source, through a channel, to a passive receiver.

The second kind of general communication model is the convergence model (Rogers & Kincaid, 1981). In convergence models (e.g., Kincaid, 1979; Pearce, Figgins, & Golen, 1984) researchers treat communication as a two-way process. Suggesting that participants in the communication process are simultaneously sending and receiving messages, researchers developing these models make less distinction between sender and receiver. Instead, they delve into the relationships among communication participants, the larger social networks in which those relationships exist, and the dynamic nature of communication (e.g., how communication changes its participants).

To ensure practical value in communication models, researchers may need to balance the simplicity of linear models with the complexity of convergence models. As Smeltzer and Leonard have suggested, a communication model should "contain enough elements so that users can

We are grateful for comments Chris Earley and three anonymous reviewers provided. We also thank Tom Cummings, Janet Fulk, Bill Gartner, Mike Kamins, Peter Kim, Peter Monge, Nandini Rajagopalan, Kathleen Reardon, and Patti Riley for their helpful comments and suggestions.

Both authors contributed equally; our names appear in alphabetical order.

relate their personal experiences and training to the model. But it must not become so complex that practitioners find it impossible to understand" (1994: 32). Thus, our model lies between the linear and convergence categories. Like linear models, its primary emphasis is on the flow of a message (gossip) from source (gossiper) to receiver (gossip recipient).[1] However, with our model we improve on traditional linear models by paying greater attention to the communication context—specifically, the culture in which gossip occurs. Also, the receiver in our model has a more active role than in strict linear models: we consider the interplay between source and receiver— that is, how the relationship between gossiper and recipient moderates the effects we propose. Additionally, we incorporate the receiver's reaction to the message in our model's dependent variable: the source's power over the receiver. The receiver's interpretation of the gossip largely determines how much power the source gains.

Power is the dependent variable in our model for several reasons. First, social scientists (e.g., Berger, 1994; Giddens, 1984; Mumby, 1988) have suggested that communication in general tends to shape power structures in organizations as well as society. Second, in extant writings on gossip, scholars have hinted at linkages to power (e.g., Emler, 1994). Third, power is a multidimensional construct (French & Raven, 1959; Hinkin & Schriescheim, 1989); as such, it has sufficient breadth to capture a variety of workplace gossip effects. Finally, power is often a critical asset to employees (Pfeffer, 1992).

Although the focus of our model is the gossiper-recipient dyad, it is important to keep in mind that such dyads are embedded in social networks. Mutual friends and acquaintances of the gossiper and recipient can influence the proliferation and impact of gossip (Burt & Knez, 1996; Jaeger, Skelder, & Rosnow, 1998). Indeed, researchers (Martin, Feldman, Hatch, & Sitkin, 1983; Martin & Siehl, 1983) have observed that even an ostensibly minor story about one employee can ultimately transform a corporate culture, if that story is shared by many organizational members.

A complete network analysis of gossip is beyond the scope of our model, for as Burt and Knez note, even "a minimal assumption of active third parties creates enormous complexity for theoretical analysis" (1996: 72). Nevertheless, at several points in this article, we touch on how such networks play a role in gossip-power linkages.

KEY CONCEPTS IN THE PROPOSED MODEL

Definition and Types of Gossip

As prior researchers have noted (Jaeger et al., 1998; Schein, 1994), gossip traditionally has been defined as *idle chatter, chitchat,* or the *evil tongue.* These negative con-

notations largely arose from religious writings (e.g., Exod. 23:1; Lev. 19:16; Prov. 25:18). Many authors (e.g., Bok, 1984) continue to treat gossip as improper and overly subjective. Some, however, recently have offered neutral definitions, such as "evaluative talk about a person who is not present" (Eder & Enke, 1991: 494) and "the process of informally communicating value-laden information about members of a social setting" (Noon & Delbridge, 1993: 25). Unlike their negative counterparts, these more even-handed definitions allow for gossip's functional as well as dysfunctional side (e.g., Dunbar, 1996; Tebbutt, 1995). Here, we draw upon and adapt these neutral conceptualizations, defining workplace gossip as *informal and evaluative talk in an organization, usually among no more than a few individuals, about another member of that organization who is not present.*

Although laypersons and academics (e.g., Ayim, 1994) occasionally may suggest that gossip encompasses informal communication about objects or events—not just people— our treatment focuses on talk about other persons. We delimit our definition in this manner for two reasons. First, in scholarly writings on gossip in larger society (e.g., Eder & Enke, 1991; Harris, 1993; Rosnow & Fine, 1976), researchers predominantly treat the concept as communication about people. Second, the American Management Association (AMA) recently asserted that the grapevine may include a wide range of informal communication, whereas gossip focuses solely on information about people (Smith, 1996).

Just as there are distinctions between gossip and other forms of informal communication, there are important distinctions among different kinds of gossip. A review of relevant literature points to three dimensions useful for making these distinctions: sign, credibility, and work-relatedness. Following writings on feedback (e.g., Ilgen, Fisher, & Taylor, 1979), we define *sign* as the positivity or negativity of the information being related. When gossip consists of favorable news about others—for example, stating that "Mary received a raise"—its sign is positive. When gossip consists of unfavorable news about others, its sign is negative.[2]

Credibility is the extent to which the gossip is believable—that is, it is seemingly accurate and truthful. Message credibility has been the subject of considerable research in the fields of communication, marketing, and social psychology (e.g., Boehm, 1994; McCroskey, 1969; Slattery & Tiedge, 1992). A recent review attests to its importance as a communication feature (Self, 1996).

Consistent with prior literature (e.g., Morrow, 1981; Tushman, 1979) in which authors have distinguished between work-related and non-work-related communication,

---

[1] The source may be either a supervisor, subordinate, or peer of the recipient. That is, the direction of gossip may either be upward, downward, or lateral.

[2] Within the categories of positive gossip and negative gossip, it is possible to make additional distinctions. For example, gossip can be negative if it describes an unfortunate event that befell someone (e.g., a broken leg), but it can also be negative if it describes unethical behavior. Here, we interpret gossip as negative when it constitutes a "smear" that could detract from a subject's reputation. Positive gossip, however, tends to enhance a subject's reputation.

we distinguish among work-related (professional) and non-work-related (social) gossip. We define *work-relatedness* as the degree to which gossip is focused on a subject's work life, such as job performance, career progress, relationships with other organizational members, and general behavior in the workplace.

Definition and Types of Power

Also essential to our model is the concept of power. Pfeffer has described power as "the potential ability to influence behavior, to change the course of events, to overcome resistance, and to get people to do things that they would otherwise not do" (1992: 30). Finkelstein has referred to power as "the capacity of individual actors to exert their will" (1992: 507). Based on these writings and the writings of others (French & Raven, 1969; House, 1988; Shackleton, 1995), we define power here as the *ability to exert one's will, influencing others to do things that they would not otherwise do*. In the model we specifically focus on the gossiper's power over gossip recipients.

The multidimensionality of power is well recognized. French and Haven (1959) advanced a typology of power that remains popular (e.g., Atwater, 1995; Davis & Schoorman, 1997; Hinkin & Schriesheim, 1994), distinguishing among five kinds of power that one individual (whom we call Person A) can have over another individual (whom we call Person B): coercive power, reward power, legitimate power, expert power, and referent power.[3] Although organizational scholars have offered other power typologies (e.g., Finkelstein, 1992; Yukl & Falbe, 1991), French and Raven's original classification is the most widely accepted and adopted. Their typology is particularly useful for describing individual-level power, which is the focus of our model. Hence, our propositions pertain to four of these power types (coercive, reward, expert, and referent) that we expect gossip to influence. (We do not consider legitimate power as an outcome because it is largely based on one's position—that is, hierarchical rank—rather than on social processes.) Our predictions refer to the French and Raven dimensions, but we draw from a range of power and influence writings to develop those predictions.

THEORETICAL BACKGROUND AND HYPOTHESES

Figure 1 presents our model. In the following sections we develop propositions about the illustrated linkages.

[3]Coercive power is the power that emerges from Person B's belief that Person A has the ability to punish him or her. Reward power is the power that emerges from Person B's belief that Person A can provide him or her with desired outcomes. Legitimate power is the power that emerges from Person B's perception that Person A has a legitimate right, based on position in the organization, to influence him or her. Expert power is the power that emerges from Person B's belief that Person A has special knowledge or expertise that Person B needs. Finally, referent power is the power that emerges from Person B's attraction for and desire to be associated with Person A.

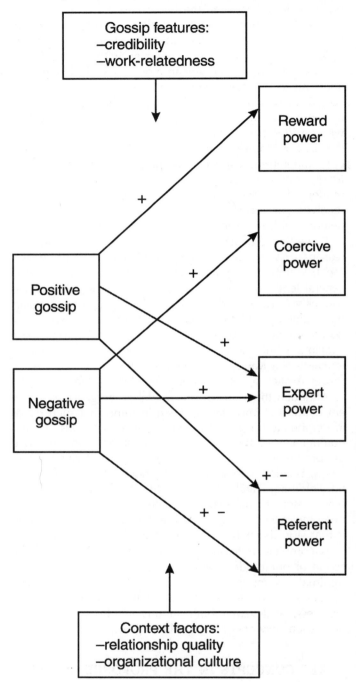

FIGURE 1
Proposed Model of Gossip and Power

Linkages Between Gossip and Power

One main effect of negative gossip may be enhanced coercive power. When the gossiper relates negative news about a third party, recipients may infer that the gossiper also could spread negative information about *them* (Yerkovich, 1977). Because such information can damage reputations and/or careers (Emler, 1994; Fine, 1977; Glazer &

Ras, 1994; Tebbutt, 1995), negative gossip may constitute an implicit threat by the gossiper. French and Raven (1959) proposed that when Person B perceives that Person A can administer punishments, Person A has coercive power over Person B. Along the same lines, other researchers (e.g., Hunt & Nevin, 1974; Tedeschi, 1972) have advanced the notion that implicit and explicit threats can enhance power and influence.[4] Those who feel threatened may comply in order to avoid retribution (Kipnis, Schmidt, & Wilkinson, 1980). Thus, negative gossip may give the gossiper coercive power over recipients.

Proposition 1: In a work setting, negative gossip will enhance the gossiper's coercive power over gossip recipients.

Positive gossip, in contrast, is likely to affect reward power. When a gossiper shares positive news about another worker, recipients may infer that the gossiper also could spread positive information about *them.* Because such information can strengthen reputations and/or careers, positive gossip shows the ability to distribute (albeit indirectly) desired outcomes. French and Raven (1959) suggested that when Person B perceives that Person A has control over valued outcomes, Person A has reward power over Person B. Along the same lines, Etzioni (1961) proposed that control of material and symbolic rewards are a basis for power. Additionally, Emerson asserted that power "resides in control over the things [another person] values. . . . In short, power resides implicitly in the other's dependency" (1962: 32). Resource dependence theorists (e.g., Salancik & Pfeffer, 1977), too, have advanced the notion that power comes from the control of relevant resources—resources that are important to others. Hence, by revealing the gossiper's ability to control an important resource (reputation), positive gossip may give the gossiper reward power over recipients.

Proposition 2: In a work setting, positive gossip will enhance the gossiper's reward power over gossip recipients.

Gossip in general, whether positive or negative, is apt to influence expert power, for it can facilitate an exchange of data and help build a knowledge base (e.g., Code, 1994; Dunbar, 1996). When a gossiper shares information about others, the recipient may learn more about the organization's values. As Heath (1994) has observed, stories shared by coworkers can help employees understand principles by which their organization operates. Additionally, gossip can reveal that the gossiper has relevant knowledge about persons in the work environment. As the gossiper demonstrates such knowledge (an ability that depends, in part, on the gossiper's network centrality), the recipient may come to view the gossiper as a source of useful information, and the gossiper may thereby gain expert power.

Proposition 3: in a work setting, gossip will enhance the gossiper's expert power over gossip recipients.

In the case of referent power, we expect gossip to have competing effects. One possibility is that gossip reduces referent power, for gossip may be seen as a small or petty activity. As mentioned earlier, in religious writings and other sources of guidance and education, gossip is often denounced as idle, immoral, or improper (Levin & Arluke, 1987). Socialized by such teachings, many persons perceive gossip as reprehensible, and they look down on those who engage in the behavior. Gossip, therefore, may detract from the referent power of the gossiper.

This effect is likely to be particularly pronounced when gossip is negative. As described earlier, positive gossip can enhance the reputation of its subjects, whereas negative gossip tends to destroy subjects' reputations. Hence, those who condemn gossip from an ethical standpoint will be especially hard pressed to find anything redeeming about negative gossip.

Proposition 4a: In a work setting, gossip will reduce the gossiper's referent power over recipients. This effect will be stronger for negative gossip than for positive gos sip.

The competing argument is that gossip enhances referent power. As gossipers share news, they draw recipients into their social circles (e.g., Dunbar, 1996; Eder & Enke, 1991). These recipients, in turn, may appreciate being included. Moreover, through gossip, recipients might realize that the gossiper is on the inside of a social network. This realization is apt to make recipients more interested in knowing and being liked by the gossiper. Consistent with this notion, impression management scholars have found that people can enhance their image by managing information about others with whom they are associated (Gardner & Martinko, 1988).

If gossip enhances referent power, this effect is apt to taper off at very high levels—that is, as the frequency of the gossip and the pool of recipients increase. As Levin and Arluke have observed, a person who gossips too much "may become defined as a 'big mouth' or a 'yenta' who will 'talk to anyone about anything,' as a person who cannot be trusted to keep a secret or to be discreet with 'privileged information' " (1987: 16). Moreover, when gossipers talk incessantly about others, they may become resented for using so much of recipients' time: Thus, we offer the following.

---

[4]There may be limits to the effectiveness of implicit threats (e.g., the threat of spreading negative information) in attempts to gain power. First, if the gossiper has few connections to others, recipients may be less concerned about the gossiper's ability to spread dark secrets. Second, some news—for example, information that is hard to remember—may be especially difficult to spread (Zimbardo & Leippe, 1991). Third, as our Proposition 7 suggests, recipients may be less afraid of the gossiper when they have a good relationship with him or her. Moreover, those who do feel threatened may strive to decrease their dependence on the person making the threat (Bacharach & Lawler, 1980; Tjosvold, 1995). As Bacharach and Lawler have noted, coercion "should be most effective when the target is highly dependent on the user" (1980: 177).

*Proposition 4b: In a work setting, gossip will have a cur-
vilinear effect on the gossiper's referent power over recipients; it will enhance referent power until it reaches a very
high level, at which point it will detract from referent
power.*

Moderators of Linkages Between Gossip and Power

The strength of the above linkages may be influenced
by characteristics of the gossip and by contextual factors,
including organizational culture and the relationship between gossiper and recipient.

Features of the gossip. As described earlier, one particularly relevant characteristic of gossip is its credibility.
Upon reviewing a variety of empirical findings and conducting their own study, Slater and Rouner (1996) concluded that message credibility has considerable influence
on judgments of source credibility.[5] Thus, gossip that lacks
credibility can lead a recipient to view the gossiper as a
noncredible source. Even if the recipient's view of the gossiper is not widely held, he or she may assume that others
share this view, for a common cognitive bias is the *false
consensus effect*: the tendency to overestimate the prevalence of one's own opinions or experiences (Kelley, 1967;
Whitley, 1998). According to Fiske and Taylor, "Researchers consistently find that consensus information (i.e.,
the opinions or experience of others) is relatively underutilized in the judgment process" (1991: 93). They explain
that those "who agree with us are more likely to come to
mind when we attempt to infer what others will believe"
(1991: 75). Recipients, therefore, may infer that the gossiper also lacks credibility with others and will not be
believed when sharing negative or positive gossip. Hence,
when gossip credibility is low, recipients are less likely to
view the gossiper as someone with coercive or reward
power.

In addition, credibility may affect the relationship between gossip and expert power. If recipients believe that
a gossiper's information is inaccurate, they may begin to
question or doubt any future information the gossiper re-
lays. As a result, that gossip will contribute less to, and
may detract from, the gossiper's expert power. In line with
this reasoning, Krackhardt (1990) has found that employees with more accurate information about the informal
network have higher reputational power than those whose
information is less accurate.

Lack of credibility also may diminish any positive link,
and enhance any negative link, between gossip and referent power. Recipients may resent the gossiper who
seems to relate far-fetched or incorrect information, for

they may perceive that the gossiper is attempting to mislead them. As Zucker (1986) has suggested, individuals
perceived as providing accurate information are more
trusted than those who share inaccurate knowledge.

*Proposition 5: The effects of gossip on coercive, reward,
expert, and referent power will be moderated by gossip
credibility. Any tendency for gossip to enhance the four
power types will be stronger when credibility is high than
when it is low. Any tendency for gossip to reduce referent
power will be weaker when credibility is high than when
it is low.*

Like credibility, the work-relatedness of gossip may play
a moderating role. Rewards (e.g., high performance ratings
and promotions) and punishments in the organization
(e.g., demotions and firings) are based largely on an employee's work-related behavior. It is, in fact, illegal to take
many personal events (topics of social gossip), such as
marriage, a major illness, or a change of housing, into
account when determining such rewards and punishments
(Hollwitz, Goodman, & Bolte, 1995; Madison & Knudson-
Fields. 1987). Although some managers still consider those
personal factors when allocating resources, legislation
(and the possibility of costly lawsuits) constrains their ability to do so. Thus, the employee who engages in work-
related gossip has a greater ability to influence rewards
and punishments in the workplace than does an employee
who engages in gossip about other topics.

Work-related gossip is also particularly likely to shape
expert power. Fiske and Taylor (1991) have pointed out
that a given context can encourage us to attend to some
information more than other information. Being in the
workplace makes employees particularly attuned to work-
related information. When the recipient is in a work context, "professional" topics such as a person's salary,
promotion, and recognition generally have more relevance
than do divorce, plastic surgery, or other "social" topics.
Thus, a gossiper who provides work-related information
about others is especially likely to be used as an information source and seen as an expert in the workplace.

In addition, the work-relatedness of gossip may diminish any negative link between gossip and referent power.
Recipients are less likely to perceive the gossiper as wasting their time at the office when the gossip is relevant to
that setting. Hence, they will be less resentful of the gossiper when the work-relatedness of gossip is high.

*Proposition 6: The effects of gossip on coercive, reward,
expert, and referent power will be moderated by the work-
relatedness of the gossip. Any tendency for gossip to enhance coercive, reward, and expert power will be stronger
when work-relatedness is high. Any tendency for gossip
to reduce referent power will be weaker when work-
relatedness is high.*

Gossiper-recipient relationship quality. Like the nature
of the gossip, the context of that gossip—specifically, the
quality of the relationship between gossiper and recipient—may act as a moderator. *Relationship quality* is the

---

[5]Although message and source credibility are conceptually distinct, they
are often closely related. Indeed, credibility is a complex feature, and
that complexity may make it more challenging to measure, compared
to other features of gossip. Those who test the proposed model should
keep this caveat in mind.

degree to which a relationship is characterized by mutual support, informal influence, trust, and frequent information exchange (Lee, 1998). Employees who have a habit of gossiping with each other, for example, can be characterized as having a high relationship quality. Much of the literature on relationship quality pertains to supervisor-subordinate dyads or leader-member exchange theory (Dansereau, Graen, & Haga, 1975), but one can also characterize peer relationships in terms of relationship quality (Kram & Isabella, 1985).

Negative gossip is less likely to enhance coercive power when relationship quality is high. If a recipient trusts a gossiper, that recipient may believe the gossiper will avoid harming him or her. Even if the gossiper is spreading negative news about others, the recipient may be confident that his or her own dark secrets will not be revealed by that gossiper.

Positive gossip, however, is more likely to enhance reward power when relationship quality is high. A recipient who is a close friend of a gossiper may believe that gossiper will try to help him or her when possible. Thus, if that gossiper is spreading positive news about others, the recipient is especially likely to think the gossiper will do the same for him or her.

Proposition 7: The effect of gossip on coercive and reward power will be moderated by gossiper-recipient relationship quality. Any tendency for negative gossip to enhance coercive power will be weaker when relationship quality is high. Any tendency for positive gossip to enhance reward power will be stronger when relationship quality is high.

Relationship quality also may shape gossip effects on referent power. Gossip is more likely to enhance referent power when the quality of a relationship is high. If the gossiper and recipient have a close and trusting relationship, the recipient is apt to view such gossip as appropriate, for informal communication is characteristic of high-quality relationships (Fairhurst, 1993; Lee & Jablin, 1995). Consistent with this logic is "halo effect" research (Nisbett & Wilson, 1977), which has revealed "a tendency to evaluate all components of a target person in the same way once a general evaluation, positive or negative, is formed" (Fiske & Taylor, 1991: 256). Thus, in the context of a strong relationship, any positive link between gossip and referent power will be stronger. Also, when relationship quality is high, recipients who frown upon gossip in general may be more forgiving of the gossiper. Hence, any negative link between gossip and referent power will be weaker.

Proposition 8: The effect of gossip on referent power will be moderated by gossiper-recipient relationship quality. Any tendency for gossip to enhance such power will be stronger when relationship quality is high. Any tendency for gossip to reduce such power will be weaker when relationship quality is high.

Organizational culture. Another moderating contextual factor may be *organizational culture*: the "system of shared values (that define what is important) and norms that define appropriate attitudes and behaviors for organizational members (how to feel and behave)" (O'Reilly & Chatman, 1996: 160). In some organizations the culture advocates considerable formal communication, while discouraging informal communication (Smeltzer & Leonard, 1994). If there is a cultural injunction against informal communication, then employees will be constrained in their use of gossip to spread news about others.

Gossip recipients may recognize these constraints and conclude that gossipers have few opportunities to help or harm reputations. The effect of gossip on reward and coercive power, therefore, will be weaker.

Also, when culture encourages formal communication and discourages informal communication, organizational members may not look to gossip as a source of information. Evidence has shown that individuals refrain from an information-seeking strategy if they expect the strategy to have high social costs (Miller & Jablin, 1991). In an antigossip culture, seeking information from a gossiper may have such costs. Consequently, it may be difficult for the gossiper to gain expert power via gossip.

The link between gossip and referent power, too, may be shaped by culture. An antigossip culture may reinforce a recipient's belief that gossip is wrong or immoral. Thus, any tendency for gossip to reduce referent power will be stronger when the culture discourages such informal communication.[6]

Proposition 9: The effects of gossip on coercive, reward, expert, and referent power will be moderated by organizational culture. Any tendency for gossip to enhance coercive, reward, and expert power will be weaker when the culture discourages informal communication. Any tendency for gossip to reduce referent power will be stronger when the culture discourages informal communication.

CONCLUDING REMARKS

The proposed model contributes to both management research and practice. On the academic side, it is—to the authors' knowledge—the first theoretical model of workplace gossip and its consequences. Noon and Delbridge (1993) took a significant step with their thought-provoking discussion of gossip in organizations and their call for research on the topic. Our model takes their work a step further, offering a refined conceptualization and specific predictions about the phenomenon. On the practitioner side, the proposed framework illustrates that, contrary to the adage "small people talk about other people," gossip can make a person quite "large" in an organization. At the same time, the model shows conditions under which

---

[6]It is possible that some employees will reject the values of the dominant culture and appreciate the individual who goes against it (e.g., by gossiping in an antigossip culture). These employees may respect that gossiper for taking such a risk.

gossip may backfire. An understanding of such dynamics of gossip is likely to help organizations and their members capitalize on this widespread genre of informal communication.

REFERENCE

Atwater, L. 1995. The relationship between supervisory power and organizational characteristics. *Group and Organization Management,* 20: 460–485.

Ayim. M. 1994. Knowledge through the grapevine: Gossip as inquiry. In R. F. Goodman & A. Ben-Ze'ev (Eds.), *Good gossip:* 85–99. Lawrence: University of Kansas Press.

Bacharach, S. B., & Lawler, E. J. 1980. *Power and politics in organizations.* San Francisco: Jossey-Bass.

Baird, J. E. 1977. *The dynamics of organizational communication.* New York: Harper & Row.

Berger, C. R. 1994. Power, dominance, and social interaction. In M. L. Knapp & G. R. Miller (Eds.). *Handbook of interpersonal communication:* 450–507. Thousand Oaks, CA: Sage.

Berlo, D. K. 1960. *The process of communication: An introduction to theory and practice.* New York: Holt, Rinehart, & Winston.

Boehm, L. E. 1994. The validity effect: A search for mediating variables. *Personality and Social Psychology Bulletin,* 20: 285–293.

Bok, S. 1984. *Secrets: On the ethics of concealment and revelation.* New York: Vintage.

Burt, R. S., & Knez. M. 1996. Trust and third-party gossip. In R. M. Kramer & T. R. Tyler (Eds.), *Trust in organizations:* 68–89. Thousand Oaks, CA: Sage.

Code, L. 1994. Gossip, or in praise of chaos. In R. F. Goodman & A. Ben-Ze'ev (Eds.), *Good gossip:* 100–106. Lawrence: University of Kansas Press.

Daniels, T., Spiker, B., & Papa, M. 1997. *Perspectives on organizational communication* (3rd ed.). Madison, WI: Brown and Benchmark.

Dansereau, F., Graen, G., & Haga, W. J. 1975. A vertical dyad approach to leadership within formal organizations. *Organizational Behavior and Human Performance,* 13:46–78.

Davis, J. H., & Schoorman, F. D. 1997. Toward a stewardship theory of management. *Academy of Management Review,* 22: 20–47.

Davis, K. 1953. A method of studying communication patterns in organizations. *Personnel Psychology,* 6: 301–312.

Dunbar, R. 1996. *Grooming, gossip, and the evolution of language.* Cambridge, MA: Harvard University Press.

Eder, D., & Enke, J. L. 1991. The structure of gossip: Opportunities and constraints on collective expression among adolescents. *American Sociological Review,* 56: 494–508.

Emerson, R. M. 1962. Power-dependence relations. *American Sociological Review,* 27: 31–41.

Emler, N. 1994. Gossip, reputation, and social adaptation. In B. F. Goodman & A. Ben-Ze'ev (Eds.), *Good gossip:* 117–138. Lawrence: University of Kansas Press.

Etzioni, A. 1961. *A comparative analysis of complex organizations: On power, involvement, and their correlates.* New York: Free Press.

Fairhurst, G. T. 1993. The leader-member exchange patterns of women leaders in industry: A discourse analysis. *Communication Monographs.* 60: 321–351.

Fine, G. A. 1977. Social components of children's gossip. *Journal of Communication,* 27(1): 181–185.

Fine, G. A., & Rosnow, B. L. 1978. Gossip, gossipers, gossiping. *Personality and Social Psychology Bulletin,* 4: 161–168.

Finkelstein, S. 1992. Power in top management teams: Dimensions, measurement, and validation. *Academy of Management Journal,* 35: 505–538.

Fiske, S. T., & Taylor, S. E. 1991. *Social cognition.* New York: McGraw-Hill.

French, J. R. P., & Raven, B. 1959. The bases of social power. In D. Cartwright (Ed.), *Studies in social power:* 150–167. Ann Arbor: University of Michigan Institute for Social Research.

Gardner, W. L., & Martinko, M. J. 1988. Impression management in organizations. *Journal of Management.* 14: 321–339.

Giddens, A. 1984. *The constitution of society: Outline of the theory of structuration.* Cambridge: Polity Press.

Glazer, I. M., & Ras, W. A. 1994. On aggression, human rights, and hegemonic discourse: The case of a murder for family honor in Israel. *Sex Roles,* 30: 269–288.

Goldsmith, D. J., & Baxter, L. A. 1996. Constituting relationships in talk: A taxonomy of speech events in social and personal relationships. *Human Communication Research,* 23: 87–114.

Harris, T. E. 1993. *Applied organizational communication: Perspectives, principles, and pragmatics.* Hillsdale, NJ: Lawrence Erlbaum Associates.

Heath, R. L. 1994. *Management of corporate communication: From interpersonal contacts to external affairs.* Hillsdale, NJ: Lawrence Erlbaum Associates.

Hinkin, T. R., & Schriesheim, C. A. 1989. Development and application of new scales to measure the French and Raven (1959) bases of social power. *Journal of Applied Psychology,* 74: 561–567.

Hinkin, T. R., & Schriesheim C. A. 1994. An examination of subordinate-perceived relationships between leader reward and punishment behavior and leader bases of power. *Human Relations,* 47: 779–800.

Hollwitz, J., Goodman, D. F. & Bolte, D. 1995. Complying with the Americans with Disabilities Act: Assessing the costs of reasonable accommodation. *Public Personnel Management,* 24: 149–157.

House, R. J. 1988. Power and personality in complex organizations. In B. M. Staw & L. L. Cummings (Eds.), *Research in organizational behavior,* vol. 10: 305–357. Greenwich, CT: JAI Press.

Hunt, S. D., & Nevin. J. R. 1974. Power in a channel of distribution: Sources and consequences. *Journal of Marketing Research,* 11: 186–193.

Ilgen. D. R., Fisher, C. D., & Taylor, M. S. 1979. Consequences of individual feedback on behavior in organizations. *Journal of Applied Psychology,* 64: 349–371.

Jaeger. M. E., Skelder, A. A., & Rosnow. R. L. 1998. Who's up on the low down: Gossip in interpersonal relations. In B. H. Spitzberg & W. R. Cupach (Eds.). *The dark side of close relationships:* 103–117. Mahwah, NJ: Lawrence Erlbaum Associates.

Katz. D., & Kahn, R. L. 1978. *The social psychology of organizations.* New York: Wiley.

Kelley. H. H. 1967. Attribution theory in social psychology. In D. Levine (Ed.), *Nebraska symposium on motivation,* vol. 15: 192–240. Lincoln: University of Nebraska Press.

Kincaid, D. L. 1979. *The convergence model of communication.* Paper 18. Honolulu: East-West Communication Institute.

Kipnis, D., Schmidt, S. M., & Wilkinson. I. 1980. Intraorganizational influence tactics: Explorations in getting one's way. *Journal of Applied Psychology.* 65: 440–452.

Krackhardt, D. 1990. Assessing the political landscape: Structure, cognition, and power in organizations. *Administrative Science Quarterly,* 35: 342–369.

Krackhardt. D., & Hanson. J. R. 1993. Informal networks: The company behind the chart, *Harvard Business Review,* 71(4): 104–111.

Kram, K. E., & Isabella, L. A. 1985. Mentoring alternatives: The role of peer relationships in career development. *Academy of Management Journal,* 28: 110–132.

Lee, J. 1998. Maintenance communication in superior-subordinate relationships: An exploratory investigation of group social context and the "Pelz effect." *Southern Communication Journal, 63:* 144–159.

Lee, J., & Jablin. F. M. 1995. Maintenance communication in superior-subordinate work relationships. *Human Communications Research,* 22: 220–257.

Levin, J., & Arluke, A. 1987. *Gossip: The inside scoop.* New York: Plenum.

Madson, R. B., & Knudson-Fields. B. 1987. The law and employee-employer relationships: The hiring process. *Management Solutions,* 32(2): 12–20.

Martin, J., Feldman. M. S., Hatch, M. J., & Sitkin, S. B. 1983. The uniqueness paradox in organizational stories. *Administrative Science Quarterly,* 28: 438–453.

Martin. J., & Siehl, C. 1983. Organizational culture and counterculture: An uneasy symbiosis. *Organizational Dynamics,* 12(2): 52–64.

McCroskey, J. C. 1969. A survey of experimental research on the effects of evidence in persuasive communication. *Speech Monographs,* 55: 169–176.

Miller, V. D., & Jablin, F. M. 1991. Information seeking during organizational entry: Influences tactics, and a model of the process. *Academy of Management Review,* 16: 92–120.

Morrow, P. C. 1981. Work related communication, environmental uncertainty, and subunit effectiveness: A second look at the information processing approach to subunit communication. *Academy of Management Journal,* 24: 851–858.

Mumby, D. K. 1988. *Communication and power in organizations: Discourse, ideology, and domination.* Norwood, NJ: Ablex Publishing.

Nisbett, R. E., & Wilson, T. D. 1977. The halo effect: Evidence for unconscious alteration of judgments. *Journal of Personality and Social Psychology,* 35: 250–256.

Noon, M., & Delbridge, R. 1993. News from behind my hand: Gossip in organizations. *Organization Studies,* 14: 23–36.

O'Reilly, C. A., III, & Chatman, J. A. 1996. Culture as social control: Corporations, cults, and commitment. In B. M. Staw & L. L. Cummings (Eds.), *Research in organizational behavior,* vol. 18: 157–200. Greenwich, CT: JAI Press.

Osgood, C. E., Suci, G. J., & Tannenbaum, P. H. 1957. *The measurement of meaning.* Urbana: University of Illinois Press.

Pearce, C., Figgins, R., & Golen, S. 1984. *Principles of business communication: Theory, application, and technology.* New York: Wiley.

Pfeffer, J. 1992. *Managing with power: Politics and influence in organizations.* Boston: Harvard Business School Press.

Podolny, J. M., & Baron, J. N. 1997. Resources and relationships: Social networks and mobility in the workplace. *American Sociological Review,* 62: 673–693.

Roethlisberger, F. J., & Dickson, W. J. 1943. *Management and the worker.* Cambridge, MA: Harvard University Press.

Rogers, E. M., & Kincaid, D. L. 1981. *Communication networks.* New York: Free Press.

Rosnow, R. L., & Fine, G. A. 1976. *Rumor and gossip: The social psychology of hearsay.* New York: Elsevier.

Ruch, W. V. 1989. *International handbook of corporate communication.* Jefferson. NC: McFarland.

Salancik, G. R., & Pfeffer, J. 1977. Who gets power—and how they hold on to it: A strategic contingency model of power. *Organizational Dynamics,* 5(3): 2–21.

Schein, S. 1994. Used and abused: Gossip in medieval society. In R. F. Goodman & A. Ben-Ze'ev (Eds.), *Good gossip:* 139–153. Lawrence: University of Kansas Press.

Self, C. C. 1996. Credibility. In M. B. Salwen & D. W. Stacks (Eds.), *An integrated approach to communication theory and research:* 421–442. Hillsdale, NJ: Lawrence Erlbaum Associates.

Shackleton, V. 1995. *Business leadership.* London: Routledge.

Shannon, C. E., & Weaver, W. 1949. *The mathematical theory of communication.* Urbana: University of Illinois Press.

Slater, M. D., & Rouner, D. 1996. How message evaluation and source attributes may influence credibility assessment and belief change. *Journalism and Mass Communication Quarterly,* 73: 974–991.

Slattery, K., & Tiedge, J. T. 1992. The effect of labeling staged video on the credibility of TV news stories. *Journal of Broadcasting and Electronic Media,* 36: 279–286.

Smeltzer, L. R., & Leonard, D. J. 1994. *Managerial communication: Strategies and applications.* Boston: Irwin.

Smith, B. 1996. Care and feeding of the office grapevine. *Management Review,* 85: 6.

Stohl, C. 1995. *Organizational communication: Connected-ness in action.* Thousand Oaks, CA: Sage.

Tebbutt, M. 1995. *Women's talk? A social history of "gossip" in working class neighborhoods, 1880–1960.* Brookfield, VT: Ashgate.

Tedeschi, J. T. 1972. *The social influence process.* Chicago: Aldine-Atherton.

Tjosvold, D. 1995. Effects of power to reward and punish in cooperative and competitive contexts. *Journal of Social Psychology,* 135: 723–736.

Tushman, M. L. 1979 Impacts of perceived environmental variability on patterns of work related communication. *Academy of Management Journal,* 22: 482–500.

Whitley, B. E. 1998. False consensus on sexual behavior among college women: Comparison of four theoretical explanations. *Journal of Sex Research,* 35: 206–214.

Yerkovich. S. 1977. Gossiping as a way of speaking. *Journal of Communication,* 27(1): 192–196.

Yukl, G., & Falbe, C. M. 1991. Importance of different power sources in downward and lateral relations. *Journal of Applied Psychology,* 76: 416–423.

Zimbardo. P. G., & Leippe, M. R. 1991. *The psychology of attitude change and social influence.* New York: McGraw-Hill.

Zucker, L. G. 1986. Production of trust: Institutional sources of economic structure, 1840–1920. In B. M. Staw & L. L. Cummings (Eds.), *Research in organizational behavior,* vol. 8: 53–111. Greenwich, CT: JAI Press.

Nancy B. Kurland is an assistant professor of management and organization in the Marshall School of Business, University of Southern California, where she teaches courses in organizational behavior, business ethics, and leadership. She received her Ph.D. from the University of Pittsburgh. She researches gossip, telecommuting, gender issues, the social impact of technology, and ethics and incentives.

Lisa Hope Pelled is an assistant professor of management and organization in the Marshall School of Business, University of Southern California, where she teaches courses in organizational behavior, managing interpersonal relations, and multicultural management. She received her Ph.D. from Stanford University. Her research areas include organizational demography, workplace emotions, communication, and conflict.

Leadership A to Z

An interview with James O'Toole about appropriately ambitious leaders.

Training & Development *spoke with James O'Toole about his new book,* Leadership A to Z: A Guide for the Appropriately Ambitious, *and other thoughts about what makes an effective leader.*

T&D: Well, I guess the first question is what do you mean by "appropriately ambitious"?

O'Toole: If you look at all of the great leaders in the world and ask what personality, trait, or characteristic they have in common, there are two kinds of ambition. There's inappropriate ambition—personal motivation. And then I think of Gandhi, who was a modest man with no desire for power or wealth but who had ambition for people in India to have pride and self-respect in being an independent nation, and he was willing to put himself on the line for that. That is what I'd call appropriately ambitious.

T&D: What prompted you to write the book?

O'Toole: People were constantly emailing me and calling me and asking, What should I read about leadership? So, I tried to summarize the key learnings about leadership from the very best minds over the past couple of decades, many of whom I've worked with. Each chapter is around a single idea and

based upon some research or experience. An example is given, and a lesson is drawn or a conclusion is made on which a reader can act.

T&D: It's a very accessible looking book. How does it depart from leaders teaching others to lead, followership, and other leadership ideas?

O'Toole: What is different—there are three things. One is how it looks on leadership as who the leader is: Anybody at any level can help build leadership throughout the entire organization. Two, the behavior of followers is a measure of leadership. Followers achieve their aspirations. Those are some insights of Max DePrees, but it goes a little bit further.

One issue for any leader is to get alignment of the behaviors of the followers with organizational goals. The problem with alignment is that by itself, it can be self-defeating. If everyone is lined up going in the wrong direction, for example, that's not going to be effective. Some organizations are well aligned, but they are bureaucracies and very inflexible.

So, what has been discovered in the past couple of years is that organizations have to be not only aligned, but also have to be adaptable. Those are two organizational capacities: Alignment and adaptability, which can actually be

measured. Those are not things you can see by looking at morale or at the charisma of an organization's leader. You actually look at them and measure them by the behavior of the organization.

In doing some research with Booz-Allen & Hamilton, and the World Economic Forums, and the Davos Group regarding the strategic leadership quotient of eight great global corporations, what we find is that when they're successful, all of their systems, processes, structures—everything they do from communication to rewards—simultaneously encourage alignment and adaptability. Moreover, this is something that is planned. This kind of leadership can be learned, it can be planned, and it can be structured.

In organizations such as those in our sample, the leaders have laid out what they have to do to get alignment and adaptability simultaneously, and they make sure there's coherence in everything they say and everything they do and in all of the actions they take to get alignment and adaptability. It's an important lesson at any level in thinking about the task of leadership.

It's also a very positive thing because it says that leadership does not have to depend on the leader. The leader doesn't have to do everything, doesn't have to be the smartest person in the organization, or do all the work. As a leader, you have to work on about a dozen dimensions that will create conditions under which the adaptability and the alignment will occur. That narrows the task of a leader and focuses on those things that will lead to effectiveness. It allows leaders to help the followers achieve their goals and their potential.

T&D: How would a person who's a CEO or manager use these skills?

O'Toole: I think you don't even have to have anyone reporting to you to be a leader. There are people who work in teams at a relatively low level in their organizations. To be effective, those teams need adaptability and alignment. They need to focus, to learn, and to be motivated to do the right things, to achieve their goals. In fact, what a member of such teams would do would be no different on the dozen or so dimensions than if he or she were the CEO or Gandhi going about trying to bring about independence in India.

I work with groups of executives, executive teams, and the way I start with them is to watch a film about Gandhi and then have a discussion. Those executives will identify about a dozen things—20 at most—that Gandhi did to be an effective leader that if they did those same things, they'd be effective as well. Down the organization with middle managers, they come up with the same list.

What this is all about is getting people focused on the things they can learn, they can do, and they can emulate to be effective.

T&D: Given that leadership filters down through all levels, do organizations still need one leader at the top?

O'Toole: If the task is change, for example, you need a leader who's supportive, who creates the conditions that will help other people bring about the change. But the work of leadership, the change, does not have to be done by that one person at the top. That person certainly has to sanction it.

Two examples from the book come to mind: two transformations at Corning. The nature of the tasks was entirely different. But, in both cases, the CEO led the change in identifying the objectives, the vision, the principles, and the values of the organization—offering rewards consistent with those—and then removed the obstacles that would prevent people from doing what they needed to do. In neither case was the actual work done by the CEO.

There are people who have thought about this and built a theory around this. And the theory is very consistent. What I tried to do in the book is show that people have thought about it and that the theory is consistent with the practice. If you look at people like Ron Heifetz and Warren Bennis, the examples I've collected since 1969 support their theories. A lot of the theory that's out there is really quite usable. I tried to give some practical examples of what it really means, what does a leader really do that is consistent with the theories.

T&D: So, teams, empowered employees can do this?

O'Toole: This approach to leadership is the most empowering of all. What we're saying is that whoever you are, whatever your weaknesses, if you have one trait—that you really care about

What they do at ABB, for example, is instill a common philosophy and approach to leadership throughout the entire organization. [Such companies] know they succeed when they see everyone behaving as leaders. When that happens, you get the alignment, you get the adaptability, you get the effectiveness in the organization.

That takes a tremendous amount of discipline on the part of leaders. They have to overcome the instinct to order people, tell them the answers, and take over when they aren't doing their jobs. They have to make people take responsibility to lead and hold them accountable. That runs counter to the instincts of most of us because being more like a teacher than a doer doesn't fit with our models of leadership—particularly if you're a man in this society, with our sports coaches, war heroes, and the like. This is much harder, I think, for men to overcome.

T&D: Do you think women lead differently?

O'Toole: Women face different problems and challenges because social expectations tend to be different for them.

> ## Those executives will identify about a dozen things—20 at most—that Gandhi did to be an effective leader that if they did those same things, they'd be effective as well.

your organization and your people, no matter what personality type you have—you can learn how to do these things to help them to be effective. That is a very empowering message.

The examples in the book are of people with all kinds of personality types and yet they were able to be very effective. In every example, the key change was made by the people doing the work. In no case do I cite a leader who's the know-it-all, see-it-all, who lays out for everybody what they have to do. That just doesn't work. The ultimate in empowerment is making other people in the organization into leaders.

I think that's changing, and I'm happy it's changing. But I think men and women start off from different places in terms of socialization and social expectations. Women have different obstacles than men do, but at least women don't have the John Wayne role model to overcome. The most damaging is the typical male role model, the commander that we subtly and constantly reinforce in our society.

You go through a training program with very bright people and you work with them, and, at the end, the rate of recidivism among men is very high. They will slip back into the old habits, and the [new learning] has to be constantly reinforced.

You can't go in one time and create these leaders and the leadership capacity is then built into the organization. In fact, in any organization there's tremendous regression toward past behavior. So, the right philosophy—this notion of cascading leadership—has to be constantly reinforced. If you look at all of the leaders mentioned in the book, they spend about 70 to 80 percent of their time communicating, not only the values and objectives of their organizations, but also the appropriate leadership model.

T&D: I think women may have latched onto the traditional male leadership model at first.

O'Toole: Read the chapter on Tina Brown. The *New Yorker* was traditionally hierarchical: Senior editors would drop little notes to their people, and it never occurred to them that wasn't the best way to deal with bright, intellectual people and bring out their capabilities. Tina got out of her office and got down in the trenches with the people. She stretched them, let them grow, and created a whole new cadre of leaders so that when she left, the organization was not dependent on Tina Brown. There were many people who could take over, who were capable of leading. I don't think you'll find a better example—in three pages—of how you go about leading people in stretching, nurturing, and holding them accountable. Never telling them what do, but never allowing them to get by with doing something easy in which they aren't learning, raising the bar, or working toward fulfilling themselves. She's a controversial person, but. . . .

T&D: Yes, not everyone would agree with what she did editorially. Do you think we're disillusioned in general with our leaders in every arena—business and politics?

O'Toole: I think we're disillusioned with the whole subject of leadership. You get people like "Chainsaw" Al Dunlap and President Clinton, and there's tremendous disillusionment. There's cynicism about leadership in the entire country today and when you consider the kinds of leaders we've had in both the private and public sectors, it's not surprising that's the case.

That's why I think we have to start thinking about leadership as an organizational capacity and not just an individual one. The organization that depends on one individual for its success is a risky proposition. Yet, we continue to associate successful organizations with a single individual—people talk about Jack Welch. We have to start thinking of companies not in terms of who the leader is, but in terms of overall organizational capacity. When we do, we'll have a different model of leadership, a much healthier one, and we will free ourselves from the cynicism and skepticism that naturally arise when you have somebody who clearly either abuses or disappoints by not having the appropriate ambition.

I love all of the leaders and others I use as examples in the book and when you call them on it, they say, "Of course, I'm not talking about there being one leader in the organization." But the usual way people talk about leadership is to point to individuals. I slip into it myself. I think we have to break ourselves of that very bad habit. When we do, I think we'll have healthier, greater, true leadership, and a lot less disappointment and dependence upon these men and women on white horses.

The idea of charismatic personalities is in our culture. George Washington is seen as a father figure, but in terms of governing, he did very little. He had Adams, Jefferson, and Hamilton. Those were the people making the decisions, the brain trust. There were people behind them too.

T&D: Is there anything else we need to know about leadership?

O'Toole: I'm hoping the study by Booz-Allen and the World Economic Forum will be a step in changing the way people think about leadership. One of the most important things in switching to an organizational focus is that the characteristics, the actions, and all of the other things associated with leadership become measurable. The discipline of leadership is often undisciplined. There are a lot of ideas and theories, it's impressionistic and anecdotal, but as long as it's about individuals, it's going to remain that way because individuals, by definition, are all different.

It's the successes, the failures, the linkages between what leaders do and the outcomes that are measurable. Then, leadership will become more of a science, and it will be possible to go into an organization and do a diagnostic and see where the organization is weak in terms of its overall organizational capacity and where it's strong. Then, you'll be able to say, "Here are some things you need to do so the organization can be led more effectively."

We're very close to a breakthrough in thinking. A lot of the work that's gone before by people like Heifetz and James MacGregor Burns is prelude to this. We're now getting ready to make the next step, and I'm excited by it. On the one hand, in the field of leadership the bloom is off the rose. But now, we're ready to move on to the next stage to be more productive.

No matter how you come out on a 360, it's hard to change who you are and how people perceive you. But the book has some practical things you can do, and ask yourself how you can apply the lessons from each chapter of the book. Each can be discussed and translated to whatever task you're doing, at whatever level you are.

James O'Toole was interviewed by **Haidee Allerton**, *managing editor of* Training & Development. *O'Toole's book,* Leadership A to Z: A Guide for the Appropriately Ambitious, *is published by Jossey-Bass (1999).*

The Manager as Political Leader:
A Challenge to Professionalism?

John Nalbandian

It has been acknowledged for a long time that city and county managers play a prominent role in policy making. It can be no other way. Managers set the council's agenda, for example, by calling to the governing body's attention infrastructure issues of which it would not otherwise be aware. They develop alternatives for the council, and they make policy recommendations. This is expected of them, and they do it well.

These administrative activities support the council's policy-making responsibility and its problem-solving capacity. Over time, local government professionals have effectively integrated this influential policy role with the sober, analytical, politically neutral foundation of their profession. But what happens when the manager is expected simultaneously to lead staff in an objective analysis of a complex project and to build political support for it?

A case-study format is ideally suited to describing both the context and some ways of thinking about the role confusion produced when a local government manager is thrust into a political role. To address the question "What happens to a politically neutral chief administrative officer when expected to act politically?" I analyzed scholarly research, examined documents, read newspaper accounts, and interviewed several public servants, including Dennis Hays, chief administrative officer of the Unified Government of Wyandotte County/Kansas City Kansas (KCK).

Reprinted with permission from the March 2000 issue of *Public Management (PM),* a magazine published by the International City/County Management Association, Washington, D.C.

Hays had just found himself in the middle of a highly visible policy debate on economic development involving the possible location of a NASCAR racing facility in Wyandotte County, Kansas. This is his story.

NASCAR Comes to KCK

In the spring of 1997, the International Speedway Corporation (ISC), headquartered in Daytona Beach, Florida, was searching for a site in the Kansas City area where it could construct a National Association for Stock Car Auto Racing (NASCAR) track. ISC is the major player in NASCAR racing; its interests include the ownership of several tracks that host this kind of racing.

Plans called for a $250 million facility in the metropolitan Kansas City area that eventually could accommodate 150,000 people. The project would develop some 1,000 acres, more than the combined area encompassed by Arrowhead Stadium (Kansas City Chiefs football) and Royals Stadium (Kansas City Royals baseball), and would require easy access from interstate highways. ISC would partially fund the project and would expect the chosen city and state to finance the rest.

NASCAR Becomes Hays's Highest Priority

The mayor and chief administrative officer were dismayed at the news that ISC might consider Kansas City, Kansas, as a site for its newly planned racetrack. "Surely, we don't want a racetrack!" Dennis Hays told Mayor Carol Marinovich when she asked him to attend a meeting with ISC and some staff members from the Kansas City Area Development Council.

If the ISC representatives were expecting a warm welcome, they were sorely disappointed. "It was almost a fiasco," said Hays. Apparently, they were expecting to be greeted as bearers of an economic jewel. Instead, "they must have thought we were really something after that first discussion. We didn't show much interest; we were not well prepared; I went through a quick dog-and-pony show about possible sites and the topography of the community and some concerns we would have about siting such a noisy, nasty facility." The economic development people reported that ISC was disappointed by the reception it received.

At the time, Hays was preoccupied with a ballot measure to consider the consolidation of city and county government. He saw the NASCAR initiative as a distraction that would force Mayor Marinovich—a champion of consolidation—into the lead publicly on what Hays thought would be an unpopular project, just before the consolidation vote.

Consolidation was approved that spring, and Hays anticipated that the next six months would be occupied with developing and implementing transition plans leading to a September vote to elect the consolidated government's new leadership. Mayor Marinovich would run for the new office of mayor and chief executive officer of the unified government of Wyandotte County/ Kansas City, Kansas. Consolidation was officially to occur on October 1, 1997.

In June, ISC officials publicly and officially announced their interest in the Kansas City area as a possible site. ISC officials met in separate sessions with officials from Kansas City, Missouri, and from KCK.

In the meantime, city officials had undertaken research on the impact of a major racing facility and had found the outlook favorable. In addition, citizens of Wyandotte County began calling the mayor and other public officials, who began to realize that they should take the initiative seriously and that the "noisy, nasty project" might not be so bad after all. "There goes the possibility for a smooth, orderly transition," Hays remembered thinking. "After the election, I thought I knew how I was going to be spending my time from April to September."

Subsequent meetings led the mayor, Hays, a councilmember, and a member of Wyandotte County's state legislative delegation to visit Fontana, California, to attend a NASCAR race at Fontana's newly built track. "I had no interest in going to a NASCAR race. My life was hell; I was working on the transition. The mayor looked at me and said, 'Hays, I'm going to Fontana, and I want you to join me.' " She left little room for discussion, Hays recalled.

But the experience was unexpected. The facility was first-rate, and the event was family-oriented. The imagined potbellied, cigarette-smoking beer drinkers in black leather did not materialize. The mayor talked with nearby residents about noise, traffic, and other possible disturbances, and, aside from the traffic on race days, Marinovich and Hays couldn't find a down side to the facility. Also, they learned at first hand why access from only one interstate highway was not acceptable to ISC.

On the return trip, Hays and the mayor tried to figure out how to lead others in the same direction as they were moving. "Mayor, they're not going to believe us," Hays remembered commenting, then adding in the sober voice of a local government manager, "What if we make an all-out effort, and we don't get it?" He recalled thinking that, like it or not, if they pursued ISC, this effort would be seen as the first test of the new unified government.

The mayor decided to appoint a fact-finding committee made up of respected citizens who were neither for nor against the track. Some owned homes in the proposed track location. The idea of the committee was

risky; if its members failed to endorse the project, their disapproval would sink negotiations with ISC before they had even begun. When the fact-finding committee took a trip to Daytona and Darlington to see these cities' NASCAR tracks, their visits confirmed Marinovich's hopes, and additional allies began lining up.

Soon after it had made another visit to the Kansas City area, ISC informed the mayor that it was requesting proposals from KCK and Kansas City, Missouri. ISC expected presentations in three weeks in its hometown of Daytona Beach!

Hays recalled: "It wasn't until that point that I realized how serious this was and how much time and energy would have to be devoted to it. I got to the mayor, and I remember saying, 'Mayor, do we want this? Do we throw everything we have at it?' She was facing a September election, and she couldn't know how this would affect her chances to become mayor of the consolidated government. But she looked at me, and she said resolutely, 'Yes, we are going for it!' "

Hays's Priorities

The city administrator got the political direction he needed. The mayor would work with the council, and Hays now knew where his priorities lay: NASCAR first, transition second. But knowing one's priorities and knowing one's role are different matters. Soon after hearing from Marinovich, Hays realized he would be cast in a role he never thought a manager would perform.

My interviews with Hays, Mayor Marinovich, and Robert Roddy, who was director of the water pollution control department and chair of a staff task force to coordinate engineering planning on the project, confirmed a cooperative relationship between the mayor and CAO.

This relationship had begun to develop years before, when Marinovich was elected to the council of KCK and Hays was deputy city administrator. She noted, "From the beginning, I had great respect for Dennis's ability from what I saw at first hand as a member of the governing body. Typically, when there was something tough to accomplish, it was given to Dennis—the deputy administrator." When she became mayor, she recommended that Hays become CAO. At the mayor's request, the contract with Hays was negotiated by one of the councilmembers, to distance Marinovich from the close working relationship she would develop.

As for Hays, his respect for Marinovich was seen in his confidence that, when she said they would go all-out for the project, he could count on her to bring the council on board and to handle other political relationships. Roddy's remarks described the relationship well. He observed, "From what I

The mayor looked at Hays and said, "I'm going to Fontana, and I want you to join me." She left little room for discussion.

have seen of Dennis and the mayor in meetings, they seem to have a common direction; they discuss what needs to be done to reach a common goal. They might have different opinions, but they are not combative. They review their opinions and try to come to a common course of action. I believe that they have the trust of the community."

What might seem like a politicized relationship, with Hays owing his job to the mayor, is anything but. In a telling statement, Marinovich said, "Respect for one another and what each other can bring to the table builds respect between me and Dennis. Our styles are different. I am more emotional. *He is our Mr. Rogers* [emphasis added]" —a characterization that Hays did not take issue with during our interviews. In fact, he joked that he has been known to wear a cardigan sweater around the office.

What more flattering characterization could be made of a midwestern local government manager? Mr. Rogers. Someone you can trust with your children (your constituents). Someone whose motives are transparent. Someone who understands that personal ambition must play second fiddle to the greater good. In short, a politically neutral figure!

It was her confidence in Hays's selfless character, his integrity, and his professionalism that permitted the mayor to push him out front when she felt it was appropriate, even when he had misgivings. His self-effacing personality and his embodiment of community values, which he had demonstrated during his years as deputy administrator, lent credibility to the project in the eyes of others, and she knew it.

The CAO Calls a Sunday Meeting and Invites the Mayor

Once the mayor had identified NASCAR as the number-one priority, Hays invested his efforts fully in the project. He recalled the

weekend after KCK was notified that the Daytona presentation was only three weeks away: "Saturday, I am wrestling with this. There is no way I can do this in the amount of time we have. The council has not endorsed this, but we can't go to them in public because there are too many unanswered questions and too many fears that could arise among the homeowners who might be displaced. But we have had no public hearings!"

Then, Hays took the first step on an uncharted path, one that might endanger his political neutrality: "I've never done this in my career, but I called a meeting at my house for Sunday. I called the mayor [and said], 'I need you at my house tomorrow!' We're still working on our relationship at this time, so I'm not comfortable about this, but I feel like I need to do it. It's my responsibility, now that [the project] is the city's number-one priority. I call people I can depend upon, whom I have worked with before, and we brainstorm."

For another manager in another context, calling a meeting like this might not have seemed out of character, but clearly it was for Hays. He did what he felt was necessary, inviting his misgivings about the role he was embarking upon.

Hays Takes the Lead at Daytona

The Daytona presentation forced Hays further into the forefront. Transition business came to a halt. The pressure leading up to the presentation was enormous, with newspaper accounts characterizing the affair as a Super Bowl showdown between Kansas City, Kansas (David), and Kansas City, Missouri (Goliath).

Hays recalled, "Somehow, we had to present an image that we could get this done when we hadn't really had any formal discussion of it [in a public meeting]. We need the council's help; we are going to need the governor's help with special legislation; we need the state legislature's help; we have to deal with the residents who will be displaced.

"But we have to make a presentation and convey the impression that we can pull this off and that we can come up with $150 million and that all their questions would be affirmatively answered." Hays was taking the lead—a highly visible and uncomfortable one.

After the lieutenant governor and the mayor had made introductory remarks, the responsibility for presenting the proposal and responding to questions fell upon Hays, who remembered: "We arrived in Daytona and worked all night on the presentation. . . .I got one hour of sleep that night. I said to the mayor, 'You are the mayor, the lieutenant governor is here, there are a lot of decisions

that are going to have to be made on the spot.' She said, 'You call it. You make the decisions, and if we see it differently, I will let you know; but otherwise, get it done.'

"We were making finance decisions down there on the fly that the city council didn't know about. Subsequently, I would try to include the mayor in the tough meetings with me, but it was understood that I would take the lead."

When Missouri Governor Carnahan vetoed special legislation supporting Kansas City, Missouri's bid, KCK held the upper hand. And the city took advantage of this position with a persuasive presentation that Hays and Marinovich later learned had made the impact they were seeking on ISC ownership.

Time Pressure Keeps Hays In Front

The leading role that had emerged for Hays in the Sunday meeting at his home and later at Daytona was reinforced when he and the mayor returned home. When ISC announced it was giving an exclusive right for 60 days to Kansas City, Kansas, to develop a final proposal, there were doubts in KCK about the timetable.

Negotiations, which ISC limited to a two-month time, required the resolution of conflicting preferences about the site, the working-out of a financial package, and an agreement on legal issues, transportation (traffic access) requirements, and a public information program. All issues involved technical questions, and consultants were hired to complement staff. The technical blended into the political, and with such a short time frame, Hays remained in charge.

These time pressures were an important part of the context. The financial package alone was incredibly complex and required meetings with consultants, the mayor and councilmembers, state legislators, ISC consultants and managers, and lobbyists. Hays had no time to slip into the background and direct the show silently. If not the producer, he was a combination of director and leading man, staging a play that was set to go on in less time than he would ever have committed himself to, had he devised the production schedule.

Hays Embodies the Story

During media announcements and public meetings, "Mr. Rogers' neighborhood" suddenly became a popular place. Hays took the lead in the next stages: announcing the successful package in October and then presiding over meetings with 600 citizens, many of whom would be affected by the project and were anxious at best. Hays said, "I am not a high-profile person. I thought we could use our public information officer or some-one from the state, but the mayor said, 'No, Hays, you are going to do this.' And no one objected.

"In fact, I was the natural one to take the lead, even if my own sense of professional-ism cautioned me not to. With so much un-certainty, it would have been political suicide for the mayor to take the lead."

Both the mayor and Hays realized that, while Hays might not have the political le-gitimacy to cheer for the project in public, he had the credibility of a respected chief administrative officer and could talk publicly about the project's benefits and costs and how the government would work to treat af-fected homeowners fairly. He could tell the NASCAR story credibly because he embod-ied trustworthiness, anchored in his past ac-complishments and in his image as "Mr. Rogers."

Mr. Rogers Goes to Topeka

State legislation was required to finance the $200 million needed to match ISC's invest-ment. The state had agreed to fund some $43 million in road improvements and economic development incentives as part of the devel-opment agreement. Special tax abatement and sales tax measures were needed, and with the Wyandotte County delegation split on the project, legislative authorization was uncertain.

As in other aspects of the project, Hays found himself at center stage. In this case, the mayor, who was persona non grata with some members of the state legislative dele-gation, was advised to stay at home. She didn't, of course, and she bristled at the ad-vice, but, knowing what had to be done, she turned to her "silent" partner, Mr. Rogers.

Hays said it turned out that "I was the one who made the contacts and who went to [legislators'] offices to try and convince them. I was fielding questions left and right on issues that were going to come to the floor on the day our legislation was to be considered. Some questions were really hos-tile, and others asked for a position: 'Would you accept . . . ?' Against my instincts, I would answer."

As of this writing, the legislation has passed and been signed, the litigation has been managed, the property acquired, the bonds sold, and construction of the track has begun.

Conclusions to Be Drawn From the Case Study

Dennis Hays's role this case was not of his choosing. When he thinks about the meaning of professionalism in local government, he still questions his role in locating the NAS-

CAR track in Wyandotte County. After all, local government managers do not see them-selves as politicians because they think of themselves as problem solvers, the balance in the wheel; they bring a long-term, sober, analytical perspective to governance. Also, they realize that political neutrality is a scarce, valued and vulnerable administrative resources. Once exhausted, it is hard to re-plenish as trust.

Effective politicians speak to our minds as they reach for our hearts. Managers will never do this. Managers do not reach for the emotions of citizens, even if they sometimes touch them. And because they will not, they do not think of themselves as politicians. But for Hays to be seen as part of the unified government's team, it seemed he had to in-vest emotionally in this project.

As a CAO, he could convey credibly the message that the project could pay for itself. But more was required in this case. He had to show his loyalty to the project in order to win full buy-in from his political superiors.

Hays was thrust into a political role, in a context not of his own making. Standing in front of so many people, with the mayor and lieutenant governor in the front row and answering questions on a project he had worked on at their direction, Hays had little to distinguish himself from a politician. In our interviews, he referred to this incident several times; it symbolized the dilemma he faced. Failing to step onstage would have jeopardized the project and his standing with the elected leadership, he said.

But as he walked onstage, he saw himself risking his credibility as a political neural. He could ingratiate himself with his political leaders by telling a story that an audience of Wyandotte County residents, desperate for a vision of economic hope, wanted to hear (even if the affected landowners didn't). But he could not escape self-doubts about his professionalism. He said, "How do you stand in front of 600 people, 300 who are losing their homes, and not sound like you are mar-keting NASCAR, telling them that this is a great deal? How do you cheerlead for a pro-ject and yet maintain the necessity of fair-ness and equity in dealing with the displaced landowners? How do you retain credibility with your staff?"

A governing body deserves to hear from its manager what it needs to know, not what it wants to hear. How far can the manager go in endorsing a project when at some point he or she may be called upon to reexamine some part of it critically?

Hays further described his self-doubts this way: "I think an elected official can say, 'This is my vision; this is what I believe.' My job as administrator is to figure out pol-icy for the governing body. The governing body has a right to know what I think, where that thinking is the product of staff's exper-tise, judgement, and experience."

> **A**lso, [managers] realize that political neutrality is a scarce, valued, and expendable administrative resource. Once exhausted, it is as hard to replenish as trust.

"Being in a high-profile role, I want to say, 'This is a great idea; I want to cheer-lead.' But I have to resist the temptation to join the bandwagon and march in the parade. My sense of professionalism tells me to stay in the operations center and manage the parade."

It was Hays's commitment to the public interest that helped him decide what to do, and this was the first of two lessons in this case. A Hays recalled, after the groundbreak-ing, " I really did personally believe after we had researched it, after we had looked at the economic impact, after visiting one of the facilities, after knowing who our partner was going to be, after understanding the governor and lieutenant governor and the level of sup-port in Topeka, that this was a good project for our community from an economic stand-point, as an economic engine."

While Hays appears to have resolved his dilemma by grounding it in the public's in-terest, it is not clear whether the public interest serves him as a rationale or a ration-alization. In large measure, I suspect that the answer to this question is not how *he* regards the choices that he made but how *others* see them. Legitimizing a role is not something the role incumbent can do alone.

How did Hays minimize the likelihood that his actions would jeopardize his political neutrality? He grounded those actions in what I assert to be a set of four fundamental values that together compose the founda-tions, the anchors of political legitimacy: representation, efficiency, social equity, and individual rights. Together, these enduring values provide the broadest base of legiti-macy for a governing role, whether admin-istrative or political. In other words, to the extent that Hays's behavior was seen as respecting these values, his claim of acting in the public's interest was more likely to be accepted.

Let's examine these values more closely:

Representation. Hays indicated that from early in the process he and the mayor were struck by the overwhelming public support for locating a NASCAR racetrack in Wyandotte County. Furthermore, he always had the mayor's support and agreement from the council that this project was a top priority and should be pursued without fail.

Efficiency. Not only was Hays able to work out a deal so that the project would pay for itself, but he also demonstrated to the governing body and to himself that he had negotiated the deal in the public's interest. In one of our interviews, he said in response to a question about whether he ever felt that he had abandoned his stance of professional neutrality: "No. I honestly don't. I think that if we had blindly pursued the NASCAR facility at all costs, I would have [felt that way].

"Knowing how hard we were battling in the negotiating room, knowing in my heart, in my gut, that we were there protecting the public's interest and we weren't giving away the farm, I can say I never felt a loss of professional credibility to the public good."

Part of embodying the value of efficiency through professionalism is conducting oneself with dignity and respect for others, maintaining and conveying a sense of integrity—not becoming emotionally caught up in the tide of events. Hays said, "I can think of several examples of individuals who did not want to move, but they called and said, 'We don't agree with it, but we want you to know that the way the meeting was handled, we thought it was fair. You listened to us, and there was a forum, and it was done professionally. We weren't talked down to; we weren't stampeded; it was respectful.'

"Some people are going to associate me personally with the project, but as an honored enemy, not necessarily as the mayor's

"Some people are going to associate me personally with the project," Hays said, "but as an honored enemy, not necessarily as the mayor's hatchet boy or the person carrying the water for the politicos."

hatchet boy or the person carrying the water for the politicos."

Social equity and individual rights. From the start of this project, there was deep concern for the landowners who were going to be displaced. Ultimately, they received 125 percent of the value of their property and a break on utilities, if they relocated within the county. Some of their stories were heart-wrenching. Hays's reaction to these stories reflects his compassion and understanding of the passion that drives issues of rights and equity: "On Christmas Eve, I went to mass with my family. The lecturer at our parish is one of the guys whose family is being relocated. He and his family are in the front aisle, and throughout the mass, all I can do is think about this poor family. And

I know who they are, and I know they are having a difficult time. My heart is going out to this family as I see him read the scripture."

One can see that Hays's actions, and the way he thought about them, reflect his deep respect for the fundamental political values that create trust in the eyes of citizens. Resolving a role conflict by claiming to have acted in the public's interest is one thing, but anchoring the claim and the resolution in enduring public values is a more convincing approach, and this may have been the second lesson in this case.

Despite their success, and with some foresight, Hays and the mayor have agreed that he should show a lower profile on issues that they are currently working on: "We've generally agreed that I would be best working on these issues from behind the scenes, keeping the elected officials in the forefront. That decision has evolved, and I think there is general agreement that we should not perpetuate my high profile. It is not in anyone's best interest." This agreement testifies to the precarious position in which Hays found himself in the NASCAR case.

Political leaders often tell others what they want to hear. But the politicians we respect the most convey stories that touch our noblest selves, our moral character as citizens. And then they ask us to reach beyond, to dignify ourselves as citizens. The manager cannot do this and remain Mr. Rogers. When Dennis Hays was invited to join in a photo opportunity celebrating the legislative victory at the statehouse, he declined.

John Nalbandian is professor of public administration, University of Kansas, Lawrence, Kansas (nalband@ukans.edu). He is a former mayor and councilmember of Lawrence, Kansas. The author wishes to thank Val Drogt, Melissa Mundt, Mary Ontko, Davin Suggs, and Kate Watson, who worked on this subject as an M.P.A. class project at the University of Kansas, and George Frederickson and Irene Rubin, who gave significant editorial assistance and encouragement.

INTEREST ALIGNMENT AND COALITIONS IN MULTIPARTY NEGOTIATION

JEFFREY T. POLZER
University of Texas at Austin

ELIZABETH A. MANNIX
Columbia University

MARGARET A. NEALE
Stanford University

This study tested hypotheses developed from the distinct literatures on negotiations and coalitions and hypotheses integrating the two. In a complex, three-person negotiation simulation, subjects had to decide jointly how to allocate two resource pools. They were given multiple pieces of information regarding their negotiation preferences, coalition alternatives, and entitlements. Coalition alternatives and entitlement cues affected only the resource pool to which they were directly linked, but compatible interests, through the coalitions they generated, affected both resource pools, including the one to which these interests were not directly linked. We discuss the importance of integrating negotiation and coalition research in a way that incorporates the social dynamics of the negotiation interaction.

Resource allocation decisions in small groups can be usefully analyzed from a negotiations perspective (Brett, 1991). Conflicting interests are resolved through multiparty negotiation in both formal and everyday social interaction, within groups ranging from governments and organizational task forces to research teams (Ancona, Friedman, & Kolb, 1991; Bazerman, Mannix, & Thompson, 1988; Brett & Rognes, 1986). In multiparty negotiations, bargainers are faced with cooperating enough to reach mutually acceptable agreements while simultaneously competing enough to satisfy individual interests—interests that may align with others' interests in ways that are distributive, integrative, or compatible (Fisher & Ury, 1981; Froman & Cohen, 1970; Kelley, 1966; Neale & Bazerman, 1991; Pruitt, 1981; Thompson, 1990). Multiparty negotiations are complex social interactions because of both the multiple sets of

preferences that must be considered in fashioning agreements and the interpersonal dynamics that grow increasingly complicated as more people interact (Bazerman et al., 1988). An especially important source of complexity in multiparty negotiations, and one that is the focus of this article, is the inherent potential for coalition membership to influence the negotiated outcomes (Caplow, 1956; Chertkoff, 1967; Gamson, 1961; Luce & Raiffa, 1957; Miller & Komorita, 1986; Murnighan, 1986).

A coalition is defined as two or more parties who cooperate to obtain a mutually desired outcome that satisfies the interests of the coalition rather than those of the entire group within which it is embedded (Komorita & Kravitz, 1983; Murnighan, 1986).[1] Coalition researchers have explored how features of a bargaining context affect coalition activity and subsequent resource allocation decisions (Miller & Komorita, 1986; Murnighan, 1978). Compared to negotiation research, however, coalition research tends to

We thank Max Bazerman, Sally Blount, Gerald Davis, Karen Jehn, and Gregory Northcraft for their assistance in data collection and Jackie Paytas for her assistance in data analysis. We also thank the three anonymous reviewers for their contributions. We collected these data while the first and third authors were at the Kellogg Graduate School of Management, Northwestern University, and the second author was at the Graduate School of Business at the University of Chicago. This research was partially supported by an award from the IBM Faculty Research Fund at the University of Chicago to the second author.

[1] This definition of a coalition is consistent with the definition found in the influence tactics literature. The coalition tactic of one party's seeking the aid of another to persuade a third or of using the support of another as an argument for the third's agreement (Yukl & Falbe, 1990) would result in a coalition as we define it: two or more parties who cooperate to obtain a mutually desired outcome. The use of this coalition tactic, if successful, results in a set of parties who form a coalition.

From *Academy of Management Journal*, February 1998, pp. 42-54. © 1998 by the Academy of Management, P.O. Box 3020, Briar Cliff Manor, NY 10510-8020. Reproduced by permission of the publisher via Copyright Clearance Center, Inc.

examine relatively constrained and information-limited problems, focusing on allocation processes that are purely distributive. One result of this focus is a prevailing view that coalitions are inherently unstable. From this perspective, coalitions are temporary alliances designed to increase individual coalition members' outcomes on a particular issue; when the issue is resolved, the coalition dissolves.

The purpose of this study was to extend this view of coalitions to incorporate the effects of both preference alignments that are not purely distributive and social psychological forces that occur within multiparty negotiations. We propose that the alignment of negotiators' preferences in multiparty negotiations has direct implications for whether and how coalition activity affects negotiated outcomes. In addition, coalitions may be more stable than coalition researchers have suggested, primarily because of the social psychological forces that accompany coalition activity. Coalition researchers have called for research that examines bargaining tasks in "a larger, more . . . social context" (Komorita & Parks, 1995: 189). Such advice led us to consider the bond between the parties who form a coalition, the boundary around the coalition, and the consequences of coalition formation that reach beyond the issue that motivated it.

We drew from the literatures on both coalitions and negotiations, two areas of research that have continued relatively independently (see Murnighan & Brass (1991) for an exception). In the next sections of this article, we first address the coalition and negotiation literatures separately. We then integrate ideas from the two literatures, along with ideas from the literature on social categorization processes, to explore an issue relevant to, but missing from, each: How are resource allocation decisions made through a multiparty negotiation process likely to be affected by relatively stable coalitions formed around compatible preferences? This integration allows us to analyze an unexplored but important connection between these research domains.

THEORY AND HYPOTHESES

Power and Entitlement in Multiparty Negotiation

Coalition researchers typically study multiparty contexts in which alternative coalitions have different values based on the inputs of the parties who form the coalition (Kahan & Rapoport, 1984; Komorita & Hamilton, 1984). In these situations, known as variable-sum or characteristic function games, power is determined by the number and value of the alternative coalitions an individual might form (cf. Aumann & Maschler, 1964; Davis & Maschler, 1965; Horowitz, 1973). High-power players are defined as those who add more value (or greater inputs, in the lexicon of coalition researchers) to the coalitions that include them (Aumann & Maschler, 1964). Adding more value to coalitions increases an individual's power

because other players are dependent on that party if they wish to acquire a portion of that value.

To clarify this type of power, consider a simple example of a two-party negotiation. Although the two parties are interdependent, the extent to which each is dependent on the other can differ. Party A may be more dependent on party B to reach an agreement than party B is on A. The more net dependence party A has on party B, the more power party B has to influence party A regarding the terms of the outcome. In this view, power is the inverse of dependence (Emerson, 1964; Pfeffer & Salancik, 1977; Thibaut & Kelley, 1959). Because parties low in power have more net dependence on parties high in power for attaining outcomes of high value, parties with high power should be able to demand a greater share of the resources (Emerson, 1964; Greenberg & Cohen, 1982; Leventhal, 1976; Thibaut & Kelley, 1959). This research implies that parties with higher power should attain higher individual outcomes than parties with lower power from the resource pool created by their combined inputs.

Social psychological models of coalitions also highlight the importance of entitlement cues in determining outcomes (Komorita, 1974, 1979; Komorita & Chertkoff, 1973; Komorita & Tumonis, 1980). Entitlement cues, which are distinct from the value a party adds to a coalition, are pieces of information that influence what an individual believes to be a reasonable or fair distribution of a resource (Homans, 1961; Komorita & Hamilton, 1984). Entitlement cues can be linked to distribution rules, such as equality (Ashenfelter & Bloom, 1984), formalized egalitarianism (Rawls, 1971), equity (Adams, 1963; Homans, 1961), need (Deutsch, 1975), precedent (Bazerman, 1985), or promised future productivity (Mannix, Neale, & Northcraft, 1995). Group members tend to diverge systematically in their perceptions of what constitutes a fair outcome because each player tends to invoke a different distribution rule, with the choice depending on which would make him or her better off (Bettenhausen & Murnighan, 1985; Kelley & Thibaut, 1978; Leventhal, 1980). For example, in many studies of coalition formation, the only cue to the appropriate distribution of resources that is given is the inputs of each party. In such cases, although low-power players may argue for an equal resource distribution, high-power players are more likely to demand a higher outcome based on their inputs, invoking the fairness of an equity distribution rule to support their claim (Kelley & Thibaut, 1978; Komorita & Chertkoff, 1973; Shaw, 1981). In this way, resources are used as a frame of reference, or a cue, to which a particular distribution rule may be applied (Komorita & Kravitz, 1983). To the extent that other parties can be persuaded to agree with the fairness of a particular distribution rule, entitlement cues are a potential source of influence in multiparty negotiation (Greenberg & Cohen, 1982; Komorita & Hamilton, 1984; Leventhal, 1976).

Cues to entitlement other than inputs often exist in multiparty negotiation. Additional entitlement cues can be consistent or inconsistent with inputs in supporting a particular allocation of resources that is based on the application of a single distribution rule. For example, the party with the highest inputs to the group may also have the highest potential for productivity, in which case both entitlement cues are consistent in indicating that this player should get the highest outcome. In another instance, the party with the highest inputs may have the lowest potential for productivity, in which case the cues are inconsistent; one cue indicates this player should get the highest outcome, but the other indicates this player should get the lowest outcome. Leventhal argued that one component determining the strength of a fairness response in a particular situation was the extent to which the "social system . . . imposes consistent, stable rules of fair procedure and fair distribution" (1980: 50). Compared to consistent cues, multiple inconsistent cues may cause greater disagreement among group members about which distribution rule (e.g., equity versus equality) is most appropriate, or about which cue (e.g., inputs versus potential productivity) they should use when applying a particular distribution rule (Bettenhausen & Murnighan, 1985; Kelley & Thibaut, 1978; Komorita & Chertkoff, 1973; Mannix & White, 1992; Shaw, 1981). This research suggests that additional entitlement cues should interact with power position (which is based on inputs) to affect individual outcomes. Specifically, parties in high-power positions should attain higher outcomes when additional entitlement cues are consistent with power, and parties with low power should attain higher outcomes when additional entitlement cues are inconsistent with their power positions.

Reviewing the coalition literature reveals that coalition researchers have focused on issues, such as the distribution of a pool of inputs, that are zero-sum, or distributive, in nature. Each player has interests that are diametrically opposed to the interests of the other parties; any gain made by one player necessarily means the other players will get less. In the current study, we built on some of the findings from this body of research. With these replications as cornerstones, we then extended these ideas by considering how social forces affected the stability of coalitions. We now turn to the negotiation literature to broaden our perspective on various alignments of interests and their effect on negotiated outcomes.

Interest Alignment in Multiparty Negotiations

Like coalition researchers, negotiation researchers examine contexts in which the interests of negotiating parties may be diameterically opposed. However, because they typically study negotiations involving multiple issues, negotiation researchers can simultaneously examine interests that are compatible and sets of interests that have integrative potential (Thompson, 1990). In studying the effects of varying degrees of interest alignment, re-searchers have found that negotiators tend to assume that their own interests are diametrically opposed to the other parties' interests, an assumption labeled the "fixed-pie bias" (Bazerman & Neale, 1983). This assumption gets tested as negotiators exchange information about their interests. New information may indicate to negotiators that their fixed pie assumptions are wrong and that other parties' interests are not completely at odds with their own. In contrast, coalition researchers typically study bargaining situations in which all parties not only have preferences that are diametrically opposed but also have full information prior to the negotiation about the inputs and preferences of the other parties (Komorita & Parks, 1995). In this study, we were especially interested in the consequences of parties' discovering, during the course of a negotiation, that their interests on some issues were compatible.

In multiparty negotiations, subsets of parties often have compatible interests on one or more issues. Indeed, the more issues that are being negotiated, the higher the probability that at least some interests among some parties will be compatible (Raiffa, 1982). The discovery of compatible interests can have a variety of effects. If the parties in a negotiation discover that they all have compatible interests on an issue, they should agree on the option they all prefer. A more complex set of consequences may unfold when only a subset of parties, rather than all parties, has compatible preferences on an issue.

When some parties share compatible interests, they can band together to influence the incompatible party. Although a single negotiator's interests are not by themselves a source of power, when two or more negotiators have compatible interests, they may coordinate their efforts, or coalesce, to influence another party to consent to an agreement more favorable to the subset. To the extent that multiple parties can be more persuasive than a single party, compatibility should help parties achieve their desired outcomes. Further, depending on the decision rule used by the group, the coalescing parties may wield enough influence based on the structure of the decision rule to dominate the final allocation of resources. For example, if the commonly used majority rule is in effect, enough parties (i.e., a majority) may have compatible preferences to forge an agreement without the consent of an incompatible party.

In this majority rule situation, the incompatible party is at a serious disadvantage, because his or her inclusion in the final agreement is dependent on the decisions of the coalesced parties. This situation is likely to result in the incompatible party's being either excluded from the final agreement or included in an agreement in which the terms are dictated by the compatible parties. The preceding discussion suggests these hypotheses:

Hypothesis 1. Parties who have compatible interests will attain higher outcomes on the issues on which their interests are compatible than will those who have incompatible interests.

Hypothesis 2. Parties whose interests are compatible will be more likely to form coalitions that completely exclude other parties from the final agreement than will parties whose interests are not compatible.

In the next section, we consider how compatible interests on one issue may influence the outcomes for other, unrelated, issues. We propose that this effect may occur through the influence of relatively stable coalitions.

The Social Process of Coalition Formation

The prevailing view in the coalition literature is that coalitions are issue-based and, as such, inherently unstable (cf. Murnighan & Brass, 1991). When parties resolve one issue and proceed to the next, the current coalition is likely to disband and a different coalition, based on new sets of preferences for the new issue, is likely to form. According to this view, preferences on one issue, even if they lead parties to form a coalition, should not affect group decisions on other issues. In contrast with this view, we present an alternative proposition that integrates to ideas: (1) that coalitions are likely to influence outcomes in multiparty contexts and (2) that compatible interests are likely to exist in multiparty negotiations. By incorporating social psychological forces, we extend this integration to predict that coalitions that form because of compatible preferences on one issue may remain intact to influence outcomes on other issues, even those for which the coalition members *do not* have compatible preferences. In other words, coalitions may be more stable than coalition researchers have suggested.

We propose that once a coalition is formed, the parties in the coalition will continue to cooperate with each other as further issues are resolved, favorably influencing their own outcomes at the expense of noncoalition members. Several mechanisms contribute to the stability of coalitions. When preferences are revealed during the process of a negotiation, coalitions based on compatibility are likely to form explicitly. As coalition members cooperate to influence others, it is likely that both members and nonmembers will perceive the coalition as a relevant social group. The boundary around the coalition, demarcating who is in it and who is not, is real, as coalition members actually are working together as a subgroup.

In addition, once a coalition begins to form, cognitive processes of social categorization may combine with motivationally based processes of (sub)group identification to amplify the salience of the boundary around the coalition (Kramer & Brewer, 1984; Tajfel & Turner, 1986; Turner, 1987). An "us versus them" categorization can emerge, whereby coalition members are viewed as distinct from nonmembers (Gaertner, Mann, Murrell, & Dovidio, 1989; Tajfel, Billig, Bundy, & Flament, 1971). Resistance from a noncoalition party that is directed at the coalition as an entity may strengthen the bond between the coalition members, making it more likely they will

continue to cooperate with each other and compete with the noncoalition party (Homans, 1950; Tajfel, 1982). Because the distinction between subgroups is based on social psychological processes as well as objective interests, we argue that identification with a coalition may not recede immediately after the issue that motivated it is resolved. The more that coalition members come to identify with the coalition rather than with the larger group, the greater the likelihood that they will continue to act in the coalition's interests (Kramer, 1993).

When compatible interests are the basis for coalition formation, coalition members are able to see their preferences satisfied without having to compete with each other (Thompson, 1990). This cooperation is likely to result in increased stability, because of the social psychological processes described above. In contrast, when coalition members have opposing preferences on the issue around which the coalition formed (that is, the issue is distributive), they must still decide how to distribute those resources among themselves after securing resources for the coalition. This distribution is an inherently competitive activity; a gain for one coalition member comes at the expense of another. Such competition between coalition members may weaken the bond between them or even drive them apart. The lack of competition in the former case may, however, lead to greater coalition stability.

For these reasons, coalitions that form because of compatible preferences on a particular issue are likely to be more stable and to have farther-reaching effects than would be predicted by a strict analysis of preference compatibility. Drawing on this reasoning, we predict:

Hypothesis 3. Interest compatibility on one issue will result in better individual outcomes for compatible parties on other, unrelated, issues.

Support for Hypothesis 3 would indicate that a coalition has effects that extend beyond the particular issue for which it was formed. In addition, the presence of such extended effects would suggest that coalition activity, to the extent that it fulfills its purpose of benefiting coalition members rather than the larger group (Mannix, 1993; Murnighan & Brass, 1991), may be more detrimental to the larger group than previously thought.

METHODS

Subjects and Procedures

Subjects were 495 graduate business students who participated in the study as a classroom exercise. The sample was 26 percent women; the average age was 27.3 years, and the average work experience was 4.6 years. Exercises were conducted in eight separate sessions, with each session including approximately 62 subjects. Each subject participated as a member of 1 of 165 three-person groups, as described below.

The experimental design was a three-by-two-by-three (power position, entitlement cues, and interest compatibility) factorial design. Power position was manipulated within-group, and entitlement cues and interest compatibility were manipulated between-groups.

The task, designed to test our hypotheses, was meant to reflect an integration of negotiation and coalition research. Subjects were randomly assigned to three-person groups, and then, within each group, randomly assigned to represent one of three departments in the research and development division of a large company. Subjects were told that the three departments currently operated separately and had little interaction. The company's CEO had expressed a desire to change that. As a result, he was willing to supply funding to start a new R&D consortium. The CEO specified that any set of two departments, or all three departments, could comprise the new consortium.

Players were told that their objective was to gain as many dollars as they could for their departments. The task of the three players, therefore, was to decide both who would be in the consortium and how the available resources would be allocated. The sequence in which subjects made decisions about these two topics was left up to them; no instructions were given to discuss the two topics in any particular order. They were also free to move back and forth between the two topics or to discuss them simultaneously. Subjects were given 45 minutes to reach an agreement. Either a majority rule agreement (Two out of three) or a unanimous agreement (three out of three) was acceptable. Agreements signed by only two players indicated that a two-way coalition had formed and the third player had received no resources. Players who did not sign the agreement could not be included or assigned resources. The experimenter who ran each session instructed subjects not to talk to people in other groups and monitored the subjects to ensure that this did not occur while they were negotiating or completing the questionnaires.

At the end of the negotiation, subjects completed a contract form and a postquestionnaire that included a manipulation check. On the contract form, subjects specified their final agreement, noting which parties were in the consortium and how the resources were allocated. After completing the questionnaire, subjects returned it immediately to the experimenter.

Experimental Manipulations

Power position. Power (high, medium, or low) was manipulated within-group. Each group contained a high-power player (the manager of department A), a medium-power player (the manager of department B), and a low-power player (the manager of department C). Power was operationally defined through the use of a

variable-sum resource pool, commonly used in coalition research (cf. Kahan & Rapoport, 1984). For simplicity, we will call this the coalition pool, although it was not referred to as such in the experimental materials. Subjects were told that they had a pool of money to divide, the size of which would vary with the composition of the consortium. The amount of money in this resource pool was based on the size of each department (the number of researchers in it). The amount of money the CEO would contribute to this fund could be calculated by summing the number of researchers in each department included in the consortium and multiplying by 10,000. Thus, the value of consortia varied with their composition.

Department A had 40 researchers, department B had 25 researchers, and department C had 10 researchers, so that the values of the coalition pools were as follows: A + B = $650,000, A + C = $500,000, B + C = $350,000, and A + B + C = $750,000. Earlier, we noted that high-power players are defined as those who add more value, or inputs, to the coalitions that include them. Thus, player A had greater power than player B, and player B had greater power than player C. The term "combined inputs," as it was used earlier in the article, refers to the total value of the coalition pool (e.g., $750,000 if A, B, and C were included).

Entitlement cues. Entitlement cues were manipulated between-groups as either consistent or inconsistent with power. The entitlement cue was operationally defined as information regarding each department's projected profitability for the coming year. Subjects were told that this information was sometimes used to allocate resources. When the entitlement cues were consistent with power, the future profitability was projected as follows: A = $400,000, B = $250,000, and C = $100,000. When entitlement cues were inconsistent, the projection was: A = $100,000, B = $250,000, and C = $400,000. Note that these figures map onto the departmental size (multiplied by 10,000), or power position, of each player.

Interest compatibility. Interest compatibility was manipulated as a between-groups variable with three conditions: (1) compatibility between the high- and medium-power players (2) compatibility between the high- and low-power players, and (3) compatibility between the medium- and low-power players. The two compatible parties had identical preferences on two issues (computer equipment and staff support) that made up a second resource pool, which we will call the negotiation pool.

Regarding the negotiation pool, players were told that they had to allocate money to be used specifically for computer equipment and staff support. Five options (A–E) were given for both computer equipment (issue 1) and staff support (issue 2) in a traditional negotiation payoff schedule with integrative potential (Bazerman, Magliozzi, & Neale, 1985). Players were told that members of the consortium had to agree on one of these options for computer equipment and on one option for staff support.

The dollar values within the payoff schedules manipulated which of the two players had compatible interests on the two issues. When two players had compatible interests, they both preferred option A for the two issues, and the third player preferred option E for the two issues. In all cases, option A for the players with compatible interests would result in a $400,000 payoff to each, and the third player would receive $0. However, a solution of higher joint gain was also available, consisting of option E for computer support and option A for staff support, resulting in a payoff of $300,000 for each of the three players.[2]

Analyses

Because we were testing hypothesized differences among the outcomes of individuals in different power positions within groups, our unit of analysis was the individual. Although power position was a within-group manipulation, our other manipulations were between-groups in the sense that they affected players in the same power positions differently across groups. We were interested, however, in the effects of these manipulations on the individual outcomes attained by the players in different power positions in each experimental condition. For example, although interest compatibility was manipulated between-groups (for instance, the high- and medium-power players had compatible interests in some groups, but the high- and low-power players or medium- and low-power players had compatible interests in other groups), we were interested in how individual outcomes were affected by a player's having interests that were compatible (versus incompatible) with another player's. Because we randomly assigned subjects to groups and groups to conditions, and because all groups had the same instructions except for our experimental manipulations, we did not expect the particular group to which subjects belonged to account for a significant amount of variance in individual outcomes. To be sure, we tested this assumption by submitting group as a factor in a multivariate analysis of variance with individual outcomes on the coalition and negotiation pools as dependent variables. The group factor did not significantly affect outcomes on either the coalition pool ($F_{157, 291} = 0.21$, n.s.) or the negotiation pool ($F_{157, 291} = 0.04$, n.s.; multivariate test, $F_{314, 578} = 0.13$, n.s.). Because it did not account for significant variance or substantively affect any of the other results when included in the equation, we excluded the group factor from all subsequent analyses.

In our analysis of the outcome data, the two-way agreements were fundamentally different from the three-way agreements, which made comparisons that com-

bined the two types of agreements difficult. The occurrence of two-way coalitions had a disproportional impact on outcome means and variances because the parties that were excluded from the coalitions always received $0 (excluded parties could not be assigned resources without their consent). The interpretation difficulty stemmed from the differential distortion of outcome means and variances across conditions caused by including the outcomes of $0. To circumvent this problem while including all of the groups in the analyses, we excluded the outcomes of individual group members who received $0 when two-way coalitions were formed but included all individuals who were part of those agreements. The tests reported in the results section include all groups (i.e., those that reached both two-way and three-way agreements) but exclude those individuals who were left out of the two-way agreements. In addition, for completeness, we conducted separate analyses for groups that reached three-way agreements and for groups that reached two-way agreements. There were no substantive differences between the two sets of results.

We used a multivariate analysis of variance (MANOVA) to test Hypotheses 1 and 3. This MANOVA examined the effects of all three independent variables (power position, interest compatibility, and entitlement cues) on the two outcome dependent variables (individual gain from the coalition pool and individual gain from the negotiation pool). If the multivariate test was significant, the univariate test for individual gain from the negotiation pool was used to test Hypothesis 1, and the univariate test for individual gain from the negotiation pool was used to test Hypothesis 3. Finally, we conducted a chi-square test for Hypothesis 2 to determine whether significantly more two-way agreements occurred between compatible than incompatible parties.

RESULTS

All of the 165 groups reached agreement. Agreements including all three players were reached by 142 groups, and 23 groups reached agreements including only two players.[2]

Manipulation Check

After they had reached an agreement, subjects completed a questionnaire in which they were asked "How powerful were you and the other two department heads?" They rated themselves and each of the other two subjects on a seven-point scale (1 = not at all, 7 = extremely). A MANOVA was conducted that examined the effects of power position (as an independent variable) on ratings of the perceived overall power of the high-, medium-, and low-power players (the dependent variables). Although the power position of the party *being rated* did affect perceived power (reported below), the

[2]The specific payoff schedules for each condition are available from the first author upon request.

119

power position of the *rater* did not affect perceptions of power (that is, there was no significant main effect for power position as an independent variable).

We analyzed the mean power of each party as rated by the other two parties in each group. Comparisons across the three dependent variables revealed that the high-power player ($\bar{X}$ = 4.94, s.d. = 1.63) had higher perceived power than the medium-power player ($\bar{X}$ = 4.42, s.d. = 1.66; t_{594} = 4.94, $p < .001$), and the medium-power than the low-power player ($\bar{X}$ = 4.07, s.d. = 1.67; t_{589} = 3.30, $p < .001$). These patterns indicate that our power manipulation worked as intended.

Negotiation Outcomes

Replications of power and entitlement effects. For our results to be consistent with those of other coalition studies, parties with higher power should have attained higher individual outcomes than parties with lower power from the resource pool created by their combined inputs. The MANOVA revealed a significant effect for power position ($F_{4, 858}$ = 57.19, $p < .001$). In the univariate tests, the effect of power position was significant for the coalition pool only ($F_{2, 431}$ = 114.57, $p < .001$, η^2 = .35). Power position did not affect distribution of the negotiation pool ($F_{2, 413}$ < 1, n.s.). We conducted Tukey post hoc comparisons at the .05 level among mean outcomes for the coalition pool. These comparisons showed the high-power player's outcome to be significantly higher than the outcome of the medium-power player and the medium-power player's outcome to be significantly higher than the outcome of the low-power player (high $\bar{X}$ = 320,390.73, s.d. = 90,916.66; medium $\bar{X}$ = 250,729.73, s.d. = 70,035.33; low $\bar{X}$ = 180,960.00, s.d. = 86,067.78).

We also expected additional entitlement cues to interact with power to affect individual outcomes. Specifically, parties with high power should have attained higher outcomes when additional entitlement cues were consistent with power, and parties with low power should have attained higher outcomes when additional entitlement cues were inconsistent with power. Consistent with our expectation, the overall MANOVA ($F_{4, 858}$ = 3.77, $p < .01$) indicated a significant interaction between power position and entitlement cues for the coalition pool only ($F_{2, 431}$ = 6.55, $p < .01$, η^2 = .03). As can be seen in the pattern of means in Table 1, the size of the differences among the outcomes of the high-, medium-, and low-power players depended on the entitlement cue condition. The significance of the interaction effect between these variables indicates that, as expected, the differences among these means are attenuated, or less extreme, under inconsistent entitlement cues. These findings for power position and entitlement suggest that our manipulations of these factors worked as intended to replicate past research in the coalition domain.

The effect of interest compatibility on the negotiation pool. Hypothesis 1 predicts that parties who have compatible interests on some issues will have higher outcomes on those issues than will parties who have incompatible interests. A significant interaction between power position and interest compatibility occurred in both the multivariate test ($F_{8, 858}$ = 59.08, $p < .001$) and the univariate ANOVA for individual gain from the negotiation pool ($F_{4, 431}$ = 113.97, $p < .001$, η^2 = .51). The pattern of means for this effect, reported in the top half of Table 2, indicates that for each power position, players obtained less from this pool when their interests were incompatible with the other parties than they did when their interests were compatible. This result supports Hypothesis 1.

Hypothesis 2 predicts that parties whose interests are compatible will be more likely to form coalitions that completely exclude one party from the final agreement than will parties whose interests are not compatible. To test this hypothesis, we looked at the agreements that included only two of the three parties. Formal two-way

TABLE 1
Mean Individual Outcomes by Power Position and Entitlement Cues for the Coalition Pool[a]

Entitlement Cue Condition	Power Position		
	High	Medium	Low
Consistent	332,486.84 (104,923.15)	257,500.00 (76,146.26)	163,094.59 (81,901.57)
Inconsistent	308,133.33 (72,766.07)	243,583.33 (62,686.06)	198,355.26 (86,982.86)

[a] Values in parentheses are standard deviations. A univariate test of interaction had the following results: $F_{2, 431}$ = 6.55, $p < .01$, η^2 = .03.

coalitions were formed in only 23 instances—less than 14 percent of the time (χ^2 [1, N = 165] = 85.82, $p < .001$). The data indicate that group members with compatible interests were more likely to form two-way coalitions than group members whose interests were incompatible—15 two-way coalitions occurred between compatible parties, and only 8 occurred between incompatible parties (χ^2 [4, N = 23] = 13.04, $p < .02$). Although this result supports Hypothesis 2, the analysis must be tempered by the fact that some of the cells had low expected frequencies (see Table 3).

The effect of interest compatibility on the coalition pool. Hypothesis 3 predicts that interest compatibility for one issue will increase the individual outcomes of compatible members on other, unrelated, issues. To test this predic-

TABLE 2
Mean Individual Outcomes by Interest Compatibility and Power Position[a]

Power Position	Interest Compatibility Condition		
	High-Medium	High-Low	Medium-Low
Negotiation pool[b]			
High	347,395.83	334,183.67	165,000.00
	(48,989.68)	(71,205.01)	(120,533.85)
Medium	348,863.64	153,888.89	334,000.00
	(44,445.73)	(112,178.27)	(80,774.31)
Low	147,340.43	336,000.00	345,212.77
	(124,480.88)	(62,507.14)	(49,077.99)
Coalition pool[c]			
High	330,812.50	349,244.90	264,177.78
	(139,312.70)	(98,222.86)	(117,896.00)
Medium	256,772.73	214,111.11	259,380.00
	(99,634.88)	(98,467.17)	(93,468.29)
Low	150,531.91	198,700.00	194,212.77
	(117,001.64)	(122,656.85)	(81,653.55)

[a] Values in parentheses are standard deviations.
[b] The results of a univariate test of interaction were $F_{4, 431} = 113.97$, $p < .001$, $\eta^2 = .51$.
[c] The results of a univariate test of interaction were $F_{4,431} = 6.91$, $p < .001$, $\eta^2 = .06$.

TABLE 3
Number of Two-Way Coalitions by Interest Compatibility and Coalition Composition[a]

Interest Compatibility	Parties in Two-Way Coalitions		
	High-Medium	High-Low	Medium-Low
High-medium	4	2	1
High-low	2	7	1
Medium-low	2	0	4

[a] χ^2 (4 df) = 13.04, $p < .02$.

for computer support and staff support of AA, AB, BA, or BB indicated the formation of an internal coalition whereby the two compatible players received the vast majority of the resources. Agreements of EA, EB, DA, and DB indicated a relatively integrative outcome of high joint benefit in which each player conceded on the issue that was less important to him or her than it was to another party. All other agreements indicated a compromise, somewhere between an agreement characterized as an internal coalition or as integrative. Almost half (47%) of the groups agreed in AA, AB, BA, or BB solutions, indicating the presence of internal coalitions. About one-third (35%) of the groups reached integrative agreements, and the remaining 18 percent of the groups reached compromise agreements. The high incidence of internal coalition agreements on the negotiation pool issues is consistent with the interpretation that compatibility on the negotiation pool issues affected outcomes on the coalition pool through the operation of relatively stable coalitions.

tion, we looked at the effect of interest compatibility on individual outcomes from the coalition pool. The multivariate test revealed a significant interaction effect between power position and interest compatibility ($F_{8, 858} = 59.08$, $p < .001$), as did the univariate ANOVA on individual gain from the coalition pool ($F_{4, 431} = 6.91$, $p < .001$, $\eta^2 = .06$), supporting Hypothesis 3. The means for this interaction are reported in the bottom half of Table 2. Inspection of the means within each row reveals that, for each power position, parties obtained the lowest mean outcome from the coalition pool when their interests on the negotiation pool issues were incompatible with those of the other parties (compared to the conditions in which they had compatible interests). Therefore, our interpretation of this significant interaction is that the outcomes for power position depended on the level of interest compatibility or, more specifically, on whether a particular power position was compatible with another position. These results support Hypothesis 3; compatible interests for one resource pool (the negotiation pool) affected outcomes on another resource pool (the coalition pool) for which the parties' interests were not compatible.

To facilitate our understanding of the negotiation pool agreements, we categorized the agreements as either internal coalition, integrative, or compromise. Agreements

DISCUSSION

The purpose of this study was to integrate negotiation and coalition research in examining resource allocations in a multiparty context. In a complex task that permitted both the formation of coalitions and the creation of integrative agreements, the value of an agreement was predicated on two potential sources of value: the coalition pool and the negotiation pool. Players who had compatible interests on the two negotiation issues were able to achieve higher individual outcomes from *both* the negotiation and coalition portions of the task. This was true even when compatible players did not form exclusive two-way coalitions. These findings indicate that compatible players formed internal coalitions, acting as allies against the incompatible third party—not necessarily to lock the third party out of the final agreement, but to force him or her to accept a reduced share of both resources pools. Power position and entitlement cues also affected the allocation of resources. However, these factors only increased or decreased players' outcomes on the coalition pool, the portion of the task to which these forms of power were directly linked.

Evidence that compatible players formed two-way internal alliances can also be seen in the pattern of the agreements that were observed. First, we noted that agreements were more likely to include all three members in a coalition rather than to leave anyone out. This result might be attributed to the dominance of group rationality in that a three-way coalition was worth more at the group level than any two-way coalition, increasing the coalition pool from a possible low of $350,000 up to $750,000. However, this concern with high joint gain did not necessarily extend to the negotiation pool, where compatible players would have had to sacrifice some gain to reach fully integrative three-way agreements, jointly worth $900,000. The pattern of agreements indicates that only one-third of the groups selected this option, compared with almost half of the groups in which the two compatible parties prevented the incompatible third party from acquiring resources from the negotiation pool. This is one piece of supporting evidence that compatible players formed internal alliances. The second, and perhaps more compelling, piece of evidence is that compatible players used their power to obtain mutually acceptable outcomes, while leaving the third player with significantly fewer resources from *both* pools.

Implications

The results of this study suggest some interesting implications for the effects of interest compatibility. Our findings indicate that interest compatibility, unlike power position or entitlement cues, can go beyond the narrow range of outcomes that are delimited by the congruence of interests. If interest compatibility on one issue has effects on multiple resource pools, its presence could lead to inefficient and possibly irrational outcomes in some contexts. Further, to the extent that interest compatibility, and the resulting correspondence of outcomes, is a necessary condition in the development of relationships among negotiators (Davis & Todd, 1985; Heidere, 1958), such compatibility signals to the players two potential outcomes: (1) the ability to extract additional resources from other parties because of the strength of the alliance *in this interaction* and (2) the likely future interdependence of the compatible parties as they find themselves again on the same side of an issue *in other interactions* (Ben-Yoav & Pruitt, 1984; Berscheid, Snyder, & Omoto, 1989; Kelley & Thibaut, 1978). These results suggest that relationships among coalition partners—which are more likely to occur when interests are compatible—not only will make coalitions more stable, but also will unify the demands of coalition members.

Another finding from this study that has implications for future research is the influence of entitlement cues. Consider the experimental condition in which additional

entitlement cues were inconsistent with power based on inputs. In this condition, the low-power party is likely to invoke entitlement based on future profitability as a justification for more resources, raising the level of ambient conflict. The high-power party should reject such a justification and, instead, press a claim to resources based on ability to add to the size of the resource pool. However, low-power parties were, in fact, able to increase their outcomes based on their entitlements, demonstrating that multiple and even ambiguous sources of power were able to affect the ability of group members to obtain resources.

These results begin to elucidate how it is that parties with different levels of power can press claims for resources based on different distribution norms (Kelley & Thibaut, 1978; Komorita & Chertkoff, 1973; Shaw, 1981). It seems necessary that for entitlement-based arguments to be effective, the medium-power party must at least partially influence the expectations of the other parties about what is reasonable. Since the medium-power position was unchanged by the entitlement conditions, its incumbents would have been most easily able to assess the quality of the arguments from a neutral vantage point (Leventhal, 1976) and thus become more influential. A medium-power party's relative neutrality combined with the ability to form a two-way coalition, if one party were viewed as making demands that were out-of-line, would have made the medium-power party's evaluation of the arguments and subsequent outcome preferences powerful predictors of the final outcomes. In effect, the medium-power player had the swing vote, influencing the outcome to a much greater extent than might initially appear possible (Mannix, 1994).

This ability for one party to draw power from the constellation of the power and interests of the other parties is a relatively unexplored aspect of personal power. There are hints of the sway that perceived neutrality can have in self-interested decision processes in both the managerial dispute intervention literature (Pinkley, Brittain, Neale, & Northcraft, 1995) and the procedural justice literature (Leventhal, 1976). Empirical research has repeatedly illustrated that the appearance of neutrality is central to the perception of a procedurally just decision process and can enhance the acceptability of managerial decisions, even when the outcome is unfavorable (Bies, Tripp, & Neale, 1993; Lind & Lissak, 1985). Thus, to the extent that an individual can argue a position that is not obviously self-interested, the power of that persuasive attempt is considerably greater (Fisher & Ury, 1981).

Another important aspect of coalitions that remains unaddressed by the current research endeavor is the process by which internal coalitions are formed. In this study, we were only able to surmise this process by the constellation of coalitions created and the outcomes associated with different interest compatibility conditions. Theoretically, interest compatibility may reflect relationship potential among the participants. More than simple expectations for future interaction (a common laboratory manipulation of relation-ship), interest compatibility signals that a basis for relation-ship formation—similarity (Heider, 1958)—already exists. Relationships have been shown to influence not only the process of negotiation but also the ways in which outcomes are evaluated (Valley, Neale, & Mannix, 1995). Thus, it is important for researchers to consider more carefully the process through which interests are discovered and internal coalitions are formed.

A key practical implication of our results is that man-agers in multiparty negotiations should anticipate how coalition activity is likely to be affected by factors other than preferences on current issues. These factors include preference alignment on seemingly unrelated issues (in-cluding issues in temporally separate negotiations), the existing relationships between parties, shared group mem-berships (defined demographically or organizationally), successful past alliances, and even shared dislike of another party. Such factors, especially when working in combina-tion, may draw certain parties together while driving other parties apart. Managers should explicitly seek information about connections between other parties that go beyond current issues. This information can be used to anticipate likely coalitions and then to analyze whether the best course of action is to attempt to join, block, dissolve, or ignore them. Considering such coalitional dynamics may help managers protect and further their own (or their or-ganizations') interests in multiparty negotiations.

Limitations

In laboratory studies such as this, one must always consider the extent to which the findings generalize to real-world settings. Neale and Northcraft (1990), in their review of work on negotiator expertise, reported that studies that directly compared the behavior of profes-sional negotiators with that of students found no differ-ence in the patterns of responses, with the exception that the professional negotiators were more likely to imple-ment integrative strategies earlier than the student sub-jects (Neale & Northcraft, 1986; Northcraft & Neale, 1987). Thus, although professional negotiators might be expected to reach integrative agreements more quickly, there is little reason to expect either that real-world man-agers or employees would differ significantly in their ne-gotiation behavior from the graduate students in this study or that the social dynamics of these two groups would differ significantly.

A second limitation is that this study used a negotiation simulation. Thus, motivations, relationships, and reputa-tional issues do not come into play at nearly the level they would in a real-world situation. However, the differences among experimental conditions we found with subjects in this relatively constrained laboratory environment suggest that the relationships we have identified may be quite pow-erful. In addition, in this study, we used a task that more closely mirrored the complexity of negotiation tasks faced

in everyday organizational life. Unlike most negotiation experiments, this one required subjects to choose with whom to negotiate, allowed development of internal coa-litions, and required distribution of the value that arose from the various pools of resources.

A further limitation concerns our manipulation check. We measured perceived power with only a one-item scale, although we did obtain a rating of each subject's power from two other players. Further, we did not pro-vide a direct check for our manipulations of additional entitlement cues or interest compatibility. Nevertheless, we hold that the most plausible explanation for these independent variables' having significant effects on our dependent variables in the predicted directions is that our manipulations worked as intended.

Conclusions

This research brings together two seemingly disparate aspects of negotiation: the search for a coalition partner and the development of a negotiated agreement. These findings suggest that negotiators can focus on these two aspects of negotiations simultaneously. In many respects, these proc-esses are analogous to, but more complex than, negotiating distributive and integrative issues simultaneously. In typi-cal negotiation tasks, the issues that are being negotiated have been clearly explicated. In this study, value was in-creased not only by the way a party negotiated the issues within the negotiation pool, but also by the way he or she attempted to claim value from the coalition pool while de-termining the particular constellation of the consortium. Clearly, adding the "with-whom-to-negotiate" component to this mixture dramatically increased the cognitive and social complexity of the interaction.

Our primary goal in this article has been to present an initial study with a large sample that combined several fac-tors identified by previous empirical research as integral to multiparty negotiation. We found that negotiators were able to understand, integrate, and use various and conflict-ing pieces of information regarding claims to resources in reaching resource allocation agreements. Some of these pieces of information—specifically, the compatibility of in-terests—have farther-reaching effects than one would pre-dict on the basis of past research. Considering the social dynamics that are likely to come into play, particularly the waxing and waning of social categorization processes, re-veals a more complex, but more complete, picture of mul-tiparty negotiations.

REFERENCES

Adams, J. S. 1963. Toward an understanding of inequity. *Journal of Abnormal and Social Psychology,* 67: 422–436.
Ancona, D., Friedman, R., & Kolb, D. 1991. The group and what hap-pens on the way to "yes." *Negotiation Journal,* 7: 155–174.
Ashenfelter, O., & Bloom, D. E. 1984. Models of arbitrator behavior: Theory and evidence. *American Economic Review,* 74: 111–124.

Aumann, R. J., & Maschier, M. 1964. The bargaining set for cooperative games. In M. Dresher, L. S. Shapley, & A. W. Tucker (Eds.), *Advances in game theory:* 443–476. Princeton, NJ: Princeton University Press.

Bazerman, M. H. 1985. Norms of distributive justice in interest arbitration. *Industrial and Labor Relations Review*, 38: 558–570.

Bazerman, M. H., Magliozzi, T., & Neale, M. A. 1985. Integrative bargaining in a competitive market. *Organizational Behavior and Human Performance*, 34: 294–313.

Bazerman, M. H., Mannix, E., & Thompson, L. 1988. Groups as mixed-motive negotiations. In E. J. Lawler & B. Markovsky (Eds.), *Advances in group processes: Theory and research:* 195–216. Greenwich, CT: JAI Press.

Bazerman, M. H., & Neale, M. A. 1983. Heuristics in negotiation: Limitations to dispute resolution effectiveness. In M. H. Bazerman & R. J. Lewicki (Eds.), *Negotiation in organizations:* 51–67. Beverly Hills: Sage.

Ben-Yoav, O., & Pruitt, D. 1984. Resistance to yielding and the expectation of cooperative future interaction in negotiation. *Journal of Experimental Social Psychology*, 20: 323–353.

Berscheid, E., Snyder, M., & Omoto, A. M. 1989. Issues in studying close relationships: Conceptualizing and measuring closeness. In C. Hendrick (Ed.), *Close relationships:* 63–91. Newbury Park, CA: Sage.

Bettenhausen, K., & Murnighan, J. K. 1985. The emergence of norms in competitive decision-making groups. *Administrative Science Quarterly*, 30: 350–372.

Bies, B., Tripp, T., & Neale, M. 1993. Procedural fairness, framing and profit seeking: Perceived legitimacy of market exploitation. *Journal of Behavioral Decision Making*, 6: 243–256.

Brett, J. 1991. Negotiating group decisions. *Negotiation Journal*, July: 291–310.

Brett, J., & Rognes, J. 1986. Intergroup relations in organizations: A negotiation perspective. In P. S. Goodman (Ed.), *Designing effective work groups:* 202–236. San Francisco: Jossey-Bass.

Caplow, T. A. 1956. A theory of coalitions in the triad. *American Sociological Review*, 21: 489–493.

Chertkoff, J. M. 1967. A revision of Caplow's coalition theory. *Journal of Experimental Social Psychology*, 3: 172–177.

Davis, K. E., & Todd, M. J. 1985. Assessing friendship: Prototypes, paradigm cases and relationship description. In S. Duck & D. Perlman (Eds.), *Understanding personal relationships: An interdisciplinary approach:* 17–38. London: Sage.

Davis, M., & Maschler, R. J. 1965. The kernel of a cooperative game. *Naval Research Logistics Quarterly*, 12(3): 223–259.

Deutsch, M. 1975. Equity, equality, and need: What determines which value will be used as the basis of distributive justice? *Journal of Social Issues*, 31(3): 137–149.

Emerson, R. M. 1964. Power-dependence relations: Two experiments. *Sociometry*, 27: 282–298.

Fisher, R., & Ury, W. 1981. *Getting to yes.* Boston: Houghton-Mifflin.

Froman, L., & Cohen, M. 1970. Compromise and logroll: Comparing the efficiency of two bargaining processes. *Behavioral Science*, 30: 180–183.

Gaertner, S., Mann, J., Murrell, A., & Dovidio, J. 1989. Reducing intergroup bias: The benefits of recategorization. *Journal of Personality and Social Psychology*, 57: 239–249.

Gamson, W. A. 1961. A theory of coalition formation. *American Sociological Review*, 26: 373–382.

Greenberg, J., & Cohen, R. L. 1982. *Equity and justice in social behavior.* New York: Academic Press.

Heider, F. 1958. *The psychology of interpersonal relationships.* New York: Wiley.

Homans, G. 1950. *The social group.* New York: Harcourt Brace Jovanovich.

Homans, G. 1961. *Social behavior: Its elementary forms.* New York: Harcourt Brace.

Horowitz, A. D. 1973. The competitive bargaining set for cooperative n-person games. *Journal of Mathematical Psychology*, 10(3): 265–289.

Kahan, J. P., & Rapoport, A. 1984. *Theories of coalition formation.* Hillsdale, NJ: Erlbaum.

Kelley, H. H. 1966. A classroom study of the dilemmas in interpersonal negotiation. In K. Archibald (Ed.), *Strategic interaction and conflict:* 49–73. Berkeley: Institute of International Studies, University of California.

Kelley, H. H., & Thibaut, J. W. 1978. *Interpersonal relations: A theory of interdependence.* New York: Wiley.

Komorita, S. S. 1974. A weighted probability model of coalition formation. *Psychological Review*, 81: 242–256.

Komorita, S. S. 1979. An equal-excess model of coalition formation. *Behavioral Science*, 24: 369–381.

Komorita, S. S., & Chertkoff, J. M. 1973. A bargaining theory of coalition formation. *Psychological Review*, 80: 149–162.

Komorita, S. S., & Hamilton, T. P. 1984. Power and equity in coalition bargaining. In S. B. Bacharach & E. J. Lawler (Eds.), *Research in the sociology of organizations:* 189–212. Greenwich, CT: JAI Press.

Komorita, S. S., & Kravitz, D. 1983. Coalition formation: A social psychological approach. In P. B. Paulus (Ed.), *Basic group processes:* 179–203. New York: Springer-Verlag.

Komorita, S. S., & Parks, C. D. 1995. Interpersonal relations: Mixed-motive interaction. In J. T. Spence, J. M. Darley, & D. J. Foss (Eds.), *Annual review of psychology*, vol. 46: 183–207. Palo Alto, CA: Annual Reviews.

Komorita, S. S., & Tumonis, T. M. 1980. Extensions and tests of some descriptive theories of coalition formation. *Journal of Personality and Social Psychology*, 39: 256–268.

Kramer, R. M. 1993. Cooperation and organizational identification. In J. K. Murnighan (Ed.), *Social psychology in organizations:* 244–268. Englewood Cliffs, NJ: Prentice-Hall.

Kramer, R. M., & Brewer, M. B. 1984. The effects of group identity on resource use in a simulated commons dilemma. *Journal of Personality and Social Psychology*, 46: 1044–1057.

Leventhal, G. S. 1976. The distribution of rewards and resources in groups and organizations. In L. Berkowitz & E. Walster (Eds.), *Advances in experimental social psychology:* 91–131. New York: Academic Press.

Leventhal, G. S. 1980. What should be done with equity theory? In K. J. Gergen, M. S. Greenberg, & R. H. Willis (Eds.), *Social exchange: Advances in theory and research:* 27–55. New York: Plenum.

Lind, E. A., & Lissak, R. I. 1985. Apparent impropriety and procedural fairness judgments. *Journal of Experimental Social Psychology*, 21: 19–29.

Luce, D., & Raiffa, H. 1957. *Games and decision: Introduction and critical survey.* New York: Wiley.

Mannix, E. A. 1993. Organizations as resource dilemmas: The effects of power balance on group decision making. *Organizational behavior and Human Decision Processes*, 55: 1–22.

Mannix, E. A. 1994. Will we meet again? The effects of power, distribution rules, and the scope of future interaction in small group negotiation. *International Journal of Conflict Management*, 5: 343–368.

Mannix, E. A., Neale, M., & Northcraft, G. 1995. Equity, equality or need? The effects of organizational culture and resource valence on allocation decisions. *Organizational Behavior and Human Decision Processes*, 63: 276–286.

Mannix, E. A., & White, S. 1992. The effect of distributive uncertainty on coalition formation in organizations. *Organizational Behavior and Human Decision Processes*, 51: 198–219.

Miller, C., & Komorita, S. 1986. Coalition formation in organizations: What laboratory studies do and do not tell us. In R. Lewicki, B. Sheppard, & M. Bazerman (Eds.), *Research on negotiation in organizations:* 117–138. Greenwich, CT: JAI Press.

Murnighan, K. 1978. Models of coalition behavior: Games theoretic, social psychological and political perspectives. *Psychological Bulletin*, 85: 1130–1153.

Murnighan, K. 1986. Organizational coalitions: Structural contingencies and the formation process. In R. Lewicki, B. Sheppard, & M. Bazerman (Eds.), *Research on negotiation in organizations:* 155–173. Greenwich, CT: JAI Press.

Murnighan, K., & Brass, D. 1991. Intraorganizational coalitions. In R. Lewicki, B. Sheppard, & M. Bazerman (Eds.), *Research on negotiation in organizations:* 283–306. Greenwich, CT: JAI Press.

Neale, M. A., & Bazerman, M. H. 1991. *Cognition and rationality in negotiation.* New York: Free Press.

Neale, M. A., & Northcraft, G. B. 1986. Experts, amateurs, and refrigerators: Comparing expert and amateur decision making in a novel task. *Organizational Behavior and Human Decision Processes*, 38: 228–241.

Neale, M. A., & Northcraft, G. B. 1990. Experience, expertise, and decision bias in negotiation: The role of strategic conceptualization. In

B. Sheppard, M. Bazerman, & R. Lewicki (Eds.), *Research in negotiation in organizations:* 55–76. Greenwich, CT: JAI Press.

Northcraft, G. B., & Neale, M. A. 1987. Experts, amateurs, and real estate: An anchoring-and-adjustment perspective on property pricing decisions. *Organizational Behavior and Human Decision Processes*, 39: 228–241.

Pfeffer, J., & Salancik, G. 1977. Organizational design: The case for a coalitional model of organizations. *Organizational Dynamics*, 6(2): 15–29.

Pinkley, R. L., Brittain, J. W., Neale, M. A., & Northcraft, G. B. 1995. Managerial third-party dispute intervention: An inductive analysis of intervenor strategy selection. *Journal of Applied Psychology*, 80: 386–402.

Pruitt, D. G. 1981. *Negotiation behavior.* New York: Academic Press.

Raiffa, H. 1982. *The art and science of negotiation.* Cambridge. MA: Belknap.

Rawls, J. 1971. *A theory of justice.* Cambridge, MA: Harvard University Press.

Shaw, M. E. 1981. *Group dynamics: The psychology of small group behavior.* New York: McGraw-Hill.

Tajfel, H. 1982. Social psychology of intergroup relations. In M. R. Rosenzweig & L. W. Porter (Eds.), *Annual review of psychology,* vol. 33: 1–39. Palo Alto, CA: Annual Reviews.

Tajfel, H., Billig, R., Bundy, C., & Flament, C. 1971. Social categorization and intergroup behavior. *European Journal of Social Psychology,* 1(2): 149–178.

Tajfel, H., & Turner, J. 1986. The social identity theory of intergroup behavior. In S. Worchel & W. G. Austin (Eds.), *Psychology of intergroup relations:* 7–24. Chicago: Nelson-Hall.

Thibaut, J. W., & Kelley, H. H. 1959. *The social psychology of groups.* New York: Wiley.

Thompson, L. 1990. Negotiation behavior and outcomes: Empirical evidence and theoritical issues. *Psychological Bulletin,* 108: 515–532.

Turner, J. C. 1987. *Rediscovering the social group: A self-categorization theory.* Oxford, England: Blackwell.

Valley, K., Neale, M. A., & Mannix, E. A. 1995. Relationships in negotiations: The role of reputation, the shadow of the future, and interpersonal knowledge on the process and outcome of negotiations. In R. J. Bies, R. Lewicki, & B. Sheppard (Eds.), *Research in bargaining and negotiation in organizations:* 65–93. Greenwich, CT: JAI Press.

Yukl, G., & Falbe, C. M. 1990. Influence tactics and objectives in upward, downward, and lateral influence attempts. *Journal of Applied Psychology,* 75: 132–140.

Jeffrey T. Polzer is an assistant professor of management in the Graduate School of Business at the University of Texas at Austin. He received his Ph.D. in organizational behavior at Northwestern University. His current research interests include intergroup relations, conflict resolution and negotiation, social dynamics in work teams, and social dilemmas.

Elizabeth A. Mannix is an associate professor in the Graduate School of Business at Columbia University. She received her Ph.D. in social and organization psychology at the University of Chicago. Her current research interests include negotiation, power, and relationships and alliances, with a focus on managerial teams.

Margaret A. Neale is the academic associate dean and a professor of organizational behavior in the Graduate School of Business at Stanford University. She received her Ph.D. from the University of Texas. Her research interests currently include negotiation, group decision making, and learning in groups.

TEAM STRUCTURE AND PERFORMANCE: ASSESSING THE MEDIATING ROLE OF INTRATEAM PROCESS AND THE MODERATING ROLE OF TASK TYPE

GREG L. STEWART
Brigham Young University

MURRAY R. BARRICK
Michigan State University

We used data from 45 production teams (626 individuals) and their supervisors to test hypotheses related to team structure. For teams engaged primarily in conceptual tasks, interdependence exhibited a ∪-shaped relationship with team performance, whereas team self-leadership exhibited a positive, linear relationship with performance. For teams engaged primarily in behavioral tasks, we found a ∩–shaped relationship between interdependence and performance and a negative, linear relationship between team self-leadership and performance. Intrateam process mediation was found for relationships with interdependence but not for relationships with team self-leadership. Overall, findings support a model of team structure and illustrate how relationships between structural characteristics and a team's performance can he moderated by its tasks.

Teams are becoming a basic building block for many contemporary business organizations, with one survey finding 68 percent of *Fortune* 1000 companies using self-managing teams (Lawler, Mohrman, & Ledford, 1995). Most of these teams are directly involved with producing goods and services. Research has generally supported the efficacy of teams for improving worker satisfaction, but studies have been inconclusive concerning the effect of teams on productivity (Banker, Field, Schroeder, & Sinha, 1996; Cohen & Ledford, 1994; Stewart, Manz, & Sims, 1999). Several researchers have hypothesized that variation in team performance can be explained by differences in team structure (Cohen & Bailey, 1997; Gladstein, 1984; Hackman, 1987; Manz, 1992; Wageman, 1995). This study was thus designed to determine how team structure relates to team performance.

We thank Tom Mahoney and Barry Gerhart for their helpful comments concerning this article. Much of Greg Stewart's work on this project was completed while he was at Vanderbilt University, and much of Murray Barick's work was completed while he was at the University of Iowa.

Organizational theorists have defined structure as the configuration of relationships with respect to the allocation of tasks, responsibilities, and authority (Greenberg & Baron, 1997; Jones, 1995). Team structure is thus defined here as team relationships that determine the allocation of tasks, responsibilities, and authority.

In their review of factors that correlate with team effectiveness, Campion, Medsker, and Higgs (1993) identified two important elements of team structure: interdependence and team autonomy/self-leadership. The importance of these two characteristics is supported by organization-level research that has identified concentration of authority and structuring of activities as the two primary categories of structure (Pugh, Hickson, & Turner, 1968; Pugh & Hickson, 1997). In their review, Cohen and Bailey (1997) also identified team autonomy and interdependence as the primary task design characteristics that influence team effectiveness through team interaction processes such as conflict and communication. Cummings (1978) also proposed group versus individual jobs (which parallels interdependence) and source of control (autonomy/self-leadership) as two fundamental features associated with team structure.

From *Academy of Management Journal*, April 2000, pp. 135-148. © 2000 by the Academy of Management, P.O. Box 3020, Briar Cliff Manor, NY 10510-8020. Reproduced by permission of the publisher via Copyright Clearance Center, Inc.

Although team self-leadership and interdependence have both received scholarly attention, inconsistent findings suggest a need to develop a deeper understanding of how these structural characteristics relate to team performance. We thus designed this study to go beyond previous studies (e.g., Campion et al., 1993; Campion, Papper, & Medsker, 1996; Saavedra, Earley, & Van Dyne, 1993; Wageman, 1995) by (1) focusing on mediating process variables to explain how team structure and performance are related and (2) exploring whether the team structure—performance relationship is consistent across tasks.

Almost every model developed to explain team performance (e.g., Cohen & Bailey, 1997; Gladstein, 1984; Goodman, Ravlin, & Argote, 1986; Guzzo & Shea, 1992; Hackman, 1987) is grounded in McGrath's (1964) input-process-output perspective. McGrath's basic proposition is that inputs such as structural characteristics combine to affect team processes, which in turn influence team outputs. Unfortunately, the input-process-output links proposed by prior researchers have received limited empirical attention. Gladstein (1984) found support for the input-process-output model when member satisfaction and team self-ratings of production were used as criterion measures, but not when external production ratings were used. Our study builds on these findings by further modeling the extent to which intrateam processes mediate the relationship between team structure and performance.

Prior research on small groups and teams (Goodman, 1986; McGrath, 1984) and sociotechnical systems (e.g., Trist, 1981) has suggested that task differences moderate the relationships between group inputs, processes, and outcomes. However, task differences have not been specifically assessed to determine whether task type moderates the relationship between team structural characteristics and team performance. Thus, the second spe-cific contribution of this study is examination of the extent to which task differences moderate how interdependence and team self-leadership relate to team performance.

RELATING TEAM STRUCTURE AND TEAM PERFORMANCE

Figure 1 shows a model of the relationships expected between team structure and team performance. According to the model, which is based on both the input-process-output model and sociotechnical systems theory (Trist, 1981), team processes mediate relationships between team performance and the structural characteristics of interdependence and team self-leadership. Task type also moderates these relationships, as a team's tasks are expected to influence the link between team processes and performance. In the following sections, we first discuss the link between team processes and team performance and look at task type as a potential moderator of this relationship. We then offer predictions about how the structural characteristics of interdependence and team self-leadership relate to team processes and thereby to team performance.

Team Processes, Team Performance, and Team Tasks

Construct definition. Intrateam processes represent interactions that take place among team members (Hackman, 1987). Most measurements of intrateam process have been based on the work of Bales (1950) and include assessments of both task and socioemotional interactions (Gladstein, 1984; McGrath, 1984). Hackman defined the socioemotional category as "the interpersonal transactions that take place within the group: who is talking with whom (or not doing so), who is fighting with

FIGURE 1
Team-Level Model of Work Design

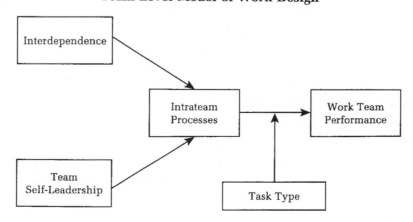

whom, who is pairing up with whom, and so on" (1987: 321). Hackman defined the task category as "those aspects of interaction that relate directly to a group's work on its task" and stated that "it should be possible, for example, to assess whether a group is using the energy and talents of its members well (rather than wasting or misapplying them), and to determine whether the group interaction develops and expands (rather than diminishes) members' performance capabilities" (1987: 321).

Numerous classification systems have been proposed to describe differences in the tasks performed by teams (e.g., Herold, 1978; McGrath, 1984; Shaw, 1973; Steiner, 1972; Tushman, 1979). Among these classification schemes, the approach taken by McGrath appears to be one of the most useful for classifying the tasks of teams operating in actual work environments (Goodman, 1986). McGrath's (1984) typology is developed around a "circumplex" that includes four task categories: generating ideas and plans, choosing between alternatives, negotiating conflicts of interest, and executing work. Along one dimension of the circumplex, tasks differ in the extent to which they are either behavioral or conceptual, with work execution tasks anchoring the behavioral end of the continuum.

However, one problem with task classification in actual work situations is that a team rarely performs only one type of task (Argote & McGrath, 1993; Goodman, 1986). In fact, McGrath (1984) suggested that teams perform tasks associated with all four of his categories, but with unequal frequency. This means that it may be inappropriate to classify the multidimensional tasks of actual work teams into mutually exclusive categories. An alternative, and often more appropriate, approach is to arrange the relative amounts of time each team spends on tasks along a continuum like the behavioral-conceptual dimension (Goodman, 1986).

The primary focus of a production team is work execution. However, because of differences in the length of production runs, variety of outputs, and stability of the environment, teams vary in the amount of time during which they actually execute behavioral tasks rather than plan, decide, and negotiate. Some production teams spend almost all of their time executing behavioral tasks—in McGrath's words, dealing with "overt, physical behavior, with the execution of manual and psychomotor tasks" (1984: 65). Other production teams, partly in response to having less clarity about which behavioral tasks are appropriate, spend a larger proportion of their time performing conceptual tasks that help them determine appropriate courses of action. The relative amount of time spent on behavioral tasks rather than on conceptual tasks like planning, deciding, and negotiating thus serves as a useful means of assessing the effects of task differences on production teams.

Hypothesized relationships. Empirical results (e.g., Barry & Stewart, 1997; Campion et al., 1993) generally support a positive, linear relationship with performance for synergistic processes (such as flexibility and open communication) and a negative, linear relationship for dysfunctional processes (such as shirking and conflict). However, the relationships exhibit substantial variation in their magnitude. Some studies have found almost no relationship between processes and performance (Gladstein, 1984), whereas others have yielded correlation coefficients exceeding .70 (Campion et al., 1996). This variability is consistent with the moderator effect shown in Figure 1, as task differences are expected to moderate process-performance relationships.

The work of production teams engaged predominantly in behavioral tasks is easily programmed, and information is centralized rather than diffused among team members (Goodman, 1986; Herold, 1978). Work requires little interaction, or interaction that is so mundane and nonproblematic that it does not create interpersonal difficulties (Herold, 1978). The ends and means of production are clear, so team members need not interact in novel ways to determine how to proceed (Herold, 1978). Teams are thus able to engage primarily in production tasks rather than in planning, deciding, and negotiating. Because they seldom need to interact in novel ways to alter their work approaches, the performance of teams engaged primarily in behavioral tasks is relatively unaffected by social interactions and team processes.

In contrast, production teams with ends and means that are not clearly defined spend a great deal of time on planning and deciding (Goodman, 1986; Herold, 1978). Lack of agreement concerning production means and ends requires the teams to engage in idea generation, decision making, and negotiating (Goodman, 1986). Interaction strongly influences and determines a team's product (Herold, 1978). Intrateam processes are therefore strongly related to performance when teams engage primarily in conceptual tasks. Hence,

Hypothesis 1. Relationships between intrateam processes and team performance are moderated by task differences in such a way that linear process-performance relationships are stronger for conceptual tasks than for behavioral tasks.

Interdependence

Construct definition. Interdependence is defined as the extent to which team members cooperate and work interactively to complete tasks. High interdependence occurs when team members interact cooperatively and depend on each other for information, materials, and reciprocal inputs (Campion et al., 1993; Emery & Trist, 1969).

Research related to interdependence has developed from two perspectives. In one perspective, flowing from organizational theory (e.g., Thompson, 1967; Van de Ven & Ferry, 1980), interdependence is conceived of as a product of technological requirements rather than as a structural feature that can be manipulated. The other perspective, which has been labeled "cooperation requirements," comes from social psychology (e.g., Shaw, 1973). In this perspective, group-level goals and feedback—areas not dependent on technology—are assumed to affect interdependence (Saavedra et al., 1993). Because several studies (Campion et al., 1996; Shea & Guzzo, 1987; Wageman, 1995) have shown that teams with similar technologies vary widely in their amount of interdependence, we adopted the social psychology conceptualization of interdependence as a feature of teams that can be controlled.

Hypothesized relationships. Gladstein (1984) examined, but found no effect for, interdependence as a moderator of the process-performance relationship. Rather than a moderator effect, the model shown in Figure 1 hypothesizes an interdependence-performance relationship that is mediated by process and moderated by task type. This conceptualization is consistent with studies showing a curvilinear relationship between interdependence and performance. For instance, Wageman (1995) found that work groups operating either primarily as individuals or cooperatively with substantial interdependence had higher performance than groups with moderate interdependence. Saavedra and colleagues (1993) also found that moderately interdependent teams received the lowest ratings for both quality and quantity of outputs. We predicted a similar ∪-shaped relationship between interdependence and team performance. However, in order to test the model presented in Figure 1, we developed hypotheses related both to mediation by process variables and to moderation by task differences.

The relationship between interdependence and process we predict is similar to the interdependence-performance relationship; interdependence is predicted to relate curvilinearly with such aspects of process as communication, conflict, shirking, and flexibility. When interdependence is very low, team members operate as individuals, and their work can be structured around the individual-level work design principles outlined by Hackman and Oldham (1980). Little interaction is required, and team members pursue their personal interests with little need for communication and low potential for conflict (Neck, Stewart, & Manz, 1996). This situation facilitates member flexibility because learning a distinct set of tasks for an individual position is much easier than developing the extensive social relationships that are necessary to coordinate interdependent roles (Manz & Newstrom, 1990). Individual contributions are also highly salient and easily identifiable, reducing the likelihood of team member shirking (Hardy & Latane, 1986; Kidwell & Bennett, 1993).

Intrateam processes are similarly expected to be synergistic for teams at the high end of the interdependence continuum. However, in this case the relationship is facilitated by group rather than individual principles of work structure. The intense interaction created by high

interdependence results in a crystallization of group norms, meaning that team members develop a high level of agreement concerning desirable and undesirable behavior (Hackman, 1992). Teams with crystallized norms tend to experience little conflict because team member behavior is guided by shared expectations rather than by individual desires (Jackson, 1975). The interactive nature of the work process itself also encourages an open flow of communication (Thompson, 1967). Team member flexibility is enhanced because boundaries between individual job assignments are de-emphasized and members learn new skills from observing and interacting closely with their coworkers (Trist, 1981). Moreover, interaction develops a cohesive team identity that creates esprit de corps and motivates team members by encouraging them to subjugate personal interests for the interests of the team as a whole (Mudrack, 1989; Murnighan & Conlon, 1991).

In contrast to teams with high and low interdependence, teams with moderate interdependence are predicted to experience process difficulties. Moderately interdependent teams have a need for intermittent dialogue between team members, but team member interactions are not consistent and intense enough to develop open communication channels. An increased dependence on others requires the sacrifice of individual autonomy and interest, which can result in conflict when interdependence is not high enough to assure the crystallization of group norms (Jackson, 1975). Flexibility is expected to decrease because it becomes critical for workers to develop the extensive social relationships that are necessary for learning how to coordinate their work with the tasks performed by their teammates (Manz & Newstrom, 1990); yet interaction is not extensive enough for members to actually develop strong ties and thereby learn informally from one another. Moderate interdependence also diffuses responsibility but fails to develop cohesion and team identity, factors that in combination suggest an increased likelihood that team members will shirk (Mudrack, 1989).

Moderate interdependence thus fails to optimize work structure from either an individual or a group perspective, suggesting that interdependence will exhibit a ∪-shaped relationship with team process. As shown in Figure 1, the curvilinear interdependence-process relationship will combine with the moderated process-performance relationship to explain the interdependence-performance relationship. Thus,

Hypothesis 2. Interdependence within work teams is curvilinearly associated with intrateam processes in such a way that low and high, but not moderate, levels of interdependence correspond with synergistic processes.

Hypothesis 3. Interdependence within work teams is curvilinearly associated with performance for teams engaged primarily in conceptual tasks in such a way that low and high levels of interdependence correspond with high team perfor-

mance and moderate levels of interdependence correspond with low team performance.

Hypothesis 4. The ∪-shaped relationship between interdependence and performance is significantly weaker for teams engaged primarily in behavioral rather than conceptual tasks.

Hypothesis 5. Intrateam processes mediate the relationship between interdependence and team performance.

Team Self-Leadership

Construct definition. Building on previous work (e.g., Hackman, 1986; Manz, 1992; Walton & Hackman, 1986), we define team self-leadership as the extent to which teams have the freedom and authority to lead themselves independent of external supervision. Teams with high self-leadership decide how tasks should be carried out, as well as what should be done and why. They are given responsibility and authority for their behavior, and team members rather than supervisors make decisions and organize work processes.

Team self-leadership does not, however, imply the absence of a leader. A self-leading team can have a leader who encourages the team to lead itself (Manz & Sims, 1987). Team self-leadership is not compromised by the leader unless he or she seeks to impose hierarchical control rather than facilitate the team's self-managing capacity (Stewart & Manz, 1995).

Hypothesized relationships. Although there has been some empirical work on interdependence, very little empirical research has examined the relationship between team self-leadership and performance. However, as shown in Figure 1, team self-leadership is expected to influence team processes. Higher levels of team self-leadership diminish the prominence of a central leader, which

encourages the development of a decentralized communication network (Shaw, 1964). Although decentralized networks can sometimes result in a dysfunctional focus on information that is already shared among team members (Larson, Christensen, Abbott, & Franz, 1996), most extant evidence supports the idea that decentralization encourages open communication within groups (Glanzer & Glaser, 1961; McGrath, 1984). Team self-leadership can also help teams effectively manage conflict, as the presence of an external leader can sometimes inhibit trust between team members (Eisenstat, 1990) and discourage the development of long-term mechanisms for resolving member conflict (Manz & Sims, 1987).

Greater team self-leadership is also expected to correspond with decreased shirking because employees have greater commitment and feelings of personal ownership (Pearce & Ravlin, 1987). Shirking decreases as team members engage in mutual monitoring to collectively control actions (Barker, 1993). Moreover, higher levels of team self-leadership should result in increased member flexibility, as variation in behavior within and among teams is expected to increase when control is decentralized (Manz & Stewart, 1997). Thus, team autonomy increases member flexibility by allowing workers to learn from one another and adjust their efforts to obtain the inputs most needed at any particular time (Trist, 1981).

Team self-leadership should thus correspond linearly with synergistic team processes. As shown in Figure 1, the linear team self-leadership relationship will combine with the moderated process-performance relationship to explain the relationship between team self-leadership and performance. Hence,

Hypothesis 6. Higher levels of team self-leadership exhibit a positive, linear relationship with synergistic intrateam processes.

TABLE 1
Means, Standard Deviations, and Pearson Correlations[a]

Variable	Mean	s.d.	1	2	3	4	5	6	7	8	9
1. Task interdependence	3.56	0.41									
2. Team self-leadership	3.43	0.33	−.27								
3. Task type	0.50	0.17	.53**	−.34*							
4. Communication	3.39	0.29	−.12	−.17	.18						
5. Conflict	2.84	0.46	.05	.02	−.10	−.85**					
6. Shirking	3.00	0.49	.04	−.02	−.04	−.58**	.74**				
7. Flexibility	3.68	0.48	.55**	−.06	.54**	.30*	−.37*	−.34*			
8. Team size	13.91	7.65	.29	−.12	.36*	−.10	.14	.22	.09		
9. Team tenure	3.47	1.33	−.07	−.30*	.24	.11	−.01	.13	.10	.16	
10. Supervisor ratings	3.50	0.42	.01	−.12	.09	.36*	−.48**	−.44*	.34*	−.10	.20

[a] $N = 45$ (teams).

* $p < .05$

** $p < .01$

Hypothesis 7. Higher levels of team self-leadership exhibit a positive, linear relationship with higher levels of team performance for teams engaged primarily in conceptual tasks.

Hypothesis 8. The positive, linear relationship between team self-leadership and team performance is significantly weaker for teams engaged primarily in behavioral rather than conceptual tasks.

Hypothesis 9. Intrateam processes mediate the relationship between team self-leadership and team performance.

METHODS

Research Sample

Our research sample consisted of employees working in teams at three different manufacturing plants. We collected data from 636 participants working in 47 teams. However, outlier analyses suggested that measures for two of the teams consistently exerted an undue amount of influence on statistical tests.[1] We thus eliminated data from these two teams, leaving a sample of 626 individuals in 45 teams. Age, gender, and tenure within firms and teams were fairly consistent. The average age of team members was 42 years; 56 percent were women, 98 percent were Caucasian, and the median level of education was high school completion (the range was from ninth grade to completion of graduate school). Average tenure within the studied organizations was almost 15 years, but teams were a relatively new innovation in these plants, and tenure within the teams averaged only 3.47 years (s.d. = 1.32, range = 1.5–5.5 years). Average team size was 14 members (s.d. = 7.65; range = 3–34).

Measures

Team performance. We assessed team performance via supervisor ratings. We adopted a common instrument measuring eight dimensions of performance, and supervisors rated each team as a unit. Consistent with appraisal research, assessments of both team outcomes and team behaviors were included (Cardy & Dobbins, 1994). The dimensions were knowledge of tasks, quality of work, quantity of work, initiative, interpersonal skills, planning and allocation, commitment to the team, and overall performance. We measured each dimension with

---

[1] Because we were concerned that the outliers might have an inordinate effect on the regression results, we assessed their influence using both the DFFITS measure and Cook's distance measure (Neter, Wasserman, & Kutner, 1989). Evaluation of these measures revealed two cases that had larger than acceptable effects on the regression equations. One team reported that they did not engage in any behavioral tasks. The other team reported a very low level of interdependence and a relatively high level of behavioral tasks. Elimination of both cases actually reduced the magnitude of the moderation effect for task type. In order to provide conservative tests, we thus eliminated data related to both teams from all analyses.

a single item using a five-point behavior-anchored scale (1 = somewhat below requirements, 5 = consistently exceeds requirements). Because factor analysis revealed a single factor underlying both the behavioral and the outcome performance measures, we combined responses to the eight items into a single score representing overall team performance. The coefficient alpha for the eight-item scale was .83.

Interdependence. We measured interdependence with a seven-item scale adapted from Kiggundu's (1983) interdependence scale. Items applicable to teams were adopted, and the scale focuses on the extent to which tasks performed by members are interrelated within a team. Items include (1) "Other members of my team depend on my performance to do their work" and (2) "How other team members do their work has an impact on my performance." The coefficient alpha of the scale was .74. However, we needed to obtain agreement among raters to aggregate the individual responses into a team-level construct.

James (1982) recommended two intraclass correlations (ICCs) for assessing agreement of team members. ICC(1) indicates the extent of agreement among ratings from members of the same team. James (1982) conducted a survey of published articles and reported a range of .00 to .50 with a median of .12 for ICC(1). ICC(2) indicates whether teams can be differentiated on the variables of interest. ICC(2) is expected to exceed the .70 reliability convention (James, 1982). For our interdependence measure, the value of ICC(1) was .21, and the value of ICC(2) was .73. These values suggest acceptable agreement and support aggregation. In order to properly test for curvilinear relationships, we also performed Z-score transformations on the interdependence scores (Aiken & West, 1991).

Team self-leadership. We assessed team self-leadership by asking team members to report whether an external supervisor or the team itself performed activities representing leadership. We reviewed lists of tasks that self-leading teams assume from traditional supervisors (i.e., Manz, 1992; Manz & Sims, 1993) and created a catalog of 20 items. Each item identified a task (for instance, conducting meetings, changing the work process, determining overall business strategy) and asked team members to respond to a forced-choice scale that indicated who was responsible for completing that task. Responses depicting sole managerial responsibility received a value of 1, responses indicating responsibility shared between a supervisor and a team, a 3, and responses suggesting total team responsibility, a 5. The mean score for the 20 items was our measurement, with higher scores representing greater team self-leadership. The ICC(1) for self-leadership was .28, and the ICC(2) was .80, indicating acceptable agreement.

Task type. We asked team members to indicate the percentage of time their teams spent working on each of the following task types taken from McGrath (1984): generating ideas and plans, choosing between alternatives, negotiating conflicts, and executing work. We used the percentage allocated to the executing work category as an indicator of task type. Higher values represent an increased amount of time for behavioral tasks. Analyses justified aggregation for task type, as the ICC(1) was .20 and the ICC(2) was .72.

Intrateam process. Following the definitions provided by Hackman (1987), we chose communication and conflict as indicators of social process, and shirking and flexibility as indicators of task-related process. We measured communication with a ten-item openness-to-communication scale originally developed by O'Reilly and Roberts (1976). The scale includes items like "It is easy to talk openly to all members of this group." Higher scores represented more open communication. The coefficient alpha for this scale was .87, the ICC(1) was .24, and the ICC(2) was .75.

We measured conflict with Rahim's (1983) eight-item measure of intragroup conflict. Example items are (1) "There is (not) harmony within my group and (2) "There are clashes between subgroups within my group." Higher values represent greater conflict. The coefficient alpha was .83, the ICC(1) was .21, and the ICC(2) was .71.

We assessed shirking with three workload-sharing items from Campion and colleagues (1993). Examples of reverse-coded items are (1) "Everyone on my team does their fair share of the work" and (2) "No one in my team depends on other team members to do the work for them." Higher values represent greater individual shirking within a team. The coefficient alpha was .82, the ICC(1) was .23, and the ICC(2) was .74.

We assessed the flexibility of team member inputs with the three-item member flexibility scale developed by Campion and colleagues (1993). Examples of items are (1) "Most members of my team know each other's jobs" and (2) "It is easy for the members of my team to fill in for one another." Higher scores represent greater team member flexibility of inputs. The coefficient alpha was .69, the ICC(1) was .27, and the ICC(2) was .79.

RESULTS

Correlation and Moderation Analyses

Table 1 provides descriptive statistics and zero-order correlation coefficients for all variables. The extent to which teams engaged in behavioral tasks correlated positively with interdependence ($r = .53$, $p < .01$) and negatively with team self-leadership (r = −.34, $p < .05$). Teams with longer tenure reported less self-leadership ($r = −.30$, $p < .05$). As expected, synergistic intrateam process variables were positively correlated with performance ($r = .36$, $p < .05$, for communication; $r = .34$, $p < .05$, for member flexibility), and the relationships between harmful processes and performance were negative ($r = −.48$, p

<.01, for conflict; $r = −.44$, $p < .05$, for shirking). The process measures were all significantly interrelated (absolute $r = .30$–.85, $p < .05$). Team size, tenure, and a dummy variable representing the firms were also explored as control variables. However, the inclusion of these controls did not alter the results of any statistical tests, and because our sample was relatively small, the following tables report statistical tests that do not include team size, team tenure, and organization source as control variables.

Hypothesis 1 predicts a moderating effect for task type. We tested Hypothesis 1 separately for each of the four process variables using hierarchical regression analysis. Moderation would be supported by a significant change in the multiple squared correlation coefficient (R^2) when an interaction between a process variable and a task type is included. As shown in Table 2, moderation was not supported for communication ($\Delta R^2 = .07$, n.s.) or flexibility ($\Delta R^2 = .02$, n.s.); moderation was supported for conflict ($\Delta R^2 = .11$, $p < .05$) and shirking ($\Delta R^2 = .28$, p < .05). The negative relationship with performance for both conflict and shirking was stronger for conceptual tasks than for behavioral tasks, as predicted.

Relationships with Interdependence

Table 3 reports a series of hierarchical models used to test Hypotheses 2 through 5. In each regression, interdependence was entered in step 1, and interdependence squared was entered in step 2. A significant change in R^2 in step 2 indicates a curvilinear relationship. Hypothesis 2 predicts a ∩-shaped relationship between interdependence and intrateam process. This prediction is

TABLE 2
Results of Hierarchical Regression Analyses Testing for Interactions Affecting Performance[a]

Step	Independent Variable	Total R^2	ΔR^2
1	Team communication	.13*	.13*
2	Task type	.13	.00
3	Team communication × task type	.20*	.07
1	Team conflict	.23**	.23**
2	Task type	.23**	.00
3	Team conflict × task type	.34**	.11*
1	Team member shirking	.19**	.19**
2	Task type	.19*	.00
3	Team member shirking × task type	.47**	.28**
1	Team member flexibility of inputs	.12*	.12*
2	Task type	.13	.01
3	Team member flexibility of inputs × task type	.15	.02

[a]$N = 45$ (teams).
* $p < .05$
** $p < .01$

TABLE 3
Results of Hierarchical Regression Analyses Testing Hypotheses 2–5[a]

Step	Independent Variable	Communication		Conflict		Shirking		Flexibility		Performance	
		Total R^2	ΔR^2	Total R^2	ΔR^2	Total R^2	ΔR^2	Total R^2	ΔR^2	Total R^2	ΔR^2
1	Interdependence	.01	.01	.00	.00	.00	.00	.30**	.30**	.00	.00
2	Interdependence squared	.36**	.35**	.24**	.24**	.05	.05	.35**	.05	.07	.07
3	Task type	.40**	.04	.25**	.01	.05	.00	.42**	.07*	.07	.00
4	Interdependence by task type	.42**	.02	.30**	.05	.13	.08	.43**	.01	.07	.00
5	Interdependence squared × task type	.42**	.00	.30*	.00	.14	.01	.43**	.00	.22	.15**

[a]$N = 45$ (teams).
*$p > .05$
**$p > .01$

supported for communication ($\Delta R^2 = .35$, $p < .01$) and conflict ($\Delta R^2 = .24$, $p < .01$), but not for shirking ($\Delta R^2 = .05$, n.s.) or flexibility ($\Delta R^2 = .05$, n.s.). Consistent with expectations, high and low levels of interdependence are associated with perceptions of more open communication and decreased conflict.

Hypothesis 3 predicts a U-shaped relationship between interdependence and performance for teams primarily engaged in conceptual tasks. Hypothesis 4 predicts that this relationship will be significantly weaker for teams primarily engaged in behavioral tasks. The results in Table 3 for step 5 reveal that task type significantly moderates the relationship between interdependence and performance ($\Delta R^2 = .15$, $p < .01$). As shown in Figure 2, Hypothesis 3 is supported, as teams primarily engaged in conceptual tasks had their highest performance with either low or high levels of interdependence. Counter to Hypothesis 4, the regression plot (Figure 2) also shows that for teams engaged primarily in behavioral tasks, in-

terdependence and performance actually exhibit an inverse curvilinear (∩-shaped) relationship, with the highest level of performance being associated with moderate interdependence.

Hypothesis 5 predicts that intrateam processes will mediate the relationship between interdependence and team performance. Because the potential mediator effect might combine with a moderator effect, an appropriate method of testing for mediation was to create a median split on the moderator variable and to then independently assess mediation in two subsamples, one subsample reporting relatively more conceptual tasks, and the other reporting more behavioral tasks.

The median value for task type, .45, served as the splitting point for the two categories. One category of teams—labeled conceptual—consisted of all teams reporting that they spent less than 44 percent of their time on behavioral tasks ($\bar{X} = 36\%$). The other category of teams—labeled behavioral—consisted of teams each re-

FIGURE 2
Regression Plot for Relationships between Interdependence and Performance[a]

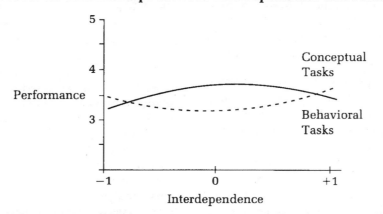

[a] As an aid to interpretation of the interaction effect, the continuous task-type variable is bifurcated at the median, and the continuous interdependence variable is plotted at −1, 0, and +1 standard deviations from the mean (Cohen & Cohen, 1983).

TABLE 4
Results of Hierarchical Regression Analyses Testing Hypotheses 6-9

Independent Variable	Communication		Conflict		Shirking		Flexibility		Performance	
	Total R^2	ΔR^2	Total R^2	ΔR^2	Total R^2	ΔR^2	Total R^2	ΔR^2	Total R^2	ΔR^2
Team self-leadership	.03	.03	.00	.00	.00	.00	.00	.00	.01	.01
Task type	.05	.02	.01	.01	.00	.00	.31	.31**	.01	.00
Team self-leadership × task type	.05	.00	.01	.00	.05	.05	.32	.01	.20*	.19**

ᵃN=45 (teams).

*$p < .05$

**$p < 0.1$

porting spending more than 48 percent of their time on behavioral tasks ($\bar{X}$ = 63%). We conducted separate regression analyses to further assess mediation in each task type.

We compared a model regressing performance on interdependence and interdependence squared with a similar model in which we first controlled for the effects of intrateam processes (Hollenbeck, Ilgen, LePine, Colquitt, & Hedlund, 1998). In the conceptual task subsample, the increase in R^2 of .21 ($p < .05$) for a curvilinear effect attenuated to an increase in R^2 of .03 (n.s.) when the effect of process was controlled. In the behavioral task subsample, the increase in R^2 of .22 ($p < .05$) attenuates to an increase in R^2 of .10 (n.s.) in the controlled model. Process thus mediates 86 percent of the effect of interdependence on performance for teams engaged in conceptual tasks and 55 percent of the effect for teams engaged in behavioral tasks. Hypothesis 5, predicting process mediation of the interdependence-performance relationship, is thus supported strongly for teams engaged in conceptual tasks and moderately for teams engaged in behavioral tasks.

Relationships with Team Self-Leadership

Table 4 reports a series of hierarchical regression models used to test Hypotheses 6 through 9. In each model, step 1 regresses the dependent variables on team self-leadership. Step 2 includes task type as an additional independent variable and provides a comparison model for hierarchically assessing a moderator effect. Step 3 includes the cross-product term as a test for moderation. Hypothesis 6, predicting linear relationships between team self-leadership and processes, was not supported, as a step 1 relationship was not detected between team self-leadership and any of the process measures.

As shown in Table 4, the relationship between team self-leadership and performance is moderated by task type (ΔR^2 = .19, $p < .01$). Hypothesis 7 is supported, as increased team self-leadership is associated with higher performance for teams engaged primarily in conceptual

tasks. However, counter to Hypothesis 8, the relationship between team self-leadership and performance goes beyond mere attenuation and actually becomes negative for teams engaged primarily in behavioral tasks.

Hypothesis 9, predicting that intrateam processes would mediate the relationship between team self-leadership and team performance, was not supported, as the tests of Hypothesis 6 failed to link team self-leadership and intrateam processes. Further tests related to mediation for team self-leadership were therefore not justified (Baron & Kenny, 1986).

DISCUSSION

Relatively little is known about whether there is an optimal structure for work teams. We hypothesized that two structural characteristics, interdependence and team self-leadership, would relate to team performance. We expected the influence of these two elements of a team's social system to be contingent on its technical system, specifically, the type of tasks that it performs. Our results illustrate that structural characteristics related to the allocation of tasks, responsibilities, and authority do indeed influence team performance. Many of our hypotheses were supported, illustrating that the optimal amount of interdependence and team self-leadership varies with the amount of time a team spends performing behavioral production tasks or conceptual tasks like planning, deciding, and negotiating.

For teams engaged primarily in conceptual tasks, our expectation of a ∪-shaped interdependence-performance relationship was confirmed. This result replicates the findings reported by Wageman (1995) and Saavedra and his coauthors (1993). However, our findings extend previous work by suggesting that this relationship may only exist for teams primarily engaged in conceptual tasks. Furthermore, the mediation focus of our study allows substantial insight into how interdependence is related to team performance when teams engage in conceptual tasks. In particular, we found that intrateam processes mediated the relationship between interdependence and performance in these teams. Very high or low levels of interdependence were related to both open communication and less conflict among team members. These socioemotional processes were in turn associated with higher team performance. The extremes of interdependence thus seem to be alternative paths to a desirable end when teams perform work that has a conceptual focus.

Consistent with much of the literature related to team autonomy, greater team self-leadership was also found to correspond with higher performance for teams primarily engaged in conceptual tasks. However, our results did not provide support for process variables as mediators of the relationship between team self-leadership and performance. This finding suggests that the input-process-output model may be in need of revision. Of particular note are the revisions suggested by Ancona and colleagues (Ancona, 1990; Ancona & Caldwell, 1992), who argued for the inclusion of factors related to external team relationships. Building on this work, in future studies researchers should examine whether structural factors like team self-leadership affect performance on some tasks through relationships with other teams and organizations rather than through intrateam relationships.

We predicted that relationships between team structures and performance would attenuate for teams primarily engaged in behavioral tasks rather than conceptual tasks, but our results suggest more than mere attenuation. Team designs that incorporated moderate levels of interdependence and greater external leadership were actually found to be more effective when teams were engaged in behavioral tasks, suggesting that relationships between structure and performance are the inverse of those for teams primarily engaged in conceptual tasks. Unfortunately, the intrateam process measures included in this study were generally unrelated to performance for teams performing these tasks, thereby providing little insight into the mechanisms that might explain why the direction of the relationships reversed. In future studies, other variables, such as external relationships and individual contributions, should be examined as potential mediators.

Finally, although the results demonstrate that type of task is an important moderator, it is instructive to look at the zero-order correlations between the two team structure characteristics and the measures of task type. These correlations suggest that teams with behavioral tasks tend to have greater interdependence. Perhaps this is because interdependence is easier to create when a task is routine and behavioral. However, our analyses suggest that teams primarily performing conceptual tasks are the very ones that can benefit most from relatively high levels of interdependence. The zero-order correlations also suggest that teams performing more conceptual tasks have more self-leadership, and our analyses suggest this greater self-leadership is functional.

A few limitations of this study should be noted. First, the data are correlational in nature. Future studies that directly manipulate interdependence and self-leadership

are needed to clearly provide evidence of causal relationships. The intrateam process variables were also collected from team members rather than supervisors, meaning that a common response bias may explain their relationships with the team structure characteristics. However, because many of these relationships were curvilinear and moderated by task type, as hypothesized, it is difficult to simply explain them as due to a common data source.

Another limitation is that the data are cross-sectional rather than longitudinal. Teams with high and low self-leadership may experience different development processes. Wellins, Byham, and Wilson (1991) argued that self-leading teams take substantial time to develop and mature. The magnitude and direction of the zero-order correlation between team tenure and team self-leadership suggests the possibility that some teams high on self-leadership did not have the opportunity to fully develop processes and thereby maximize performance. Nevertheless, average tenure on the teams was nearly three and a half years, decreasing the likelihood that short tenure explains our negative finding, but at the same time making it unclear whether our findings generalize to newly formed work teams.

An additional limitation is the relatively small sample. Even though our findings are based on data provided by 626 individuals, the team level of analysis required comparisons based on the sample of 45 teams. Although this sample size is similar to those in many other team-level studies, statistical power is limited. Yet, the relatively strong effects, particularly the interactive effects, that we observed across dependent variables seem to provide evidence for robust relationships between team structure, team processes, type of task, and team performance. The absolute size of the effects also suggests that gaining insight into team structure is critical for understanding work teams.

With these limitations taken into account, the data do have important implications for practice, theory, and research. Practically, the results have important implications for determining optimal methods of work team design. Organizations using teams to complete conceptual tasks can benefit from either very high or very low levels of interdependence, as well as greater self-leadership. In contrast, when work tasks are primarily behavioral in nature, moderate amounts of interdependence and greater external leadership seem best.

From a theoretical perspective, we built on organization-level findings and showed that differences in how responsibilities are apportioned and coordinated correspond to variance in performance at the team level. Consistent with sociotechnical systems theory, the effect of these social elements is moderated by technical demands (tasks). Our results also support the efficacy of the input-process-output model for explaining some aspects of teams. In particular, the model effectively explains relationships between interdependence and performance for teams primarily engaged in conceptual tasks. However, the input-process-output model was less effective for explaining performance differences on behavioral tasks and relationships with team self-leadership. This finding adds to previous acknowledgments that the input-process-output model may be incomplete (Ancona, 1990; Cohen & Bailey, 1997; Hackman, 1987) and suggests that alternative models need to be developed and empirically tested.

In view of our findings, researchers should acknowledge that a single optimal structure for work teams does not exist. It is important for researchers to explore the boundary conditions of their models, particularly in relation to task differences. As organizations continue to design work around teams, future studies that account for task differences and systematically examine the mechanisms through which structural characteristics affect teams will become increasingly beneficial. The pursuit and application of such research will help organizations realize the full potential of using teams to accomplish work.

REFERENCES

Aiken, L. S., & West, S. G. 1991. *Multiple regression: Testing and interpreting interactions.* Newbury Park, CA: Sage.

Ancona, D. G. 1990. Outward bound: Strategies for team survival in the organization. *Academy of Management Journal,* 33: 334–365.

Ancona, D. G., & Caldwell, D. F. 1992. Bridging the boundary: External activity and performance in organizational teams. *Administrative Science Quarterly,* 37: 634–665.

Argote, L., & McGrath, J. E. 1993. Group processes in organizations: Continuity and change. In C. L. Cooper & I. T. Robertson (Eds.), *International review of industrial and organizational psychology,* vol. 8: 333–389. New York: Wiley.

Bales, R. F. 1950. *Interaction process analysis: A method for the study of small groups.* Reading, MA: Addison-Wesley.

Banker, R. D., Field, J. M., Schroeder, R. G., & Sinha, K. K. 1996. Impact of work teams on manufacturing performance: A longitudinal field study. *Academy of Management Journal,* 39: 867–890.

Barker, J. R. 1993. Tightening the iron cage: Concertive control in self-managing teams. *Administrative Science Quarterly,* 38: 408–437.

Baron, R. M., & Kenny, D. A. 1986. The moderator-mediator variable distinction in social psychological research: Conceptual, strategic, and statistical considerations. *Journal of Personality and Social Psychology,* 6: 1173–1182.

Barry, B., & Stewart, G. L. 1997. Composition, process, and performance in self-managed groups: The role of personality. *Journal of Applied Psychology,* 82: 62–78.

Campion, M. A., Medsker, G. J., & Higgs, A. C. 1993. Relations between work group characteristics and effectiveness: Implications for designing effective work groups. *Personnel Psychology,* 46: 823–850.

Campion, M. A., Papper, E. M., & Medsker, G. J. 1996. Relations between work team characteristics and effectiveness: A replication and extension. *Personnel Psychology,* 49: 429–452.

Cardy, R. L., & Dobbins, G. H. 1994. *Performance appraisal: Alternative perspectives.* Cincinnati: Southwest.

Cohen, J., & Cohen, P. 1983. *Applied multiple regression/ correlation analysis for the behavioral sciences* (2nd ed.). Hillsdale, NJ: Erlbaum.

Cohen, S. C., & Bailey, D. E. 1997. What makes teams work? Group effectiveness research from the shop floor to the executive suite. *Journal of Management,* 23: 239–290.

Cohen, S. G., & Ledford, G. E. 1994. The effectiveness of self-managing teams: A quasi-experiment. *Human Relations,* 47: 13–43.

Cummings, T. 1978. Self-regulated work groups: A socio-technical synthesis. *Academy of Management Review,* 3: 625–634.

Eisenstat, R. A. 1990. Fairfield coordinating group. In J. R. Hackman (Ed.), *Groups that work (and those that don't: Creating conditions for effective teamwork.* San Francisco: Jossey-Bass.

Emery, F. L., & Trist, E. L. 1969. Socio-technical systems. In F. E. Emery (Ed.), *Systems thinking:* 281–296. London: Penguin.

Gladstein, D. L. 1984. Groups in context: A model of task group effectiveness. *Administrative Science Quarterly,* 29: 499–517.

Glanzer, M., & Glaser, R. Techniques for the study of group structure and behavior: Empirical studies of the effects of structure in small groups. *Psychological Bulletin,* 58: 1–27.

Goodman, P. S. 1986. Impact of task and technology on group performance. In P. S. Goodman (Ed.), *Designing effective workgroups:* 120–167. San Francisco: Jossey-Bass.

Goodman, P. S., Ravlin, E., & Argote, L. 1986. Current thinking about groups: Setting the stage for new ideas. In P. S. Goodman (Ed.), *Designing effective work groups:* 1–33. San Francisco: Jossey-Bass.

Greenberg, J., & Baron, R. A. 1997. *Behavior in organizations* (6th ed.). Upper Saddle River, NJ: Prentice-Hall.

Guzzo, R. A., & Shea, G. P. 1992. Group performance and intergroup relations in organizations. In M. D. Dunnette & L. M. Hough (Eds.), *Handbook of industrial and organizational psychology:* 269–313. Palo Alto, CA: Consulting Psychologists Press.

Hackman, J. R. 1986. The psychology of self-management in organizations. In M. S. Pallak & R. O. Perloff (Eds.), *Psychology and work: Productivity, change, and employment:* 85–136. Washington, DC: American Psychological Association.

Hackman, J. R. 1987. The design of work teams. In J. W. Lorsch (Ed.), *Handbook of organizational behavior:* 315–342. Englewood Cliffs, NJ: Prentice-Hall.

Hackman, J. R. 1992. Group influences on individuals in organizations. In M. D. Dunnette & L. M. Hough (Eds.), *Handbook of industrial and organizational psychology,* vol. 3: 199–268. Palo Alto, CA: Consulting Psychologists Press.

Hackman, J. R., & Oldham, G. R. 1980. *Work redesign.* Reading, MA: Addison-Wesley.

Hardy, C., & Latane, B. 1986. Social loafing on a cheering task. *Social Science,* 71(2–3): 165–172.

Herold, D. M. 1978. Improving the performance effectiveness of groups through a task-contingency selection of intervention strategies. *Academy of Management Review,* 3: 315–325.

Hollenbeck, J. R., Ilgen, D. R., LePine, J. A., Colquitt, J. A., & Hedlund, J. 1998. Extending the multilevel theory of team decision making: Effects of feedback and experience in hierarchical teams. *Academy of Management Journal,* 41: 269–282.

Jackson, J. 1975, Normative power and conflict potential. *Sociological Methods and Research,* 4: 237–263.

James, L. R. 1982. Aggregation bias in estimates of perceptual agreement. *Journal of Applied Psychology,* 67: 219–229.

Jones, C. R. 1995. *Organizational theory.* Reading, MA: Addison-Wesley.

Kidwell, R. E., & Bennett, N. 1993. Employee propensity to withhold effort: A conceptual model to intersect three avenues of research. *Academy of Management Review,* 18: 429–456.

Kiggundu, M. N. 1983. Task interdependence and job design: Test of a theory. *Organizational Behavior and Human Performance,* 31: 145–172.

Larson, J. R., Jr., Christensen, C., Abbott, A. S., & Franz, T. M. 1996. Diagnosing groups: Charting the flow of information in medical decision-making teams. *Journal of Personality and Social Psychology,* 71: 315–330.

Lawler, E. E., III, Mohrman, S. A., & Ledford, G. E., Jr. 1995. *Creating high performance organizations: Practices and results of employee involvement and total quality management in Fortune 1000 companies.* San Francisco: Jossey-Bass.

Manz, C. C. 1992. Self-leading work teams: Moving beyond self-management myths. *Human Relations,* 45: 1119–1140.

Manz, C. C., & Newstrom, J. 1990. Self-managing teams in a paper mill: Success factors, problems, and lessons learned. *International Human Resource Management Review,* 1: 43–60.

Manz, C. C., & Sims, H. P., Jr. 1987. Leading workers to lead themselves: The external leadership of self-managing work teams. *Administrative Science Quarterly,* 32: 106–128.

Manz, C. C., & Sims, H. P., Jr. 1993. *Business without bosses: How self-managing teams are building high-performing companies.* New York: Wiley.

Manz, C. C., & Stewart, C. L. 1997. Attaining flexible stability by integrating total quality management and socio-technical systems theory. *Organization Science*, 8: 59–70.

McGrath, J. E. 1964. *Social psychology: A brief introduction.* New York: Holt, Rinehart & Winston. McGrath, J. E. 1984. Group interaction and performance. Englewood Cliffs, NJ: Prentice-Hall.

Mudrack, P. E. 1989. Defining group cohesiveness: A legacy of confusion? *Small Group Behavior*, 20: 37–49.

Murnighan, J. K., & Conlon, D. E. 1991. The dynamics of intense work groups: A study of British string quartets. *Administrative Science Quarterly*, 36: 165–186.

Neck, C. P., Stewart, G. L., & Manz, C. C. 1996. Self-leaders within self-leading teams: Toward an optimal equilibrium. In M. M. Beyerlein, D. A. Johnson, & S. T. Beyerlein (Eds.), Advances in interdisciplinary studies of work teams: Team leadership, vol. 3: 43–66. Greenwich, CT: JAT Press.

Neter, J., Wasserman, W., & Kutner, M. H. 1989. *Applied linear regression models* (2nd ed.). Homewood, IL:Irwin.

O'Reilly, C. A., III, & Roberts, K. H. 1976. Relationships among components of credibility and communication behaviors in work units. *Journal of Applied Psychology*, 61: 99–102.

Pearce, J. A., & Ravlin, E. C. 1987. The design and activation of self-regulating work groups. *Human Relations*, 40: 751–782.

Pugh, D. S., & Hickson, D. J. 1997. *Writers on organizations* (5th ed.). Newbury Park, CA: Sage.

Pugh, D. S., Hickson, D. J., & Turner, C. 1968. Dimensions of organizational structure. *Administrative Science Quarterly*, 13: 289–315.

Rahim, M. A. 1983. Measurement of organizational conflict. *Journal of General Psychology*, 109: 189–199.

Saavedra, R., Earley, P. C., & Van Dyne, L. 1993. Complex interdependence in task-performing groups. *Journal of Applied Psychology*, 78: 61–72.

Shaw, M. E. 1964. Communication networks. In L. Berkowitz (Ed.), *Advances in experimental social psychology*, vol. 1: 111–147. New York: Academic Press.

Shaw, M. E. 1973. Scaling group tasks: A method for dimensional analysis. *JSAS catalog of selected documents in psychology*, 3(8): MS No. 294.

Shea, G. P., & Guzzo, R. A. 1987. Group effectiveness: What really matters? *Sloan Management Review*, 28(3): 25–31.

Steiner, I. D. 1972. *Group process and productivity.* New York: Academic Press.

Stewart, G. L., & Manz, C. C. 1995. Leadership for self-managing work teams: A typology and integrative model. *Human Relations*, 48: 747–770.

Stewart, G. L., Manz, C. C., & Sims, H. P., Jr. 1999. *Team work and group dynamics.* New York: Wiley.

Thompson, J. D. 1967. *Organizations in action.* New York: McGraw-Hill.

Trist, E. L. 1981. The sociotechnical perspective: The evolution of sociotechnical systems as a conceptual framework and as an action research program. In A. Van de Ven & W. F. Joyce (Eds.), *Perspectives on organization design and behavior:* 19–75. New York: Wiley.

Tushman, M. L. 1979. Work characteristics and subunit communication structure: A contingency analysis. *Administrative Science Quarterly*, 24: 82–97.

Van de Ven, A. H., & Ferry, D. L. 1980. *Measuring and assessing organizations.* New York: Wiley.

Wageman, R. 1995. Interdependence and group effectiveness. *Administrative Science Quarterly*, 40: 145–180.

Walton, R. E., & Hackman, J. R. 1986. Groups under contrasting management strategies. In P. 5. Goodman & Associates (Eds.), *Designing effective work groups:* 168–201. San Francisco: Jossey-Bass.

Wellins, R. S., Byham, W. C., & Wilson, J. M. 1991. *Empowered teams: Creating self-directed work groups that improve quality, productivity, and participation.* San Francisco: Jossey-Bass.

Greg L. Stewart is an associate professor of organizational behavior at the Marriott School of Management, Brigham Young University. He earned his Ph.D. in human resource management at Arizona State University. His research interests include the design, composition, and leadership of work teams, as well as the influence of personality traits on work performance.

Murray R. Barrick is a professor of management at the Eli Broad Graduate School of Management, Michigan State University. He earned his Ph.D. in industrial/organizational psychology from the University of Akron. His research interests include assessing the impact individual differences in behavior and personality have on job performance, methods of measuring and predicting such differences, and organizational processes associated with developing compensation systems.

Unit 4

Unit Selections

Key Points to Consider

❖ Does structure drive strategy of the organization, or does strategy drive structure? Defend your answer.

❖ What do you think is the future of jobs in the workplace? Do you think you could be doing a job in the future that does not even exist today? Explain.

❖ How do you think the function of human resources will be changing in the future?

❖ What do you think the importance is of organizational culture? Do you think that people in organizations can violate the organization's culture and be successful?

 **Links**   **www.dushkin.com/online/**

19. **Center for Organization and Human Resource Effectiveeess**
   http://socrates.berkeley.edu/~iir/cohre/cohre.html
20. **Global Business Network (GBN)**
   http://www.gbn.org
21. **Human Resources—Corporate Culture**
   http://www.auxillium.com/culture.htm

These sites are annotated on pages 4 and 5.

People live in groups, but for groups to be successful and to survive, they must have a purpose. When the earliest tribes first settled in fertile river valleys, one of the objectives of the tribe was to establish the city-state that would provide the members of the tribe with safety from marauding bands of less civilized people that threatened the city-state. This is a function that is still provided by nations in the form of armies and other defense functions. Religion then became the next large-scale organization and was often a function of the state, but religious leaders learned to distance themselves from the state. The key to the long-term success of religious beliefs was to not tie them too closely to one particular nation, empire, or king.

Christianity became greater than the Roman Empire, and while the empire contracted, Christianity expanded to the peoples who were bent on the destruction of the empire. This left the Church standing when the empire in the West fell, and, after things had become somewhat sorted-out, left the Church in the position of the supreme organization in Western Europe. Kings and emperors derived their authority from God, and the Church established the legitimacy of that authority as the representative of God on Earth.

Commercial organizations began to rise in power as the industrial revolution began in England in the 1700s. As the production of goods and services moved from craftsmen and cottages to machinery and factories, organizations were formed that could successfully produce those goods and services. As organizations grew larger, it became clear that work needed to be divided into various subfunctions. Specialization of labor was the obvious key to efficient production, with individuals performing tasks for which they were the best suited. Early management theorists such as Max Weber, who developed the theory of bureaucracy, still the basis for the organization of most corporations, and Henri Fayol, whose 14 points can still be seen in the writings of Peter Drucker, Tom Peters, and W. Edwards Deming, both addressed these issues of organization. It is still an issue that faces all corporations. Forward-looking organizations are in the process of looking "Beyond the Org Chart," and are trying to create different and more responsive organizations. The problem is that things are moving so fast that it is difficult to tell what that shape is likely to be. It could be "The Future That Has Already Happened" (see article 20), as Peter Drucker writes. Organizations may simply not have even a semipermanent shape, but rather be an ever-changing entity, growing, shrinking, and changing as conditions and circumstances demand.

What organizations cannot control is the environment. Conditions outside of the corporation are changing very rapidly and the factors that are driving this change are beyond the control of the organization. These factors include rapid technological change at an ever-increasing rate. There was more technological advancement in the twentieth century than in the rest of recorded history. Social changes are also moving at a faster rate than ever before. The role of women and minorities in the workplace has changed and the attitudes of individuals toward these groups must also change. There is no room for racial prejudice or gender bias. The market is simply too competitive for organizations to indulge in discrimination against any individual or group for reasons that have nothing to do with the task at hand. In some ways, the future has already happened in that certain trends in society have become clear and their impact can be predicted. Among them has been the change in the meaning of work and the workplace. The workplace is evolving. Perhaps it may be changing to the point where it will no longer be recognized.

This, of course, means changes in work design, the way people actually perform their jobs. Computers will offer the employee and the company greater flexibility in the design of the work day and how work is done. Companies and employees are bound to recognize the advantages of "Telework: The Advantages and Challenges of Working Here, There, Anywhere, and Anytime" (see article 22). The real question is how organizations are going to address and cope with these changes in the future. Given all of the various factors that have an impact on organizations and the workforce, how will organizations attract and keep their best employees, those who are absolutely necessary for these organizations to survive and prosper?

To keep people focused on the tasks before them it is necessary to guide and reward them appropriately. Performance appraisal, feedback, and rewards are the keys to keeping good people, and continuously pointing them in the right direction. In today's environment, the competition is always looking for the best possible people to have in their organization and some of those people are going to be in your organization. To keep the best employees, they must be allowed to perform and to be given the appropriate feedback and rewards.

The area most directly concerned with the development of the members of an organization is its human resources department. Human resources has come a long way in its development from an employee welfare office to personnel to human resources. For organizations to be successful they can no longer look upon their employees as a simple cost of doing business but as an asset. Organizations are demanding more from the human resources function than they have in the past and will demand even more in the future, as "What Do CEO's Want From HR?" discusses. The problem is that organizations, society, the economy, technology, indeed, virtually everything is becoming more and more complex. As organizations grow, they will begin doing business in different parts of the world, in different environments, with different people, whose experiences, beliefs, and expectations will be different from those on the domestic front.

Every organization has a system of beliefs, ideas, and goals that were developed by the history of the company, the experiences of the people in the organization, and the guidance and examples provided by senior management. The culture of an organization directly reflects the ideals of that firm and the people who work there. It has a direct impact on their commitment to the company and the ideals of that company. If the company values its employees, then that will be reflected in how those employees are treated; if it does not, the employees will soon learn the facts. An organization that wants to be successful and effective must engage in building the heart and soul of the organization because people who are committed to an organization are going to be more effective employees. To be truly effective, organizations must also recognize that they are not living in the 1950s anymore and that the emergence of women and minorities has brought a cultural change. The needs and demands of employees will be different and successful organizations will meet those needs and keep those employees that will be the key to the success of the organization in the future.

Organizational Systems

Structure-Driven Strategy and Virtual Organization Design

William B. Werther, Jr.

Successful organizations adapt to their environment. They do so by monitoring technological, competitive, legislative, or other changes that affect their strategies and competencies. In turn, needed organizational competencies are strengthened, acquired, or, if time permits, developed internally. The firm's competencies (present and prospective) are then blended into a revised strategy with which to exploit the opportunities or defend against the threats found in the environment. Finally, the firm's structure is redesigned, if needed, to better support its strategy. The theory is that form (structure) should follow function (strategy).

> **The bigger, the better? Hardly. Sometimes it's better even not to be "real."**

There is, however, a special case in which structure can drive strategy—or at least reconfigure it. This article explores that special case.

Structural Evolution: From Tradition to Special Case

Functional organization designs are the traditional case. Even today, most businesses and virtually all other organizations are structured functionally; similar activities or functions are grouped together for administrative purposes into departments. Evidence abounds, with most structures having accounting, finance, marketing, and production departments. When the external environment is stable, functional organizations tend to be efficient. Attention is focused on doing the functional activity better, often resulting in an inward view that asks how to improve the function's productivity or quality. But many functionally organized manufacturing industries in North America responded poorly to an environment made more turbulent by strong international competitors.

Back in the 1960s and 1970s, when Japanese products began flooding into the United States, "Japan Inc." targeted manufacturing industries such as automobiles, photocopiers, and televisions. These industries (among others) are of particular note because the U.S. firms were the worldwide productivity, quality, technological, and volume leaders. With variations, the Japanese strategy was fairly consistent: Enter the market at the low-end segment, with low-margin products that domestic manufacturers would not rigorously defend. As a result, the U.S. witnessed low-priced "rice-burners" (as Japanese cars were derisively referred to in Detroit), slow desktop copiers (initially aimed at home and professional offices in the days of centralized photocopier services), and portable 13-inch televisions (targeted for the kitchen or bedside).

Many manufacturers all but abandoned the low end to the Japanese, giving them a beachhead. Detroit continued to rely on middle-range cars for the bulk of its profits (Pontiac, Buick, and Oldsmobile, at General Motors, for example); Xerox pushed increasingly sophisticated, high-end machines that were beyond what the Japanese could produce or service; and RCA and Zenith stressed their ever larger and more profitable console models with the big 21- and 25-inch screens.

Reprinted from *Business Horizons*, March/April 1999, pp. 13-18. © 1999 by the Board of Trustees at Indiana University, Kelley School of Business.

Essentially, industry after industry in the U.S. went "upscale"–moving into "bigger," "better," and more sophisticated products that had higher profit margins, with only token efforts to counter the Japanese. Even so, the Japanese were able to establish brand and quality recognition, distribution, and service capabilities. Then the Japanese moved upscale in the 1980s with Lexus, color copiers, and 35-inch televisions.

A quarter of a century ago, U.S. firms in these industries were the domestic and world leaders in both sales volume and technology. Today the Japanese have the number one selling car in the U.S. (the Toyota Camry) and more than 50 percent market shares in photocopiers and televisions. Initially they beat the Americans with superior productivity, then superior quality, and more recently with superior time-to-market, while relying on traditional organizational structures. Neither the Japanese nor the Americans, however, gained a strategic advantage through structure-driven changes.

Hollow Organizations. In more recent decades, downsizing, reengineering, and other forms of "permanent" restructuring can be seen as delayed reactions to competitive pressures. Many of these efforts simply sought to do more with less. The search for competitive advantage through structural change has led to a renewed and widespread application of "make-or-buy" analysis. Janitorial, payroll, and data processing services are long-standing examples. More recently, this "hollowing out" has expanded to include functions formerly deemed essential to competitive success. Examples include inbound or outbound logistics, which have been taken over by Ryder for Xerox and the Saturn Division of General Motors. Or, consider how Chrysler transformed its structure and the operations strategy of the company.

Chrysler management moved toward a hollowed-out form, with subcomponent design and production activities increasingly contracted to suppliers. One result was the highest per-car profitability levels among the "Big Three" auto makers. Another result was that Chrysler barely produced more than half the content of the cars it sold, putting the company on the verge of transforming itself from a manufacturer of automobiles to an assembler.

Although there is nothing wrong with changing one's status from a manufacturer to an assembler, Chrysler's strategic revision was driven in large measure by the search for competitive advantage through structural change, particularly in the manufacturing operations. Carried to an extreme, hollowing out leads to "virtual" organization designs.

Virtual Organizations. As used here, the difference between "hollow" and "virtual" organizations is one of intent and extent. Hollow firms seek economies within the current structure; virtual firms externalize all but core activities. Thus, virtual firms may be little more than a shell, performing only one or two key functions and not much more. Traditional, in-house organizational functions are the exception in virtual designs, because talent and capital are focused on value-added, core competencies.

> "Hollow firms seek economies within the current structure; virtual firms externalize all but core activities."

Consider Smith Corona, the long-time leader in portable typewriters. Word processing software combined with personal computers and laptops have made typewriters all but obsolete. Even moving production facilities from New York and Singapore to Mexico in 1993 could not prevent a 1995 bankruptcy. To emerge from bankruptcy in 1997, the firm sold its remaining factory and began the process of transforming itself into a virtual organization.

Today, 82 percent of Smith Corona's revenues come from products made by others. Any future growth in its targeted small-office, home-office (SOHO) market will depend on phones, fax machines, and other electronic devices designed and made by others but sold under its name.

If Smith Corona has core competencies, they are its ability to leverage its 112-year reputation and coordinate its supplies with market demands. Although this transformation into a virtual organization is an example of strategy-driven structural change, it suggests that structure—or at least a virtual structure—can be the basis of competitive survival. Will Chrysler, Sunbeam Appliances, and other manufactures follow Smith Corona's lead? Will Chrysler's structural changes reshape its new "partner," Daimler Benz?

Outside of manufacturing, we already see a clear example of structure used to define strategy. Consider Amazon.com, the Internet book seller. Amazon.com is little more than a Web page and a series of computer servers. Orders are placed electronically over the Internet to its offices in Seattle. Virtually no physical inventory is stocked, except high-volume best sellers, but the company boasts that it is the world's largest bookstore. Instead of maintaining an extensive physical inventory, it keeps a virtual one by being connected to the computers of major publishers through which it can handle order fulfillment electronically.

In the case of Amazon.com, its structure is its source of competitive advantage. Being an Internet-based bookstore, its virtual structure essentially externalizes such expenses as inventory carrying costs, warehousing facilities, and related staff. One result is the need for *less* management time and talent to coordinate all these activities among consumers and publishers. While Amazon.com appears to be a book retailer, it acts more like a value-added wholesaler with order fulfillment capabilities. Other costs are avoided, such as expensive store frontage, stockouts, and steep discounts for overstocks.

> "Compared to the self-contained citadel mentality of functionally designed organizations, virtual forms are more responsive and possess the ability to adjust competencies to the shifting sands of competition."

Amazon.com's virtual organization structure has created a new market segment and helped to redefine the industry. Now, traditional competitors such as Barnes & Noble and Borders Books are being forced to copy this structure-based competitive advantage. Because traditional strategists and theorists would argue the "right" organizational structure can be evaluated only with respect to how it supports the strategy, structure-driven strategy might be viewed as the "tail wagging the dog." However, under special circumstances, having the right structure can create strategic possibilities—as illustrated by Amazon.com's rapid success.

Competencies, Responsiveness, and Structure

Virtual and hollow organizations are not necessarily superior. Given stability in competitive, technological, legal, and other environments, a functional design works well because it is efficient. In less developed economies, which lack sophisticated business infrastructure, functional designs may be the only viable alternative. But when the environment is turbulent, responsiveness may be a more important competency than efficiency.

Turbulent environments may not allow a firm to develop necessary competencies. Smith Corona lacked the time and resources needed to develop its own design and manufacturing competencies for the fast-changing SOHO market. Instead, those competencies

were acquired to compete with Hewlett-Packard and Lucent Technologies. Selling off assets to emerge from bankruptcy made a virtual design a necessity.

Functionally designed organizations devote considerable attention to efficiency, quality, and other indices of "doing things right." This inward focus can distract leadership from the more important task of doing the "right things." Smith Corona was successful because it innovated typewriters with upper and lower case characters, cartridge ribbons, and portability. Early in its existence, it did the right things. But the technological shift from typewriters to word processing spelled doom for the company. No amount of restructuring, downsizing, or offshore production could save it.

As a virtual organization, the details of a functional firm are largely left to others, allowing management to key on the external strategic issues—such as matching SOHO customer needs with vendor capabilities under the Smith Corona distribution system. Whether Smith Corona can regain its former glory and economic success is uncertain—perhaps even doubtful when one looks at its more successful, better-known, and bigger competitors. Nevertheless, stripped of most assets through bankruptcy, faced with major competitors, and confronted with rapidly changing product technologies, the remaining structure and resources (primarily its name recognition) are driving its broker-like strategy.

When an environment is turbulent, the firm's competencies at detecting and responding to change are crucial. Virtual, and to a lesser extent hollow, designs focus the organization on its limited, value-added competencies. When new competencies are needed, they are added by acquisition or contract. Compared to the self-contained citadel mentality of functionally designed organizations, virtual forms are more responsive and possess the ability to adjust competencies to the shifting sands of competition.

SUCCESS CONDITIONS

Whether emerging out of necessity at Smith Corona or out of innovations at Amazon.com, structure-driven strategy is a special case. Teasing out the circumstances under which strategists should consider structure as a source of innovative strategies includes the following conditions for success.

Advanced Infrastructure

The citadel mentality of largely self-contained organization designs that once embraced all business functions was often a necessity. Henry Ford needed the world's largest steel works at the River Rouge facility to ensure adequate quantity and quality of steel to meet Ford Motor Company's needs. Today, Ford does not run a fully integrated steel mill, finding it more sensible to contract with others. However, if it were not for the advanced infrastructure of producing and shipping steel, Ford undoubtedly would still carry on the steelmaking function. In fact, it may be this lack of infrastructure that sees many developing countries rely heavily on conglomerate corporate strategies. South Korea's *chaebols* (large, diverse conglomerates, such as Daewoo or Hyundai, composed of affiliates and unrelated industries) suggest an example of this.

Surplus Capacity

The advanced infrastructure also must exhibit surplus capacity. Normally, excess capacity is found in mature industries, which exist when an industry's ability to supply products or services exceeds demand across the business cycle, even though demand may still be growing. This excess capacity invites price competition as a means of gaining incremental sales. Carried to an extreme, severe price competition in the face of surplus capacity can lead to *deflation*, especially if market forces do not allow high-cost producers to fail and withdraw their contribution to the industry's over-supply.

Chrysler's success in moving from a manufacturer to an assembler depends on the surplus capacity in the auto parts industry. Likewise, Dell and Gateway Computers could not exist without the surplus capacity in supplier industries. In turn, the fierce price competition associated with these surpluses may be driving innovators to seek radical, rather than incremental, ways of attaining lower costs in potentially deflationary markets. Structure-driven strategies—though contrary to strategy-driven structures—may be one radical solution for some industry players.

Turbulent Environment and Speed

Even with an advanced infrastructure and surplus capacity, competition, technology, or other factors must create turbulence in the environment to provide impetus for structure-driven strategies. Turbulence demands fast response times. The historically short sales life of most books makes the publication and distribution aspects of the book industry turbulent. By externalizing most aspects of book selling (such as retail stores, stockouts, overstocks, and the like), Amazon.com's structure is better able to respond to changing customer tastes. And this structure seems to do so with less potential risk of obsolescent inventory or surplus retail capacity.

Capital Limitations and Risk

As with many strategic alliances, capital limitations may drive an organization's structure/strategy relation-

ship. Chrysler, Volkswagen, and Motorola are just three illustrations.

- Chrysler's need for fast time-to-market, combined with its precarious financial situation in the late 1980s and early 1990s, led it toward an increasingly hollow structure, dependent on vendors for design and manufacture of increasingly larger and more complex subcomponents. Lacking capital and in need of spreading risks associated with new designs, Chrysler hollowed out the firm through forceful make-or-buy analysis.
- Volkswagen's new Brazilian production system goes even further by leasing floor space on the assembly line for suppliers to actually install their parts and subcomponents.
- Motorola's multibillion-dollar Iridium project, which encircles the Earth with scores of low-orbiting telecommunication satellites, is yet another example of capital risk limitations creating structure that drives the company's alliance strategy for the project.

> "In fact, the self-contained citadel remains appealing (and perhaps appropriate in stable settings) because its design ensures control and communications, even if at the price of responsiveness."

Control and the Rule-of-Law

Structural innovations can give rise to successful strategies only if the leaders can maintain control. These virtual and hollow designs use contractual networks to replace the hierarchy-based controls that traditionally cemented functional and matrix organizations together. If the rule-of-law does not exist—if contracts cannot be enforced through courts—then these design options may be too risky to implement, unless exceptional ethics, extended family, or some other device ensures execution of agreements. The use of extended families and personal relationships as the basis for building allies, even organizational structure, in Eastern societies may prove to be a greater limitation in eastern Asia than the current financial turmoil when there is a need for structural-driven strategies. Simply put, innovative designs may fail when enforcement depends on non-meritorious factors such as reputation, contacts, graft, or the like.

Communications

Ford's self-contained approach to automobile building at the beginning of this century was also required by limited communications. For a hollow or virtual structure to shape an effective strategy assumes easy, quick, and efficient communications, which are often electronically facilitated. In fact, the self-contained citadel remains appealing (and perhaps appropriate in stable settings) because its design ensures control and communications, even if at the price of responsiveness.

> "Thus, the pursuit of a responsive structure at the expense of a firm's core competencies may prove to be a Faustian bargain, destined to fail."

Core Competency

Structural change that undermines core competencies is of dubious merit. Success conditions assume that the firm provides a value-added benefit, presumably tied to its core competency. If Honda Motor Company contracted out its motor design and manufacture, it might quickly find that this adds limited value, and its competitive position might erode quickly.

Smith Corona is potentially in a similar situation. Presumably, its core competency lies in the distribution of products made by others. Because it is selling mostly "me-too" products, however, it is hard to see how it is going to survive, even with its low overhead and streamlined virtual organization design. Because the Smith Corona name recognition is hard to duplicate, consumer trust and brand recognition will undoubtedly carry it for awhile, just as Honda's name would if it contracted out its core competency of engine design and manufacturing. Thus, the pursuit of a responsive structure at the expense of a firm's core competencies may prove to be a Faustian bargain, destined to fail.

Virtual and, to a lesser extent, hollow organization designs imply a key competency in the area of managing the contractual relationships and the coordination such a diverse organization implies. It is conceivable that those who master this core competency may be able to build virtual conglomerates, with the core competency being relationship management.

FUTURE IMPLICATIONS

So what? As the necessary conditions for structural-driven strategy spread to other industries and countries, these strategic approaches will become more important and obvious. Large and largely self-contained traditional designs will remain, particularly in nonprofit, quasi-monopoly, or government organizations. Hollow and virtual organizations will become more commonplace as declining coordination costs parallel the drop in electronic hardware expense and the growth of Internet-facilitated commerce. Some specific implications include the following considerations.

Business Support Services

Make-or-buy analysis will be applied more and more often. Traditional cost evaluations of outside versus inside supply will be blurred by strategic considerations. While core competencies will be deemed central to survival, other functions will be more willingly spun off for economic *and* strategic reasons. Extending the cost effectiveness and strategic logic of make-or-buy analysis, competitive pressures will move more and more companies to spin off non-core functions as a means of lowering costs, increasing responsiveness, and enhancing strategic focus on the application of core competencies. Existing organizations, with their leaders stuck in traditional paradigms, will move toward the hollow form; increasingly, new players will spring full-form as virtual organizations—as Barnes & Noble discovered with the appearance of Amazon.com.

Here the implications are for a proliferation of business support services, suggesting healthy growth for staffing agencies, consultants, and third-party contractors as organizations reduce their bench strength. Included will be traditional data processing, accounting, payroll services, janitorial, and the like along with contract logistics, design, manufacturing, benefits, and related human resource activities. Hierarchical designs and control will give way to network structures of contractors and alliances, glued together by contractual relationships.

Human Resource Implications

Traditional employment relationships will, for all but a few key employees, gravitate toward temporary contractual relationships, with employment patterns more likely to reflect practices in the construction industry or other project-based employment. Career management responsibilities will fall squarely on the individual, who must obtain and maintain skills and networks of contacts. Those with the coordination skills and wide-ranging contacts may create virtual organizations that form and reform on an ad hoc, project-by-project basis. These organizational designs will be ideally suited to nimble leadership and skill mixes that respond seamlessly to client demands. Careers are likely to be a random blend of employee and contractor status—sometimes as a project leader, sometimes as a team member, sometimes as a solo-practitioner. Networking and negotiating will be increasingly important career tools, holding powerful implications for educational curriculum redesign and networking groups such as professional associations, trade shows, and community-wide business support groups.

As independent contractors replace employees, compensation packages are more likely to be based on incentives and tied to preset objectives and performance measures. Benefits may be provided more commonly by professional, fraternal, or other affinity groups—not necessarily granted by the employer. Pressures for portable benefits should continue to grow.

Organizational Development

Leaders will become even more concerned with developing responsive organizations that can be adapted to, and even exploit, the changing environment. Superior responsiveness among firms in a turbulent industry suggests a source of competitive advantage and, therefore, developmental focus. Speed, the ability to create new strategies and shift among them, may be the best defense against competitors, seen and unseen.

Fast responders are less likely to become targets of innovation by competitors. Just the ability to respond quickly may become a cherished, strategic defense. Innovations in organizational development and the creation of strongly embedded cultures that em-brace change may increasingly become a source of competitive advantage. Increasingly, too, the work of leaders and organizational development specialists may blur to an even greater degree.

Simply put, says Galbraith (1982), "Innovative ideas are destructive: they destroy investments in capital equipment and people's careers." Organizations and leaders addicted to size and comprehensive citadels may find that competitors are not the enemy or the cause of failure. Rather, failure may arise from the internal burden of bureaucracy and outdated structural components that slow responsiveness to an ever-changing competitive environment.

References

Joseph L. Badaracco, Jr., *The Knowledge Link* (Boston: Harvard Business School Press, 1991).

Claudia Deutsch, "Using a Key that Still Works," *New York Times,* March 23, 1998, p. C1.

Kenneth J. Fedor and William B. Werther, Jr., "Making Sense of Cultural Factors in International Alliances," *Organizational Dynamics,* Spring 1995, pp. 43–48.

Jay R. Galbraith, "Designing the Innovating Organization," *Organizational Dynamics,* Winter 1982, pp. 5–25.

William B. Werther, Jr. and Jeffrey L. Kerr, "The Shifting Sands of Competitive Advantage," *Business Horizons,* May–June 1995, pp. 11–17.

Joan Woodward, *Industrial Organization: Theory and Practice* (London: Oxford University Press, 1965).

William B. Werther, Jr. is the Office Depot Management Scholar at the University of Miami's School of Business Administration in Coral Gables, Florida.

The Future That Has Already Happened

By Peter Drucker

In human affairs—political, social, economic, and business—it is pointless to try to predict the future, let alone attempt to look ahead 75 years. But it is possible—and fruitful—to identify major events that have already happened, irrevocably, and that therefore will have predictable effects in the next decade or two. It is possible, in other words, to identify and prepare for the future *that has already happened.*

The dominant factor for business in the next two decades—absent war, pestilence, or collision with a comet—is not going to be economics or technology. It will be demographics. The key factor for business will not be the *over*population of the world, of which we have been warned these last 40 years. It will be the increasing *under*population of the developed countries—Japan and those in Europe and in North America.

The developed world is in the process of committing collective national suicide. Its citizens are not producing enough babies to reproduce themselves, and the cause is quite clear. Its younger people are no longer able to bear the increasing burden of supporting a growing population of older, nonworking people. They can only offset that rising burden by cutting back at the other end of the dependence spectrum, which means having fewer or no children.

Of course, birthrates may go up again, though so far there is not the slightest sign of a new baby boom

> Managers face two converging trends: the declining work force and the ascent of knowledge work.

in any developed country. But even if birthrates increased overnight to the three-plus figure of the U.S. baby boom of 50 years ago, it would take 25 years before those new babies would become fully educated and productive adults. For the next 25 years, in other words, the underpopulation of the developed countries is accomplished fact and thus has the following implications for their societies and economics:

- **Actual retirement age**—the age at which people stop working—will go up in all developed countries to 75 for healthy people, who are the great majority. That rise in retirement age will occur well before the year 2010.

- **Economic growth** can no longer come from either putting more people to work—that is, from more resource input, as much of it has come in the past—or from greater consumer demand. It can come only from a very sharp and continuing increase in the productivity of the one resource in which the developed countries still have an edge (and which they are likely to maintain for

a few more decades): the productivity of knowledge work and of knowledge workers.

- **There will be no single dominant world economic power,** because no developed country has the population base to support such a role. There can be no long-term competitive advantage for any country, industry, or company, because neither money nor technology can, for any length of time, offset the growing imbalances in labor resources. The training methodologies developed during the two world wars—mostly in the United States—now make it possible to raise the productivity of a preindustrial and unskilled manual labor force to worldclass levels in virtually no time, as Korea demonstrated 30 years ago and Thailand is demonstrating now. Technology—brand-new technology—is available, as a rule, quite cheaply on the open market. The only comparative advantage of the developed countries is in the supply of knowledge workers. It is not a qualitative advantage; the educated people in emerging countries are every whit as knowledgeable as their counterparts in the developed world. But quantitatively, the developed countries have an enormous lead. To convert this quantitative into a qualitative lead is one—and perhaps the only—way for the developed countries to maintain their competitive position in the world economy. This means continual, systematic work on the productivity of knowledge and knowledge workers, which is still neglected and abysmally low.

Implications of Knowledge As a Resource

Knowledge is different from all other resources. It makes itself constantly obsolete, so that today's advanced knowledge is tomorrow's ignorance. And the knowledge that matters is subject to rapid and abrupt shifts—from pharmacology to genetics in the health-care industry, for example, or from PCs to the Internet in the computer industry.

The productivity of knowledge and knowledge workers will not be the only competitive factor in the world economy. It is, however, likely to become the decisive factor, at least for most industries in the developed countries. The likelihood of this prediction holds implications for businesses and for executives.

The first—and overarching—implication is that the world economy will continue to be highly turbulent and highly competitive, prone to abrupt shifts as both the nature and the content of relevant knowledge continually and unpredictably change.

The information needs of businesses and of executives are likely to change rapidly. We have concentrated these past years on improving traditional information, which is almost exclusively information about what goes on *inside* an organization. Accounting, the traditional information system and the one on which most executives still depend, records what happens within the firm. All recent changes and improvements in accounting—such as activity-based accounting, the executive scorecard, and economic value analysis—still aim at providing better information about events inside the company. The data produced by most new information systems also have that purpose. In fact, approximately 90%

or more of the data any organization collects is information about inside events.

Increasingly, a winning strategy will demand information about events and conditions *outside* the institution: noncustomers, technologies other than those currently used by the firm and its present competitors, markets not presently served, and so on. Only with this information can a business decide how to allocate its knowledge resources to produce the highest yield. Only with such information can a business also prepare for new changes and challenges arising from sudden shifts in the world economy and in the nature and the content of knowledge itself. The development of rigorous methods for gathering and analyzing outside information will increasingly become a major challenge for businesses and for information experts.

Knowledge makes resources mobile. Knowledge workers, unlike manual workers in manufacturing, own the means of production: They carry that knowledge in their heads and can therefore take it with them. At the same time, the knowledge needs of organizations are likely to change continually. As a result, in developed countries more and more of the critical work force—and the most highly paid part of it—will increasingly consist of people who cannot be "managed" in the traditional sense of the word. In many cases, they will not even be employees of the organizations for which they work, but rather contractors, experts, consultants, part-timers, joint-venture partners, and so on. An increasing number of these people will identify themselves by their own knowledge rather than by the organization that pays them.

Implicit in all this is a change in the very meaning of *organization*. For more than a century—from J.P. Mor-

gan and John D. Rockefeller in the United States to George Siemens in Germany, to Henri Fayol in France, through Alfred Sloan at GM, and up to the present infatuation with teams—we have been searching for the one *right* organization for our companies. There can no longer be any such thing. There will be only "organizations," as different from one another as a petroleum refinery, a cathedral, and a suburban bungalow are, even though all three are "buildings." Each organization in the developed countries (and not only businesses) will have to be designed for a specific task, time, and place (or culture).

There are also implications for the art and science of management. Management will increasingly extend beyond business enterprises, where it originated some 125 years ago as an attempt to organize the production of *things*. The most important area for developing new concepts, methods, and practices will be in the management of society's *knowledge resources*—specifically, education and health care, both of which are today overadministered and undermanaged.

Predictions? No. These are the implications of a future *that has already happened*.

About the Author

Peter Druker is the founder of the Drucker Foundation for Non-Profit Management and the author of many books on the study and practice of management. He may be contacted through Harvard Business School Press, 60 Harvard Way, Boston, Massachusetts 02163.

This article is reprinted with permission from his latest book, Peter Drucker on the Profession of Management, which is available from Harvard Business School Press (telephone 1–888–500–1016; Web site www.hbsp.harvard.edu) or from the Futurist Bookstore for $29.95 ($26.95 for Society members), cat. no. B–2147.

Creating a hybrid organizational form from parental blueprints: The emergence and evolution of knowledge firms

ABSTRACT

Using a case study of a new biotechnology firm, we examine the formation of a new organizational form as a hybrid emerging from two 'parent' organizational forms. We focus on key internal labor processes that are selected from existing organizations and replicated in the hybrid form and argue that this inheritance process strengthens the likelihood of survival of the new form. We propose that analyzing the micro-level processes of inheritance contributes to the understanding of macro-level phenomena of organizational births and deaths, examined by population ecologists.

KEYWORDS

biotechnology ■ genealogical processes ■ hybrid organizational forms ■ knowledge firms ■ new organizational forms ■ organizational evolution

Amalya L. Oliver and Kathleen Montgomery

Introduction

In this paper, we propose that our understanding of organizational evolution and the emergence of new organizational forms can be enhanced by taking into account the complex interplay of the dual processes of (ecological) selection and (genealogical) replication. We analyze the selection of various elements from previously existing organizational forms, as a genealogical organizational 'blueprint', which are transferred and modified into elements appropriate to the new hybrid form. We use a micro lens, focusing on internal processes in the management of human capital to illustrate how a mixture of 'ingredients' can be 'inherited' from existing organizational forms and turned into a new hybrid form. We highlight the particular importance of this selection and transfer process in new knowledge firms and use as an example a case study of the formation of a new biotechnology firm.

Theoretical background

Fundamental questions about organizational change have been the object of substantial theoretical development from several perspectives. Researchers have sought to understand explanations for both why and how organizations change and new organizational forms emerge. In terms of 'why' organizations change, scholars have identified changes in the social structure of societies, in environmental resources, or in technologies as constituting the grounds and creating the resource space for new organizational forms (Stinchcomb, 1965; Van de Ven & Garud, 1989; Romanelli, 1991). For example, Chandler (1962) and Fligstein (1985) point to historical and economic changes that led to diversification in many large companies as fostering the emergence of the multi-divisional or M-form organization. Ouchi and Jagger (1978) argue that the Type Z organizational form, offering holistic concern

From *Human Relations*, Vol. 53, No. 1, 2000, pp. 33–56. © 2000 by Sage LTD. Reprinted by permission.

for employees, emerged when social organizations such as churches and neighborhoods no longer satisfied individuals' needs for affiliation. Similarly, Powell (1990) proposes that network organizations, based on trust, reputation, and friendship, emerged in response to the need for long-term interdependent organizational exchanges whose commodity values are not easily measured.

In approaching the 'how' question, several theories have been proposed to guide our understanding of the process through which organizations change and new organizational forms emerge. Two of the major theoretical approaches that have been used to study such questions are population ecology and organizational systematics. Population ecology theories (Aldrich & Pfeffer, 1976; Hannan & Freeman, 1977; Carroll, 1984) introduce the natural selection process through which various organizational forms are selected or extinguished; organizational systematics theory (McKelvey, 1982; Baum & Singh, 1994) deals with genealogical processes of transmission and inheritance of organizational structures. These two approaches employ different foci and levels of analysis (Baum & Singh, 1994). Population ecologists generally observe macro-level changes in populations of organizations and focus on the structure and integration of a hierarchy of jobs, work groups, organizations, populations, and communities. In contrast, the genealogical approach is concerned with the conservation and transfer of production processes, routines, skills, and knowledge at the micro-firm level.

We suggest that insights from these two approaches can be usefully integrated to provide a richer understanding of the emergence and potential survival of new organizational forms. That is, we propose that the ecological processes of selection and retention at the population level (Hannan & Freeman, 1977) can be examined at the internal-firm level as well, by examining micro-level firm information related to selection and retention (i.e. replication) of routines and procedures from 'parental' organizations (Romanelli, 1991), as examples of a genealogical inheritance process.

Further, we propose that the successful emergence and evolution of a hybrid form may be importantly related to its ability to capture salient key features of its parents. The key features that are most strongly related to the emergence of a hybrid form will, of course, differ across organizational types and industry, depending on the nature of the parents and the intended purpose of the emergent hybrid. Hence, it is vital that key features be appropriately recognized and selected for their potential to impact the successful emergence of the hybrid firm. In this paper we demonstrate this phenomenon through an examination of the internal process of a particular form of new organizational hybrid known as the 'knowledge' firm.

In this new organizational form, advanced knowledge generated by scientific professionals is used in the creation of new products, such as in the biotechnology or computer industries. Thus, we suggest that the knowledge firm can be viewed as a hybrid of an established knowledge-creating organization—the research university—and an established production-oriented, market-driven enterprise—the large corporation. This is consistent with the observation by Powell and Owen-Smith (1998) that the boundaries between universities and firms in the life sciences are crumbling, with new organizational arrangements that blur the distinction between academic research and commercial development.

Despite the blurring of boundaries between universities and firms, the genealogical parents of knowledge firms are distinguished from each other in terms of their goals, labor, and production processes. Most importantly, in the research university, knowledge is an individual commodity that is generated by and resides with individual scholars. These individuals may choose to pass on their knowledge through teaching and publishing, but they remain the 'owners' of their original ideas. In the industrial setting, on the other hand, knowledge is an organizational commodity (Nonaka, 1994), in that the organization 'owns' the knowledge that is produced by its actors, and the organization chooses how it will be used and marketed.

The challenge, therefore, to the new knowledge firms is to obtain from the knowledge creators (i.e. individual scientists who have been socialized in a research university framework) the commitment to produce organizational knowledge consistent with the market-oriented goals of the new hybrid firm. In order to do this, the hybrid firms must establish a context and incentives that enable and encourage individual scientists to willingly create 'organizational knowledge' rather than 'individual knowledge' (Nonaka, 1994).

In the next section, we present a case study of a new biotechnology firm to illustrate the key features of both parents that have been inherited and modified to fit the needs of the new firm and its knowledge producers. To provide a context for the case study, we begin first with a brief overview of the biotechnology industry and its organizational actors.

The biotechnology industry

Evolving organizational actors

The biotechnology industry is composed of various organizational actors involved in the discovery, development, and production of biotechnology products. During the 1970s, the development of new technologies such as recombinant DNA in the United States and monoclonal antibodies in the United Kingdom shifted science in the area of microbiology, molecular biology, and biochemistry from basic to highly applied research. The potential of genetically engineered products in the therapeutic, diagnostic, agricultural, veterinary, and food and waste areas carried enormous economic possibilities.

Some might have predicted that the primary organizational actors to emerge in this new industry would have been existing profit-seeking institutions such as large pharmaceutical firms, because of the high level of financing needed to bring such products to the market. The incumbent pharmaceutical companies had well established research and development (R&D) facilities, had the stability and resources to adapt the new technologies, and were vertically integrated. Thus, given the commercialization needs, a logical collaboration would be between universities or research centers and incumbent pharmaceutical companies. Yet, this model did not become the organizational form that captured the potential in biotechnology products.

Part of the explanation may be found in Hannan and Freeman (1984), who emphasize that many larger and older firms suffer from internal inertia (p. 157) that prevents them from being able to reorganize and quickly adapt their strategies and structure to new technological opportunities. This structural inertia provides a window for external entrepreneurs who can more rapidly take advantage of new opportunities.

Further, when a new technology constitutes a dramatic breakthrough, it acts both to reduce the value of an existing company's ability to adjust, as well as to create the grounds for generating new kinds of organizations able to exploit the new technology (Abernathy & Clark, 1985; Tushman & Anderson, 1986). For this reason, Schumpeter (1934/1975: 83) refers to such 'broad and rapid changes to core technologies' as 'gusts of creative destruction'. As Powell and Brantley (1992: 368) note, '[b]iotechnology is a dramatic case of competence-destroying innovation because it builds on a scientific basis (immunology and molecular biology) that differs significantly from the knowledge base (organic chemistry and its clinical applications) of the more established pharmaceutical companies'. As well, 'biotechnology represents a competence-destroying technology because it required technical skills that were fundamentally different from those with which established pharmaceutical firms were familiar' (Pisano, 1990: 154). He adds that 'for this reason, most of the early commercial biotechnology R&D was conducted by new ventures that formed in the United States between 1976 and 1982 and not by established pharmaceutical firms' (Pisano, 1990: 155).

The emergence of NBFs

Thus, the biotechnology industry is characterized by the emergence of a new form of knowledge organization: the new biotechnology firm (NBF). In the early stages of the biotechnology industry, the new form was developed through a creative collaboration between leading scientists and venture capital entrepreneurs to capture the new opportunity (Kenney, 1986; Kornberg, 1995). In this way, venture capital provided the mechanism for introducing the new technologies important for future economic growth. This direction of organizational evolution is consistent with Van de Ven and Garud's (1989) observation that environmental niches do not pre-exist but are constructed through a continuous interaction of entrepreneurs and organizations toward the establishment of new organizations that can take advantage of underutilized and non-redundant opportunities of a 'structural hole' (Burt, 1992).

To illustrate, the birth of the industry is commonly marked by the formation of Genentech in 1976, which was established by Professor Herbert Boyer, from the University of California at San Francisco, one of the inventors of the Cohen-Boyer gene-splicing technique, and Robert Swanson, a venture capitalist (Kenney, 1986). The rapid 'birth rate' of similar NBFs, such as Amgen, Biogen, Genetic Systems, and Immunogen, suggests that this new organizational form quickly gained legitimacy as the prominent adaptive form (Hybels & Popielarz, 1996). By 1994, over 1200 such new companies were formed in the United States (Kornberg, 1995), and the same form simultaneously emerged in many countries around the world, including the United Kingdom, Japan, Germany, Italy, Switzerland, and Israel (Oliver, 1993).

Challenges confronting NBFs

As Kornberg (1995: 95) cautions, 'good science and good technology might not be sufficient to make a company profitable'. To enhance their prospects for survival and success, and to compensate for the 'liability of newness' (Stinchcomb, 1965; Hannan & Freeman, 1977, 1984), NBFs may seek to retain elements of their genealogical organizational 'parents'—research university and the large corporate pharmaceutical firms—that have already achieved institutional legitimacy. The process allows NBFs to borrow from both parents various routines and competence elements (McKelvey, 1982; McKelvey & Aldrich, 1983) appropriate to the new form.

The effort to inherit a 'blueprint' from the parental organizations, however, generates potential incompatibilities for NBFs. As noted by Kenney (1986: 176), 'the norms of "doing science" in the university are very different from those necessary for economic success'. These potential incompatibilities manifest themselves in various aspects of the management of the scientific labor process. For example, while Teece (1992) has argued that R&D may be more efficiently governed by hierarchies than by markets, governance and control in a typical firm hierarchy are inconsistent with such procedures in a research university environment. Of particular concern are expectations and norms about autonomy and about information sharing. In their study of the Danish biotechnology industry, Kreiner and Schultz (1993) found that management may have little direct control over how, when, and with what consequences employees participate in networking activities. This dilemma is particularly acute with respect to soliciting external knowledge resources, while simultaneously protecting their own knowledge resources from expropriation.

Powell et al. (1996) also studied networking relations among biotechnology firms and found that beneath the formal ties exists a 'sea of informal relations of knowledge exchanges', similar to a university laboratory, where scientists enjoy autonomy, work on their own projects, and share their knowledge with the wider scientific community. Liebeskind et al. (1996) and Argyres and Liebeskind (1998) report similar findings. Argyres and Liebeskind (1998) observe that universities were created to uphold their social-contractual commitment to society to create and sustain an 'intellectual commons'—a knowledge archive openly accessible to all members of society. The universities support the practice of 'open science' in order to allow for the evaluation and potential replication of findings by other scientists, helping to ensure the quality of research and facilitation of further discoveries. As a result, scientists typically expect and receive greater autonomy in their choices of research topics than do their counterparts in large established firms, publish widely, and draw on their network of relations with university scientists for obtaining scientific know-how (Liebeskind et al., 1996). All of these activities may run counter to the market-driven needs of NBFs.

In the following section, we analyze some of the mechanisms by which NBFs have confronted the challenge of establishing legitimacy, by selecting the advantages offered by their genealogical parents and modifying them to address the potential incompatibilities of professional norms and market demands.

NBF hybridization case study: New Genetics

Our analysis employs a case study of a large and successful NBF located in California, referred to by the pseudonym of 'New Genetics'.

Case example selection and rationale

The rationale for qualitative case studies is well established in management research (Yin, 1984; Eisenhardt,

1989; Sutton, 1997). Our intent in this case study example is to focus on the theoretical development of new organizational forms as hybrids from genealogical parents, in general, and on the emergence of NBFs as a particular type of new organizational hybrid. In this work, we do not use the case study to develop and systematically test specific formal hypotheses; rather, we employ the qualitative data as a basis for theoretical insights, as well as to highlight areas where further extensions are called for in theory development and hypothesis testing. Toward this end, we have selected a new firm that many consider to be a model for success within the industry.[1]

New Genetics is one of the first NBFs formed in the United States (North Carolina Biotechnology Center, 1991), established within the first four years of the industry formation by a leading scientist. The firm is located in California, the geographical area with the highest number of NBFs in the United States (of a total of 554 NBFs 'born' between 1976 and 1990, 133 were located in California) (North Carolina Biotechnology Center, 1991).

Since its founding, the firm has grown significantly on virtually every growth parameter: it has increased its product diversification and entered new technologies; it has substantially increased its workforce and enlarged its physical facilities; it has become vertically integrated, has launched international units, and has established several subsidiaries. Despite these dramatic changes, however, the firm has retained the unique features upon which it was established, especially those pertaining to the internal scientific-labor processes drawn from its parental blueprints, as described below.

Methodology

Data from qualitative interviews with scientists and top executives at New Genetics were collected in 1993 and supplemented with information collected from many of the same individuals in 1996. These data have been augmented by observations and analysis of internal documents of the firm (newsletters and publication list) and by descriptive information on internal processes from business journals and other recent studies of NBFs.

Interviews average one to four hours. To enhance the validity and reliability of the case-study data, the researchers took detailed notes and/or taped the interviews, and transcribed the notes without delay. Further, we interviewed organization members of different ranks, positions, and tenure, to assure that analyses of the data were not based on idiosyncratic individual responses. The principal interviews were conducted over a three-month period in 1993, and confirmatory interviews were conducted over a one-month period in 1996. While background firm information was obtained from several interviewees to provide a comprehensive picture of procedures and norms at the time of the study, the study was not designed to examine process issues over time; such a goal would require different data-collection strategies. Thus, an in-depth temporal analysis would be inappropriate from these data.

Analytical framework: human resources management

As knowledge organizations, the way NBFs manage their human capital is extremely important to their success (Youndt et al., 1996). Yet, as we have proposed above, the two parental forms of NBFs are the research university and large pharmaceutical corporations, whose procedural norms and routines related to their human capital may contrast sharply. We have argued that a viable strategy for the hybrid NBF would be to capture and modify salient key features related to the labor process in such a way as to best accommodate the socialized expectations of its organizational participants as knowledge creators, while attending to its market-oriented production goals. This is because, as studies in human resources management have shown, optimum effectiveness is achieved when there is a 'fit' between organizational structures and practices, and the expectations of the organization's personnel (Arthur, 1994; Ledford & Lawler, 1994; Huselid, 1995; Jackson & Schuler, 1995).

Because of the centrality of human capital in knowledge firms, we place our analysis within a framework of the functions of human resources management. These basic functions are: personnel selection, work assignment, training, coordination and control, motivation and rewards, and person-organization 'fit' (DeCenzo & Robbins, 1996). As shown in Table 1 and discussed below, we have identified several representations of human resources functions, as they are found in the parents and the hybrid organizational forms. They do not constitute an exhaustive list, but rather a set of illustrative examples that we believe demonstrate the hybridization process of selection and retention.

Capturing the salient features of its parents

1 Human resources function: personnel selection
Project team development Scientists in universities have independence in selecting their research team members, who are frequently based at other institutions. Although members may differ in seniority and a senior scientist or a member with special expertise may be deferred to by others, the team structure is generally collaborative among equals. In the industrial setting, assignment of team members and projects is a managerial decision, and team structure is likely to be hierarchical.

At New Genetics, teamwork was encouraged to facilitate collaboration on creation of a new concept, and norms of academia and industry were both evident in team selection and structure. In recognition of scientists' norms of autonomy in determining collaborators, New Genetics allowed team leaders some flexibility in the team selection process. However, more consistent with industry practices, team leaders were constrained in their choice of team members since selections were generally restricted to firm personnel. For example, the process of team organization upon launching a new R&D project called for the head scientist to select the other scientists within the firm with whom he wanted to work. If the head scientist expressed a need to recruit an external scientist who possessed particular expertise, the head scientist—as in academia—would be involved in the search for the new external team member. Final approval of team composition, however, was retained by the firm's management, reflecting in part the firm's concerns with privacy protection, as elaborated under item 3(b) below.

In terms of team structure, New Genetics adopted a self-organized team structure, also more common in universities than in industry, with the understanding that heads of departments worked for the teams, which determined their own needs for equipment and other resources. Because of the trust and shared perspective required within the team, generated through continuous exchanges (Nonaka, 1988), the use of self-organized project teams was considered an important organizing strategy to enhance organizational effectiveness and survival.

2 Human resources function: work assignment and training
Selection and guidance in research projects Scientists in a university setting expect to develop their own research agenda, determining what is, to them, important work, irrespective of the economic implications of the outcome. Funding is commonly solicited from external sources, and constraints on project selection generally arise from the competition for scarce research funds. In industry, economic potential is the major factor influencing selection of projects, and funding for projects is internal, based on the organization's assessment of the market-based demand for the outcome.

Like any new firm, New Genetics' first strategic challenge was generating project ideas and deciding which projects to pursue. As a knowledge firm, New Genetics depended on its research scientists as the source of new ideas. This created a critical challenge for New Genetics, since it required the delicate act of increasing the scientists' awareness of the economic imperatives of their work, without dampening their creative enthusiasm and norm of independence in the selection of research projects to pursue.

Table I Labor-process routines and procedures represented in the two parent forms and the new hybrid form

		Parent Form		Hybrid Form
Generic human resources function	*Specific routines and procedures*	*Research university*	*Pharmaceutical corporation*	*Entrepreneurial NBF*
1 Personnel selection	Project team development	Self-selected by individual researchers from profession at large	Structured by management from intra-firm personnel	Selected by head scientist from internal pool, with occasional extra-firm additions
2 Work assignment	Selection of research projects	High flexibility, only constrained by availability of external funding	Low flexibility, often constrained by economic potential and internal funds	Moderate flexibility, with some internal economic constraints
3(a) Coordination and control (internal)	Work scheduling and monitoring	Highly flexible, no monitoring	Restricted by organization's scheduling	Flexible within loose target dates
3(b) Coordination and control (external)	Exchanges across organizational boundaries	Highly flexible	Low flexibility	Permeable boundaries, primary inflow
4 Motivation and rewards	Incentives and basis for compensation	Individual productivity and reputation	Constrained by firm performance	Individual and firm performance
5 Person–organization fit	Organizational culture	Stable environment promoting slow-changing, risk-averse culture	Dynamic environment necessitating more responsive, higher risk culture	Turbulant environment, requiring innovative, high-risk, high-return culture

At New Genetics, this was accomplished by mimicking several aspects of the research proposal process of universities. For example, every year, all scientists were asked to write one or more short research proposal describing the projects they wished to develop. Although there was no limit placed on the number of proposals a scientist could submit, each proposal was required to contain an explanation of how the research could lead to a marketable product. This was similar to the requirement of academic funding agencies that proposals contain a discussion of how the research would contribute to the scientist's body of knowledge.

In addition, recognizing that scientists may be less aware of the market constraints or the competitive conditions of their research interests, New Genetics created a position of 'strategy executive' with responsibility for helping the scientists to evaluate the profit-potential of the products. This executive serves as a technical resource for gathering information from the environment about the potential competitiveness of their projects and disseminating it to New Genetics'

scientists. This is similar to the technical support provided by universities to enable scientists to comply with proposal-writing guidelines often imposed by external funding agencies, thus enhancing their potential to be awarded competitive grants.

These managerial procedures replicated the academic routine of writing scientific grant proposals for external funding, while modifying the scientists' behavior by instilling a recognition of the market potential of scientific discovery. Thus, the firm institutionalized a new form of 'doing science'—internal competition for scientific excellence, augmented by adjustments to market potential. Kornberg's (1995) study of two NBFs (DNAX and Aleza) also indicates the recognition of the importance of scientific norms, describing the emphasis in recruitment at these NBFs of promises of a far greater free-choice research environment than that found in large pharmaceutical companies.

After generating a set of proposals from its scientists, New Genetics' management had to decide which of the proposals to approve. While maintaining the model of a competitive process, New Genetics, in fact, approved many of the research proposals developed by its scientists. The firm followed this approach not necessarily because they believed that approved proposals had equal commercial potential or because there was unlimited internal funding. Rather, this represented a calculated decision that the firm's prospects for success were improved by having more projects in the pipeline and by developing a diversified portfolio of research projects.

In this way, by opting for increased variation, New Genetics' management were able to respond both to the norms of scientific independence of their employees and to the processes enhancing organizational survival. This strategy is supported by findings from other knowledge firms (Quinn, 1986; Nonaka, 1988; Rappa, 1989). For example, Miner (1994) indicates that high tech managers who permit employees (scientists) to pursue individual projects have basically decided to strengthen the variation process. In accepting inconsistencies in research projects and local inefficiency, the managers sacrifice some retention of resources in return for possible benefits of increased variation, which has been recognized by Weick (1977) and McKelvey and Aldrich (1983) as a way to enhance organizational adaptability.

3(a) Human resources function: coordination and control (internal)

Work scheduling and monitoring In the university setting, scientists are accustomed to enormous flexibility in terms of scheduling their work, from short-term daily work schedules to long-term project schedules, with few reporting and monitoring mechanisms (Latour & Woolgar, 1979). In industrial settings, such extreme flexibility is rare, and employees must conform to externally imposed and monitored time and scheduling.

At New Genetics and at other NBFs, a recognition of the norm of scheduling autonomy held by scientists was reflected in attempts to allow similar flexibility, within limits of expectations for project completion targets. Scientists were encouraged to follow the timetable convenient to them, including working nights and weekends, so long as the project was completed within the allotted period. This organizational strategy suggested an expectation that organizational effectiveness would be achieved through placing trust in scientists' personal judgment, rather than imposing external monitors, thereby enhancing their commitment and dedication to their research.

3(b) Human resources function: coordination and control (external)

Exchanges across organizational boundaries Scientists in university settings consider a major aspect of their occupational role to be publishing their scientific work, as well as participation in seminars and scientific con-

ferences. These channels reflect the expectation of an open exchange of information among scientists, following the notion of the 'invisible college' (Crane, 1972). Indeed, the exchange of ideas is embedded in the norms of the scientific community as a key element in the process through which scientific knowledge is produced and reproduced (Liebeskind et al., 1996). In contrast, such exchanges are not common in the industrial setting because of the dangers of expropriation of ideas by competitors.

New Genetics had to confront the scientific norm of open exchanges of knowledge across organizational boundaries, either via collaborations of inter-organizational team members or via contacts through professional interactions, without loss of proprietary information. While the firm's scientists were encouraged by the firm to participate in many scientific conferences and to engage in external collaborations, strict secrecy was maintained about current research endeavors. For example, firm's scientists would not disclose to outsiders the identity of their university collaborators, out of fear that this information might lead competitors to learn about projects the firm had in the pipeline. Indeed, the intensity of the competition over ideas and research directions led some New Genetics scientists to generate 'false searches' when they needed to search on a network database of scientific publications. Thus, in addition to searching for material on topics relevant to their work-in-progress, New Genetics' scientists would generate numerous searches on irrelevant topics, to mislead 'espionage' agents who monitored the searches of other NBFs to learn about the sort of research work carried out by competitors.

Further, New Genetics prohibited its scientists from sending out any work for publication prior to an internal review by the firm's chief scientist. One estimate held that the firm's researchers published only about 30 percent of the internal scientific work in academic journals and that most of the published information concerned basic science. In contrast, unpatented applied scientific work that could be expropriated by rival firms was not published. However, the firm did not restrict external scientific collaborations over time. That is, the NBF allowed joint scientific publications with external scientists but imposed a time lag that provided the firm with sufficient time to patent the knowledge and transfer it into the commercialization process.

This process served the dual purposes of accommodating, at least partially, the scientific norm of collaboration, while preserving important economic survival goals of the hybrid firm. Thus, it allows inter-organizational scientific collaborations to produce knowledge needed for the firm, thereby acquiring external knowledge at a relatively low cost. For example, Liebeskind et al. (1996) demonstrate that, although there were ongoing joint inter-organizational scientific collaborations, most patents assigned to the NBFs were not shared with external entities, universities, or firms.

4 Human resources function: motivation and rewards

Incentives and basis for compensation A university setting offers rewards (rank and salary) that are strongly related to the scientist's publication rate and quality. Thus, the reward structure encourages commitment to one's own accomplishments, with the goal of attaining recognition within the scientific profession. In industry, however, it is increasingly common for rewards to be tied to firm performance. The mechanism of profit-sharing is designed to enhance the employees' interest in and commitment to the overall firm's performance as well as their individual performance.

New Genetics used a composite form of compensation to reward its scientists that would sufficiently motivate them for individual productivity while still being cost-effective for the firm. Thus, the firm recognized individual scientific excellence through salaries, incentive rewards for successful projects, and shared rights to patents. At the same time, a profit-sharing policy provided all scientists with stock options in the company (Burrill, 1989), thereby enhancing their commitment to overall organizational excellence. Scientists interviewed at New Genetics universally declared that their income working in an NBF was substantially higher than that of their university counterparts and that their commitment to the firm was strengthened by this combination of rewards based on individual and firm accomplishments.

5 Human resources function: person-organization fit

Organizational culture The environment of most university settings is generally stable, encouraging a systematic, risk-averse, less time-bound pursuit of knowledge. In contrast, the environment of industry is more dynamic; hence, organizations are more susceptible to changes in the environment and must respond more rapidly. These demands result in a greater likelihood of an organizational culture that fosters the pursuit of higher-risk projects.

New Genetics had to establish an organizational culture that fostered research efforts consistent with its turbulent environment (North Carolina Biotechnology Center, 1991). This need was dramatically different from the more stable, often risk-averse research environment of the university, and closer to the dynamic environment of industry in general, which was more susceptible to changes in the environment and must respond more rapidly. Smaller entrepreneurial firms such as New Genetics are especially vulnerable to environmental shifts and hence are at great risk of failure unless they adopt a high-risk, high-return strategy. Such a strategy is facilitated through an innovative or-

ganizational culture, fostered by the charismatic leadership of its founder.

New Genetics reflected such a culture, having been established by a leading PhD scientist, uniformly described as highly innovative and charismatic, who generated a sense of excitement about joint 'science making'. This entrepreneurial culture persisted and has been reinforced and passed down to newer generations of scientists through organizational stories and rituals, even though New Genetics has grown rapidly and the founder has left the firm to establish a new NBF. Scientists at New Genetics reported that it was the spirit of entrepreneurship possible in NBFs in general, and at New Genetics in particular, that enticed them to quit a permanent academic position, despite the early high risk of firm failure.

Further, many New Genetics scientists remarked on the compelling intangible presence of its founder, even in his absence, and the strong trust they felt in his ability to create a successful firm. His portrait hung in every office of the firm. Managers who knew him universally remarked in the interviews about his unique abilities and original vision. New scientists in the firm who were interviewed unfailingly mentioned that, although they had never met the founder, his standard of excellence and excitement over scientific work were transmitted to them when they joined the firm.

These observations are consistent with Dodgson's (1993) and Liebeskind and Oliver's (1998) emphasis on the necessity to organizational survival of establishing a basis of commitment and trust that can transcend individual relationships as organizational personnel change over time. Thus, at New Genetics, the strong identification with the charismatic entrepreneur, along with the shared spirit of entrepreneurship, built a highly motivated and committed research team, strengthening the potential for organizational survival.

Discussion

Summary

As Lewin et al. (1997) have observed, the transformation of organizational forms can be seen as the result of a confluence of major forces of environmental changes and significant organizational responses to the perceived shift in the 'rugged landscape'. The emergence of new biotechnology firms demonstrates how changes in environmental opportunities foster the creation of an organizational niche for innovative entrepreneurs to fill. In particular, NBFs have emerged as a response to opportunities presented by the discovery of new scientific technologies that created the basis for a new kind of marketable product. Two resources acted together in establishing the new form:

venture capital provided the seed money for research-lab-like new firms; and leading scientists oriented to making science profitable have joined with research ideas, reputational scientific networks to recruit the needed intellectual capital, and current knowledge of the possibilities of the new technological development.

Population ecology studies have shown how organizations evolve and thrive by fitting into advantage niches through competition for resources (Hannan & Freeman, 1984; Hannan & Carroll, 1992). However, as noted by Aldrich and Pfeffer (1976), environmental selection is concerned not only with organizations as wholes, but also with particular structures and behavior within organizations. Further, the structures and behavior within new organizational forms are importantly related to the individuals who constitute the core of the firm; and, as both Selznick (1957) and Stinchcomb (1965) observe, organizations tend to take the characteristics of people and environments that surround their early establishment. Our analysis of the case study of New Genetics supports these arguments, by showing how both the scientists as a professional community, as well as the organizational genealogical parents—the university and market-oriented corporations—have contributed to the structure of the new form.

In essence, the hybrid form represents a selection of the features seen as advantages of the genealogical parents, and a modification where the features raise potential incompatibilities. The set of features recognized as important for selection and modification will, of course, differ according to the purpose and goals of the new organizational hybrid. For hybrid firms in the biotechnology industry, we have argued that the key features relate to the firm's human capital; namely, the management of the vital human resources of scientific labor. For example, New Genetics transformed the academic expectation for scientific freedom into firm strategy and utilized the norms of inter-organizational scientific collaborations in order to import knowledge into the firm. Additionally, it provided corporate-style incentives that exceeded those possible in academic settings, while supporting a team structure and scheduling flexibility not common in industry; and it fostered an entrepreneurial organizational culture not common in research universities.

Empirical research directions

Other case studies
Studies investigating the emergence of hybrids in different industries and with different types of genealogical parents, and hence different key features to select and replicate, will provide an important point of comparison to this analysis.

The health care industry contains several examples of new hybrid organizations that may lend themselves to an analysis of genealogical inheritance from paren-tal forms. A case study could be proposed of the production of medical services, focusing on the emergence of health maintenance organizations (HMOs) as a hybrid derived from the parental forms of private physician practices and large for-profit insurance firms.[2] The challenge to the hybrid HMO would be, first, selecting the procedures and norms most salient to physicians, such as physician autonomy and physician–patient privacy, along with the procedures important to a market-driven enterprise, such as cost control of scarce resources and advertising; and, second, modifying these norms and procedures in the hybrid form in such a way as to preserve their advantages and reduce their potential incompatibilities. The emergence of physician practice management companies (PPMCs), whose genealogical parents are private physician practices and large management consulting firms (Burns, 1997), may present another opportunity for an illustrative case study.

In the communications industry, an example of a new organizational hybrid may be seen with the emergence of new firms providing comprehensive Internet access, where the parental forms are traditional utility firms (e.g. telephone companies) and the newsprint media. In this case, the challenge to the new hybrid form is selecting and retaining key features relating to the service expectations of traditional utility firm customers, coupled with the service expectations of consumers of the news media. Thus, in this example, the analysis may be framed with a focus on marketing management—the expectations of the external customers—rather than on the human resources management of the expectations of the internal labor supply, as in the current study.

Hypothesis testing
Our analysis leads us to the hypothesis that a hybrid such as New Genetics would be better positioned to survive than new organizational forms that do not explicitly draw key features, important both to their core participants and their organizational purpose, from their genealogical parents. Indicators of New Genetics' organizational growth and survival, mentioned earlier, would lend support for this hypothesis, and anecdotal evidence suggests that NBFs that do not replicate key features from their genealogical parents are less successful than those that strive to transfer parental elements. Volberda's (1996) work on the survivability of flexible organizational forms in turbulent environments is compatible with this projection. Of course, corroboration requires more rigorous empirical testing of this hypothesis, in the biotechnology industry and elsewhere, and analysis of the long-term evolution and success of the hybrids would require different data from those presented here.

Implicatons for theory

Much research devoted to organizational change uses a macro-level ecological approach, which emphasizes the impact of environmental factors on changes in populations of organizations. Yet, the difficulty in defining 'organizational death' or 'structural inertia' in the population ecology paradigm (Young, 1988) generates problems in specifying the time and space dimensions of what constitutes a 'new organizational form'. Several unanswered questions include, at what point is an organization considered a new form? Is the emergence of new forms discrete or continual? Once a new form is detected, at what point do further structural changes in the new form constitute yet another new form? Can a new form emerge within an existing organization, or must it be an entirely new organization?

We suggest that a micro-level approach may be a useful addition to the theoretical search for these answers. In the current study, we have used a micro-level perspective to examine changes in organizations as an evolutionary phenomenon through the transmission of internal routines and procedural norms as a form of genealogical inheritance. By widening the focus to the inheritance of key features from existing parental forms, we may move closer to finding answers to the more fundamental questions related to the definition of a new organizational form.

With respect to the biotechnology industry, we concur with the observation of Arora and Gambardella (1994: 109) that 'The growing perception that universities can, and ought to, play a more important role in promoting national competitiveness places the linkages between private firms and universities squarely on the agenda for further research'. We offer this case study analysis of a highly visible and successful new biotechnology firm as one contribution to that research effort.

Acknowledgements

This study was supported by a National Science Foundation dissertation improvement grant and a US-Israel bi-national science foundation (to A. Oliver) and from the UC Riverside Academic Senate and the Center for Ideas and Society (to K. Montgomery). The authors thank Phillip Bonacich, Julia Liebeskind, and Lynne Zucker for valuable comments on earlier drafts.

Notes

1. 'The fact that we came out with a new product has managed to promote the stock values of all NBFs, since the success of our firm has an impact on the perceived investment value of the entire industry' (New Genetics' financial executive for investors' relations).

2. HMOs are increasingly popular in the United States as a cost-effective model for delivering private-sector health care by combining in one organization the functions of direct patient care and financing of care.

References

Abernathy, W. J. & Clark, K. B. Innovation: Mapping the winds of creative destruction. *Research Policy*, 1985, *14*, 3–22.

Aldrich, H. E. & Pfeffer, J. Environments of organizations. *Annual Review of Sociology*, 1976, *2*, 79–105.

Argyres, N. S. & Liebeskind, J. P. Privatizing the intellectual commons: Universities and the commercialization of biotechnology. *Journal of Economic Behavior and Organization*, 1998, *35*, 427–54.

Arora, A. & Gambardella, A. Evaluating technological information and utilizing it: Scientific knowledge, technological capabilities, and external linkages in biotechnology. *Journal of Economic Behavior and Organization*, 1994, *24*, 91–114.

Arthur, J. B. Effects of human resource systems on manufacturing performance and turnover. *Academy of Management Journal*, 1994, *37*, 670–87.

Bacharach, S. Organizational theories: Some criteria for evaluation. *Academy of Management Review*, 1989, *14*, 496–515.

Baum, J. A. C. & Singh, J. V. Organizational hierarchies and evolutionary processes: Some reflections on a theory of organizational evolution. In J. A. C. Baum and J. V. Singh (Eds), *Evolutionary dynamics of organizations*. New York: Oxford University Press, 1994, pp. 3–22.

Burns, L. R. Physician practice management companies. *Health Care Management Review*, 1997, *22*, 32–46.

Burrill, S. G. with the Ernst and Young High Technology Group. *Biotech 90: Into the next decade*. New York: Mary Ann Liebert, 1989.

Burt, R. *Structural holes: The social structure of competition*. Cambridge, MA: Harvard University Press, 1992.

Carroll, G. R. Organizational ecology. *Annual Review of Sociology*, 1984, *10*, 71–93.

Chandler, A. *Strategy and structure: Chapters in the history of the American industrial enterprise*. Cambridge, MA: MIT Press, 1962.

Crane, D. *Invisible colleges: Diffusion of knowledge in scientific communities*. Chicago: University of Chicago Press, 1972.

DeCenzo, D. A. & Robbins, S. P. *Human resource management*. New York: John Wiley and Sons, 1996.

Dodgson, M. Learning, trust, and technological collaboration. *Human Relations*, 1993, *46*, 77–95.

Eisenhardt, K. M. Building theory from case research. *Academy of Management Review*, 1989, *4*, 532–50.

Fligstein, N. The spread of the multidivisional form among large firms, 1919–1979. *American Sociological Review*, 1985, *50*, 377–91.

Hannan, M. T. & Carroll, G. R. *Dynamics of organizational populations*. New York: Oxford University Press, 1992.

Hannan, M. T. & Freeman, J. The population ecology of organizations. *American Journal of Sociology*, 1977, *83*, 929–84.

Hannan, M. T. & Freeman, J. Structural inertia and organizational change. *American Sociological Review*, 1984, *49*, 149–64.

Huselid, M. A. The impact of human resource management practices on turnover, productivity, and corporate financial performance. *Academy of Management Journal*, 1995, *39*, 635–72.

Hybels, R. C. & Popielarz, P. A. The iron law revisited: The formation of an interorganizational oligarchy through joint ventures in US biotechnology. Paper presented at the Academy of Management annual meeting, Cincinnati, August 1996.

Jackson, S. E. & Schuler, R. S. Understanding human resource management in the context of organizations and their environments. *Annual Review of Psychology*, 1995, *46*, 237–64.

Kenney, M. *Biotechnology: The university industry complex*. New Haven, CT: Yale University Press, 1986.

Kornberg, A. *The golden helix: Inside biotech ventures*. Sausalito, CA: University Science Books, 1995.

Kreiner, K. & Schultz, M. Informal collaboration in R&D: The formation of networks across organizations. *Organization Studies*, 1993, *14*, 189–209.

Latour, B. & Woolgar, S. *Laboratory life: The social construction of scientific facts*. Beverly Hills, CA: Sage, 1979.

Ledford, G. E. & Lawler, E. E., III Research on employee participation: Beating a dead horse? *Academy of Management Review*, 1994, *19*, 633–6.

Lewin, A. Y., Long, C. P. & Carroll, T. N. The evolution of new organization forms. Working Paper 97-07-01, Duke University Fuqua School of Business, 1997.

Liebeskind, J. P. & Oliver, A. L. From handshake to contract: Intellectual property, trust and the social structure of academic research. In C. Lane and R. Bachmann (Eds), *Between Organizations*. New York: Oxford University Press, 1998, 118–45.

Liebeskind, J., Oliver, A. L., Zucker, L. & Brewer, M. Social networks, learning, and flexibility: Sourcing scientific knowledge in new biotechnology firms. *Organization Science*, 1996, *7*, 428–43.

McKelvey, B. *Organizational systematics: Taxonomy, classification, evolution*. Berkeley, CA: University of California Press, 1982.

McKelvey, B. & Aldrich, H. Populations, natural selection, and applied organizational science. *Administrative Science Quarterly*, 1983, *28*, 101–28.

Miner, A. S. Seeking adaptive advantage: Evolutionary theory and managerial action. In J. A. C. Baum and J. V. Singh (Eds), *Evolutionary dynamics of organizations*, New York: Oxford University Press, 1994, pp. 76–89.

Nonaka, I. Creating organizational order out of chaos: Self-renewal in Japanese firms. *California Management Review*, 1988, *12*, 53–65.

Nonaka, I. A dynamic theory of organizational knowledge creation. *Organization Science*, 1994, *5*, 14–37.

North Carolina Biotechnology Center. US Company Database. Research Triangle Park, NC, 1991.

Oliver, A. New biotechnology firms: A multilevel analysis of interorganizational relations in an emerging industry: Bringing process into structure. PhD dissertation, UCLA, 1993.

Ouchi, W. J., & Jagger, A. M. Type Z organization; Stability in the midst of mobility. *Academy of Management Review*, 1978, *3*, 305–14.

Pisano, G. P. The R&D boundaries of the firm: An empirical analysis. *Administrative Science Quarterly*, 1990, *35*, 153–76.

Powell, W. W. Neither market nor hierarchy: Network forms of organization. In L. L. Cummings and B. Staw (Eds), *Research in organizational behavior*. Greenwich, CT: JAI Press, 1990, pp. 295–336.

Powell, W. W. & Brantley, P. Competitive cooperation in biotechnology: Learning through networks? In N. Nohria and R. G. Eccles (Eds), *Networks and organizations: Structure, form and action*. Cambridge, MA: Harvard Business School Press, 1992, pp. 366–94.

Powell, W. W. & Owen-Smith, J. Universities and the market for intellectual property in the life sciences. *Journal of Policy Analysis and Management*, 1998, *17*, 253–77.

Powell, W. W., Koput, K. W. & Smith-Doerr, L. Interorganizational collaboration and the locus of innovation; Networks of learning in biotechnology. *Administrative Science Quarterly*, 1996, *41*, 116–45.

Quinn, J. B. Innovation and corporate strategy: Managed chaos. In M. Horwitch (Ed.), *Technology in the modern corporation: A strategic perspective*. Elmsford, NY: Pergamon Press, 1986, pp. 107–83.

Rappa, M. A. Assessing the emergence of new technologies: The case of compound semiconductors. In A. H. Van de Ven, H. L. Angel and M. S. Poole (Eds), *Research on the management of innovation*. Cambridge, MA: Ballinger, 1989, pp. 439–64.

Romanelli, E. The evolution of new organizational forms. *Annual Review of Sociology*, 1991, *17*, 79–103.

Schumpeter, J. A. *The theory of economic development*. Cambridge, MA: Harvard University Press, 1934/1975.

Selznick, P. *Leadership in administration*. New York: Harper and Row, 1957.

Stinchcomb, A. L. Social structure and organizations. In J. G. March (Ed.), *Handbook of organizations*. Chicago: Rand McNally, 1965, pp. 153–93.

Sutton, R. The virtues of closet qualitative research. *Organization Science*, 1997, *8*, 97–106.

Teece, D. J. Competition, cooperation, and innovation: Organizational arrangements for regimes of rapid technological progress. *Journal of Economic Behavior and Organization*, 1992, *18*, 1–25.

Tushman, M. & Anderson, P. Technological discontinuities and organizational environments. *Administrative Science Quarterly*, 1986, *31*, 439–65.

Van de Ven, A. H. & Garud, H. L. A framework for understanding the emergence of new industries. In R. S. Rosenbloom and R. A. Burgelman (Eds), *Research on technological innovation, management and policy*. Greenwich, CT: JAI Press, 1989, pp. 195–225.

Volberda, W. H. Toward the flexible form: How to remain vital in hypercompetitive environments. *Organization Science*, 1996, *3*, 359–74.

Weick, K. Re-punctuating the problem. In P. S. Goodman, J. M. Pennings and Associates (Ed), *New perspectives on organizational effectiveness*. San Francisco, CA: Jossey-Bass, 1977, pp. 193–225.

Yin, R. *Case study research*. Beverly Hills, CA: Sage, 1984.

Youndt, M. A., Snell, S. A., Dean, J. W. & Lepak, D. P. Human resources management, manufacturing strategy, and firm performance. *Academy of Management Journal*, 1996, *39*, 836–66.

Young, R. Is population ecology a useful paradigm for the study of organizations? *American Journal of Sociology*, 1988, *94*, 1–24.

Amalya L. Oliver is Assistant Professor of Sociology at The Hebrew University. She earned her PhD from UCLA's Department of Sociology. Her dissertation research involved a multi-level analysis of interorganizational relationships in the biotechnology industry. Currently, she is studying comparisons between formal and informal collaborations for intellectual capital in the biotechnology industry; country-level differences for the governance of intellectual capital exchanges; new organizational forms; and network theory and methods. She is also interested in the role of trust within and between organizations. Her work has appeared in *Organization Science, Organization Studies, Social Networks, Sociological Inquiry, Health Services Research,* and elsewhere. [E-mail: amalyao@shum.cc.huji.ac.il]

Kathleen Montgomery is Associate Professor of Organizations and Management at the University of California, Riverside's Anderson Graduate School of Management. She has been a post-doctoral fellow at UCLA and a visiting scholar at Stanford University's Graduate School of Business. Her PhD in Sociology is from New York University. Her research interests include changes in the professional/organizational relationship, especially as they reflect professional and organizational responses to environmental pressures and threats. Currently, she is developing a theoretical and empirical study of the phenomenon of organizational dysempowerment, and physician–patient relationships within managed care. She has published in *Organization Studies, Work and Occupations, Current Research on Occupations and Professions, Human Resources Management,* the *Academy of Management Best Papers Proceedings, Health Services Research, Medical Care,* the *Journal of the American Medical Association,* among others. [E-mail: kmont@mail.ucr.edu]

There are four breaks from the traditional 9-to-5 routine of employees who share a work location and see each other on a daily basis. Each of these offers challenges for companies and their managers but also opportunities. We can also expect telework to look very different in the next few years.

Telework:

The Advantages and Challenges of Working Here, There, Anywhere, and Anytime

NANCY B. KURLAND   **DIANE E. BAILEY**

Twenty-five years ago, Jack Nilles coined the term "telecommuting" while stuck in traffic in Los Angeles. It is not surprising then that initial interest in telecommuting was driven by concerns about traffic congestion and pollution in densely populated areas such as southern California. In the 1980s, as companies focused increasingly on cutting costs, they pointed to telecommuting as a means to reduce the expense of maintaining office space. More recently, organizations have begun to view telecommuting as a tool to attract and retain top personnel in fields with short labor supplies. Over the years, the substitution of computer-based technology for physical travel has led to a number of alternative work forms beyond home-based telecommuting, including satellite centers, neighborhood work centers, and mobile working. Together, these forms constitute "teleworking." What they have in common is a transition from in-person supervision to remote managing, from face-to-face communication to telecommunications-mediated communication, from on-site working to off-site or multiple-site working, and, in the case of groups, from side-by-side collaboration to virtual teamwork.

Estimates of the number of telecommuters in the U.S. vary, but most figures range between three and nine million people (three to eight percent of the workforce). These figures include people who work from home at least several days per month of their normal work schedule. Many forecasters predict these numbers will continue to rise, but forecasts for the U.S. in the year 2000 vary considerably: from 15 million workers to 44 million workers or 57% of the workforce. Further evidence of telecommuting's growing popularity is found in the creation in 1993 of a national trade organization, the International Telecommuting Advisory Council (ITAC), dedicated to promoting telework and telecommuting. Recently, ITAC published the premier issue of *Telecommute*, a monthly magazine devoted to "today's flexible workplace."

One troubling element of this trend in new work forms is that many companies are allowing employees to telework without adequately informing employees and managers about the benefits and challenges. In this ar-

Originally from *Organizational Dynamics*, Autumn 1999, pp. 53-68. © 1999 by Elsevier Science. Reprinted with permission.

Nancy B. Kurland is assistant professor of management and organization in the Marshall School of Business, University of Southern California, where she teaches courses in organizational behavior and business ethics. Her research focuses on telecommuting, gossip (informal communication), the social impact of technology, and ethics and incentives. She has published in *Academy of Management Review, Business Ethics Quarterly, Business & Society, Business and Society Review, Human Relations, Journal of Applied Psychology, The Information Society, Journal of Business Ethics,* and *Organization Science.* She is an active telecommuter.
E-mail: nkurland@marshall.usc.edu

Diane E. Bailey was awarded her B.S. in industrial engineering and operations research (IEOR) in 1988 from the University of California, Berkeley. She received her master's degree in 1990 in operations research and her Ph.D. in IEOR in 1994, both from Berkeley. She currently is assistant professor of industrial engineering and engineering management at Stanford University. She was assistant professor of industrial and systems engineering at the University of Southern California from 1994–1998. Bailey's dissertation on the relation between work team structure and performance in semiconductor manufacturing won the 1995 Institute of Industrial Engineering Doctoral Dissertation Award. Her research on the effectiveness of work teams has appeared in both engineering and business journals.
E-mail: debailey@stanford.edu

ticle, we differentiate among the previously mentioned alternative work forms of teleworking, describe advantages and challenges of each form, and provide recommendations to address these challenges. We base our insights on previous research, as well as on conversations Kurland had with 54 traditional on-site and remote supervisors and the teleworkers and non-teleworkers they manage in two high technology firms.

DEFINING TYPES OF TELEWORK

To begin the discussion, we define the four types of telework: home-based telecommuting, satellite offices, neighborhood work centers, and mobile working.

Home-based telecommuting refers to employees who work at home on a regular basis, though not necessarily (and, in fact, rarely) every day. For example, employees at Hewlett-Packard can opt to telecommute several hours to several days each week. (We do not consider as telecommuters the home-based workers who are self-employed or who otherwise have no connection to a central workplace.) A person can be said to be a telecommuter if her telecommunications link to the office is as simple as a telephone; however, telecommuters often use other communications media such as electronic mail, personal computer links to office servers, and fax machines. Either the firm or the employee purchases the home-based equipment. Hewlett-Packard covers most expenses for employees when they telecommute, including installing ISDN lines in employees' homes. In 1993, 100 American Express travel agents in 15 locations telecommuted. The company connected these employees' homes to American Express' phone

and data lines for a modest one-time expense of $1300 each, including hardware.

In *satellite offices*, employees work both outside the home and away from the conventional workplace in a location convenient to the employees and/or customers. A satellite office houses only employees from a single firm; it is in some sense a branch office whose purpose is to alleviate employees' commute. The satellite office is equipped with office furniture and equipment provided by the firm; in addition, administrative help may be available there. Fuji Xerox has a satellite office near Shin-Yurigaoka Station on the Odakuy Line in a suburb of Tokyo. It has PCs, teleconferencing, and other equipment so employees can work there without having to go to the headquarters office in the city. The people who work there belong to different departments within the firm so no whole unit is present at the satellite center.

A *neighborhood work center* is essentially identical to a satellite office with one major difference: the neighborhood work center houses more than one company's employees. In other words, several companies may share the lease on an office building and maintain separate office areas within the building for employees of each company. Office suites may be furnished by the site owner or by each renting firm. Satellite and neighborhood work centers are alternatives to home-based telecommuting; the employee avoids a long commute to the conventional workplace but remains in an office rather than a home setting. For example, Southern California has numerous telecenters in which employees from different companies can rent space monthly.

TABLE 1: ORGANIZATIONAL ADVANTAGES AND CHALLENGES OF TELEWORKING

	Advantages	Challenges	
Home-Based Telecommuting	• Greater productivity • Lower absenteeism • Better morale • Greater openness • Fewer interruptions at office • Reduced overhead • Wider talent pool • Lower turnover • Regulation compliance	• Performance monitoring • Performance measurement • Managerial control • Mentoring • Jealous colleagues • Synergy • Informal interaction • Organization culture • Virtual culture	• Organization loyalty • Interpersonal skills • Availability • Schedule maintenance • Work coordination • Internal customers • Communication • Guidelines (e.g. expenses) • Technology
Satellite	• Greater productivity • Better morale • Wider talent pool • Lower turnover • Customer proximity • Regulation compliance • Corporate culture intact	• Performance monitoring • Performance measurement • Managerial control	• Jealous colleagues • Virtual culture • Internal customers
Neighborhood Work Center	• Greater productivity • Better morale • Wider talent pool • Lower turnover • Customer proximity • Regulation compliance	• Performance monitoring • Performance measurement • Managerial control • Mentoring • Jealous colleagues • Synergy	• Informal interaction • Organization culture • Virtual culture • Organization loyalty • Schedule maintenance • Work coordination • Internal customers
Mobile Work	• Greater productivity • Lower absenteeism • Customer proximity	• Performance monitoring • Performance measurement • Managerial control • Synergy • Informal interaction • Organization culture • Virtual culture	• Organization loyalty • Availability • Schedule maintenance • Work coordination • Communication • Guidelines (e.g. expenses) • Technology

These centers sport conveniences such as private office spaces, cubicles, fax machines, data hookups, teleconferencing, and videoconferencing technology.

In contrast to telecommuters who work from one designated location outside the main office and who communicate with the office using electronic communication, *mobile workers* are frequently on the road, using communications technology to work from home, from a car, from a plane, or from a hotel—communicating with the office as necessary from each location. Mobile workers thus are accustomed to working in an assortment of locales. In an airport waiting lounge, one author recently overheard a woman ask a mobile worker, working on his laptop, where his office was. "Actually," he responded, "you're sitting in it." Most companies have employees who are intimately familiar with mobile work, like marketing managers, salespersons, investment bankers, investigative reporters, and any other personnel who need to be on the move to get their jobs done.

Telework, in any form, has ramifications beyond simply changing the way or place in which an individual employee performs work: It can extend to remote managing and virtual teams.

Remote managing occurs when managers are physically separated from their direct reports because the manager and/or the employee

TABLE 2: INDIVIDUAL ADVANTAGES AND CHALLENGES OF TELEWORKING

	Advantages	Challenges	
Home-Based Telecommuting	• Less time commuting • Cost savings • Less stress • No need for relocation • More autonomy • Schedule flexibility • Comfortable work environment • Fewer distractions • Absence of office politics • Work/family balance • Workplace fairness • More job satisfaction	• Social isolation • Professional isolation • Organization culture • Reduced office influence • Work/family balance • Informal interaction	• Conducive home environment • Focusing on work • Longer hours • Access to resources • Technical savvy
Satellite Office	• Less time commuting • Cost savings • Less stress • No need for relocation • Work/family balance • More job satisfaction	• Professional isolation • Reduced office influence	• Access to resources
Neighborhood Work Center	• Less time commuting • Cost savings • Less stress • No need for relocation • More autonomy • Absence of office politics • Work/family balance • More job satisfaction	• Social isolation • Professional isolation • Organization culture	• Reduced office influence • Access to resources
Mobile Work	• More autonomy • Schedule flexibility • Absence of office politics	• Social isolation • Professional isolation • Organization culture • Reduced office influence	• Longer hours • Access to resources • Technical savvy

teleworks, and thus manages these employees remotely. For example, a manager in Irvine, California at Fujitsu Business Systems supervises two employees, one based in Boston and the other in Dallas. Both employees telecommute full-time from home and the manager telecommutes part-time. Remote managing is characterized by this inability of a manager to observe her employees' work processes.

Virtual teams consist of team members who are geographically dispersed and who come together by way of telecommunications technology (e.g., video conferencing). Each team member may be located in a traditional office setting, but the offices are not proximate to one another. Additionally, virtual team members may telework, such as a telecommuter who is a member of a multiple-site team. A project manager at Hewlett-Packard sits in Northern California, while his team members abide in Southern California, Florida, and Brussels.

Thus, telework may have additional advantages and challenges that emerge when consideration extends beyond the isolated teleworker—both up (to managers) and across (to teammates) the traditional organization.

TABLE 3: SOCIETAL ADVANTAGES AND CHALLENGES OF TELEWORKING

	Advantages	Challenges
Home-Based Telecommuting	• Less traffic congestion • Less pollution • Less neighborhood crime • Greater community involvement	• Telework culture • Loss of ability to interact with others
Satellite Office	• Less traffic congestion • Less pollution • Greater community involvement	
Neighborhood Work Center	• Less traffic congestion • Less pollution • Greater community involvement	
Mobile Work	• Telework culture	

IDENTIFYING ADVANTAGES AND CHALLENGES OF TELEWORK

These alternative work forms bring both benefits and challenges to organizations, individuals, and society. Many of the advantages and challenges we discuss (see Tables 1 through 3) assume that the teleworker is away from the office a significant percentage of working time. The impact of each advantage and challenge may diminish for individuals who telework a small fraction of their working time.

HOME-BASED TELECOMMUTING

Organizational level. From the organization's perspective, home-based telecommuting provides an opportunity to improve workplace productivity. Because telecommuting employees experience greater schedule flexibility, they can work when they prefer, and thereby improve their productivity.

Also, popular press accounts of successful telecommuting programs often report that telecommuters take fewer sick days, are absent less, have higher job satisfaction, and have higher work performance ratings. These factors may positively affect productivity. A prime example of such success can be found at TeleService Resources, which was founded

in 1984 as a unit of American Airlines Reservations to handle the growing demand for call marketing services. In response to growing concerns over Texas state commuter legislative restrictions, as well as employee retention and alternative capacity solutions, TSR began a pilot project to allow their telephone agents to work from home. Over 25 agents now work from home, using state-of-the-art call center technology, providing a seamless connection with TSR's Dallas-Ft. Worth call center. TSR management believes the teleworkers have been more productive, and that they are more satisfied with their jobs compared to their office-based counterparts.

Furthermore, telecommuting provides employees with a relatively distraction-free environment, as noted by one on-site manager, "[F]rom time to time [I telecommute] just to get away from here, so that [when] I have specific things I want to get done, then I can get away from the phones and the people walking in." Also, because telecommuters have relatively distraction-free environments, they are more open to receiving interruptions while at the traditional office. For example, one telecommuter commented, "Before I started telecommuting, [if] somebody would come along and interrupt me it would irritate me. So today . . . certainly I have days when I am annoyed by interruptions but they're fewer because I think, 'Okay, I'm not going to worry about it because I'm going to focus on this when I get home.'" Together, these factors, relating to the location of work, the timing of work, and the quality of work life, can increase productivity.

Home-based telecommuting benefits organizations in ways beyond productivity. It enables them to cut costs related to office space, as well as to address space constraints. For example, IBM recently reported a $75 million annual savings in real estate expenses as a result of telecommuting. In 1994, AT&T saved $80 million in real-estate and office overhead costs from having employees telecommute. And more modestly, the Energy Usage Analysis Service for the General Services Administration in Ft. Worth, Texas, saved $30,000 a year in office space costs when a group leader convinced his management to let a seven-member staff, slated to move to another office space, telecommute from home full-time instead.

Another reason to implement telecommuting is that it widens the talent pool available to the organization. It also may stem turnover by providing workers with flexibility that allows them to keep their jobs in the face of external demands or desires. As one on-site manager commented about his telecommuting employee: "I think that one very good [advantage] is the fact that we have her here. . . . [I]f we do not have this flexibility, I think that we might lose her to some other department here or to another organization."

Finally, telecommuting programs enable firms to comply with regulations such as the Clean Air Act and the Americans with Disabilities Act. The City of San Diego boasts an extensive telecommuting program that it implemented in response to the federal and state mandates to clean up the air. Telecommuting gets people off the freeways and provides opportunities to people who stay at home or who might otherwise have difficulty traveling to a workplace. The organizational advantages of telecommuting thus cover a wide spectrum, including behavioral outcomes, productivity, and legal issues.

On the other hand, several challenges may hamper an organization's willingness to integrate telecommuting into the traditional office environment. A major challenge for managers is their inability to physically observe their employees' performance. They question, "How do you measure productivity, build trust, and manage people who are physically out of sight?" If a manager can't see her subordinates in action, then she can't note where the employee is struggling and where he is strong, and may not be able to provide reliable and constructive performance feedback. Some managers can just focus on outcome, rather than process, assuming that these outcomes are easy to measure and monitor. Salespeople, for example, are prime contenders for telecommuting, and may be one reason both IBM and Merrill Lynch are staunch supporters of telecommuting. But for many other types of employees, monitoring and measuring their performance remain problematic and a source of concern. One manager in our research complained, "At this point, I don't have any measure at all, none whatsoever, and that's one of the pieces of this that bothers me about the telecommuter; there needs to be a better way to measure productivity."

Further, telecommuting can negatively affect the social network in the workplace, and thereby pose other challenges for managers. For example, telecommuting may negatively impact those who remain in the workplace (i.e., non-telecommuters) by (1) disrupting teamwork, (2) fragmenting the local social network [of those left behind], and (3) creating possible resentment among employees NOT chosen to telecommute. For example, in one case, a telecommuter complained that because he lived next to a golf course, his colleagues teased that when he worked at home, he had gone "tele-golfing."

Other entities may also face challenges in dealing with telecommuting. Unions, for example, fear that telecommuting may adversely affect worker solidarity because telecommuters are more physically dispersed and less able to organize collectively.

Additionally, managers may find it difficult to create team synergy and to overcome the absence of informal, interactive learning—learning that takes place by the water cooler, over lunch, or in the hallways. On the challenge to synergy, one manager commented, "Productivity gains are measured when you put people into an office environment and a lot of synergy's created. . . . When you telecommute . . . there's a lack of energy that I notice in the office. . . ." On the challenge to informal, interactive learning, another manager commented: "It's much more difficult to communicate with [the telecommuter]. [M]ost communication here tends to be informal communication, not meetings, not memos, or things like that. We find that he is probably the least in touch with the general things that are going on in the division in terms of product ideas, concepts. I mean he can make it for a formal presentation but those don't happen very often compared to work getting done as people just run into folks, have lunch with folks, and that kind of thing."

This manager affirmed that participating in formal, scheduled meetings is not enough. When employees work off-site, they miss the learning that occurs, informally, spontaneously—learning that cannot be scheduled, and is sometimes known as "in place career development."

Other issues concern developing and transmitting organization culture. First, organizations may find it difficult to transmit their cultures to individuals who often are physically remote. How can organizations communicate and instill values to and in these employees? How can organizations develop and express norms? Will telecommuters be less loyal to a company than non-telecommuters? Will telecommuters fail to develop interpersonal skills, some of them firm-specific, that help people communicate and cooperate in the workplace?

A second concern is the issue of creating a virtual culture: How does an organization make telecommuting acceptable among telecommuters and non-telecommuters, among subordinates and managers, and among employees and customers? For example, some non-telecommuters may believe that teleworkers are not working when they are not regularly seen in the traditional office, as with the so-called tele-golfing employee mentioned above. Others may be reluctant to phone telecommuters for fear of interrupting them at their homes. Clearly, cultural concerns, both of conveying a corporate culture to the individual telecommuter and of expanding the corporate culture to include virtual etiquette and understanding, pose tremendous challenges to the organization. Merrill Lynch may have one solution. It has over 130 employees working from home an average of three days per week. In its formalized program, Merrill Lynch provides training and equipment along with the same software that exists in its office. It has also created a "telecommuting simulation lab" where prospective telecommuters are required to train for two weeks prior to working from home. However, to fully develop a virtual culture, Merrill Lynch will need to expand its labs to include interactions with office-based colleagues.

Other challenges relate to coordinating and organizing work. One challenge has to do with the telecommuter's availability. When telecommuters take advantage of flexibility in scheduling their work, they may be unavailable to work peers and clients who maintain traditional office hours. Another challenge relates to how organizations distribute tasks between telecommuters and office workers. Who should handle what? How should handoffs be carried out? Should work-related items (e.g., files, contacts, physical objects) be transferred from office to home and back? Still other difficulties spring from arranging linkages between telecommuters and internal customers if the latter are unaware that the telecommuters work at home. Lastly, despite advances in communications technology, communicating with a remote employee teleworker can still pose challenges, such as conveying non-verbal messages. As such, there is a greater need to establish contingency plans in the event that the telecommuter cannot be reached by, or cannot reach, an office counterpart.

Finally, telecommuting challenges organizations to establish clear telecommuting policy guidelines. Some telecommuters are concerned with how to handle expenses. For example, if the firm has supplied the printer, can the telecommuter also use it for personal purposes? If so, how should subsequent costs (e.g., toner and paper) be expensed? Others worry about their telecommuting colleagues' technological competence. One telecommuter complained that he works with other telecommuters who cannot send e-mail, who cannot use basic software such as PowerPoint®, and who are unable to transfer files electronically. He loses his own time (and patience) when forced to help them. Although not as frequent a concern, determining employees' eligibility for workers' compensation is also difficult, largely because no one is around to witness accidents in the home. Establishing guidelines and requirements for telecommuting may be an easier challenge to overcome. The state of Oregon provides a very detailed, easy-to-follow workbook to help a company devise its own guidelines, as do other sources available through the Internet.

Individual level. From the individual's perspective, telecommuting offers a number of advantages. The most obvious benefit is that it eliminates (for full-time telecommuters) or reduces (for partial-week telecommuters) commute time. Reduced commute time saves gas and car maintenance, as well as lessens traffic-related stress. Moreover, for workers whose long commutes may cause them to consider relocating (either to a new firm or to a new neighborhood), telecommuting saves them the expense and upheaval of such major change. Telecommuting further provides employees with more autonomy and control over their work lives via schedule flexibility and an invisibility from managers and co-workers. They can work in comfortable and familiar environments with fewer distractions. Since few people see them, they have no need to dress up, and thus they save money on dry cleaning and dress clothes. Moreover, their at-home situation allows them to avoid office politics. For many employees, telecommuting provides an even greater advantage: It permits a more effective balance of work demands with responsibilities at home—a major reason Hewlett-Packard strongly supports telecommuting. Telecommuting also allows for workplace fairness by enhancing employment opportunities for disabled individuals. Hence, because telecommuting can improve individuals' overall work-life quality, telecommuters may be more satisfied with their jobs.

By comparison, probably the most commonly expressed challenge of telecommuting is overcoming the isolation caused by the separation of the telecommuter from the social network in the traditional work space. Ursula Huws referred to this isolation as a "trapped housewife syndrome." While isolation can lead to social frustration that arises from a lack of interaction with work peers, it can also lead to feelings of professional isolation. Telecommuters may fear that when they're out of sight, they're out of mind for promotions and other rewards. Because telecommuting encourages autonomy rather than solidarity, still other telecommuters report that their commitment or loyalty to the organization diminishes because they're not "around" the traditional workplace often enough. Isolation may inhibit an individual's ability to learn the corporation's culture and may also serve to reduce the telecommuter's influence within the firm.

Another challenge commonly voiced about telecommuting relates to its perceived role as a panacea for employees, especially women, who face family obligations. Telecommuters may have difficulty establishing a home environment that is conducive to work. Children and spouses alike may not respect the sanctity and privacy of a home office. Children, especially, may have a tough time learning not to interrupt their working parent. Indeed, telecommuting may hinder employees' productivity if they are expected to simultaneously raise children who may need constant attention, "trapping" women in the dual roles of caretaker and employee while working at home. Conversely, with work located right in the home, and thus so much more accessible, telecommuters may find themselves working longer hours, further straining family relationships.

Another issue in work and family balance centers on the function of the commute. Employees may need the transition time between home and work to refocus themselves from home challenges to work challenges and vice versa. In other words, the daily commute may serve as a "warm-up" period in the morning and a "cool-down" in the evening. Thus, telecommuting, by placing workers in the home and eliminating the commute to work, serves to blur distinctions between family life and work life. Quite possibly, this blurring is a disadvantage for the individual.

Two other challenges should be noted. Telecommuters must overcome the challenge of maintaining access to resources at work, as failure to do so could lead to performance losses. Telecommuters may need to be more technically savvy than their office peers, since support services are not accessible on-site.

Societal level. Telecommuting provides societal benefits as well. It can decrease traffic congestion on strained highways and reduce automobile-related air pollution—though its impact may be negligible if only a few people telecommute. By working at home, telecommuters discourage community crime that might otherwise occur in bedroom communities. Further, because telecommuters have more flexible schedules and gain time by not commuting to work, they can spend more time building community ties.

However, telecommuting does pose challenges to society. Society as a whole needs to come to terms with telecommuting; it needs to develop a culture of telework. One issue that this culture must resolve is zoning regulations that forbid business parcel delivery within residential neighborhoods. Another is the assumption (by friends, relatives, neighbors, etc.) that anyone at home during the day is free to chat, to watch a child, or to run an errand. A greater, but we suspect much less likely, concern that has been put forward is that, by transforming work from a sensual activity to an abstract, computer-mediated one, telecommuting may cause a gradual degradation of a person's ability to interact with other people in a personal, intimate, and human manner. Over time, and with enough people involved, this degradation could change the nature of social intercourse in disturbing and undesirable ways.

SATELLITE OFFICES AND NEIGHBORHOOD WORK CENTERS

Telework, via satellite offices or neighborhood work centers, shares many of the organizational, individual, and societal benefits and challenges associated with home-based telecommuting. For example, consistent with telecommuting advantages, satellite office and neighborhood work center employees will spend less time commuting, will be better able to balance work demands with family demands, and can be located closer to external customers. A shared disadvantage is that being off-site invites managerial concerns about measuring employee productivity.

Nevertheless, several differences exist. On the plus side, employees who work in satellite offices may experience less professional and social isolation than do home-based telecommuters. Because the satellite office houses only employees of a single firm, much of the corporate culture may be replicated in the satellite site. Informal interactions are more likely; thus, mentoring and informal learning may again take place, reducing professional isolation. Likewise, in contrast to home-based workers, satellite office and neighborhood work center employees should feel less socially isolated because other people are present in their work environments. However, neighborhood work center employees may continue to feel professionally isolated. Because the neighborhood center services a community rather than an organization, it most likely will not house sufficient numbers of employees from any single firm to provide a firm-specific learning environment. Hence, impediments to productivity, such as those related to a lack of informal interaction and remoteness in relation to internal customers, may persist in neighborhood work centers.

MOBILE WORKING

The implications of mobile working stand in contrast to those of home-based telecommuting, satellite offices, and neighborhood work centers. Whereas telecommuting brings the employee home, mobile work sends the employee away. Extant technology enables employees to work anywhere and anytime. Employees are further freed from physical office constraints. Organizations benefit as employees work more closely with customers and other stakeholders, which is one reason that Fujitsu Business Communications encourages its account executives to telecommute mobilely.

However, advantages associated with telecommuting for the individual prove to be absent in the mobile work environment. Mobile workers find it more difficult to balance work demands with home demands. They are often away from home for days and weeks, and may spend a considerable amount of time in hotels—all of which may chip away at the mobile worker's morale. Two mobile workers discussed the disadvantages of this work form:

"[When I was mobile, I was] always away from my family. Lots of travel. I put on 20,000 miles on my car [in less than one year]. Just trying to communicate with . . . many people is very difficult. Just the fact that I was always traveling I think was frustrating . . . being away from my family, [and always] in hotels."

"Well, I don't know that I personally derive any benefit. I gain freeway time. I gain less face time with individuals. My travel time goes up. I have the ability to access information anywhere I'm at. Personally the only way that it affects me is that I have to spend more time driving and I have less time to see people face to face."

Mobile working has few societal benefits except that it promotes frequent interaction among people outside the organization. It thus enables mobile workers to build and refine their interpersonal skills and in turn to contribute to a milieu of healthy, human social interaction. However, a more likely result for society is that mobile workers merely add to air pollution and traffic congestion.

FURTHER RAMIFICATIONS: REMOTE MANAGING AND VIRTUAL TEAMS

Remote Managing. When employees telework, managers necessarily manage them remotely. Most often, managers do so only part-time and from short distances, since employees usually telecommute or work on the road for only part of each week. During the remainder of the week, these employees come to the main office; managers can interact with them face-to-face. In such scenarios, managers have ample opportunity to observe, counsel, and mentor subordinates. In addition, teleworking employees are able to associate with their peers both formally and informally. Through this collegial interaction, organizations can foster shared values and norms between on-site workers and frequently remote employees.

The situation becomes complicated, however, when teleworkers "hotel." Hoteling refers to the process by which companies assign office space to employees on an as-needed, temporary basis. In a hoteling environment, employees have no permanent office or desk; rather, they may be in a different space each time they go to the office. For example, Cisco Systems converted to hoteling in its Freemont, California, office. At the time, the Freemont office served 33 employees (account managers, systems engineers, and support staff). After converting to a hoteling environment, these employees shared four private phone booths, six cubicles, one team cube, four carrels, and a lab for the systems engineers. Such arrangements can cut costs tremendously. But companies need to be wary that under a hoteling arrangement, teleworkers don't often find that each time they visit the main office, they are located at some distance from their work groups, and thus they miss out on some of the interactions these employees expect and need to participate in when at the office.

Remotely managing employees full-time and from great distances is difficult and of greater concern. Although truly remote managing has undeniable benefits (e.g., it enlarges the pool from which to choose talented workers and may place the remote employee closer to external customers), it constrains managers' ability to communicate across time zones and to mentor teleworkers. As one remote mobile manager remarked:

"In our business and in a lot of other people's business, the coaching and counseling that you do with people is really, really critical. And it's a constant process as a manager. So that's one of the challenges: How do you develop your people? How do you have enough face-to-face [time], or enough time in a professional environment with them to be able to see the things they need to improve on and to be able then to spend that coaching and counseling time with them? If you do

everything remotely, at the end of the quarter, at the end of the half, how do you do somebody's review? How do you assess their performance? It's easy to identify their performance based upon activity and, you know, the results. But how about those personal development or skills development issues that you really need to focus on?"

Virtual teams. Virtual teams consist of members who are separated organizationally or geographically, sometimes by continents. The number of virtual teams is growing as more people work across internal functional boundaries and across external boundaries with vendors, customers, complementary enterprises, and direct competitors. More so than other forms of telework, virtual teams depend on e-mail, video-conferencing, audio-conferencing, and the like to meet, collaborate, and share ideas. Virtual teams benefit from their diverse memberships, cross-cultural links, access to wider talent pools, and broader ranges of customer service.

However, virtual teams face a number of challenges. One engineer we interviewed spoke of problems he faces on a virtual team spread out among two California locations and a European one. The team must overcome considerable cultural barriers. For example, the Europeans on the team prefer formal modes of communication, while the Americans prefer more informal ones. Reliance on e-mails and telephone calls (which must be coordinated across time zones) complicated processes of informal communication, which frustrated the American side of the team. Team members must also strive to create synergy and shared values; their attempts in these domains is made more difficult by their remote locations. This problem is likely to exist even for teams whose teleworking members are located in the same city, as lack of face-to-face time severely hampers the development of a team's sense of itself. All of these factors may delay decision time in the team and, ultimately, may negatively affect its performance.

A continuum of remote managing. We summarize the discussion of remote managing and virtual teams by building a continuum showing the degree of difficulty, in terms of coordination, observation, and so on, involved in various remote managing situations. In Figure 1, the employee's work arrangement is located along the continuum; we assume for purposes of argument that the manager is located at the main office. Local,

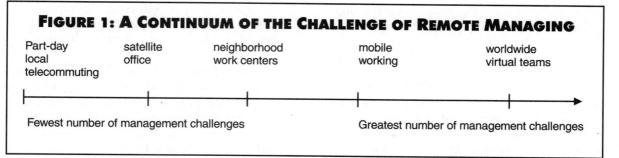

FIGURE 1: A CONTINUUM OF THE CHALLENGE OF REMOTE MANAGING

| Part-day local telecommuting | satellite office | neighborhood work centers | mobile working | worldwide virtual teams |

Fewest number of management challenges   Greatest number of management challenges

part-time telecommuting represents the least challenging remote managing situation for the manager based at the main office. Remote managing becomes more challenging the further the subordinate is from the office (in terms of physical distance for satellite offices, in terms of both distance and association for neighborhood work centers), with virtual teams presenting the most difficult situation.

PREPARING FOR AND MANAGING TELEWORK ENVIRONMENTS

Managers can address many of the teleworking challenges described in this article through careful preparation and on-going involvement. We provide recommendations to aid this process.

Guidelines. Organizations need to prepare themselves and their employees for telework. Guidelines can prepare teleworkers and managers by covering topics such as scheduling, communication expectations, telecommuting eligibility, performance expectations, expense policies, and how to maintain healthy collegial relationships.

The State of California Telework Program, a collaborative effort undertaken by the Department of Personnel Administration (DPA) and the Department of General Services (DGS), provides extensive information regarding its policies and procedures online at *http://www.dpa.ca.gov/jobsnpay/telework/telemain.htm.*

Infrastructure. Managers need to guarantee that prospective teleworkers have basic technical tools, such as e-mail access and responsive communication links (e.g., ISDN lines) to ensure successful off-site work. Further, managers should help teleworkers address work-family issues, including the design of conducive home environments for work. For example, one manager we spoke with is himself a full-time, home-based telecommuter who manages full-time, home-

based telecommuters. He personally visits his telecommuting employees' home work spaces early in the process, advising improvements as necessary.

Availability. Many firms require teleworkers to maintain working schedules consistent with the office schedule (e.g., 8 to 5 schedule, with lunch at noon) to facilitate coordination with work peers. We caution, however, that such a practice may reduce productivity gains associated with telework. Whether a company requires a fixed schedule will obviously vary by the type of job; for example, it may be more essential for customer service representatives than for design engineers. Managers may choose instead to negotiate a certain number of hours during which the teleworker will be available. Teleworkers may enhance their availability by carrying a pager or by proactively contacting the main office by e-mail or phone.

Communication. Another element of preparation should address communication needs. To solve many communications problems, off-site workers can let a centralized communications center know where they are working. If the teleworking employee services internal customers, then these customers must be alerted to the employee's remote days. Some customers may find contacting the employee at home an inconvenience, while others will continue to demand face-to-face interaction. These specific concerns can be handled on a case-by-case basis.

Training may need to focus on time zone and cross-cultural communication barriers, especially for virtual teams. Often several time zones separate supervisors from their employees, thus allowing only a few hours during which their work schedules overlap. Issues that could otherwise be handled through face-to-face communication any time in a work day may go unaddressed unless individuals make a conscious effort to set aside time. It is critical that both supervisors and employees feel they can share their concerns, and that they are capable of communicating their concerns cogently. Managers and employees may need to improve their ability to communicate effectively with electronic media.

Task scheduling. Part-time telecommuters can learn to reserve certain work for their telecommute days—work that does not require access to on-site resources or that does demand hours of uninterrupted quiet time.

Meeting scheduling. Organizations periodically should bring on site non-collocated individuals whose work is interdependent to enable them to get to know one another. Establishing initial bases of trust and familiarity through face-to-face interaction strengthens subsequent virtual communication. The process is particularly important for virtual teams. In addition, supervisors may wish to schedule regular meetings, "peacock sessions," either face-to-face or electronically mediated, in which employees share their accomplishments and "strut their stuff." Such meetings counter the view that when workers are out of sight, they must not be working.

Trips to the main office. Organizations may require employees to be on site at regular intervals to help enmesh them in the organization's culture. Some other firms require teleworkers to work in the main office for a given amount of time prior to teleworking to allow the company's culture to sink in. Subsequent office visits and interactive idea-sharing forums, visits, including time set aside by managers for employees to voice concerns, allow employees to develop social and professional ties. These ties foster teleworkers' beliefs that they actively participate in the processes that govern them, and subsequently combat professional isolation. Also, frequent e-mail may increase off-site employees' commitment to the organization, although it may reduce solidarity in existing social groups.

Performance measurement. Supervisors can begin to manage teleworkers by outputs rather than inputs. However, for managers who want to actively mentor their employees or for employees whose work is not easily quantifiable, a focus on outputs may be limiting. Organizations can supplement an output focus with frequent communication. Computer technology further alleviates the problem of in-person observation for many other types of workers. Teleworkers can electronically submit observable, quantifiable outputs such as reports, files, graphs, and other work-specific data. For example, one manager

we spoke with monitors his telecommuters' performance daily using computerized statistics of product orders, number of buys, and the like.

Non-teleworker buy-in. Managers should cultivate non-teleworker buy-in as part of the preparation process. On-site employees may find that their workload increases and disruptions multiply if they become the resource for questions while the teleworker works away from the main office. Thus, managers must estimate the impact of teleworking on non-teleworkers and devise appropriate business procedures to limit this impact as much as possible. Moreover, organizations should discourage the perspective that teleworkers do not work, or that they do not work as hard as office employees.

In sum, effective preparation and subsequent managing can foster a healthy and productive telework culture. Clearly, current and expected advances in telecommunications technology will facilitate a growing number of teleworkers. Thus, creating a positive culture now for remote workers will reap numerous future benefits for individuals, organizations, and society alike.

THE FUTURE OF TELEWORK

Many forecasters predict a steady and considerable increase in the number of teleworkers in the years to come. The increase, they claim, will be precipitated by tremendous advances in telecommunications and multimedia technology that will make communication between a remote site and a main office even smoother and easier than it is today. The technological advances will come at a time when the U.S. economy will experience continued growth in service industries. When no physical product is associated with work, as in the service industries, teleworking becomes a more viable option. Even in some industries where there is a physical product, its creation may not require hands-on attention in a central site. For example, the growth of the software industry provides a large pool of programmers who quite easily can contribute to the creation of an application program from the comfort of a home office. Thus, we expect that teleworking in the future—even in the next few years—will look very different than it does today.

One short-term change, already evident in some locales, is that new homes will be designed with a home office as a standard feature, and housing developments will include ISDN lines as commonly as they do telephone and sewer lines. Already in the Silicon Valley one sees newspaper advertisements for apartments with ISDN lines.

Some small firms may go completely virtual. For example, Janet Caswell describes how a small accounting firm established all its employees in home offices, gave up the lease on a main office, and placed the remaining office supplies in storage, with plans to go completely paperless in the near future. Other firms will sport main offices that are less crowded than before. Already in universities, empty hallways are common, as professors opt to work at home, using computers to communicate with students and colleagues. Efforts in distance learning (where the students, the professor, or both, are located away from the traditional classroom) suggest a possible decline in an on-campus presence. In the corporate world, being in the main office soon could be minimally effective in increasing one's visibility should telecommuting become increasingly popular, as there may be no one else there to do the seeing.

Teleworking may fulfill the desire of many workers to leave large urban areas behind them. Currently, the Sierra Nevada mountains in California are becoming much more populated as workers take to the hills, computers in tow. The surge in population in previously remote areas will grow dramatically, and in many cases there will be unfavorable effects on the rural environment and on local economies. Meanwhile, back in the cities, we might expect to see fewer large office parks and ultimately less congestion. Teleworking may conceivably spark a long-term spreading out of the U.S. population that will alter, among other things, tax bases and transportation needs.

Also, we are beginning to see telecities or villages in which "information technologies are used for mobility, economic growth, and other long-term public interests, as well as the short-term private interests usually satisfied by competitive markets." The Blue Line Televillage in Compton, California, is comprised of four different levels of structure (from largest to smallest): central tele-district centers, sub-regional centers, televillage centers and neighborhood communication centers. The telecity Blue Line architects wanted to spatially redesign urban areas, making everything (all services, public and private)

available within walking distance or a short public shuttle ride from each home. The Blue Line Televillage includes a small telework center, a computer center, videoconference center, meeting rooms and information kiosks. Many services are available there, including ATM machines, distance education classes, computer and internet classes, and public access computers. Future televillages might also have connections to government offices, retailers, and medical clinics.

The long-term ramifications of teleworking on a global scale may include a lessening of immigration to the U.S. and the diminishment of U.S. engineering and business schools as premier degree-granting institutions. For example, as communication technology allows software development to spread to India, fewer Indian engineers will seek higher degrees—and ultimately employment—in the U.S. Domestic high-technology firms will find it more difficult to attract talent, but they also may have less need for it. U.S. workers may face lower wages and fewer opportunities if positions in service industries, like those in manufacturing industries before them, move overseas. The technology that will enable U.S. workers to work at home, similarly, will allow foreign workers to remain in their home country. The result may at once bring both benefits and hardships to U.S. workers.

Finally, telework might open up new market opportunities for innovative companies. Already, companies such as Cisco Systems, Fujitsu Business Communications, KPMG Peat Marwick LLP, Flextime Corporation, and Synergy Planning are marketing products and advice designed to address teleworkers' unique needs.

We have listed here a few of the expected impacts associated with a predicted rise in teleworking. We add the caveat that the forecasts of large numbers of future telecommuters are simply that—forecasts. Quite possibly, individual workers and managers may determine the challenges of telework outweigh the advantages, and thus decline to set up teleworking arrangements. Or, more likely, individuals may telecommute on a part-time basis, thereby muting the impact caused by a large teleworking population. Nonetheless, in the face of this phenomenon, small businesses, large corporations, local, state, and federal government agencies, and the public at large do well to begin to develop public policies to address the needs, challenges, and ramifications associated with telework. Rural towns should plan for new development. For example, towns and cities should revisit zoning codes, managers should design methods for mentoring and evaluating remote employees, and teleworkers should seek ways to ensure their employment while allowing themselves to benefit from telework. Although some outcomes are unavoidable, careful planning may serve to make the transition to the new future world of work easier for all.

SELECTED BIBLIOGRAPHY

A joint effort among the Arizona Department of Administration Travel Reduction Programs (602-542-3637), the Oregon Department of Energy Telecommuting Resources (503-378-4040), and the Washington State Energy Office, Telecommuting Resources (360-956-2000) produced an excellent Telecommuting Training Kit. It contains guidelines, a workbook, and a video to foster cooperation and understanding among prospective telecommuters, co-workers, and supervisors. Also visit any bookstore in person or online and ask for sources on telecommuting. Many consultants estimate the number of people who telecommute. We found our numbers in part from J. Langhoff's "Telework in the Year 2000: Consultants Give Their Predictions," *Tele-Trends: The Official Newsletter of ITAC (The International Telework Advisory Council)*, 5:2, p. 1+ (1997). Also, visit the web sites of the U.S. Department of Transportation *(http://www.bts.gov/ntl/DOCS/telecommute.html)* and ITAC *(http://www.telecommute.org/index.html)*.

For theory, reviews, and empirical studies of telecommuting and alternative work forms, read P. L. Mokhtarian and I. Salomon's "Modeling the Choice of Telecommuting: Setting the Context," *Environment and Planning*, 1994; 26: 749–766. F. D. Becker, "Loosely-Coupled Settings: A Strategy for Computer-Aided Work Decentralization," *Research in Organizational Behavior, 1986*, Vol. 8, 199–231 (JAI Press); U. Huws's "Telework: Projections," *Futures*, 1991, January/February, 19–30; J. G. Caswell's "Going Virtual: How We Did It," *Journal of Accountancy*, 1995, December, 64–67; and Kurland and Egan's "Telecommuting: Justice and Control in the Virtual Organization," *Organization Science* (forthcoming).

Knowledge Transfer: A Basis for Competitive Advantage in Firms

Linda Argote
Carnegie Mellon University
and
Paul Ingram
Columbia University

This concluding article in the special issue of *Organizational Behavior and Human Decision Processes* on the foundations of knowledge transfer in organizations argues that the creation and transfer of knowledge are a basis for competitive advantage in firms. The article builds on a framework of knowledge reservoirs to show why knowledge transfer can be difficult and to identify the kinds of knowledge that are most difficult to transfer to different contexts. The article develops the proposition that interactions among people, tasks, and tools are least likely to fit the new context and hence are the most difficult to transfer. This theoretical result illuminates how organizations can derive competitive advantage by transferring knowledge internally while preventing its external transfer to competitors. Because people are more similar within than between organizations, interactions involving people transfer more readily within than between firms. By embedding knowledge in interactions involving people, organizations can both effect knowledge transfer internally and impede knowledge transfer externally. Thus, knowledge embedded in the interactions of people, tools, and tasks provides a basis for competitive advantage in firms. ©2000 Academic Press

The ability to transfer knowledge from one unit to another has been found to contribute to the organizational performance of firms in both the manufacturing (Epple, Argote, & Murphy, 1996; Galbraith, 1990) and service sectors (Baum & Ingram, 1998; Darr, Argote, & Epple, 1995). Although the benefits of knowledge transfer have been documented in many settings, the effectiveness of knowledge transfer varies considerably among organizations (Argote, 1999; Szulanski, 1996).

The current article, the concluding article in this special issue of *Organizational Behavior and Human Decision Processes* on the psychological foundations of knowledge transfer in organizations, presents a conceptual framework for analyzing knowledge transfer in organizations. The article begins by defining knowledge transfer and discussing its measurement. A framework of knowledge reservoirs (repositories where knowledge is embedded in organizations) that was developed by McGrath and Argote (in press) is used to demonstrate why knowledge transfer can be difficult and to organize the evidence on the kinds of knowledge that are more readily transferred. The article argues that the creation and transfer of knowledge in organizations provide a basis for competitive advantage in firms.

KNOWLEDGE TRANSFER DEFINED

Knowledge transfer in organizations is the process through which one unit (e.g., group, department, or division) is affected by the experience of another. This definition is similar to definitions of transfer at the indi-

We thank Joel Baum, Aimée Kane, Bill McEvily, Dick Moreland, Ron Ophir, Ray Reagans, and Peter Roberts for their helpful comments.

Address correspondence and reprint requests to Linda Argote, Graduate School of Industrial Administration, Carnegie Mellon University, Pittsburgh, PA 15213. E-mail: argote@cmu.edu.

vidual level of analysis in cognitive psychology. For example, Singley and Anderson (1989, p. 1) defined transfer at the individual level as "how knowledge acquired in one situation applies (or fails to apply) to another." Although knowledge transfer in organizations involves transfer at the individual level, the problem of knowledge transfer in organizations transcends the individual level to include transfer at higher levels of analysis, such as the group, product line, department, or division. For example, one manufacturing team may learn from another how to better assemble a product or a geographical division may learn a different approach to product design from its counterpart in another division.

Knowledge transfer in organizations manifests itself through changes in the knowledge or performance of the recipient units. Thus, knowledge transfer can be measured by measuring changes in knowledge or changes in performance. For example, a performance-based approach to measuring knowledge was used by Darr, Argote, and Epple (1995) to estimate the extent to which the productivity of fast-food stores was affected by the experience of the other stores in their franchise. Similarly, Baum and Ingram (1998) analyzed the extent to which the survival of hotels was affected by the experience of other hotels in their chain. Benkard (in press) analyzed the extent to which experience producing one model of a product affected the amount of labor required to produce a subsequent model. A particular challenge in assessing transfer through measuring changes in performance is controlling for factors in addition to the experience of other units that may affect the performance of the recipient unit (see Argote, 1999).

Knowledge transfer in organizations can also be assessed through measuring changes in the knowledge of the recipient unit, although this approach also poses challenges. A significant component of the knowledge that organizations acquire may be tacit and not easily articulated (Nonaka, 1991). Tacit knowledge may not be captured through the verbal reports often used to measure knowledge. Performance-based measurement approaches are better suited to capture tacit knowledge than approaches that attempt to measure the knowledge more directly. For example, a series of studies by Berry and Broadbent (1984, 1987) showed that individuals were able to transfer their experience from one management simulation to another: The performance of participants with significant experience on a previous simulation was better than that of participants with little or no experience. Although experienced participants performed better on a subsequent simulation, they were not able to articulate why they performed better. Neither self-report questionnaire measures nor verbal protocols showed differences in the knowledge of experienced and inexperienced participants. Thus, unlike performance-based measures, verbal measures of knowledge were not able to capture the knowledge that experienced participants had acquired.

Another challenge to measuring knowledge transfer in organizations through measuring changes in knowledge is that knowledge in organizations resides in multiple repositories (Levitt & March, 1988; Starbuck, 1992; Walsh & Ungson, 1991). For example, Walsh and Ungson posited that there are five retention bins or repositories for knowledge in organizations: (a) individual members, (b) roles and organizational structures, (c) the organization's standard operating procedures and practices, (d) its culture, and (e) the physical structure of the workplace. In order to measure transfer through changes in knowledge, one must capture changes in knowledge in these different repositories.

Most existing techniques for measuring knowledge, such as questionnaires or verbal protocols, measure changes in knowledge embedded in individuals. Although knowledge change is initially mediated through individuals in organizations, subsequent knowledge change can occur without individual involvement. For example, an individual in one branch of a firm may learn through experience how to modify a piece of software to produce a better quality product. The software may then be transferred to another site in the organization where it may improve the performance of the recipient unit without any individual at the recipient unit being able to articulate why the performance improved. Attempts to measure changes in knowledge at the recipient site through measuring the knowledge of individuals would not be informative in this example because individuals' knowledge did not change. Knowledge embedded in other repositories, however, changed with the introduction of the new software.

The knowledge repositories play a dual role in knowledge transfer in organizations. On the one hand, the knowledge repositories are changed when knowledge transfer occurs. Thus, changes in the knowledge repositories reflect the outcomes of knowledge transfer. On the other hand, the state of the knowledge repositories affects the processes and outcomes of knowledge transfer. Just as an individual's readiness and past knowledge affect his or her ability to acquire new knowledge (e.g., see Goldstein, 1991), an organization's current knowledge affects its ability to assimilate new knowledge (Cohen & Levinthal, 1990).

RESERVOIRS OF KNOWLEDGE IN ORGANIZATIONS

The framework of knowledge reservoirs used here was developed by McGrath and Argote (in press). We use the term "reservoir" here, derived from the French "reserver" meaning "to keep for future use," because it connotes that the knowledge can be used again. The McGrath and Argote framework builds on previous theoretical frameworks (Argote, 1999; Argote & McGrath, 1993; Arrow, McGrath, & Berdahl, 2000; Levitt & March,

1988; McGrath, 1991; Starbuck, 1992; Walsh and Ungson, 1991). According to the framework of McGrath and Argote, knowledge is embedded in the three basic elements of organizations—members, tools, and tasks—and the various subnetworks formed by combining or crossing the basic elements. Members are the human components of organizations. Tools, including both hardware and software, are the technological component. Tasks reflect the organization's goals, intentions, and purposes.

The basic elements of organizations combine to form subnetworks (McGrath & Argote, in press). The member–member network is the organization's social network. The task–task network is the combination of technologies used by the organization. The member–task network (or the division of labor) maps members onto tasks. The member–tool network assigns members to tools. The task–tool network specifies which tools are used to perform which tasks. The member–task–tool network specifies which members perform which tasks with which tools.

According to the framework, organizational performance improves with increases in both the internal compatibility of the networks and their external compatibility with other networks (McGrath & Argote, in press). For example, organizational performance is enhanced when the member–task network allocates tasks to the members most qualified to perform them. Similarly, when members have the appropriate tools to perform the tasks allocated to them, the member–task network is compatible with the member–tool network. The former is an example of internal compatibility of the networks, while the latter is an example of external compatibility or compatibility between the different networks. Other researchers have also emphasized the importance of the compatibility or congruence of organizational components as a contributor to organizational effectiveness (e.g., Argote, 1982; Leavitt, 1965; Nadler & Tushman, 1980).

A significant component of the knowledge that organizations acquire, especially tacit knowledge, is embedded in individual members. For example, Engeström, Brown, Engeström, and Koistinen (1990) described a urology clinic where most of the organization's knowledge was embedded in one administrator. Similarly, Starbuck (1992) argued that in professional service organizations, such as law firms or consulting firms, a significant component of the organization's knowledge is embedded in individual members.

Knowledge can also be embedded in an organization's tools and technology. For example, Argote (1999) described how the software of a truck assembly plant was modified to capture knowledge about how to apply paint with less scrap material. Similarly, Argote and Darr (in press) analyzed how fast-food franchises adapted their tools to capture knowledge about how to produce products more cost effectively.

Knowledge can also be embedded in an organization's tasks and their interrelationships. The task network is the sequence of tasks or the routines and standard operating procedures the organization uses (see Gersick & Hackman, 1990; Nelson & Winter, 1982, for discussions of routines). Argote (1999) described how a truck assembly plant developed a more cost-effective method for painting trucks that was embedded in a routine or task sequence that all workers used. Similarly, Darr, Argote and Epple (1995) analyzed how the knowledge acquired at a fast-food franchise about how to produce a higher quality product was embedded in a routine.

Finally, knowledge can be embedded in the various networks formed by combining members, tools, and tasks. The member–task network or the division of labor specifies which member performs which tasks in the organization. Knowledge of who in the organization is good at which task is embedded in the member–task network. Studies of organizational learning have shown that an important source of the productivity benefits that organizations typically gain with experience is learning which member is good at which tasks and assigning tasks accordingly (Argote, 1993). Studies have also shown that, with experience working together, dyads and small groups improve their performance by acquiring knowledge of who knows what (e.g., see Hollingshead, 1998; Liang, Moreland, & Argote, 1995). The term "transactive memory" was coined to capture this concept of who knows what (Wegner, 1986). Transactive memory systems embed knowledge of who is proficient at which tasks (the member–task network) and who is proficient with which tools (the member–tool network). As organizations acquire knowledge, they also learn which tasks are best performed by people and those which are best performed by tools or automation. The latter knowledge is embedded in the task–tool network that also contains information about which tasks are best performed by which tools. Last, organizations acquire information about which members best perform which tasks with which tools. This knowledge is embedded in the coordination network.

Knowledge transfer occurs when experience in one unit of an organization affects another unit. Knowledge transfer can occur explicitly when, for example, a unit communicates with another unit about a practice that it has found to improve performance. Knowledge transfer can also occur implicitly without the recipient unit being able to articulate the knowledge it has acquired. For example, if an individual uses a tool that has been modified to improve its performance, the individual can benefit from the productivity enhancement in the tool without necessarily understanding the modifications or being able to articulate why the modifications improved the tool's performance. Similarly, norms or routines can be transmitted to group members without the members being able to articulate the norm or being aware of the knowledge embedded in it.

In general terms, knowledge can be transferred by moving a knowledge reservoir from one unit to another or by modifying a knowledge reservoir at a recipient site. Members can be moved from one unit to another. Similarly, technology can be moved and routines can be transported from one organization to another. The reservoirs at the recipient unit can also be modified through communication and training.

KNOWLEDGE AS A BASIS OF COMPETITIVE ADVANTAGE

Our goal is now to show how the framework of knowledge reservoirs can be combined with behavioral evidence on knowledge transfer to understand the differential performance of organizations. First, we describe the emerging role of knowledge as a basis for the competitive advantage of organizations. Then we apply our framework to explain why successful knowledge transfer is difficult and to organize the evidence regarding knowledge that is more easily transferable. Finally, we present evidence indicating how organizations can develop the knowledge that is a basis for competitive advantage.

The recent trend in the field of strategic management has been to emphasize the role of organizational knowledge as a basis of the competitive advantage of particular organizations. Explanations of competitive advantage that rely primarily on the positioning of organizations in an industry (e.g., Porter, 1980) or the deployment of organizational assets through competitive interaction with rival firms (e.g., Dixit, 1980; Shapiro, 1989) have been relatively deemphasized. Novel work continues on industry structure, but that work integrates organizational knowledge perspectives with industry (Williams, 1998) or rivalry perspectives (e.g., Korn & Baum, 1999). Empirical findings have shown that differences between organizations may account for more variance in firm performance than differences between industries (Rumelt, 1991). Although important industry effects may be present (e.g., see McGahan & Porter, 1997), organizational-level differences are now acknowledged as a critical source of variation in firm performance over and above industry differences.

Although empirical findings make the case for organizational resources as a basis of competitive advantage, theoretical arguments have been powerful for identifying the types of resources that are key. Barney (1986) pointed out that for resources acquired through competitive markets, the value that the resource brings to the organization should be reflected in its price to the organization. For this reason, the focus for competitive advantage should be on resources developed or made valuable inside the organization rather than those purchased from outside it. The set of relevant resources is further limited by the recognition that resources cannot be the source of competitive advantage if many competitors have them.

Therefore, to be the source of competitive advantage, resources must also be difficult for competitors to imitate (Lippman & Rumelt, 1982).

The focus on resources that are developed within the organization and difficult to imitate puts organizational knowledge in a preeminent position as the principal source of competitive advantage (Spender & Grant, 1996; Teece, Pisano, & Shuen, 1997). Despite variance in terminology for organizational knowledge (competencies, capabilities, routines, or innovations), there is growing agreement that it is what the organization comes to know that explains its performance. The problem for those who want to develop competitive advantage for their organizations, however, is that, in the field of business strategy, more effort has gone into identifying knowledge as the basis of competitive advantage than into explaining how organizations can develop, retain, and transfer that knowledge. As Spender and Grant (1996, p. 6) observed, "The surge of interest into organizational capabilities and competencies has directed attention to organizationally embedded knowledge, but has made only limited progress in understanding its anatomy and creation." To the extent there has been progress, it has been at the level of identifying consistencies in organizations' knowledge development paths (e.g., Teece, 1988) and almost never at the level of the human interactions that are the primary source of knowledge and knowledge transfer.

Against this backdrop, there is a clear opportunity for the research effort represented in this special issue to contribute to the understanding of how organizations gain competitive advantage through knowledge. The framework of knowledge reservoirs outlined in this article represents the "anatomy" of knowledge in organizations. We show how the framework can be applied to illuminate the problem of knowledge transfer, indicating when organizations can be expected to derive competitive advantage by transferring knowledge internally and preventing its transfer to competitors. Other articles in this special issue, and the literature they build on, illuminate the process by which organizations can create knowledge. We describe how the articles contribute social-psychological guidance for the task of developing competitive advantage in firms.

MOVING KNOWLEDGE BY MOVING RESERVOIRS AND NETWORKS

The framework of knowledge reservoirs and their interconnecting networks provides insight into why some types of knowledge are difficult to transfer within the organization and to imitate outside the organization. In principle, knowledge can be moved by moving the networks on which it is embedded. In practice, however, this is difficult to accomplish. As noted previously, organizational performance depends on the internal and external compatibility of the networks. Compatibility of members, tools, and tasks moved from one unit to another can be problematic. In order for members, tools, and tasks to be effective at the new unit, they may have to adapt or be adapted to the new context. The issue of compatibility in moving the networks from one site to another, however, is even more complex than moving the basic elements of people, tools, or tasks. For example, a division of labor developed in one organizational unit that fits the skills of its members may not work in another unit where members have different skills and areas of expertise. Thus, moving networks is difficult to do effectively because they embody interactions that may not fit the new context. It is less likely that the networks will fit the new contexts than the basic elements (member, tools, and tasks) because the networks consist of more components that must be internally compatible with one another, and compatible with the new context in order for the transfer to be successful.

Strategy scholars have also recognized that the interdependence of various components of knowledge inhibits transfer (Teece, Pisano, & Shuen, 1997). The advantage of the framework we present is that it highlights the fact that interdependencies between knowledge reservoirs may vary, making some types of knowledge easier to transfer than others. Research may then proceed to examine the transfer success of particular networks.

More research has been done on moving members and moving tools or technology than on moving the other knowledge reservoirs. Moving members is generally seen as a powerful mechanism for facilitating knowledge transfer in organizations (Galbraith, 1990; Rothwell, 1978). Individuals are able to adapt and restructure knowledge so that it applies to new contexts (Allen, 1977). Individuals are also able to transfer both tacit and explicit knowledge to new contexts (Berry & Broadbent, 1984, 1987). A recent empirical study of the effect of moving members found that the mobility of engineers between firms contributed to the transfer of knowledge about innovations in the semiconductor industry (Almeida & Kogut, 1999).

Gruenfeld, Martorena, and Fan (2000) demonstrated that moving individual members can have subtle effects on knowledge transfer across groups. Moving members did not result in ideas moving directly from one group to another in their study. On the contrary, the ideas of "itinerants" who changed groups were not particularly influential in the new groups and were used significantly less often than the ides of "indigenous" members after the itinerants returned to their groups of origin. New knowledge, however, was generated in groups upon their itinerant members' return from sojourns in other groups: Both "itinerant" and "indigenous" members generated significantly more unique ideas after the itinerants returned to their groups of origin than before or during the period of membership change.

Considerable research has been done on technology transfer to study the effect of moving tools from one site to another on outcomes at the organizational, interorganizational, and societal levels (see Zhao & Reisman, 1992, for an overview). Although transferring knowledge through moving technology can be effective, the success of technology transfer attempts varies considerably. The technology often needs to be adapted to the context at the recipient site in order to be effective (Leonard-Barton, 1988).

Explicit, codifiable knowledge that is embedded in technology has been found to transfer more readily than knowledge not embedded in technology (e.g., see Zander & Kogut, 1995). Similarly, technology transfer attempts have been found to be more successful when the technology is not complex and is well understood (Galbraith, 1990). In addition, attempts to move knowledge by transferring technology within firms have been found to be more effective when they are accompanied by moving personnel (e.g., see Galbraith, 1990).

Although embedding knowledge in technology is an effective way to transfer knowledge within the firm, it is also a way to facilitate knowledge transfer externally. Studies of how rapidly knowledge "leaks out" to competitors have found that technological knowledge embedded in products spills over to other firms more quickly than knowledge embedded in organizational processes or routines (Mansfield, 1985). Making knowledge explicit enough to be embedded in technology eases its internal transfer but also speeds its spillover to other organizations.

Many studies of knowledge transfer recognize the relevance of knowledge embedded in tasks when they invoke the concept of routines. Only a few studies, however, have attempted to explicitly examine or describe the routines or task sequences used by organizations (e.g., see Argote & Darr, in press; Baum & Berta, 1999; Gersick & Hackman, 1990; Szulanski, in press) and to analyze their transfer to new settings. A major theme in these studies is that transferring knowledge through moving routines can be effective, although specific characteristics of the routine, as well as features and interrelationships of the originating and receiving units of the organization, influence the likelihood of successful knowledge transfer.

Similarly, only a few studies have examined knowledge transfer through moving subnetworks. The results of these studies document the difficulty of transferring knowledge through moving subnetworks that involve members. For example, Moreland, Argote, and Krishnan (1996) examined whether a "transactive memory system" (a network of member–task relations and member–tool relations) transferred from the group in which it was developed to a group composed of different members. Results indicated that these transactive memory systems that embodied knowledge about which group members were good at which tasks did not transfer to groups composed of different members. Devadas and Argote (1995) found that membership change was harmful for groups when the member–task network and the member–tool network did not fit the skill and expertise of the new member. Similarly, Wegner, Erber, and Raymond (1991) found that imposing a division of labor (a member–task network) on an ongoing dyad that had already developed its own knowledge about who was good at what hurt the performance of the dyad. By contrast, imposing a division of labor on a newly formed dyad improved the dyad's performance.

These findings provide insights into the observation that new organizations seem particularly open to learning from the experience of others (e.g., see Argote, Beckman, & Epple, 1990; Ingram & Baum, 1997). Knowledge provided to an established organization may not be as useful because it conflicts with networks already in place at the organization. By contrast, knowledge provided at the start of operation is less likely to create such conflict because networks of knowledge are not yet fully established.

In contrast to the emerging evidence on the effects of moving subnetworks involving people, evidence suggests that moving the task–tool network can be an effective way to transfer knowledge. One study found that the knowledge embedded in the task–tool network of a plant transferred quickly and effectively to new members (Epple, Argote, & Murphy, 1996). The study analyzed the productivity of a manufacturing plant that added a second shift almost 2 years after operating with one shift. The second shift, composed primarily of members who were new to the organization, used the same tools and task sequences embedded in the assembly line that the first shift had used. The second shift achieved a level of productivity in a couple of weeks that the first shift took many months to achieve. The second shift benefited from knowledge embedded by the first shift in the tools and tasks sequences.

Several theoretical results emerge from our analysis of knowledge transfer through moving the knowledge reservoirs and subnetworks. The strengths of moving people as a knowledge-transfer mechanism complement the strengths of moving tools or technology. People are able to transfer tacit as well as explicit knowledge when they move and to adapt their knowledge to new contexts. Although tools lack the sensitivity and flexibility of people, they provide consistency and enable the organization to transfer knowledge on a large scale in a way that is relatively independent of the idiosyncrasies of individual members. The effects of transferring knowledge through moving tasks are similar to those of moving tools. Tasks, however, usually require people to perform them, whereas tools may require less human intervention. Thus, transferring knowledge through moving tasks or task–task subnetworks is somewhat more flexible and somewhat less consistent than transferring knowledge through moving technology.

In order for knowledge transfer to be successful, the reservoirs or subnetworks that are moved must fit or be compatible with the new context. As noted previously, the compatibility of members, tools, and tasks moved from one unit to another cannot be taken for granted. In order for these elements to be effective knowledge conduits, they may have to adapt or be adapted to the new context. Attaining compatibility between subnetworks moved from one site to another, however, is even more problematic than attaining compatibility of people, tools, or tasks moved to the new context because the subnetworks consist of more elements and involve interactions among them. It is less likely that the interactions will fit the new contexts than the single elements will.

Further, interactions involving people are more problematic than those involving tools or tasks. People are likely to vary more across sites than tools or tasks. Thus, it is more difficult to transfer knowledge by moving the member–member, member–task, member–tool, or member–task–tool network to a new setting than it is to transfer knowledge through moving the other knowledge reservoirs.

Our analysis indicates that the most problematic knowledge conduits are the subnetworks involving people and not the people in them per se. Although social psychological processes mediate the effect of moving people on knowledge transfer (e.g., see Gruenfeld et al., 2000), people can be effective knowledge conduits. People are likely to be especially effective conduits of general principles or abstract knowledge that is relatively invariant to context, such as that embedded in patents (e.g., see Almedia & Kogut, 1999).

The observation that it is difficult to transfer knowledge from one organization to another by moving the subnetworks involving members has important managerial and strategic implications: It suggests that embedding knowledge in the member–member, member–task, member–tool, or member–task–tool network minimizes knowledge spillover to other firms because knowledge in these networks is the most difficult to transfer or copy. Further, to the extent that people are more similar within than between organizations (which seems likely, in light of the selection, socialization, training, and communication that go on within organizations, e.g., see Jackson, Brett, Sessa, Cooper, Julin, & Peyronnin, 1991), moving the subnetworks involving people will be a more effective way to transfer knowledge within than between organizations. Thus, embedding knowledge in the subnetworks that involve people makes it difficult for external knowledge transfer to occur while permitting some (albeit challenging) internal knowledge transfer.

MOVING KNOWLEDGE BY MODIFYING RESERVOIRS AND NETWORKS

In addition to moving a knowledge reservoir from one unit to another, the other main method of knowledge transfer is to modify the knowledge reservoirs of the recipient unit, primarily through communication or training. Several articles in this volume examine how communication and training can modify the knowledge of the recipient.

Building on work on analogical reasoning, Thompson, Gentner, and Lowenstein (2000) found that dyads who were trained to compare across cases and abstract a common principle performed better on a subsequent task than dyads who were trained to give advice about the cases. These results provide important insights into how organizations can facilitate the codification of knowledge into principles. As noted previously, codified knowledge transfers more readily than knowledge that is not codified.

Two studies in the special issue examined how communication affected the development of knowledge of "who knows what" in groups and organizations. Moreland and Myaskovsky (2000) compared the effect of providing opportunities to communicate and providing feedback about individual group members' skills on the creation of transactive memory systems in groups. These transactive memory systems embed knowledge of who is good at performing which tasks (the member–task network) and who is good at operating which tools (the member–tool network). Providing feedback about individual skills and providing opportunities to communicate were found to be equally effective (and more effective than training individuals) in creating transactive memory systems with compatible member–task and member–tool networks. Further, the performance of groups with well-developed transactive memory systems exceeded that of groups lacking such memory systems.

Rulke, Zaheer, and Anderson (2000) also examined the creation of knowledge about who knows what. Focusing at the organizational level of analysis, the researchers contrasted the effect of communication channels on an organizations's knowledge of its own capabilities. They found that relational channels both inside and outside the organization and nonrelational internal channels (e.g., company newsletters, formal training programs) contributed more to knowledge of an organization's capabilities than external nonrelational channels, such as trade association publications and newsletters. These findings underscore the importance of relationships in knowledge transfer.

Two articles in this special issue analyzed how the task network affected the generation and transfer of knowledge. Paulus and Yang (2000) found that procedures for sharing knowledge that exposed group members to the ideas of others while allowing them to generate ideas continuously and maintain their own identity led to the creation of more novel ideas than did procedures that simply pooled the ideas of individual group members. Levine, Higgins, and Choi (2000) demonstrated that task instructions shaped the development of a shared reality in groups that affected their problem-solving strategies.

Stasser, Vaughan, and Stewart (2000) provided evidence on how member–task networks affected knowledge sharing in groups. This study replicated previous work demonstrating that during group discussion, groups focused more on shared information that members held in common than on unshared information that members uniquely possessed. Further, the bias favoring shared information was reduced by publicly identifying members' expertise at the onset of group discussion but not by forewarning individual members of their areas of expertise before they prepared for the group discussion. Thus, awareness of the member–task network by all groups members improved group performance.

FACTORS AFFECTING KNOWLEDGE TRANSFER

Articles in this special issue as well as other research identify factors that affect knowledge transfer in organizations. Darr and Kurtzberg (2000) examined how the similarity between tasks affected the transfer of knowledge between fast-food stores. "Strategic similarity" (similarity of the stores' strategies and tasks) positively affected transfer of knowledge, whereas similarity of customers or location had no effect.

Szulanski (2000) analyzed how characteristics of the source of knowledge, the recipient, the context, and the knowledge itself affected transfer. Szulanski found that the importance of these factors varied over stages of the transfer process. Factors that affected the perception of an opportunity to transfer knowledge, such as the reliability of the source, predicted difficulty of transfer during the early initiation stage, whereas factors that affected the execution of transfer, such as the recipient's ability to absorb knowledge, affected difficulty during the implementation phases. The "causal ambiguity" of the knowledge or the extent to which it was not well understood predicted the difficulty of transfer throughout all phases of the transfer process.

Other research has examined the factors affecting knowledge transfer in organizations (see Argote, 1999, for a review). Research has been done, for instance, on how characteristics of individual members, such as their ability and motivation, affect the transfer of knowledge from training to transfer contexts (see Baldwin & Ford, 1989, for a review).

The question of how characteristics of the member–member or social network affect knowledge transfer is receiving increasing attention. One important finding to emerge from this work is that knowledge transfers more readily across organizations that are embedded in a network or subordinate relationship, such as a franchise, chain, or alliance, than across independent organizations (Baum & Ingram, 1998; Powell, Koput, & Smith-Doerr, 1996). For example, Darr, Argote, and Epple (1995) found that fast-food stores benefited from the experience of other stores in the same franchise but not from that of stores in different franchises (see also Darr & Kurtzberg, 2000). Similarly, Baum and Ingram (1998) found that hotels benefited from the experience of local hotels (but not nonlocal hotels) that belonged to the same chain. Ingram and Simons (1999) found that kibbutzim were positively affected by the experience of other kibbutzim in the same federation.

Studies have also found that characteristics of the social network affect the extent of knowledge transfer. For example, in a study of knowledge transfer among small manufacturers, McEvily and Zaheer (1999) found that, consistent with structural hole theory (Burt, 1992), nonredundancy in organizations' social networks predicted their ability to acquire knowledge and new capabilities. Organizations with nonredundant social ties to other organizations had access to more information that enabled them to acquire more new capabilities than organizations whose ties to other organizations were redundant or overlapping.

Research has also shown that the nature of the social ties interacts with characteristics of the knowledge being transferred to affect transfer outcomes. In a study of new product development projects, Hansen (1999) found that "weak ties," characterized by infrequent and distant relationships between units, facilitated the search for knowledge in other units and reduced the time to complete projects when knowledge was not complex and could be codified. By contrast, when knowledge was not codified, strong ties that allowed for repeated interaction promoted knowledge acquisition and shortened project-completion times. Along similar lines, Baum and Berta (1999) found that learning between student groups in a business simulation was higher when there was a higher degree of social contact between them.

Characteristics of the task have also been found to affect knowledge transfer. The most fundamental task characteristic found to affect transfer is the similarity across tasks in different contexts. The more similar the number of elements across the tasks, the greater the likelihood of transfer (Thorndike, 1906). The finding that similarity increases the likelihood of transfer has been found at different levels of analysis, ranging from the individual (Singley & Anderson, 1989) to the organizational (Darr & Kurtzberg, 2000). At the individual level, research has also been done on the effect of other task characteristics such as the amount of feedback that participants receive or the conditions of their practice on knowledge transfer (see Baldwin & Ford, 1989, for a review). At the organizational level, research has been done on the extent to which the task was well understood on knowledge transfer.

Characteristics of the technology or tools being transferred have also been found to affect the success of the transfer. Galbraith (1990) compared the productivity at the "recipient" site to the productivity of the "source" at the time the technology was transferred. Galbraith found that the recipient's productivity recovered faster when the technology was not complex, when the source and recipient were close geographically, when coproduction continued at the donor site, and when the engineering team at the source organization moved for a significant time period to the recipient site. Continuing production at the source site and moving personnel may have facilitated transfer by enabling the recipient to access tacit knowledge at the source that was not written down or embedded in documents, plans, tools, and products.

Our framework of knowledge reservoirs also provides insights into when knowledge transfer can negatively affect the performance of the recipient unit. If the knowledge to be transferred is inappropriate for and cannot be adapted to the new context, negative effects on performance can occur (e.g., Baum & Ingram, 1998; Greve, 1999). For example, Greve provided evidence of how knowledge acquired outside the local market of radio stations can negatively affect their performance. Following Baum and Ingram, Greve suggested that the negative effect occurred because routines imported from other markets were not appropriate for the local markets, where competitors were different.

The framework of knowledge reservoirs also provides insights into "situated cognition" (Lant, 1999; Lave, 1993), the research tradition that views cognition as dependent on particular features of the context. Because cognition is so dependent on the context, knowledge transfer from other contexts is conceived as playing little or no role in learning. By providing a more fine-grained framework for analyzing where knowledge is embedded in organizational contexts, our analysis identifies when knowledge will be relatively easy to transfer from one context to another and when such transfer will be problematic. Thus, the framework provided here is positioned between frameworks that posit virtually no transfer across contexts and those that posit virtually instantaneous and complete transfer across contexts.

CONCLUSION

The more nuanced view of knowledge transfer presented in our framework is more consistent with empirical evidence on knowledge transfer, which shows both that transfer often occurs and that it is often incomplete. The more fine-grained framework presented here provides a deeper understanding of the conditions under which knowledge transfer occurs and the conditions under which knowledge transfer is problematic or incomplete. Thus, the framework advances theory about knowledge transfer in organizations and provides practical insights for the management of knowledge in firms.

Our framework illuminates the dual role of people in knowledge transfer. On the one hand, differences in the subnetworks involving people across contexts make knowledge transfer problematic. As noted previously, in order for knowledge transfer to be successful, the knowledge reservoirs or subnetworks imported from one context must be compatible with or fit the new context. Compatibility across contexts of the subnetworks involving people is more problematic than compatibility of the other subnetworks because people are likely to vary more across contexts than tools or tasks.

On the other hand, people are capable of adapting knowledge from one context to another. As noted previously, moving technology or tasks from one site to another has been found to be more effective when accompanied by moving people because people are capable of adapting the tools and technology to the new context. Thus, although adapting to differences in people across contexts poses challenges to knowledge transfer, people's ability to adapt knowledge they possess facilitates transfer.

Because people play the most critical role in the success of technology transfer, further research on the role of members and the subnetworks involving them is needed. A fundamental question is identifying the conditions under which moving people will result in knowledge transfer. As noted in the Gruenfeld et al. article in this special issue, the success of knowledge transfer through moving people is not automatic and depends on social influence processes. When people are moved to a new context to transfer knowledge, they often become "minorities" in the context of the majority at the new site (see Levine & Thompson, 1996; Wood, Lundgren, Ouelette, Busceme, & Blackstone, 1994, for discussions of minority influence). Thus, understanding how minorities who are moved to new sites can influence knowledge transfer should be a fruitful area for future research.

As noted previously, "modifying" people is also an important general mechanism for transferring knowledge. A greater understanding is needed of the socialization and training processes that modify, or change, people and how they affect knowledge transfer. Because differences in context pose particular challenges to knowledge transfer, research on socialization and training that takes context into account is likely to be especially promising.

The member–member or the social network also plays an important role in knowledge transfer. The social network can link organizational units to new sources of knowledge and aid interpretation of the new knowledge. More research is needed on the properties of social networks that facilitate (or impede) transfer. Future research should also examine the strong group identities that are often associated with dense social networks in organizations. The identification with a social unit can lead to in-group favoritism where the members of one's own group are perceived much more favorably than members of other groups (Kramer, 1991; Messick & Mackie, 1989). Research is needed on how this in-group favoritism can affect knowledge transfer in organizations.

Research is also needed on the implications of the many levels of potential identification for knowledge transfer in organizations. For example, members may identify primarily with their own work group, with the department in which their group is embedded, with the larger division of which the department is a part, or with the firm (Moreland & Levine, 2000). An organization where members identify most strongly with their work groups may have more difficulty transferring knowledge across groups than an organization where members identify mainly with the superordinate organization. Understanding factors that lead members to identify with one level over another as well as the consequences of their identification for knowledge transfer is an important area for future research.

More generally, future empirical studies should examine the conditions under which knowledge is embedded in the various reservoirs. For example, how do the member–member, the member–task, and the member–tool networks develop? Research should also empirically determine the extent to which knowledge in the various reservoirs transfers to new contexts. Factors that support or impede such transfer should be identified. Information about these issues will greatly advance our understanding of knowledge transfer in organizations.

The framework of knowledge reservoirs discussed here provides insights into the reasons why it is difficult to transfer knowledge and into the conditions under which knowledge transfer is most likely. We have shown here that attaining compatibility between the subnetworks moved from one site to another is even more problematic than attaining compatibility of the basic elements of people, tools, or tasks. The subnetworks consist of two or three elements that have coevolved to fit their current context and are less likely than the basic elements to fit the new context.

The observation that the subnetworks involving people are the most problematic from a knowledge-transfer perspective provides important insights into the fundamental paradox of knowledge management in firms: Firms are most effective when they manage both to facilitate internal knowledge transfer and to block external knowledge spillover. The framework described here provides insights into how firms can accomplish both. Embedding knowledge in the subnetworks that involve people minimizes the likelihood of transfer to external organizations because knowledge in these reservoirs is least likely to fit other contexts. Because selection, socialization, training, and communication processes within organizations make people more similar within than between firms, the subnetworks involving people are more likely to be compatible with other subnetworks internal to the organization than with external subnetworks. Thus, achieving transfer through moving the subnetworks involving people is more problematic between than within organizations. Our framework shows how organizations can minimize transfer to external organizations while they achieve internal knowledge transfer. Thus, the processes underlying knowledge transfer provide a basis for understanding the competitive advantage of firms.

REFERENCES

Allen, T. J. (1977). *Managing the flow of technology: Technology transfer and the dissemination of technological information within the R&D organization.* Cambridge, MA: MIT Press.

Almeida, P., & Kogut, B. (199). Localization of knowledge and the mobility of engineers in regional networks. *Management Science,* **45,** 905–917.

Argote, L. (1999). *Organizational learning: Creating, retaining, and transferring knowledge.* Norwell, MA: Kluwer.

Argote, L. (1993). Group and organizational learning curves: Individual, system and environmental components. *British Journal of Social Psychology,* **32,** 31–51.

Argote, L. (1982). Input uncertainty and organizational coordination in hospital emergency service units. *Administrative Science Quarterly,* **27,** 420–434.

Argote, L., Beckman, S. L., & Epple, D. (1990). The persistence and transfer of learning in industrial settings. *Management Science,* **36,** 140–154.

Argote, L., & Darr, E. (in press). Repositories of knowledge in franchise organizations: Individual, structural, and technological. In G. Dosi, R. Nelson, & S. Winter (Eds.), *The nature and dynamics of organizational capabilities.* Oxford: Oxford Univ. Press.

Argote, L., & McGrath, J. E. (1993). Group processes in organizations: Continuity and change. *International Review of Industrial and Organizational Psychology,* **8,** 333–389.

Arrow, H., McGrath, J. E., & Berdahl, J. L. (20000). *Small groups as complex systems: Formation, coordination, development and adaptation.* Thousand Oaks, CA: Sage.

Baldwin, T. T., & Ford, J. K. (1988). Transfer of training: A review and direction for future research. *Personnel Psychology,* **41,** 63–105.

Barney, J. B. (1986). Strategic factor markets: Expectations, luck and business strategy. *Management Science,* **32,** 1231–1241.

Baum, J. A. C., & Berta, W. B. (1999). Sources, timing, and speed: Population-level learning by organizations in a longitudinal behavioral simulation. In A. S. Miner & P. Anderson (Eds.), *Population-level learning and industry change, Advances in Strategic Management* (Vol. 16, pp. 155–184). Stamford, CT: JAI Press.

Baum, J. A. C., & Ingram, P. (1998). Survival-enhancing learning in the Manhattan hotel industry, 1898–1980, *Management Science,* **44,** 996–1016.

Benkard, C. L. (in press). Learning and forgetting: The dynamics of aircraft production. *American Economic Review.*

Berry, D. C., & Broadbent, D. E. (1984). On the relationship between task performance and associated verbalizable knowledge. *The Quarterly Journal of Experimental Psychology,* **36A,** 209–231.

Berry D. C., & Broadbent, D. E. (1987). The combination of explicit and implicit learning processes in task control. *Psychological Research,* **49,** 7–15.

Burt, R. S. (1992). *Structural holes: The social structure of competition.* Cambridge: Harvard Univ. Press.

Cohen, W. M., & Levinthal, D. (1990). Absorptive capacity: A new perspective on learning and innovation. *Administrative Science Quarterly,* **35,** 128–152.

Darr, E., Argote, L., & Epple, D. (1995). The acquisition, transfer and depreciation of knowledge in service organizations: Productivity in franchises. *Management Science,* **41,** 1750–1762.

Darr, E. D., & Kurtzberg, T. R. (2000). An investigation of partner similarity dimensions on knowledge transfer. *Organizational Behavior and Human Decision Processes,* **82,** 28–44.

Devadas, R., & Argote, L. (1995, May). *Collective learning and forgetting: The effects of turnover and group structure.* Paper presented at Midwestern Psychological Association Meetings, Chicago.

Dixit, A. (1980). The role of investment in entry deterrence. *Economic Journal,* **90,** 95–105.

Engeström, Y., Brown, K., Engeström, R., & Koistinen, K. (1990). Organizational forgetting: An activity theoretical perspective. In D.

Middleton & D. Edwards (Eds.), *Collective remembering* (pp. 139–168). London: Sage.

Epple, D., Argote, L., & Murphy, K. (1996). An empirical investigation of the micro structure of knowledge acquisition and transfer through learning by doing. *Operations Research,* **44,** 77–86.

Galbraith, C. S. (1990). Transferring core manufacturing technologies in high technology firms. *California Management Review,* **32**(4), 56–70.

Gersick, C., & Hackman, J. R. (1990). Habitual routines in task-performing groups. *Organizational Behavior and Human Decision Processes,* **47,** 65–97.

Gruenfeld, D. H., Martorana, P. V., & Fan, E. T. (2000). What do groups learn from their worldliest members? Direct and indirect influence in dynamic teams. *Organizational Behavior and Human Decision Processes,* **82,** 45–59.

Goldstein, I. L. (1991). Training in work organizations. In M. D. Dunnette & L. M. Hough (Eds.), *Handbook of industrial and organizational psychology* (2nd ed.). Palo Alto, CA: Consulting Psychologists Press.

Greve, H. R. (1999). Branch systems and nonlocal learning in populations. In A. S. Miner & P. Anderson (Eds.), *Population-level learning and industry change, Advances in Strategic Management* (Vol. 16, pp. 57–80). Stamford, CT: JAI Press.

Hansen, M. (1999). The search-transfer problem: The role of weak ties in sharing knowledge across organization subunits. *Administrative Science Quarterly,* **44,** 82–111.

Hollingshead, A. B. (1998). Group and individual training: The impact of practice on performance. *Small Group Research,* **29,** 254–280.

Ingram, P., & Baum, J. A. C. (1997). Opportunity and constraint: Organizations' learning from the operating and competitive experience of industries. *Strategic Management Journal,* **18,** 75–98.

Ingram, P., & Simons, T. (1999). *The exchange of experience in a moral economy: Embedded ties and vicarious learning in Kibbutz agriculture,* Academy of Management Proceedings.

Jackson, S. E., Brett, J. F., Sessa, V. I., Cooper, D. M., Julin, J. A., & Peyronnin, K. (1991). Some differences make a difference: Individual dissimilarity and group heterogeneity as correlates of recruitment, promotions, and turnover. *Journal of Applied Psychology,* **76,** 675–689.

Korn, H. J., & Baum, J. A. C. (1999). Chance, imitative, and strategic antecedents of multimarket contact. *Academy of Management Journal,* **42,** 171–193.

Kramer, R. M. (1991). Intergroup relations and organizational dilemmas: The role of categorization processes. *Research in Organizational Behavior,* **13,** 191–228.

Lant, T. (1999). A situated learning perspective on the emergence of knowledge and identity in cognitive communities. In J. Porac & M. Vantresca (Eds.), *Advances in management cognition and organizational information processing.* (Vol. 6, pp. 171–194). Stamford, CT: JAI Press.

Lave, J. (1993). Situated learning in communities of practice. In L. B. Resnick, J. M. Levine, & S. D. Teasley (Eds.), *Perspectives on socially shared cognition* (pp. 63–82). Washington, DC: American Psychological Association.

Leavitt, H. J. (1961). Applied organizational change in industry: Structural, technological and humanistic approaches. In J. G. March (Ed.), *Handbook of organizations* (pp. 1144–1170). Chicago: Rand McNally.

Leonard-Barton, D. (1988). Implementation as mutual adaptation of technology and organization. *Research Policy,* **17,** 251–267.

Levine, J. M., Higgins, E. T., & Choi, H-S. (2000). Development of strategic norms in groups. *Organizational Behavior and Human Decision Processes,* **82,** 88–101.

Levine, J. M., & Thompson, L. (1996). Conflict in groups. In E. T. Higgins & A. W. Kruzlanski (Eds.), *Social psychology: Handbook of basic principles* (pp. 745–776). New York: Guilford.

Levitt, B., & March, J. G. (1988). Organizational learning. *Annual Review of Sociology,* **14,** 319–340.

Liang, D. W., Moreland, R. L., & Argote, L. (1995). Group versus individual training and group performance: The mediating role of transactive memory. *Personality and Social Psychology Bulletin,* **21,** 384–393.

Lippman, S. A., & Rumelt, R. P. (1992). Demand uncertainty and investment in industry-specific capital. *Industrial and Corporate Change,* **1,** 235–262.

Mansfield, E. (1985). How rapidly does industrial technology leak out? *The Journal of Industrial Economics,* **34,** 217–224.

McEvily, B., & Zaheer, A. (1999). Bridging ties: A source of firm heterogeneity in competitive capabilities. *Strategic Management Journal,* **20,** 1133–1156.

McGahan, A. M., & Porter, M. E. (1997). How much does industry matter, really? *Strategic Management Journal,* **18,** 15–30.

McGrath, J. E., & Argote, L. (in press). Group processes in organizational contexts. In M. A. Hogg & R. S. Tindale (Eds.), *Blackwell handbook of social psychology:* Group processes (Vol. 3). Oxford, UK: Blackwell.

McGrath, J. E. (1991). Time, interaction, and performance (TIP): A theory of groups. *Small Group Research, 22,* 147–174.

Messick, D. M., & Mackie, D. M. (1989). Intergroup relations. *Annual Review of Psychology, 40,* 45–81.

Moreland, R. L., Argote, L., & Krishnan, R. (1996). Socially shared cognition at work: Transactive memory and group performance. In J. L. Nye & A. M. Brower (Eds.), *What's so social about social cognition? Social cognition research in small groups* (pp. 57–84). Thousand Oaks, CA: Sage.

Moreland, R. L., & Levine, J. M. (2000). Socialization in organizations and groups. In M. Turner (Ed.), *Groups at work: Advances in theory and research* (pp. 69–112). Mahwah, NJ: Erlbaum.

Moreland, R. L., & Levine, J. M. (2000). Exploring the performance benefits of group training: Transactive memory or improved communication? *Organizational Behavior and Human Decision Processes, 82,* 117–133.

Nadler, D. A., & Tushman, M. L. (1980). A model for diagnosing organizational behavior: Applying a congruence perspective. *Organizational Dynamics, 9* (2), 35.

Nelson, R. R., & Winter, S. G. (1982). *An evolutionary theory of economic change.* Boston: Belkman Press.

Nonaka, I. (1991). The knowledge-creating company. *Harvard Business Review, 69* (6), 96–104.

Paulus, P. B., & Yang, H-C. (2000). Idea generation in groups: A basis for creativity in organizations. *Organizational Behavior and Human Decision Processes, 82,* 76–87.

Powell, W. W., Koput, K. W., & Smith-Doerr, L., (1996). Interorganizational collaboration and the locus of innovation: Networks of learning in biotechnology. *Administrative Science Quarterly, 41,* 116–145.

Porter, M. E. (1980). *Competitive strategy.* New York: Free Press.

Rothwell, R. (1978). Some problems of technology transfer into industry: Examples from the textile machinery sector. *IEEE Transactions on Engineering Management,* **EM-25,** 15–20.

Rulke, D. L., Zaheer, S., & Anderson, M. H. (2000). Sources of managers' knowledge of organizational capabilities. *Organizational Behavior and Human Decision Processes, 82,* 134–149.

Rumelt, R. P. (1991). How much does industry matter? *Strategic Management Journal, 12,* 167–182.

Shapiro, C. (1989). The theory of business strategy. *RAND Journal of Economics, 20,* 125–137.

Singley, M. K., & Anderson, J. R. (1989). *The transfer of cognitive skill.* Cambridge, MA: Harvard Univ. Press.

Spender, J. C., & Grant, R. M. (1996). Knowledge and the firm: Overview. *Strategic Management Journal, 17,* 5–9.

Starbuck, W. H. (1992). Learning by knowledge-intensive firms. *Journal of Management Studies, 29,* 713–738.

Stasser, G., Vaughan, S. I., & Stewart, D. D. (2000). Pooling unshared information: The benefits of knowing how access to information is distributed among group members. *Organizational Behavior and Human Decision Processes, 82,* 102–116.

Szulanski, G. (in press). Appropriability and the challenge of scope: BancOne routinizes replication. In G. Dosi, R. Nelson, & S. Winter (Eds.), *The nature and dynamics of organizational capabilities.* Oxford: Oxford Univ. Press.

Szulanski, G. (2000). The process of knowledge transfer: A diachronic analysis of stickiness. *Organizational Behavior and Human Decision Processes, 82,* 9–27.

Szulanski, G. (1996). Exploring internal stickiness: Impediments to the transfer of best practice within the firm. *Strategic Management Journal, 17,* 27–43.

Teece, D. F. (1988). Technological change and the nature of the firm. In G. Dosi, C. Freeman, R. Nelson, G. Silverberg, & L. Soete (Eds.), *Technical change and economic theory* (pp. 256–281). New York: Pinter.

Teece, D. F., Pisano, G., & Shuen, A. (1997). Dynamic capabilities and strategic management. *Strategic Management Journal, 18,* 509–533.

Thompson, L., Gentner, D., & Lowenstein, J. (2000). Avoiding missed opportunities in managerial life: Analogical training more powerful than individual case training. *Organizational Behavior and Human Decision Processes, 82,* 60–75.

Thorndike, E. K., (1906). *Principles of teaching.* New York: A. G. Seiler.

Walsh, J. P., & Ungson, G. R. (1991). Organizational memory. *Academy of Management Review, 16,* 57–91.

Wegner, D. M. (1986). Transactive memory: A contemporary analysis of the group mind. In B. Mullen & G. R. Goethals (Eds.), *Theories of group behavior* (pp. 185–205). New York: Springer-Verlag.

Wegner, D. M., Erber, R., & Raymond, P. (1991). Transactive memory in close relationships. *Journal of Personality and Social Psychology, 61,* 923–929.

Williams, J. R. (1998). *Renewable advantage.* New York: Free Press.

Wood, W., Lundgren, S., Oullette, J. A., Busceme, S., & Blackstone, T. (1994). Minority influence: A meta-analytic review of social influence processes. *Psychological Bulletin, 115,* 323–345.

Zander, U., & Kogut, B. (1995). Knowledge and the speed of the transfer and imitation of organizational capabilities: An empirical test. *Organization Science, 6,* 76–92.

Zhao, L. & Reisman, A. (1992). Toward meta research on technology transfer. *IEEE Transactions on engineering management, 39,* 13–21.

Received June 21, 1999

What Do CEOs Want from HR?

*CEOs agree on HR's increasingly important role.
Here's how they say HR can fulfill it.*

BY BILL LEONARD

What do chief executive officers really think of the human resource profession? And how do CEOs think HR should change to meet the growing needs of their organizations? To find out, *HRMagazine* recently interviewed five CEOs who represent a broad spectrum of industries, company sizes and geographic locations. One CEO spent many years working in HR; the others have less experience with human resource management.

Despite these varied backgrounds, the comments from all five CEOs reveal common themes—and common areas where HR can stand to improve.

A UNIQUE RELATIONSHIP

As HR professionals increasingly strive to become strategic partners with top management, their relationship with CEOs takes on new significance. All the CEOs interviewed for this article agree that—of all the members of their management teams—their relationship with the top HR professional may be the most important.

The amount of time CEOs spend with HR executives underlines the importance of this relationship.

"I'm probably speaking with our senior v.p. of human resources about 40 percent of my time at work," says Robert McDonald, CEO of the North American division of Standard Chartered Bank in New York. "It seems that I am always talking to her and seeking her advice and input."

Likewise, Mike R. Bowlin, chairman and CEO of ARCO, the Los Angeles-based oil and energy giant, constantly consults his top HR executive.

"I believe that I spend as much time with John Kelly (senior vice president of HR) as anyone else who works for me," he says. "There is no major decision that takes place in the company that John is not involved with, and I fully expect him to have an opinion on business decisions. As CEO, I use John as a personal consultant and sounding board for ideas and problem solving. Many times, he and I go to lunch and just bounce ideas off each other, which works well for us."

All five CEOs say that as HR has gained more access to their offices, the head of HR has assumed a unique relationship with the CEO. But how can HR make sure that relationship remains solid?

"The key to a good relationship between the CEO and the head of HR is honesty," believes Craig Sturken, chief executive officer of Farmer Jack Supermarkets in Detroit. "For the relationship to really work well, there has to be a trust, closeness and almost intuitive understanding between the CEO and the head of HR. The last thing that you want to do as CEO is stifle that relationship; it's crucial to the success of your business."

Girard Miller, president and CEO of ICMA Retirement Corp. in Washington, D.C. says HR must relate well to both employees and top management. "It's a hard role to play, I believe. A good HR professional must have the ability to thoroughly develop a trusting relationship with the employees, while at the same time be something of a collaborator and serve as a confidant to the CEO."

Miller adds that HR must work closely with CEOs. "I'm a firm believer that the HR function must be a direct report to the CEO," he says. "I think that there are just too many opportunities for mischief, if it is not."

THE STRATEGIC ROLE OF HR

Why do these CEOs place such emphasis on the strategic role of HR in their organizations? The answer lies in the evolving and strategic role of the profession.

"HR has become a very important component in our strategic planning processes," says Mike Goodrich, president and CEO of BE&K Inc., an engineering and construction company based in Birmingham, Ala. "We need to anticipate where our company is going to be five to six years down the road, and HR is crucial to understanding the

**T. Michael Goodrich
President and
Chief Executive Officer
BE&K Inc., Birmingham, Ala.**

Goodrich became president of BE&K in 1989 and was named CEO in 1995. He began working for BE&K in 1972 as assistant secretary and general counsel.

BE&K is one of the largest privately owned engineering and construction companies in the United States. Last year, the company had nearly $1 billion in sales and currently has a workforce of nearly 8,000.

changing demographics and expectations of our workforce."

The other CEOs agree that HR executives must understand and embrace their evolving strategic role, which includes helping track the skills of the workforce and matching them up with the organization's needs.

"HR management is one of the critical resources that we have to carry on our business plan," says Bowlin. "Our people are what will truly build a sustainable competitive advantage. In the long run, everyone has the same access to capital and technology, so a company's human resources is what makes the difference and makes it successful. It is the key resource."

**Robert P. McDonald
Chief Executive Officer
North America
Standard Chartered Bank,
New York**

McDonald began working for Standard Chartered Bank in 1992, when First Interstate Bank was acquired by Standard Chartered. Prior to 1991, McDonald worked for 20 years with Chase Manhattan Bank in London and New York.

Standard Chartered is an international bank, which focuses most of its activities on Asia, Africa, the Middle East and Latin America. The bank has more than 26,000 employees worldwide, with nearly 600 in the United States.

McDonald fully expects "HR to be the guardian of information as to where your best people are in the organization and what their talents are."

Miller adds that "HR needs to know how the personnel talent of the organization can make a difference to the short-term business plans as well as the long-term strategy."

THE BOTTOM-LINE APPROACH

As HR's role as a strategic partner has evolved, the focus and knowledge necessary to be a successful HR executive have also changed. For example, the CEOs interviewed for this article emphasized that—although HR has improved its

understanding of financial issues—more work needs to be done.

"When it comes to the bottom line, I would say that HR generally has been a bit out to lunch," says McDonald. "But their understanding of the bottom line has improved over the past few years, and I do believe most HR executives are striving to better understand how their decisions and actions can truly affect the bottom line."

Miller goes so far as to characterize HR's comprehension of financial issues as "soft." "HR professionals are not as far along as I, as a CEO, would like to see them," he says. "I believe they get the idea when it comes to their own budget but have a tough time understanding concepts such as variable costs versus fixed costs."

Miller says this is true with his current vice president of HR but adds that she has been a willing student. "And her willingness to learn is really the key here and clearly shows that she is interested and committed to improving the bottom line of this organization," he adds.

Sturken's experience mirrors that of McDonald and Miller; a solid financial orientation has not been a strength of most of the HR professionals he has worked with.

"I believe there has been a lack of concentration on the bottom line among many of the HR people I have known," Sturken says. But, like Miller, he sees improvement.

"I will hand it to my current vice president of HR," he says. "She is trying hard to learn and improve her knowledge and skills, and I believe that her efforts will pay off for both her and our company in the long run."

Sturken encourages HR professionals to strengthen their financial knowledge by taking advantage of educational opportunities. "I always advise my HR staff to take courses in business finance and financial planning," he says. "There are a lot of seminars and workshops on the fundamentals in accounting for nonfinancial managers. I have had managers come back from these courses and give suggestions and ideas to our accounting department on streamlining and improving some systems."

OTHER SKILLS

Besides a strong bottom-line orientation, several of the CEOs say their HR executives and managers need to be more aggressive and work on their powers of persuasion.

"At my company, we have a saying that you need to push the envelope," says Goodrich. "And HR has never really pushed the envelope with me. I have no problem saying 'no' if I think it's too much. I have said 'no' plenty of times to our information technology department. But HR has never pushed hard enough or far enough for me to say 'no' yet."

Bowlin says that HR has moved into the role of internal consultants at ARCO, but he is quick to point out that the term "consultants" does not mean he wants a bunch of "yes men or women" on his staff. He wants people who will challenge and question decisions that they believe are flawed.

"The people who acquiesce too quickly are usually gone quickly," he says. "But then if you have someone who tries to be too controlling, that's not good either. What we want is a team player who is knowledgeable, bright and aggressive and has good consulting skills," Bowlin says.

Part of being a good consultant, says Bowlin, is being persuasive. "This is a skill that HR needs to work on, I believe," he says. "To succeed, you must have the ability to be persuasive and move the organization forward and to influence key business decisions."

To be more persuasive, however, many HR professionals need more education in business fundamentals.

"Clearly, HR professionals today are better trained than I was when I began my career 30 years ago [in HR]. But they do need sufficient and fundamental business training to participate and contribute to the company."

Miller goes a step further, saying that HR managers seem to lack some business training that is necessary to perform in today's workplace.

"I find generally that many HR professionals' business math skills and dimensions are fairly weak," Miller says. "I believe that the skill level is slowly improving and that's largely due, in part, to the fact that it is changing from the personnel function to the HR function."

Miller also believes that HR professionals have a "lack of vision" when it comes to the big picture of the organization.

"HR professionals have been getting by focusing on the day-to-day. They need to develop a broader and farther-reaching vision and understand where their organization is headed and how they can help steer the company in that direction," Miller adds.

McDonald says that HR is "being a bit insular." He says that one of the major problems with HR is that the profession's executives and managers have tended to focus solely on their HR departments.

"Their primary focus was HR, and the company was secondary to that. All the company did was provide them a paycheck, and that was the prevailing attitude 20 years ago," says McDonald. "It has improved, but I think because of that at-

**Mike R. Bowlin
Chairman and
Chief Executive Officer
ARCO, Los Angeles**

Bowlin was appointed president and CEO of ARCO in July 1994 and was named chairman of the ARCO board of directors one year later.

Bowlin began his career with ARCO in 1969 as an HR representative and moved steadily up the ranks, holding positions such as manager of HR of ARCO's Alaska operations, vice president of human resources for ARCO Oil and Gas Co. and senior vice president of ARCO Resources.

ARCO, an acronym for the Atlantic Richfield Co., is the seventh largest oil company in the United States. The Fortune 100 company has 24,000 employees worldwide and annual sales of more than $18.6 billion.

titude, HR's reputation among other departments was a bit tainted. That reputation has improved vastly in recent years, but there's always room for improvement."

McDonald believes that improvement comes when HR sees itself as an internal consultant. "It really makes my job easier if I'm working with someone who sees themself as working with internal clients rather than seeing themself as just a part of the HR group," says McDonald. "Those who think outside the four dots and believe that they are serving internal clients get my vote."

BEYOND SKILLS

The CEOs interviewed for this article tend to agree that the best and most successful HR professionals have a real passion for their jobs.

"The better HR professionals that I have worked with have been compassionate and have deep feelings for our employees," says Goodrich. "They have a burning desire to see our employees succeed and build better lives for themselves. It's a trait that I have truly admired among most of the really good and successful HR professionals that I have known."

Bowlin agrees that true success comes from a passion for your job. "To really truly succeed, you have to be passionate about your work. You have to feel that you can make a difference," he says. "And if you are really good and passionate about your job, and you work in HR, you can really make one of the most positive impacts of any group within a company."

THE FUTURE OF HR

All five of the CEOs have to think strategically about the short- and long-term issues that confront their organizations. Two of the key issues they identified for their organizations—and, consequently, for HR—are recruiting and diversity.

Sturken says that the primary problem his company faces is a drastic labor shortage. The tight labor market has made recruiting and retention top priorities at his company.

"Retail is really tough right now," Sturken says. "It's a quality of life issue. The question that we face is, How can we improve our employees' lifestyle? People don't want to work weekends and evenings, and that's the lifeblood of retail. None of the old rules work when it comes to recruiting and hiring people. HR has to be very creative and market and merchandise our company and the advantages of working here. It's a very different ball game now."

Goodrich agrees that the labor market's rules have changed but attributes many of the changes to a dramatic shift in demographics.

"We really have been paying close attention to the changing demographics of our workforce," Goodrich says. "We have more women and more Latinos working in the construction industry today, and we must be prepared to respond to these changes."

He adds that the aging of the workforce will present some interesting challenges to the workplace. That is a trend that will also profoundly affect Miller's organization, which manages retirement funds for local governments.

"As the baby boom generation ages, we will have a powerful growth curve over the next five to six years in this organization," Miller says. "The demand for more retirement benefits and retiree medical care will be tremendous and will affect all businesses. We have to begin considering how we are going to pay for those benefits."

Bowlin believes that effectively managing multicultural diversity is the primary challenge that faces HR and corporate America.

"ARCO has to design HR systems that recognize cultural differences and help the company be more effective in those cultures. It's a high priority for us," Bowlin says. "As this company becomes more global, how we manage diversity will be key to our success."

The workplace challenges of multicultural diversity only emphasize the importance of developing a global focus when dealing with HR issues, according to McDonald.

"The challenge of HR is cross-cultural. It is a huge job to make that cultural bridge," he says. "HR professionals can prepare to meet these challenges by making themselves available for international assignments, and by that I mean living outside the country for three to four years. International mobility is key. Today's economy is a global economy, and HR has to be ready to accept the roles and challenges that the global marketplace brings."

Bill Leonard is senior writer for HRMagazine. *Patrick Mirza, managing editor of* HRMagazine, *contributed to this article.*

Managing Social Capital

By Lovemore Mbigi

Social capital–an organization's emotional and spiritual resources–is a distinctive competitive factor akin to intellectual capital. Social capital affects the impact of any strategic intervention and the ultimate effectiveness of policies, procedures, and processes. But modern management thinking, practices, and literature are weak in managing emotional and spiritual resources, which also help determine the value of an organization.

Science is not instructive on how to manage social capital in organizations. Social capital is a different form of energy and level of consciousness, and requires a different knowledge base. The practices of ancient African religions can contribute to social capital management and its transformation. One can use the hierarchy of African spirits, which is transtribal, as a model for managing cultural, emotional, and spiritual resources in an organization.

In African spirit religion, the spirit represents our ultimate real self, our inner self and total being, and our total consciousness. The spirit is who we really are. In terms of management, spirit is the ultimate energy and consciousness of an organization. The spirit is an organization's values and essence. The African spirit model serves as a metaphor to capture an organization's prevailing climate, culture, energy, and consciousness. This model can be used as a tool for auditing the dominant spirits and cultural values of an organization in a live, collective, and participative manner. The model can also be used as a framework for managing and transforming an organization's social capital–its emotional and spiritual resources. It can be more effective than sophisticated cultural surveys and psychological techniques, which some employees might not understand because they lack basic literacy skills, a factor that can skew the results of traditional surveys.

The model has been used to transform and create social capital in large business and state organizations in South Africa, such as the South African Post Office (26,000 employees), Spoornet–SA national railway (66,000 employees), and Agricultural Rural Development Corporation. Huge, burning platforms of 100 to 200 employees debate gut issues that will determine the social capital resources of their organization. The workshops are a ritual of integration

The Gist

☐ Social capital—an organization's emotional and spiritual resources—is as crucial to competitiveness and strategic efforts as intellectual capital.
☐ The Hierarchy of African Spirits can serve as a model of modern management.
☐ It's important to dispel negative spirits for a positive organizational climate to flourish and make renewal efforts sustainable and high-impact.

accompanied by music, drumming, and dancing. They are offsite, residential, multilevel, multifunctional, and multirational. The debates and outputs center around selected strategic themes. The workshops are run by trained facilitators who must be open to various outcomes and be prepared to pioneer new methods for entire communities. The focus is on raising consciousness regarding world views, power, and public accountability. The world views are co-created through public debate and dissent on critical issues facing the country and the organizations involved, and on the mobilization of action around those issues.

The other focus is on helping people think through who they are, why they are, and what they can become. That's done through collective dancing, singing, drumming, and storytelling, as well as mythography—a technique that requires the facilitator to capture the collective story of the group in the form of a heroic mythology with distinctive events and characters to dramatize the message. The ritualistic elements of the workshop are as important as the content and discussions.

I rely heavily on the use of myths in running my workshops on transformation and strategy. The approach varies, depending on the issues and themes of the workshop. Here are some of the common elements.

Storytelling. Factual accuracy isn't as important as the message. Each story must have a heroic character struggling with survival, competitive, and moral issues. Each story should be brief and build to a climax, include the anticipatory circumstances, and have a dramatic ending.

Organizational myths and spirits. There are many ways to extract the myths and spirits of an organization. You can ask participants to share their most memorable experiences, or ask them to share stories of the most remarkable characters in the organization. If the stories are negative, it

African Spirit Hierarchy

Rainmaker Spirit **GOBWA**

Hunter Spirit **SHAVI RUDZIMBA**

Divination Spirit **SANGOMA**

War Spirit **MAJUKWA**

Clan/Family Spirit **MUDZIMU WEMHURI**

Wandering Spirit **SHAVE**

Avenging Spirit **NGOZI**

Witch Spirit **MUTAKATI**

Cultural Values	Spirit
Morality and dignity	Rainmaker Spirit GOBWA
Performance and enterprise	Hunter Spirit SHAVI RUDZIMBA
Authority: Know the truth	Divination Spirit SANGOMA
Power and conflict	War Spirit MAJUKWA
Survival of one's self and one's group	Clan/Family Spirit MUDZIMU WEMHURI
Particular obsession, ability, and creativity	Wandering Spirit SHAVE
Bitterness, anger, revenge	Avenging Spirit NGOZI
Cynicism, negativity, destruction	Witch Spirit MUTAKATI

means that the myths and spirits of the organization are negative.

Constructing new stories and myths can create a positive spirit within the organization. That can be accomplished in various ways:

- The history of the organization can be reconstructed in a heroic, mythological drama with a particular theme and well-selected positive aspects.
- The history of the various social groups participating in the workshop can be reconstructed in a way that focuses on the heroic and mythical aspects.
- You can select individuals in the organization who have tried to do what it seeks and create hype

around them, thereby transforming them into mythical and real heroes.

The sessions should be punctuated with humor, collective singing, or dancing in order to access the spiritual and emotional resources of the organization. The physical setting should have

- appropriate decoration and colors to portray the theme of the session
- physical evidence or props representing the emotional and spiritual elements of the theme
- appropriate background music
- a place with a positive spirit
- facilitators who convey the emotional and spiritual message
- a seating arrangement that allows symbolic expression of the or-

ganization's spirit and emotional energy.

The ritualistic elements are based on a Shona renewal ceremony called *Dandaro*. Literally translated, it means "relaxing together in a meaningful and renewing way." The ceremony is open to all and is facilitated by an outside soothsayer. It includes collective singing, dancing, drumming, and eating, as well as a search for future direction.

The spirits of management

The destructive spirit. Witch Spirit Mutakati is the lowest spirit in the hierarchy of African spirits. This is an evil spirit that wants to spoil everything in life and on Earth. In terms of the corporate collective spirit, it's characterized by destructive cynicism, negative thinking, and passive and active sabotage. This spirit devours an organization's energy. It is a dominant spirit in sluggish businesses and government bureaucracies.

The powerless spirit. Avenging Spirit Ngozi is usually good but has been treated unjustly. As a result, it harbors anger, bitterness, and revenge. It is the dominant spirit among marginalized and powerless groups in society and organizations. This is the predominant spirit in dispossessed groups and the underclass of any society and organization. Unless such groups can overcome their bitterness and anger, they won't be able to negotiate a new reality and new vision for themselves or their organizations. They can also become a danger to themselves and society as a whole.

The innovative spirit. Wandering Spirit Shave is the spirit of an outsider who comes to the family or clan as a White Knight on a specific issue or area. This is an unusual individual who has a particular obsession and unique creative ability. It is the spirit of innovation. This is a weak spirit in many modern organizations in which innovators aren't accepted or re-

> **The African Spirit Hierarchy has lessons for managing an organization's emotional and spiritual resources.**

warded but, at best, just tolerated. The key strategic lesson is that innovative ideas may have to come from outside the organization and from outsiders to the accepted corporate system. That suggests a strong case for employment practices that can attract mavericks, who usually have incomplete or unusual résumés. Organizations may also have to make use of reputable consultants to generate creative ideas. The insiders may be too close to their systems to envision potential realities. It's difficult to challenge a corporate culture from within, as it is career limiting. The second strategic lesson is that innovation may have to be managed outside of the formal structure, giving rise to the need to create parallel structures for innovation.

The family spirit. Clan Spirit Mudzimu Wemhuri is a family spirit that is interested in the survival of its group. This spirit enhances group solidarity through specified rituals, activities, ceremonies, and symbols. It's important for building team-based, world-class organizations. It also serves to emphasize the importance of ritu-

For More Reading

UBUNTU: The African Dream in Management, by Lovemore Mbigi. Johannesburg: Knowledge Resources Ltd.
UBUNTU: The Spirit of African Transformation Management, by Lovemore Mbigi with J. Maree. Johannesburg: Knowledge Resources Ltd.

als, ceremonies, and symbols in designing organizational teams.

The personal spirit. War Spirit Majukwa is a spirit of personal power, conflict, and gamesmanship. It helps us understand power cultures and how to create power and influence in organizations. The rise of spider-web structures in modern organizations makes it imperative for individuals to develop power skills for personal influence in order to accomplish objectives.

The spirit of truth. Spirit of Divination Sangoma knows the whole truth, its truth, and is not open to other views. Experts and specialists in organizations typically personify this spirit, as do most traditionalists. This spirit reduces the rate of learning in an organization and its ability to adapt to change. Therefore, we should populate action learning teams with nonexperts and mavericks.

The restless spirit. Hunter Spirit Shavi Rudzimba is a restless spirit and is the spirit of entrepreneurship. It has an eye for opportunity and deal making. This spirit has a marked quest for pragmatic, creative solutions to survival and competitive challenges. The rituals and ceremonies surrounding this spirit help us develop practices to manage entrepreneurship in organizations.

The relationship spirit. Rainmaker Spirit Gobwa is concerned about our relationship with the organization and other people, as well as with our ecological, social, political, economic, and spiritual environments. This spirit takes care of our whole universe and is concerned with truth, morality, balance, and human dignity. This spirit helps clarify the stewardship role of the CEO and the need to take accountability for the whole organization, as well as being its conscience. The primary role of a CEO is to look after the spirit of the organization and its total social capital.

Strategic lessons

In any given situation, there will be two or more dominant spirits that determine the social capital of an organization. The dominant spirits determine the organization's outcomes, consciousness, culture, and energy levels.

The African Spirit Hierarchy model can be used to audit the dominant culture and values, as well as the organizational climate in a collective, participative manner through dialogues and bonding rituals that allow group psychological departure and rebirth. The ceremonies and symbols that are integrated into the process provide access to the collective unconsciousness of the organization. The whole process is enhanced by one or more elements of storytelling, singing, dancing, and mythography.

It's important to dispel negative spirits for a positive organizational climate to flourish and make renewal efforts sustainable and high-impact. Organizations can't let go of a negative past and embark on the critical path of corporate renewal as long as there are deadening, routine activities and processes. There's a need to design rituals and ceremonies of departure and rebirth. As a general rule, competent and charismatic outside consultants must facilitate those. Organizations can't embark on a cultural renaissance without dealing with past grievances.

Organizations have to know where they are coming from to find out where they can go. They have to know who they are before they can know what they can become. Strategic visioning and values exercises have failed because of their lack of a spiritual dimension, for want of a better term. Such exercises have ended up with empty slogans that are neither practiced nor taken seriously.

Organizational transformation isn't just an intellectual journey; it's also an emotional and spiritual journey. In order to access the emotional and spiritual resources of an organization, appropriate bonding symbols, myths, ceremonies, and rituals are needed.

Lovemore Mbigi *is a professor and a principal of Rainmaker Management Consultants, Johannesburg, South Africa; wmc@icon.co.za.*

EFFECTS OF LEADERSHIP STYLE AND FOLLOWERS' CULTURAL ORIENTATION ON PERFORMANCE IN GROUP AND INDIVIDUAL TASK CONDITIONS

DONG I. JUNG
San Diego State University

BRUCE J. AVOLIO
State University of New York at Binghamton

We manipulated transformational and transactional leadership styles and compared them in individual and group task conditions to determine whether they had different impacts on individualists and collectivists performing a brainstorming task. Results showed that collectivists with a transformational leader generated more ideas, but individualists generated more ideas with a transactional leader. Group performance was generally higher than that of individuals working alone. However, contrary to expectations, collectivists generated more ideas that required fundamental organizational changes when working alone.

There has been considerable interest in whether the attitudes, behavior, and motivation of managers and employees differ across cultures and in the effects those differences have on work group performance (Chen, Chen, & Meindl, 1998; Hofstede, 1980a). The need to learn more about these potential cross-cultural differences coincides with the rapid globalization of the world's economy as well as with the cultural diversification of the U.S. workforce, in which the majority of new entrants over the next 20 to 30 years will be women, Asians, Hispanics, and African Americans (Johnston & Packer, 1987). These changes have produced a sense of urgency among many organizational leaders regarding the practical importance of understanding, addressing, and meeting the needs of culturally diverse work groups (Hofstede, 1993).

The changing composition of the U.S. workforce raises an important question: Are current leadership and management models valid for explaining the behavior and motivation of culturally different work groups? Supporting the need for cross-cultural research, Hofstede (1980b) argued that many differences in individual motivation and leadership styles could be traced to differences in cultural programming. Erez (1994) also challenged the appropriateness of simply assuming that United States–centric leadership theories can be generalized to other cultures.

Should one lead differently in different cultural settings? This question was formulated on the basis of preliminary evidence showing that culturally different groups prefer different ways of being led (Hofstede, 1993; Triandis, 1993). Although there are several theoretical models to help explain cultural differences regarding what constitutes effective leadership (see, for example, Dorfman [1996] and Triandis [1993]), only a handful of studies have actually examined the effects of differences in cultural orientation on the effectiveness of leader-follower interactions.

We thank the three anonymous reviewers for their valuable and constructive comments on earlier versions. We also thank Bernard Bass and Francis Yammarino for their helpful comments. This research was in part supported by the Center for Leadership Studies at the State University of New York at Binghamton.

Here, we set out to compare how transformational and transactional leadership affected the performance of ad hoc work groups comprised of either individualists or collectivists. We also examined different task conditions and their interaction with leadership style, since prior research has reported that cultural orientation may interact with an individual's preferred way of working (Wagner, 1995).

THEORETICAL BACKGROUND AND HYPOTHESES

Transactional and Transformational Leadership

Transactional leadership was described by Burns (1978) as motivating followers primarily through contingent-reward-based exchanges. Typically, the main focus of transactional leaders is on setting goals, clarifying the link between performance and rewards, and providing constructive feedback to keep followers on task (Bass, 1985).

In contrast, transformational leadership involves developing a closer relationship between leaders and followers, one based more on trust and commitment than on contractual agreements. Transformational leaders help followers to see the importance of transcending their own self-interest for the sake of the mission and vision of their group and/or organization. By building followers' self-confidence, self-efficacy, and self-esteem, such leaders are expected to have a strong, positive influence on followers' levels of identification, motivation, and goal achievement (Gardner & Avolio, 1998; Klein & House, 1995; Shamir, House, & Arthur, 1993).

Transactional and transformational leadership have been examined in various cultures. For example, Yokochi (1989) reported that the top managers in several large Japanese firms rated by followers as more transformational also had higher ratings on their followers' level of effectiveness. Koh (1990) reported a similarly positive relationship between ratings of transformational leadership, levels of trust, and school effectiveness for secondary school principals in Singapore.

However, previous cross-cultural research on transformational leadership has mainly focused on replicating the augmentation effects of transformational leadership over transactional leadership on followers' performance. There have been no systematic efforts made to link leadership styles, followers' cultural orientation, and followers' performance taking a cross-cultural perspective (Jung, Bass, & Sosik, 1995). In the current study, we undertook to address this gap by testing hypotheses on the main characteristics of both leaders' styles and followers' cultural orientations.

Followers' Cultural Orientation and Leadership Style

A number of cross-cultural studies have shown that collectivists tend to have a stronger attachment to their organizations and tend to subordinate their individual goals to group goals (Earley, 1989; Triandis, 1995). Collectivists maintain longer-term relationships with their organizations and view interpersonal skills and relationships as being more valuable than specific job knowledge and skills. Indeed, many organizations in collectivist cultures highlight the importance of maintaining long-term relationships as well as in-group solidarity (Ungson, Steers, & Park, 1997). The central role the group plays in collectivist cultures parallels some of the main value orientations associated with transformational leadership. For example, transformational leaders emphasize the importance of subordinating individual needs to group goals, a central feature of collectivist cultures. Collectivists are expected to identify with their leaders' goals and the common purpose or shared vision of the group and organization. They also typically exhibit high levels of loyalty and commitment to the leader (Jung et al., 1995).

People in individualist cultures are expected to be more motivated to satisfy their own self-interests and personal goals (Hofstede, 1980a). In such cultures, individuals take care of themselves, and they tend to place higher priority on individual initiative and achievement, as well as on personal rewards based on satisfying transactional agreements. The person or self is defined more as an independent entity, whereas the self is defined in association with groups or organizations in collectivist cultures (Triandis, 1995). As such, individualists are expected to be more motivated by transactional leadership. Transactional leadership is typically more short-term-focused and in line with the values orientation in more individualistic cultures (Hofstede, 1993).

In collectivist cultures, the strong tendency to support organizational values and norms should fit with a transformational leader's efforts to align followers' personal values with a new mission or vision (Avolio & Bass, 1988). Followers from collectivist cultures are expected to more readily internalize their leader's vision than will individualist followers for at least two reasons. First, collectivists tend to accept their leader's beliefs more readily, because of the high power distance that exists in those cultures (Hofstede, 1980a, Triandis, 1995).[1] Although there may be some countries, such as Norway and Sweden, where individuals are collectivists but prefer equal distribution of power, most collectivist countries, such as those in Asia, tend to demonstrate high degrees of power distance. Second,

---

[1] Power distance refers to the extent to which individuals accept an unequal distribution of power.

there is typically a high level of value congruence between followers and leaders owing to extensive socialization processes in collectivist cultures. Consequently, we expected that a transformational leader's emphasis on achieving collective goals would be more readily accepted when group members' cultural orientation was more collectivist (Jung et al., 1995).

The congruence between followers' cultural values and a transformational leader's attempts to build identification with a collective vision is expected to enhance motivation and performance among followers. Hence, we predicted that such leaders would maximize the efforts and performance of followers who have a more collectivistic orientation.

Taken together, our consideration of different leadership styles and their relationship with followers' cultural orientations led us to the first hypothesis tested in the current study:

Hypothesis 1a. The performance of individualists will be higher working with a transactional leader than with a transformational leader.

Hypothesis 1b. The performance of collectivists will be higher working with a transformational leader than with a transactional leader.]

Followers' Cultural Orientation and Task Structure

Generally, collectivists are considered to be more concerned than individualists with maintaining solidarity in their groups. Collectivism is also associated with a higher attachment to the group and greater acceptance of group norms. These specific cultural differences may have some implications for the design of work tasks in different cultures (Cox, Lobel, & McLeod, 1991: Wagner, 1995). For example, Gabrenya, Latane, and Wang (1983) compared American and Chinese students and reported that the performance of Chinese students working in groups was significantly higher than that of Chinese students working alone. They suggested the collectivist Chinese may have viewed their individual actions as an important contribution to their group's efforts and received greater levels of satisfaction and feelings of accomplishment from group outcomes. The collectivist's tendency to display cooperative behavior in a group setting may also contribute to differences in performance (Chen et al., 1998; Cox et al., 1991).

Earley (1989) explained collectivists' strong tendencies to prefer to work in groups and to perform better in groups than when working alone on the basis of social loafing theory. Earley found that collectivist Chinese managers did not engage in social loafing when working in groups because they valued achieving group goals over self-interest. In contrast, individualist American managers performed better on an individual than on a group task and were more likely to loaf when their individual contributions to group performance were not easily monitored.

Erez and Somech (1996) explained collectivists' low degree of social loafing in work group situations in terms of "independent" and "interdependent" selves and their different motivational effects on a person's desire to contribute to group performance. In Erez and Somech's formulation, collectivists view themselves as an integral part of social relationships and are more likely to define their self as being tied to others in their social network. Erez and Somech (1996) argued that working with others and making contributions to group performance help collectivists fulfill the interdependent self and strengthen their group identity. Individualists, who value the independent self more than the interdependent self, view their contributions to groups as being less important than enhancing their self-accomplishment.

Our discussion of cultural orientation leads to the following set of hypotheses:

Hypothesis 2a. The aggregate performance of individualists will be higher when they work alone than when they work in a group.

Hypothesis 2b. The aggregate performance of collectivists will be higher when they work in a group than when they work alone.

In sum, taking into consideration our review of followers' cultural orientation, leadership style, and task structure, we advance the following hypotheses on their interaction:

Hypothesis 3a. The aggregate performance of individualists will be higher when they work alone and have a transactional leader than it will be under all other leadership and task conditions.

Hypothesis 3b. The aggregate performance of collectivists will be higher when they work in groups and have transformational leaders than it will be under all other leadership and task conditions.

METHODS

Participants and Research Design

A total of 347 students participated in this study (153 Asians and 194 Caucasians).[2] The mean age of participants was 21.5 years (s.d. = 4.1) and 52 percent were male. Eighty-six percent of the students were juniors and seniors in college. The Asian students' average length of time in the United States was 10.6 years (s.d. = 6.7). There were 31 Asian students who were born in the United States. Only a small percentage (8

---

[2] The 153 Asian participants consisted of Chinese (59), Japanese (37), and Korean (57) individuals.

percent) of the Caucasian students indicated that they had lived outside of the United States. Their average length of stay abroad was less than a year (s.d. = 2.76).

Most participants were business majors in the school of management of a large public university in the northeastern United States. Additional Korean students ($n = 27$) were recruited from two Korean language courses because not enough Asian students were enrolled in the school of management. These Korean students were randomly assigned to groups of Asians from the school of management, so that each group had a similar ratio of students from business and language courses. Further, in order to counterbalance potential effects of gender, we assigned two male and two female students to each group.

This study employed a completely crossed two-by-two (transformational/transactional leadership by group/individual task) experimental design. Leadership style was manipulated by having groups led by either an individual exhibiting transactional leadership or an individual exhibiting transformational leadership. Task structure was manipulated by having half of the students work as individuals and having the remaining half work in groups. This two-by-two experimental design was repeated for the Caucasian and Asian samples.

Experimental Task, Procedures, and Leadership Manipulations

The task performed by participants was to provide recommendations to support the school of management's application for reaccreditation to the American Assembly of Collegiate Schools of Business (AACSB). Participants were asked to generate as many ideas as they could in a 35-minute session on how the school could improve the quality of education it offered to students. Prior to actual experimental sessions, participants were given a short overview of the project and a questionnaire measuring their cultural orientation, ethnicity, and other demographic information. Each experimental session lasted about two hours and had two phases. Phase 1 involved a 30-minute orientation period in which the group leader, one of two male instructors working for us, introduced himself and explained the purpose of the project following a script. There were two scripts, one for transactional leadership and one for transformational leadership. After participants spent 10 minutes for group member introductions, the leader handed out an information package, which included a letter from the school's dean highlighting the importance of their input for the project and information about reaccreditation.

Phase 2 began with a 5-minute pretrial exercise designed to acquaint participants with the task. We used participants' pretrial performance as a covariate in the hypothesis tests to control for individual differences.

Participants then worked on the main task for 35 minutes. In the group task condition, group members designated one person to write down their recommendations. In the individual task condition, participants worked alone to provide and record recommendations. The group leader made several statements based on predefined scripts at 10-, 25-, and 33-minute intervals to reinforce one of the two leadership styles. At the end of phase 2, participants were instructed to complete a posttask questionnaire measuring the intended leadership manipulations.

As noted above, we manipulated leadership style by using two trained male confederates as session leaders. The transactional and the transformational leadership scripts cited identical work experience. The two confederate leaders were also similar in terms of their personal characteristics: they were both Caucasian, male, middle-aged, and of similar height. During the introduction phase, each man gave verbal cues associated with either transformational or transactional leadership using scripts adapted from a training program developed by Bass and Avolio (1997). For example, for the transformational leadership conditions, the instructor emphasized the importance of the task and its broader contribution to management education. He also encouraged participants to come up with new and creative ways to analyze problems in the school. For the transactional leadership condition, the instructor emphasized what needed to be done to accomplish the task and assured participants tangible outcomes would be derived from accomplishing their work.

Measures and Coding

Seventeen items adapted from the Multifactor Leadership Questionnaire (MLQ) Form 5X (Bass & Avolio, 1997) were used to measure transformational and transactional leadership. Items were rated on a five-point scale (1 = strongly disagree to 5 = strongly agree). Transformational leadership was measured with 11 items (sample: "My leader seeks differing perspectives when solving problems"). Transactional leadership was measured with 6 items (sample: "My leader makes clear what one can expect to receive when performance goals are achieved.").

As a manipulation check, we used a collectivism/individualism scale developed by Bass and Avolio (1997). Participants indicated their response by placing an X in one of five places equally spaced between two bipolar statements. A sample item is "I prefer to work toward individual goals" (1)/"I prefer to work toward group goals" (5).

In order to assess *quantity*, two raters counted the total number of unduplicated recommendations independently. Their initial agreement rate prior to discussion was over 90 percent. The dimensions used to assess the *quality* of performance were practicality and

TABLE 1
Results of Leadership Manipulation Checks[a]

| | Leader 1 | | | | Leader 2 | | | |
| | Transformational Leadership | | Transactional Leadership | | Tranformational Leadership | | Transactional Leadership | |
Raters[b]	Ratings of Transformational	Ratings of Trans-actional	Ratings of Transformational	Ratings of Trans-actional	Ratings of Transformational	Ratings of Trans-actional	Ratings of Transformational	Ratings of Trans-actional
Under-graduate students	2.72	2.21	1.85	2.69	2.64	2.04	1.87	2.87
Doctoral students	3.56	3.00	0.75	3.38	3.00	2.83	0.69	2.96
Experimental sample	3.86	3.32	3.58	4.07	3.62	3.18	3.06	3.73

[a]All ratings are based on a five-point (0 to 4) scale.
[b]Undergraduate $n = 4$. For the experimental sample, n's slightly varied depending on the confederate leaders and leadership condition. Participants in actual experimental sessions rated only their own leader. All of the mean differences under each leader and leadership condition were significant at p .001 or lower.

long-term versus short-term orientation. Practicality was defined in terms of ease of implementation and the extent to which implementation was in the control of the school. Long-term orientation was defined as requiring substantial and fundamental efforts by change by the school over an extended period of time. Although we did not intend to imply that short-term ideas and solutions were necessarily of less value than long-term ones, we did assume that long-term ideas were more in line with the school's interest in developing a strategic mission, values, and plan for launching a "new" school of management. In addition, the dean emphasized in his letter to participants that the school needed to develop a long-term and mission-based focus to achieve reaccreditation.

Overall, initial interrater agreement was 77.6 percent for practicality and 89 percent for long-term orientation. Discrepancies were resolved through discussion between the two raters working together to arrive at a single score for each category. The final interrater agreement for all categories was above 90 percent.

RESULTS

Manipulation Checks

After 15 hours of leadership training, the confederate leaders' portrayal of the two leadership styles was videotaped without any participants present. A group of undergraduate business students unfamiliar with this study evaluated the videotapes using the 17 MLQ

Form 5X items (Bass & Avolio, 1997). Drawing on feedback provided by student raters, each confederate leader then spent an additional 5 hours of training with the authors to further refine his portrayal of the two leadership styles. After the second training session, a panel of doctoral students who were also unfamiliar with the study rated a second videotape of each leader.

Mean scores for each confederate leader are shown in Table 1. Results of these comparisons were significant ($p < .001$) and in the intended direction, indicating that students perceived each leader's behavior as more or less transformational or transactional in the appropriate condition. Furthermore, students' ratings confirmed that the same leadership style was being portrayed similarly by both confederates. None of the t-tests were significant, indicating the two confederate leaders portrayed the leadership styles similarly. Results of mean comparisons for actual experimental participants, shown in Table 1, revealed a similar pattern.

As predicted, the mean score for collectivism among Asian students (3.42) was significantly higher than it was among Caucasian students (3.10; $F = 6.50$, $p < .01$). In order to test for the effects of the length of their stay in the United States on the Asians' cultural orientation, we split all Asians into two groups based on mean length of time (10.6 years) in the United States. Results of an analysis of variance (ANOVA) indicated there was no significant difference in terms of collectivist orientation between the two Asian groups ($F_{1,151} = 2.43$, n.s.). Also, the correlation between the col-

TABLE 2
Means, Standard Deviations, and Correlations

Variable	Mean	s.d.	1	2	3	4
Caucasians						
1. Quantity	19.85	12.89				
2. Practicality	3.20	0.62	−.08			
3. Long-term orientation	3.13	0.72	−.10	−.13*		
4. Leadership condition[a]			−.25**	−.11**	.25**	
5. Task condition[b]			.24**	.04	.16*	.06
Asians						
1. Quantity	19.74	9.51				
2. Practicality	2.75	0.58	.29**			
3. Long-term orientation	3.05	0.64	.12**	−.09		
4. Leadership condition[a]			.18*	.16*	.04	
5. Task condition[b]			.14*	.03	−.18*	.05

[a] Coding: 1 = transactional, 2 = transformational.
[b] Coding: 1 = individual, 2 = group.
* $p < .05$
** $p < .01$

lectivism score and length of stay in the United States was not significant.

Table 2 presents means for each dependent measure summarized within ethnic groups. Mean scores for quantity were similar for Asians and Caucasians. (Table 4 summarizes the means for the dependent measures by leadership and task condition within the ethnic groups.) Table 2 also shows correlations among the dependent measures. Results of a confirmatory factor analysis also supported the development of the two leadership scales. Alpha coefficients were .79 and .85 for transactional and transformational leadership, respectively.

Results of the Hypothesis Tests

Multivariate analysis of covariance (MANCOVA) was used to test all main and interactive effects of leadership style and task structure on performance. We controlled the effects of individual differences on participants' performance using each individual's performance during a pretrial period as a covariate. We tested potential confounding effects of having nonbusiness majors (the Korean language students) participating in this study by running parallel MANCOVAs without these students included and obtained results identical to those reported below for the entire sample. Consequently, subsequently reported analyses include the 27 non-business majors.

The MANCOVA results produced significant F values for the two main effects as well as for the two-way interaction terms in both samples. These results are summarized in Table 3. Since all results from the

MANCOVAs were significant, analyses of covariance (ANCOVAs) were run next. The ANCOVA results are also summarized in Table 3. For the Caucasians, leadership and task conditions were highly significant for quantity performance. Neither the main nor the two-way interaction effects were significant for the practicality measure. Leadership, task, and their interaction were each significant for the long-term orientation measure. It appears that for the Caucasians, the significant multivariate results for leadership were mainly due to differences on the quantity and long-term orientation measures. The same pattern emerged for the effects of task condition. For the two-way interaction term, the main differences occurred with the long-term orientation measure.

For the Asians, the main and interaction effects were all significant for quantity, but only leadership had a significant effect on the practicality measure. Task condition had a significant effect on the long-term orientation measure of performance. It appears that for Asians the significant multivariate effects for leadership were due to differences on the quantity and practicality measures; for the task condition, the significant effects appeared to be primarily due to differences on the quantity and long-term orientation measures; and the interaction effect appeared to be mainly the result of differences on the quantity measure.

Next, we ran a series of one-way ANOVAs using the cell means to test our first two hypotheses. Comparisons of means and results of these one-way ANOVAs are summarized in Table 4. Results shown in Table 4 support Hypothesis 1a on two of the three per-

TABLE 3
Summary of ANCOVA and MANCOVA Results by Leadership and Task Condition[a]

Variable	Caucasians			Asians		
	F[b]	p	n^2	F[b]	p	n^2
MANCOVA						
Leadership	11.20	.01	.15	3.19	.02	.06
Task	3.71	.01	.07	3.00	.03	.06
Leadership × task	5.29	.01	.08	2.55	.05	.05
ANCOVA						
Quantity						
Leadership	12.23	.01	.06	7.20	.01	.05
Task	7.80	.01	.04	4.39	.04	.03
Leadership × task	2.62	.11	.05	5.92	.01	.04
Practicality						
Leadership	1.16	.28	.00	4.63	.03	.03
Task	0.43	.51	.00	0.42	.52	.00
Leadership × task	3.17	.07	.02	1.15	.29	.00
Long-term orientation						
Leadership	12.22	.01	.11	0.30	.58	.00
Task	3.87	.05	.03	3.65	.05	.02
Leadership × task	9.56	.01	.05	2.18	.14	.01

[a] Pretrial performance was used as a covariate to control individual differences.
[b] MANCOVA Fs are for the Wilks's lambda of each main and interactive effect.

formance measures. As expected, Caucasians working in the transactional leadership condition generated more recommendations than Caucasians in the transformational leadership condition, while also generating more practical recommendations. However, failing to support Hypothesis 1a, Caucasians in the transformational leadership condition generated more ideas that were long-term-oriented than their counterparts in the transactional leadership condition. The performance of Asians was in the expected direction and significant for both quantity and practicality, supporting Hypothesis 1b for two of the three performance measures. The mean difference between the two leadership conditions on the long-term orientation measure among Asians was not significant.

Tests for the main effects of task condition did not support Hypothesis 2a in that Caucasians working in groups outperformed their counterparts working alone on both quantity and long-term orientation. Hypothesis 2b was not supported. Mean differences between the two task conditions on measures of quantity and practicality for Asians were not significant. However, performance in terms of the number of long-term ideas was significantly higher when the Asians performed the task alone versus in groups.

ANOVA results did not support Hypothesis 3a. Caucasians working in a group led by a transactional leader had significantly higher scores on quantity than their counterparts in the other three conditions. Although the mean score for practicality was highest in the individual task and transactional leadership condition, it was not significant ($p < .09$). Caucasians who worked in a group with a transformational leader generated more long-term-oriented recommendations than their counterparts in the remaining conditions. Hypothesis 3b was supported in that Asians in the group task and transformational leadership condition generated significantly more ideas than Asians in any other conditions.

DISCUSSION

Independent Effects of the Leadership Style and Task Conditions

Caucasians in the transactional leadership condition produced more ideas than those working in the transformational leadership condition. These results may be partially explained by the transactional leader's strong instrumental orientation, which could have led

TABLE 4
Comparisons of Means under Different Leadership and Task Conditions with One-Way ANOVAs[a]

Variable	Transactional Leadership	Transformational Leadership	F	Individual	Group	F	Leadership by Task				
							Transactional Leadership		Transformational Leadership		
							Individual	Group	Individual	Group	F
Caucasians											
Quantity	**23.34**	16.95	12.51**	**17.99**	24.81	11.38**	**20.23**	29.06	16.46	18.82	8.07**
Practicality	**3.27**	3.14	2.30	**3.21**	3.16	0.27	**3.36**	3.11	3.11	3.23	2.04
Long-term orientation	**2.93**	3.29	12.79**	**3.08**	3.34	3.43*	**2.99**	2.83	3.19	3.72	8.40**
Asians											
Quantity	18.23	**21.56**	4.81*	18.64	**21.21**	2.80	18.46	17.95	18.83	**25.64**	4.79**
Practicality	2.67	**2.85**	3.95*	2.73	**2.77**	0.18	2.68	2.64	2.79	**2.95**	1.79
Long-term orientation	3.03	**3.07**	0.19	3.14	**2.92**	4.40*	3.20	2.84	3.07	**3.04**	2.23

[a] The first three columns show results of the tests of Hypothesis 1a and 1b; the next three are for Hypothesis 2a and 2b; and the final five are for Hypotheses 3a and 3b. Bold values are those expected to be higher or highest in each manipulated conditions.
* $p < .05$
** $p < .01$

the Caucasians to generate as many practical, short-term ideas as they could within the limited time allotted. Given the short duration of the experimental session, participants may have chosen to simply generate more recommendations. Sosik (1995) reported that giving instructions to followers that are framed in terms of goals and rewards may enhance the quantity of ideas without necessarily enhancing quality.

In contrast, transformational leadership appeared to promote Caucasians' generating ideas with a long-term orientation. In keeping with the longer-term goals and vision articulated by transformational leaders, participants may have seen the importance of such ideas, as opposed to short-term solutions. This pattern of influence would be consistent with the idea that transformational leaders encourage followers to go beyond their immediate needs to address the long-term interests of their organizations (Avolio & Bass, 1988).

Asians working with a transformational leader outperformed their Asian counterparts working with a transactional leader on the measures of quantity and practicality. Perhaps the transformational leader's emphasis on having a collective sense of mission and sacrificing self-interest for the collective interests of the school resonated more positively with the collectivist Asian students' cultural norms. However, the transformational leader did not have a significant impact on the Asians' generation of long-term ideas. Their strong tendency toward face saving, maintenance of group harmony, and fear of evaluation may explain this find-

ing (Earley, 1997). Possibly the Asians were more apprehensive about being criticized by group members and/or about losing face if their long-term and fundamentally different ideas were not well accepted. Additionally, Asians may have felt less comfortable questioning the authority of the institution and its professors by proposing fundamental changes in what the school was currently doing. This hesitancy, coupled with the need to maintain group harmony, may have reduced the number of long-term ideas generated.

Contrary to Hypothesis 2a, Caucasians produced a greater number of long-term-oriented recommendations in the group than in the individual task condition. The number of practical recommendations was similar in the two task conditions. Overall results for the group versus the individual task condition were consistent with findings of previous group brainstorming research. On the average, people can think up twice as many ideas when working in a group than they can when working alone (Diehl & Stroebe, 1987). Unlike the Asians, the Caucasians may have generated more long-term ideas in their groups because of a lack of concern for maintaining group harmony or saving face, which may have resulted in the higher evaluation apprehension noted earlier for Asians.

Interaction Effects

First, for the Caucasians in the sample, the quantity of ideas was highest in the group task and transactional leadership condition. It appears the transactional leader's emphasis on goals and expectations had a stronger impact on the Caucasians' total output in the group condition. Second, the number of ideas classified as having a long-term orientation was highest in the group task and transformational leadership condition. Apart from achieving their groups' goals, Caucasians may have been reinforced by the transformational leader's emphasis on taking a longer-term view and offering ideas for fundamental change. Finally, Asians performed best in terms of their total output of ideas working in groups guided by a transformational leader. Perhaps the transformational leader's emphasis on working toward collective goals for the sake of the school motivated Asians to generate a higher number of recommendations in the group than in the individual task condition.

Implications for Research

Our results illustrated that the same leadership style can be perceived differently and can have different effects on motivation and performance for followers from different cultural groups. For example, a transformational leader's encouraging followers to come up with long-term ideas that challenged the current state of the school, the focal organization, appeared to have different motivating effects among Caucasians and Asians. Hence, researchers need to be cautious about assuming that the same leader behaviors and statements will be interpreted similarly by followers with different cultural orientations. Smith, Misumi, Tayeb, Peterson, and Bond (1989) found that leaders' consideration and task styles emerged as universally relevant dimensions across several different cultures but that how followers evaluated actual leader behaviors in terms of these styles differed across cultures. For example, a leader who discussed followers' personal problems with others in their absence was viewed as considerate in Japan but was seen as invading the followers' privacy in the United States (Smith et al., 1989). Future cross-cultural leadership research should examine whether the same leader behavior will have different effects on the motivation and performance of followers with different cultural orientations.

The second implication of the current study is that confounding effects of individual differences may also affect the different levels of motivation and performance observed in the present study. For example, the Caucasian participants here performed better on the group than on the individual task, while the Asians' performance did not differ across the two task conditions. A group versus individual "psychological orientation" may or may not be the same as a cultural orientation (Triandis, 1995). In this regard, future research needs to separate the effects that personal attributes have on individual attitudes and behavior from the effects that cultural orientation has on attitudes and behavior. To the extent that culture emerges through the social interaction among individuals who have different personal dispositions, future researchers should now focus on how an individual's cultural orientation affects his or her collective work motivation and performance in group settings while also taking personal dispositions into consideration.

Another implication of the current study for future cross-cultural researchers to consider involves the composition of the groups that were labeled "collectivist." For instance, the Asian groups in our study consisted of individuals from various ethnic and/or national backgrounds. Perhaps the Asian groups were more ethnically heterogeneous than the Caucasian groups, since the former could contain Korean, Japanese, and Chinese individuals. Higher variation among the groups considered to be collectivist in this study may in part explain some of the patterns in our results. For example, we reported that Caucasian participants performed better in the group than in the individual task condition. This finding may be due to the group identity of the Caucasians being stronger than the group identity of the more heterogeneous Asians. Indeed, perceptions of in-group versus out-group among the Asian participants could have had a significant effect on group members' attitudes toward each other as well as on their willingness to cooperate in the group task condition (Earley, 1989). Clearly, future cross-cultural researchers need to examine ethnic or cultural heterogeneity and its impact on the collective motivation among Asian and Caucasian participants in studies similar to the present investigation.

Finally, the current research demonstrated that transactional and transformational leadership affected followers' performance as measured by the quantity and quality of the ideas generated. However, as with other complex task projects, the success of the school's reaccreditation process might not solely depend on creative and innovative ideas, since the process is a long-term one over the course of which many organizational stakeholders would need to put forth their maximum efforts. Future research could examine whether a group's ideas, once generated, can be turned into effective performance using more standard measures of performance. Leadership effectiveness measured taking such a long-term perspective might be more in line with real-world job requirements for effective managerial leadership.

Implications for Practice

The results reported here may also have practical implications for managing cultural diversity in the United States. The different effects that transformational and transactional leadership had on both Caucasian and Asian followers' performance may suggest that companies can help their leaders manage culturally diverse groups more effectively by providing training on the differential effects of various leadership styles. Certain leadership styles may be more or less effective than others depending on the ethnic group followers belong to and the tasks that are being performed. Results from this study indicated that individuals with different cultural orientations may prefer different ways of performing their tasks. For example, when employees are more collectivist, managers may want to design tasks in such a way that group members can work together (Earley, 1989). Performing tasks in a group can by itself satisfy collectivist followers' social motives, which in turn may enhance their motivation and performance. Yet one must also keep in mind that collectivists' concern for maintaining group harmony and tendency to avoid intragroup conflicts may warrant keeping certain tasks individually rather than group based. This recommendation is particularly important if one is concerned about the effects of evaluation apprehension on idea generation or the offering of innovative, radical solutions. Thus, when managers are soliciting ideas from collectivist followers for long-term organizational planning or about more sensitive issues, they need to make sure their followers feel comfortable suggesting ideas that challenge current organizational norms and authority (Joplin & Daus, 1997).

One potentially useful tool for helping collectivist participants to challenge each other more openly is to use group decision-making support systems (GDSS), which allows members to discuss and exchange challenging ideas without worrying about pressures to conform (Kahai, Sosik, & Avolio, 1997). These symptoms provide anonymity for participants, which can directly enhance the level of creativity observed in brainstorming tasks (Kahai et al, 1997). Using GDSS tools and technology, collectivist followers may provide more ideas without jeopardizing harmony and face saving.

Limitations

Although the present study's use of an experimental design to examine cultural differences was in line with recent recommendations by Chen and colleagues (1998), several limitations of the study warrant further attention in future research. First, since this study used Caucasian and Asian students to represent cultural orientation, further validation of these results with more culturally and occupationally diverse participants is obviously required. Second, not all our Asian participants came from the school of management that was the subject of the task; their lack of knowledge about the business school may have increased their inhibition about generating ideas, poten-

tially introducing some sampling bias in our results. Third, the two instructors who acted as group leaders were Caucasians; the results reported here may have differed if the leader's ethnicity had been varied. In a more diverse workforce, the chances of a leader's ethnicity being different from his or her followers' is increasingly more likely (cf. Yammarino & Jung, 1998). Finally, even though we went through several training phases and carefully designed manipulation checks to make sure leadership style was accurately conveyed, the mean transactional ratings in the transformational leadership condition were higher than intended, perhaps reducing the differential impact of these two leadership styles. This result could be due to the brevity of the experimental leadership manipulation, the lack of time for interaction between the leader and followers, and the type of instructions delivered by the leaders.

Conclusion

Results of this study showed that the effects of transformational and transactional leadership may not always generalize across Caucasian and Asian followers. Thus, future leadership research should be based on a broader theoretical framework that includes both the type of cultural contingencies examined here and a broader range of tasks and cultural value orientations.

REFERENCES

Avolio, B. J., & Bass, B. M. 1988. Transformational leadership, charisma and beyond. In J. G. Hunt, B. R. Balaga, H. P. Bachler, & C. Schriesheim (Eds.), *Emerging leadership vista:* 29–50. Emsford, NY: Pergamon Press.

Bass, B. M. 1985. *Leadership and performance beyond expectations.* New York: Free Press.

Bass, B. M., & Avolio, B. J. 1997. *Full range of leadership development: Manual for the Multifactor Leadership Questionnaire.* Redwood City, CA: Mind Garden.

Burns, J. M. 1978. *Leadership.* New York: Harper & Row.

Chen, C. C., Chen, X., & Meindl, J. 1998. How can cooperation be fostered? The cultural effects of individualism-collectivism. *Academy of Management Review,* 23: 285–304.

Cox, T., Lobel, S., & McLeod, P. 1991. Effects of ethnic group cultural differences on cooperative and competitive behavior on a group task. *Academy of Management Journal,* 34: 827–847.

Diehl, M., & Stroebe, W. 1987. Productivity loss in brainstorming groups: Toward the solution of a riddle. *Journal of Personality and Social Psychology,* 53: 497–509.

Dorfman, P. 1986. International cross-cultural leadership. In B. J. Punnett & R. Shenkar (Eds.), *Handbook of international management research:* 267–349. Cambridge, MA: Blackwell.

Earley, C. 1989. Social loafing and collectivism: A comparison of the United States and the People's Republic of China. *Administrative Science Quarterly,* 34: 565–581.

Earley, C. 1997. *Face, harmony, and social structure.* New York: Oxford University Press.

Erez, M. 1994. Toward a model of cross-cultural I/O psychology. In M. D. Dunnette & L. Hough (Eds.), *Handbook of industrial and organizational psychology:* 559–607. Palo Alto, CA: Consulting Psychologists Press.

Erez, M., & Somech, A. 1996. Is group productivity loss the rule or the exception? Effects of culture and group-based motivation. *Academy of Management Journal,* 39: 1513–1537.

Gabrenya, W., Latane, B., & Wang, Y. 1983. Social loafing in cross-cultural perspective. *Journal of Cross-Cultural Psychology,* 14: 368–384.

Gardner, W. L., & Avolio, B. J. 1998. The charismatic relationship: A dramaturgical perspective. *Academy of Management Review,* 23: 32–58.

Hofstede, G. 1980a. *Culture's consequences: International differences in work-related values.* Beverly Hills, CA: Sage.

Hofstede, G. 1980b. Motivation, leadership, and organization: Do American theories apply abroad? *Organizational Dynamics,* 10(1): 42–63.

Hofstede, G. 1993. Cultural constraints in management theories. *Academy of Management Executive,* 7(1): 81–94.

Johnston, W. B., & Packer, A. 1987. *Workforce 2000: Work and workers for the 21st century.* Indianapolis: Hudson Institute.

Joplin, J., & Daus, C. S. 1997. Challenges of leading a diverse workforce. *Academy of Management Executive,* 11(3): 32–47.

Jung, D., Bass, B., & Sosik, J. 1995. Bridging leadership and culture: A theoretical consideration of transformational leadership and collectivistic cultures. *Journal of Leadership Studies,* 2: 3–18.

Kahai, S., Sosik, J., & Avolio, B. J. 1997. Effects of leadership style and problem structure on work group process and outcomes in an electronic meeting system environment. *Personnel Psychology,* 50: 121–146.

Klein, K., & House, R. 1995. On fire: Charismatic leadership and levels of analysis. *Leadership Quarterly,* 6: 183–198.

Koh, W. 1990. *An empirical validation of the theory of transformational leadership in secondary schools in Singapore.* Unpublished doctoral dissertation, University of Oregon, Eugene.

Shamir, B., House, R. J., & Arthur, M. B. 1993. The motivational effects of charismatic leadership: A self-concept based theory. *Organizational Science,* 4: 577–594.

Smith, P. B., Misumi, J., Tayeb, M., Peterson, M. F., & Bond, M. 1989. On the generality of leadership style measures across cultures. *Journal of Occupational Psychology,* 62: 97–109.

Sosik, J. 1995. *The impact of leadership style and anonymity on performance, creative outcome, and satisfaction in GDSS-supported groups.* Unpublished doctoral dissertation, State University of New York at Binghamton.

Triandis, C. H. 1993. The contingency model in cross-cultural perspective. In M. M. Chemers & R. Ayman (Eds.), *Leadership theory and research perspectives and directions:* 167–188. San Diego: Academic Press.

Triandis, C. H. 1995. *Individualism and collectivism.* Boulder, CO: Westview Press.

Ungson, G. R., Steers, R. M., & Park, S. 1997. *Korean enterprise: The quest for globalization.* Boston: Harvard Business School Press.

Wagner, J. 1995. Studies of individualism-collectivism: Effects of cooperation in groups. *Academy of Management Journal,* 38: 152–172.

Yammarino, F. J., & Jung, D. 1998. Asian-Americans and leadership: A level of analysis perspective. *Journal of Applied Behavioral Science,* 34: 47–67.

Yokochi, N. 1989. *Leadership styles of Japanese business executives and managers: Transformational and transactional.* Unpublished doctoral dissertation, United States International University, San Diego.

Dong I. Jung is an assistant professor of management at San Diego State University. He received his Ph.D. in management from the State University of New York at Binghamton. His current research interests include transformational leadership, group development, and cross-cultural comparative management.

Bruce J. Avolio earned his Ph.D. at the University of Akron and is currently a professor in the School of Management, State University of New York at Binghamton, and the director of the Center for Leadership Studies. His current research interests include examining how computer mediation affects the impact of leadership on team processes and performance.

Unit 5

Key Points to Consider

❖ How important do you think change is to the success of the organization? Why do organizations need to change?

❖ Do you think that international organizations need to face change differently than domestic ones?

❖ What are some things that organizations can do to help people relieve stress?

❖ Do you think synergy is important? Why or why not?

DUSHKIN ONLINE **Links**   **www.dushkin.com/online/**

These sites are annotated on pages 4 and 5.

Organizations must change and develop to meet the changing environment in which they must exist. Two things are certain: (1) the environment will change, and (2) the organization will change. The question is how can the organization change to successfully meet the changes in the environment. History is full of once-highly successful organizations that have ended on the ash heap. In 1920, the Pennsylvania Railroad was the third-largest corporation in the United States. Today, there is no Pennsylvania Railroad. This is not to say that the functions and tasks once performed by the Pennsylvania Railroad have ceased; they continue to be performed by Amtrak and Conrail, both of which are heavily subsidized by the government. What it does say is that the Pennsylvania Railroad, at the height of its success, did not do what it needed to do to survive. Conditions changed and alternative means of transportation for both freight and passengers became available: an interstate highway system was developed that is used extensively by trucks, and airlines span the country in hours instead of days. The Pennsylvania Railroad was not able to adjust and the company declined into bankruptcy.

Today, organizations are constantly trying to change in an effort to meet a changing environment that is, perhaps, little understood by executives. Corporations merge, divest, privatize, go public, in what seems to be an endless machination of buyouts and takeovers with little or no thought given to what the long-term consequences will be. Just because a merger is hailed by Wall Street does not mean that it will be successful in the long run. When AT&T took over NCR a few years ago, it was hailed as one of the best possible fits that could be arranged between two companies. Unfortunately, a few years later, AT&T divested itself of NCR, admitting that the merger had been a mistake and that the two companies were never really able to make it work. This does not mean that all mergers are failures. Chrysler Corporation's purchase of American Motors a few years ago looks like a great success for Chrysler, but it remains to be seen if the more recent merger with Daimler-Benz will pay dividends. It is, perhaps, one of the great ironies of multinational corporations that the Jeep, the most successful and identifiably American product to come out of World War II, is now owned, produced, and marketed by a German company.

Perhaps the biggest single challenge to organizations is the international economy that exists today. This segment of the economy has grown significantly over the past 30 years. In the early 1970s and late 1960s, international trade represented less than 10 percent of the gross national product (GNP), while today it accounts for over 30 percent. When a particular segment represents over 30 percent of the economy, it is difficult to ignore. Multinational organizations do not view the world as ending at the national border of their home country. They view it as a global economy where resources, competition, and personnel come from all over the globe. General Motors competes in a worldwide market. It is no accident that Toyota has factories in the United States, because the United States is the largest automobile market in the world, just as it is no accident that Ford Motor Company has had production facilities in Germany since before World War II.

Multinational organizations must learn that "Building Teams Across Borders," (see article 27) is going to be one

of their primary activities in the years ahead. For multinational corporations to be truly successful in taking advantage of all of their assets in this highly competitive world, they must avail themselves of all of the talents of all of their employees. Multinationals are faced with the problem of integrating a corporate culture with roots from all over the world. That cultures in different countries are different is a given in the global economy. Being able to deal successfully with those differences will be a factor that will lead to success. The employees will, of course, have to adapt to the organization and, to a certain extent, the organization will have to adapt to the employees. Developing people and organizations that can do this successfully will be a major task for the future.

One of the factors that will certainly have an impact on the success of global organizations, and one that many people are simply ignoring, is the impact of AIDS, especially in the lesser developed countries.

One of the consequences of this change is emotional stress. Change causes stress, and stress is one of the major health concerns for individuals in an organization. Dealing with stress will no doubt continue in the twenty-first century. Some organizations are trying to help their employees to deal with stress better and, as a result, to become more productive, as Phillip Perry writes in "Less Stress, More Productivity."

Organizations continue to seek to become more than what they really are. They are constantly seeking advantages over their competition in an effort to become more successful, and more profitable. The only way that they can do this is to become greater than just the sum of the parts, and this they must do through their people. In an era where all the major players in an industry have essentially the same equipment, financial resources, and access to the same raw materials, the only way to build a lasting competitive advantage is by having the best people do the job, and the way to maximize those efforts is to create synergy in an organization. Corporations are "Desperately Seeking Synergy" (see article 29), in an effort to become increasingly more competitive. This does not mean that all attempts at seeking synergy are successful, because they are not. But it does mean that organizations will continue to attempt to create situations in which the whole is greater than the sum of the parts. Companies need to continue to attempt to create synergy if they want to be successful, because it is only through the maximum use of their human assets that they can hope to achieve competitive advantage and prosper in the millennium.

Building Teams Across Borders

Today your organization may have the technology to make global teams a reality. But all the wiring in the world won't be enough if you haven't started with a solid foundation.

By Charlene Marmer Solomon

A dmit it. If you think about it, global teams are probably one of the toughest games around, with little chance to succeed. And if you're really honest about it, you'd confess that it's astounding when intercultural teams have any success at all. Luckily, they do. And the credit, in no small measure, goes to the managers—both HR and line—who realize what a complex task awaits the global team. They improve the odds by providing tools to help team members make their groups work.

Global teams come in various configurations. Generally, they fall into one of two categories: *intercultural teams,* in which people from different cultures meet face-to-face to work on a project, and *virtual global teams,* in which individuals remain in their separate locations around the world and conduct meetings via different forms of technology. Obviously, both kinds are fraught with enormous challenges.

Given the communications and cultural obstacles, what do companies gain from these units? Teams help global companies, preventing them from needing to reinvent the game with each new project. They enable organizations to realize 24-hour productivity via the latest in technology. They allow cross-pollination between cultures as well as business units, adding depth of knowledge and experience to the endeavor.

But effective global teams are not simple to create or maintain. With myriad challenges—from time and space logistics, to cultural assumptions that no one articulates because each individual believes them to be so universal—teams must continually overcome considerable obstacles. While you may be eager to capitalize on the expertise of individuals from around the world, and even have the technology to do so, it's important to remember that global teams must master the basics, understand the rules, learn to harness both cultural and functional group diversity and become adroit at communication and leadership.

Mastering the basics and understanding the rules.

"Everybody wants to know what's happening at the edge and the next wave of things to come, but we still

---

Charlene Marmer Solomon is a contributing editor for GLOBAL WORKFORCE. *E-mail charsol@aol.com to comment.*

find people who don't do the basics very well," says Mary O'Hara-Devereaux, coauthor with Robert Johansen of *Global Work: Bridging Distance, Culture and Time* (Jossey-Bass Inc., 1994). "People need some understanding of what a team is—the variations of the team's work and the variety of cultures that are on it, ways to communicate effectively, and how to work with distributed leadership so that everyone on the team has leadership roles."

Covering the basics means ensuring everyone associated with the venture appreciates the difficulties involved with participating in a global team. There should be solid business reasons for forming one. And it's important that team members and associated managers understand the following considerations:

• The team champion should have the mandate to choose the people with the right skills for the job.

• The team should have measurable goals that participants have had the opportunity to discuss and agree with.

• Meetings must have clearly established objectives and predetermined agendas.

• Team members must make time to discuss the lines of communication. What methods will members use to communicate? Does everyone have equal access to the communication? (See "Make the Most of Teleconferencing" and "Develop an E-mail Protocol.")

• Participants should recognize the role of language difficulties and manner of speaking in cross-border teams. For example, individuals from various English-speaking countries will speak in different dialects that may be troublesome for some members. Allow time for group members to acclimate to each other.

• Members must realize that people need to understand each other's differences before they can effectively come together as a group. Teambuilding sessions and cross-cultural training can help with this.

Of course there's a lot more to creating a team than a simple list of do's and don'ts. Clear expectations, defined responsibilities and an appreciation of cultural differences are among the basics to be accomplished by each team at the outset. Every member must know and comprehend the business objectives, understand the timetables and agree to follow a set of team rules. These are basic elements to success, but they require time and careful consideration if the team is going to consent and abide by them.

Fairfax, Virginia-based Mobil Corp. knows this lesson first-hand. About 10 years ago, Mobil undertook a companywide study and determined that it had to change significantly if it was going to be able to remain a profitable oil company in a volatile marketplace. Its assessment initiated global teams. The company realized that these work groups maximize an individual's knowledge by sharing it throughout the company with others via natural work teams, as well as transferring best practices within the company. In other words, the best practices from one group would be carried to another via team members.

With more than 43,000 employees—only 16,500 of whom are in the United States—and with operations in more than 140 countries, most natural work teams have representation from all over the world, such as the Speed-Pass™ program initiated by Mobil in the United States.

Working with Texas Instruments, Mobil developed electronic transaction payment systems for service stations. These are like bank debit cards that are customer-activated at pay-at-the-pump terminals. Mobil first tested Speed-Pass™ in the States with excellent results. The next step was to form a global team to lob that learning from one country to another.

"A project champion, who was the individual who had implemented SpeedPass™ in the U.S., was in charge of creating the team with others from the Fuels Advisory Council who nominated individuals to participate," recalls Bill Cummings, who represented Japan on the team and is currently Mobil's media relations advisor at the U.S. headquarters. Desiring cross-pollination, Mobil charged the individual who had successfully implemented Speed-

Make the Most of Teleconferencing

Teleconferences are so much a part of conducting everyday business that it's easy to forget the basics of making these communications work effectively. Here are some ideas for intercultural teams.

• Obtain the best equipment within budget. The quality of sound varies tremendously.

• Be sure all locations have equal access to communications links.

• Allow individuals ample opportunity to learn to use the technology.

• The group should choose a conference leader and rotate that leadership. The leader should make sure the group works as a team and isn't at the mercy of the most vocal individuals.

• Written agendas should be distributed to everyone before the meeting.

• The group should decide ahead of time what the length of the phone conference will be.

• The conference leader should recap the goals of the discussion before starting. He or she should review updates since the last meeting.

• The leader should encourage everyone to participate. If someone is quiet, the leader should try to draw out the individual—or encourage the individual later with a phone call or e-mail.

• The group should be sensitive to time zones. Naturally, someone will be inconvenienced, so it's important to rotate the times meetings are held.

• Someone should write a brief recap of the main points of the conference and distribute it after the call.

—CMS

Develop an E-mail Protocol

While e-mail is necessary and beneficial, it's important to recognize that it's a medium that uses only text and offers no visual or nonverbal clues. It's wise to develop an e-mail protocol among global group members, minimizing the chances for misunderstandings when using this tool. Cornelius Grove, partner at Brooklyn-based Cornelius Grove & Associates LLC, offers the following list of considerations as you develop your guidelines.

Topics. Which topics are appropriate for e-mail and which are not? Which topics should be addressed in person or over the phone instead?

Frequency. How frequently should members use e-mail?

Urgency. What constitutes urgency? Is it possible to define the terms "ASAP" and "urgent"?

Participation. Who should participate? Does every team member need to be a recipient of every e-mail?

Showing respect. How can team members demonstrate respect for each other? (This is important with hierarchical cultures.) Are titles necessary?

Time of day. Should there be "blackout" periods when e-mails are not sent or received?

Jokes, profanity, intimacies. What kinds of guidelines should exist regarding topics, language or personal relationships?

Communication guidelines. Should there be guidelines for handling situations that arise in e-mail, but dictate voice-to-voice communication?

—*CMS*

Pass™ in the U.S. with the project leadership. Not only did this individual choose the team representatives, but he communicated to them that their global expertise was critical to the success of the project. He encouraged them to express their different viewpoints.

For example, it was clear that it had taken 20 years for Americans to move from full-serve to mini-serve to self-serve to pay-at-the-pump. Countries like Japan were still accustomed to full-service. Other countries were at different points along the same journey. Only people who had first-hand knowledge of the cultures of countries such as Japan, Australia and Singapore could help take this U.S. best practice and transplant it successfully overseas.

"The concept of taking lessons learned and applying them across as many different countries, cultures and experiences as possible is a fundamental part of Mobil's corporate culture," says Cummings. "Clearly, individuals from the different regions would bring their cultural know-how and business perspectives to the team effort. It was their job to evaluate whether or not it was possible to transplant the lessons learned into other cultures."

Harnessing group diversity.

Even though almost all of the dozen individuals in the group already had been on other global teams, they first gathered face-to-face in Los Angeles. Mobil generally has its team members huddle in one location at the launch of a new effort so they can begin to build relationships with each other and clearly understand the team's business mission.

This initial meeting was also the occasion in which team members began to understand their roles, confirmed their commitments and decided the rules by which the team would operate. This particular team consisted of marketing and line managers, technology specialists, information technology experts and retail specialists. There were individuals from Texas Instruments present, as well, creating a global virtual team across two companies.

Mobil gave the team members ample time (five days) to get acquainted with the product so they could understand it thoroughly and begin to contribute their ideas for marketing it in their respective regions. This face-time together is when the team leader typically solidifies the group and guides it toward working jointly. Again, several points should be established clearly at this stage: specific team objectives, how to accomplish them, who is responsible for what and when, and general project timetables.

Cross-cultural training is a basic prerequisite for these meetings. Says O'Hara-Devereaux, "I think we haven't done it very well, so we like to pretend that we are through with it now, and everybody did it." She continues, "I do think, however, people have grown acclimated and accustomed to working with people who are different than they are. They go into teams expecting things to be a little bumpier. But they've done it enough times now that there is a whole set of new expectations and experience and awareness that people bring different elements to the team. They're comfortable with the relationships that are formed."

Communicating across the field.

Once the basics are addressed and cultural differences acknowledged, communication takes center field. But communication is achieved through experience, not necessarily through rigid training. "We saw that the workforce was becoming global, so we decided to teach people how to use technology and be sensitive in global teams," says Santa Clara, California-based 3Com's Debra Engel, currently executive advisor, and for the past 15 years senior vice president of corporate services. That personal experience accelerates the learning immensely. Says Engel, "It's amazing how quickly it has switched from a world in which you so rarely had contact with others outside your

Try These Books and Articles for More Information

Try the following list of resources as you conduct additional research. Many relate details about teams in general. Others discuss global teams.

ARTICLES
You can find the following articles in the WORKFORCE ONLINE archives. Go to *www.workforceonline.com,* where you can click on "Research Center." Scroll down to the Topic Index, and select the designated categories.

1. Global Teams: The Ultimate Collaboration
Index Category: Global HR
Subcategory: Global HR
Work teams already have become an established institution in the American workplace. But what happens when a company such as Maxus or Intel transplants the concept abroad? Many of the same rules apply, but you must also help global teams cope with different cultures, languages, locations and time zones. This article was written by Charlene Marmer Solomon and published in the September 1995 issue of PERSONNEL JOURNAL.

2. Motorola's HR Learns the Value of Teams Firsthand
Index Category: HR Trends and Strategies
Subcategory: Teams
After training many business functions to work in teams, HR staff members realized that they must do the same. Two HR departments at Motorola have learned to practice what they preach. This article was written by Kate Ludeman and published in the June 1995 issue of PERSONNEL JOURNAL.

3. Self-directed Skills Building Drives Quality
Index Category: HR Trends and Strategies

Subcategory: Teams
By Instituting a TQM process that supports employee empowerment, Granite Rock Co. gained an edge over its competition. For this, it won the 1994 Personnel Journal Optimas Award for Competitive Advantage. This article was written by Dawn Anfuso and published in the April 1994 issue of PERSONNEL JOURNAL.

4. Team Staffing Requires New HR Role
Index Category: HR Trends and Strategies
Subcategory: Teams
In team-based organizations, staffing can't be handled in a traditional manner. Instead, HR must play an advisory role and allow team members to help make hiring decisions. This article was written by Shari Caudron and published in the May 1994 issue of PERSONNEL JOURNAL.

5. Teamwork Takes Work
Index Category: HR Trends and Strategies
Subcategory: Teams
When rugged individualists are faced with working as part of a well-coordinated group, turmoil often results—but only if they're unprepared. Ongoing training and communication are the keys to unlocking each team's potential as its members learn that their number one priority is to satisfy customers, not management. This article was written by Shari Caudron and published in the February 1994 issue of PERSONNEL JOURNAL.

BOOKS
Each of the following books is available for purchase online through Amazon. Go to *www.amazon.com* and search by title.

1. Capitalizing on the Global Workforce: A Strategic Guide for Expatriate Management
Written by Michael S. Schell and Charlene Marmer Solomon
Published by Irwin Professional Publishing
November 1996
ISBN: 0786308958

2. Cross Cultural Team Building: Guidelines for More Effective Communication and Negotiation
Edited by Mel Berger
Published by McGraw-Hill Book Co. Ltd.
June 1996
ISBN: 0077079191

3. Global Work: Bridging Distance, Culture and Time
Written by Mary O'Hara-Devereaux and Robert Johansen
Published by Jossey-Bass Publishers
May 1994
ISBN: 1555426026

4. International Human Resource Management
Written by Dennis R. Briscoe
Published by Prentice Hall Press
April 1995
ISBN: 0131910086

5. Teams at the Top: Unleashing the Potential of Both Teams and Individual Leaders
Written by Jon R. Katzenbach
Published by Harvard Business School Press
November 1997
ISBN: 0875847897

6. Virtual Teams: Reaching Across Space, Time and Organizations With Technology
Written by Jessica Lipnack and Jeffrey Stamps
Published by John Wiley & Sons
May 1997
ISBN: 0471165530

7. The Wisdom of Teams: Creating the High-Performance Organization
Written by Jon R. Katzenbach and Douglas K. Smith
Published by Harper Business
March 1994
ISBN: 0887306764

—CMS

own work to one where the customer base and marketplace segmentation is disappearing and groups need to communicate all the time."

3Com distinguishes itself through its use of technology. The company, a networking giant, naturally attracts people who want to push the edge of technology as part of their work. Interestingly, though you might expect 3Com to use whiz-bang high-tech gymnastics in its teamwork, the organization has created a different mentality in the way

people operate. With 5,000 employees in its offices in London, Dublin, Tel Aviv, San Diego and Boston, it pursues the ultimate in the virtual office. 3Com's work with global teams concentrates on obtaining peak performance from solid use of the traditionals: voice, e-mail and teleconferencing.

In fact, phone conferencing handles a huge percentage of the real time interaction. If there is a need for visuals in teleconferences, the team members receive e-mailed documentation. They'll look at the document on their individual computers while participating in the teleconference. This offers better resolution and clarity than video, and people also have the opportunity to make changes in the document right there on the screen.

Indeed, while the company is so technologically progressive that all 3Com employees have the ability to watch the chairman's address via live video at their desks, it also knows how to use technology effectively, rather than randomly. It has actually moved away somewhat from videoconferencing. "It wasn't as productive as telephones when you take into account the time to get to the video-conference facility," says Engel. "We also found that some of the video is actually distracting—the delay and extraneous visual effects detracted from the information."

3Com's global team members (about 80 percent of whom are senior managers) have also become more experienced and efficient with teleconferencing. They have learned the behaviors that make teleconferencing more productive: speaking louder and more clearly, having extensions of the phone speakers, being adept at describing the materials they're discussing, and making sure they ask for people's opinions—whether they're physically present or not.

"People get better and better at teleconferencing and they develop new habits," says Engel. Even when a large percentage of the team is present at the meeting location and others are teleconferencing in, speakers will not project their visuals. Instead, they hand them out, making it easier for them to remember what to describe since some of their audience isn't in the room. "If you're projecting the visuals, you tend to take verbal shortcuts. But if you don't have them projected, you describe them to the people in the room the same way as the people on the phone," she explains.

Most team members simply call one of the conferencing systems and enter the meeting via a telephone from an office, home or a cellular phone anywhere in the world. These are not mere squawk-boxes that distort sound and cause callers to scream every time they can't hear. Sophisticated teleconferencing technology allows several callers to join the conversation in a very natural way, and even listen to prior minutes of the meeting so they can hear what they've missed. 3Com uses a system called Meeting Place, with which the caller uses a series of codes. One code allows access to minutes of the meeting, and another allows immediate entry to the meeting.

Because people are distributed globally, one of the biggest challenges is the timing of the meetings. If you have people in the United States and Europe, you just choose an early morning Pacific time; if you have conferences that include Europe, the Americas and Asia, you should rotate the time so that the same group isn't inconvenienced on every occasion.

Cultivating distributed leadership.

With the fundamentals considered, and communication tackled, the teams must next grapple with leadership issues. This is especially important because work in the late 1990s has become more fragmented. Global teams can be severely penalized if leadership isn't adequate.

And it's important that there isn't just one leader. Instead, each team member should have a shared leadership role. One major barrier to global teams is that most people have multiple job responsibilities. Since they have several roles throughout the organization, it's difficult for everyone to respond in a timely, effective manner. You can imagine this becomes exacerbated when one supervisor is in the States and another is the team leader 10,000 miles away. Individuals will frequently report that their managers require them to perform tasks that interfere with their global teamwork. "People have more roles than they used to," says O'Hara-Devereaux. "Creating a sense of leadership for everyone so it's their job to manage other competing demands is important. It needs to be pushed deeper down into the organization."

Some people may be on four, five or six teams, so they must have a sense of ownership of the processes. This establishes not only division of leadership, but rotation of the overall leadership role, as well. Different people take responsibility for convening and running remote meetings, and measuring progress.

Consequently, global leadership training is another skill that must be developed. People should be selected for team participation with leadership in mind, and they must also be trained, supported and monitored.

In the beginning of the team building, however, there typically is a more traditional team leader who helps define the leadership role, as well as the goals and responsibilities for each person on the team. This individual must ensure everyone has explicit enough information so they can clearly visualize what they'll be doing and where they'll be going.

Finally, people need to provide solutions to the team. They can't be shy about offering their ideas. In many business situations, groups come together to work out solutions from the bottom upward. But most global teams don't have that luxury. Part of the leadership function is to be responsible for coming up with solutions that fit into the overall context of the team's goals.

Challenged from all fronts, successful global teams need guidance to overcome the substantial barriers they encounter. When you think about the tasks your global teams must accomplish—and you consider the language obstacles, the cultural barriers, the business challenges—it becomes apparent that your role as global HR manager is equally complex. You can help your organization's cross-border teams enormously by offering cultural preparation and training on successful teamwork, and by providing ongoing assistance with the maintenance of the team.

Less Stress, More Productivity

Six workplace psychologists provide practicable suggestions for alleviating employee stress and thereby enhancing productivity.

By Phillip M. Perry

THE HEAT IS ON.

Gone are the days when businesses responded to increased workloads by hiring more people. Nowadays, faced with the need to wring more profits from limited resources, employers are demanding better performance from their already overburdened staffs. Today, everyone is expected to work smarter and faster.

But there's a downside to this mad rush to greater productivity. Workplace stress has become a costly business issue. Overworked personnel become uncooperative. They call in sick; they sabotage projects; they even jump ship for other employers where the atmosphere is more congenial.

The workers are not the only ones who suffer—customers who are ignored or even mistreated by a stressed-out staff start buying from competitors. "Stress creates a major negative impact on creativity, innovation, and business profits," asserts Dr. Richard Hagberg, president of Hagberg Consulting Group, Foster City, Calif. "That's counter to the traditional thinking of many managers. They have the idea that if they pour on the pressure, people perform better. In reality, stressed-out workers patch together short-term fixes to business problems, while costly, deep-rooted issues remain unaddressed and take their toll on the bottom line."

So what to do? Well, here's some help. In this article, six renowned workplace psychologists give solid, nuts-and-bolts techniques for reducing costly stress in your place of business. Let's see what they have to say.

Spot Signs of Stress

Before you can cure the disease, you have to spot the symptoms. "Supervisors can become attuned to signs of employees experiencing stress," confirms Dr. Rodney Lowman, a professor of organizational psychology at the San Diego campus of the California School of Professional Psychology. He points to the following common signs that the general stress level is on the rise:

- Absenteeism is increasing, whether from illness or for other reasons. Just when individuals are needed the most, they come down with the flu.
- People seem to need more vacation time.
- Everyone becomes more irritable and difficult to get along with.
- There's a general rise in comments such as, "We're really stressed out around here."
- People exhibit confusion and make mistakes at tasks they usually perform well.
- You yourself are feeling stress. "If the boss is stressed, the whole staff will be," says Dr. Lowman. "This is the trickle-down theory of management."

Bonus tip: Stimulate upward communication by regularly asking individuals, "What can we do to make your job less stressful"

Identify the Sources of Stress

Now that you've spotted stress in the workplace, how do you get at what's causing it? "Stressors can result from a variety of situations," Dr. Lowman continues. "These include downsizing, with fewer people left to do more work; a bad boss; a difficult match between a boss and a subordinate; and conflicts between people in the workplace who can't get along with each other."

To find out which specific stressors are causing grief, go right to the source: Get people to open up and tell you. In general, you should encourage people to speak up when they feel as though they are being overloaded with work, or when they are getting mixed signals about their work roles from managers.

But you can do even better, according to Dr. Peter Chang, a professor of organizational psychology who is at the Alameda, Calif., campus of the California School of Professional Psychology. He recommends scheduling regular meetings during which the staff can discuss what they like and don't like about their work environment. "It can make a world of difference to have meetings where people express what is on their minds, and the management does more listening than talking." The trick is to open up a valve to allow people to "let off steam."

Sounds good. But how do you keep these meetings from deteriorating into gripe sessions? Dr. Chang suggests that prior to each meeting, hand out a questionnaire to be filled out by each employee. Ask each participant to describe the five tasks they perform most often, the five things they like the best about their work, and the five things they like the least.

Dr. Chang points to a number of advantages to a questionnaire: "It saves time by keeping the forthcoming meeting focused on work-related issues in a productive manner. It also alerts the staff that management is interested in this topic, and gets everyone to start some real thinking before the meeting."

Once the meeting is over, don't let the issues drop. "It is vital to follow up on the employees' requests and suggestions," says Dr. Chang. "Ideally, you should hold a loosely structured initial meeting where employees say what is on their minds. Then for efficiency's sake there ought to be a subsequent meeting that is action-focused. This is where you provide responses to specific employee suggestions. List which recommendations seem reasonable and which are out of the question."

Bonus tip: Hold the meetings often enough to communicate ongoing concern, but not so often that they become redundant. A quarterly schedule may be just right.

Is There "Good Stress"?

Maybe too much stress is damaging. But can a little stress stimulate performance? It depends on your definition of stress.

"There's is a misconception that stress is motivational," says Dr.David C. Munuz, a professor of psychology at Saint Louis University, St. Louis, Mo. "But stress is really wear and tear on the individual, and there is no way that can motivate. What *is* motivational is the demand of a task—if we see the demand as a challenge. Rather than stress, workers need a challenging environment, a measure of control over their workday, and the tools to complete their tasks."

Dr. Munz states that while some people may use the term "good stress," they are really referring to an environmental in which the business demands that the individual perform at 100 percent of capabilities. "Most people do not want to be exhausted at the end of the day, but neither do want a boring job."

Encourage Humor in the Workplace

Humor can go a long way toward reducing workplace stress. "Maybe we can't control what happens in our workday, but we can control what goes on in our minds," notes

Smart Ways to Handle Stress

1. Pause to re-evaluate yourself and your workday. Look at your performance and come up with ways to feel successful.

2. If you are going through a dry spell, set small goals that you can meet to establish a success attitude.

3. Relax and take deep breaths, do some push-ups, or stretch.

4. Schedule more time to get a certain task done. Ask for another full day to put together a proposal.

5. Use techniques such as meditation, yoga, and positive self-talk.

David Granirer, a consultant based in Vancouver, Canada. "Studies show that being able to respond to a situation with humor gives people back their cognitive control: That's the ability to focus on their sphere of influence and to respond creatively to difficult situations."

Barring the hiring of a workplace jester, just how do you stimulate humor? One technique, says Granirer, is to have the staff make ridiculous statements that pretend bad things are good. "Humor often involves an attitude reversal," he explains. "You often see a stand-up comic take something that's a negative and pretend it's great. For example, you often hear variations of the joke, 'It's great going bald because I have less hair to comb.'"

You can do the same in your workplace, says Granirer. Assign people to groups of four or five. Then have each group come up with three or four outrageous reasons why they love being overworked, dealing with bad clients, and other stressors. For example, one attitude reversal might be: "I love dealing with the so-and-so client. I really needed to have my self-esteem beaten down today."

"This approach allows people to say the things they are not supposed to say because they are doing it in a humorous way," Granirer observes. "When people laugh, the stressors become less threatening. Later, when they deal with the difficult client, they remember the humorous statement they had made and it's difficult to be so serious about it."

Bonus tip: Encourage your staff to compartmentalize each task and concentrate on it until it is completed. When the task is over they should take a deep breath and move on. Avoid being overwhelmed by thoughts of many tasks still to do.

Create a Positive Work Environment

"Groups of workers can create positive or negative cultures," observes Dr. David C. Munz, a professor of psychology at Saint Louis University, St. Louis, Mo. "When the language used by your staff is positive, affirmative thinking becomes contagious."

Dr. Munz suggests encouraging positive language when people communicate with one other. Recommend the empowering "I will" rather than the passive "I should." If an employee says something like "I don't have enough time," persuade him to change

his goal so he can state, "I have just enough time." Has a staff member not become computer-literate? Prompt the employee to say, "I will learn a program by the end of this month" rather than "I am not that good at computers."

Finally, influence your staff to avoid negative self-talk inside their head. Phrases such as "That won't work" and "That was stupid" need to make way for "To make this work, I will . . ." and "From this experience, I have learned to . . ."

Bonus tip: Establish a "What's Good" bulletin board, where the staff posts photos and notes about the positive aspects of the workplace.

Create Work Flexibility

Individuals feel less stress if they have the power to manage the time they spend on business and personal life. "People are having difficulty balancing their family and work lives," says Paul Gibson, an attorney and human resources analyst at CCH Human Resources Group, Chicago. "Our surveys show that a paid-leave bank is the most successful way to reduce the stress that results when people have too few hours to do too many tasks."

A "paid-leave bank" system lumps all time off—vacation, sick, and personal days—into one bank that the employee can use as appropriate. This reduces stress because it allows the employee to schedule time as needed. It benefits the employer as well; the person who needs to take care of a family task can now let the supervisor know about a necessary absence well in advance. This avoids the last-minute scrambling—and increased staff stress level—that occurs when employees call in sick.

Bonus tip: Simple things such as the ability to take breaks freely, to augment desk lighting, and select their own work apparel can also contribute to employees' sense of flexibility.

Tackle Stress the Right Way

The information age is bringing rapid change to the workplace. It will take time for people to develop coping mechanisms for the increase in stress that is the result of the need to achieve more productivity from limited resources.

One thing's for sure: We can't reverse the clock. "Today, everything is moving in technology time," Dr. Hagberg concludes. "People who want things to be the way they were will be frustrated over the next few years. Handling stress will continue to be a major challenge for every business."

*A healthy dose of skepticism can help executives
distinguish real opportunities from mirages.*

Desperately Seeking Synergy

BY MICHAEL GOOLD AND ANDREW CAMPBELL

THE PURSUIT OF SYNERGY pervades the management of most large companies. Meetings and retreats are held to brainstorm about ways to collaborate more effectively. Cross-business teams are set up to develop key account plans, coordinate product development, and disseminate best practices. Incentives for sharing knowledge, leads, and customers are built into complex compensation schemes. Processes and procedures are standardized. Organizational structures are reshuffled to accommodate new, cross-unit managerial positions.

What emerges from all this activity? In our years of research into corporate synergy, we have found that synergy initiatives often fall short of management's expectations. Some never get beyond a few perfunctory meetings. Others generate a quick burst of activity and then slowly peter out. Others become permanent corporate fixtures without ever fulfilling their original goals. If the only drawbacks to such efforts were frustration and embarrassment, they might be viewed benignly as "learning experiences." But the pursuit of synergy often represents a major opportunity cost as well. It distracts managers' attention from the nuts and bolts of their businesses, and it crowds out other initiatives that might generate real benefits. Sometimes, the synergy programs actually backfire, eroding customer relationships, damaging brands,

---

Michael Goold and Andrew Campbell are directors of the Ashridge Strategic Management Centre in London, England. They are the authors of The Collaborative Enterprise: Why Links Between Business Units Fail and How to Make Them Work *(Perseus Books, 1999). They also wrote, with Marcus Alexander,* Corporate-Level Strategy: Creating Value in the Multibusiness Company *(John Wiley & Sons, 1994).*

or undermining employee morale. Simply put, many synergy efforts end up destroying value rather than creating it.

The pursuit of synergy often distracts managers' attention from the nuts and bolts of their businesses.

Avoiding such failures is possible, but it requires a whole new way of looking at and thinking about synergy. Rather than assuming that synergy exists, can be achieved, and will be beneficial, corporate executives need to take a more balanced, even skeptical view. They need to counter synergy's natural allure by subjecting their instincts to rigorous evaluation. Such an approach will help executives avoid wasting precious resources on synergy programs that are unlikely to succeed. Perhaps even more important, it will enable them to better understand where the true synergy opportunities lie in their organizations. (See the insert "What Is Synergy?")

We believe that synergy can provide a big boost to the bottom line of most large companies. The challenge is to separate the real opportunities from the illusions. With a more disciplined approach, executives can realize greater value from synergy—even while pursuing fewer initiatives.

Four Managerial Biases

When a synergy program founders, it is usually the business units that take the blame. Corporate executives chalk the failure up to line managers' recalcitrance or incompetence. We have found, however, that the blame is frequently misplaced. The true cause more often lies in the thinking of the corporate executives themselves.

Because executives view the achievement of synergy as central to their jobs, they are prone to four biases that distort their thinking. First comes the *synergy bias,* which leads them to overestimate the benefits and underestimate the costs of synergy. Then comes the *parenting bias,* a belief that synergy will only be captured by cajoling or compelling the business units to cooperate. The parenting bias is usually accompanied by the *skills bias*—the assumption that whatever know-how is required to achieve synergy will be available within the organization. Finally, executives fall victim to the *upside bias,* which causes them to

concentrate so hard on the potential benefits of synergy that they overlook the downsides. In combination, these four biases make synergy seem more attractive and more easily achievable than it truly is.

Synergy Bias. Most corporate executives, whether or not they have any special insight into synergy opportunities or aptitude for nurturing collaboration, feel they *ought* to be creating synergy. The achievement of synergy among their businesses is inextricably linked to their sense of their work and their worth. In part, the synergy bias reflects executives' need to justify the existence of their corporation, particularly to investors. "If we can't find opportunities for synergy, there's no point to the group," one chief executive explained to us. In part, it reflects their desire to make the different businesses feel that they are part of a single family. "My job is to create a family—a group of managers who see themselves as members of one team," commented another CEO. Perhaps most fundamentally, it reflects executives' real fear that they would be left without a role if they were not able to promote coordination, standardization, and other links among the various businesses they control.

The synergy bias becomes an obsession for some executives. Desperately seeking synergy, they make unwise decisions and investments. In one international food company that we studied—we'll call it Worldwide Foods—a newly appointed chief executive fell victim to such an obsession. Seeing that the company's various national units operated autonomously, sharing few ideas across borders, he became convinced that the key to higher corporate profits—and a higher stock price—lay in greater interunit cooperation. The creation of synergy became his top priority, and he quickly appointed global category managers to coordinate each of Worldwide Foods' main product lines. Their brief was to promote collaboration and standardization across countries in order to "leverage the company's brands internationally."

Pressured by the CEO, the category managers launched a succession of high-profile synergy initiatives. The results were dismal. A leading U.K. cookie brand was launched with considerable expense in the United States. It promptly flopped. A pasta promotion that had worked well in Germany was rolled out in Italy and Spain. It backfired, eroding both margins and market shares. An attempt was made to standardize ingredients across Europe for some confectionery products in order to achieve economies of scale in purchasing and manufac-

What Is Synergy?

The word synergy is derived from the Greek word *synergos*, which means "working together." In business usage, synergy refers to the ability of two or more units or companies to generate greater value working together than they would working apart. We've found that most business synergies take one of six forms.

Shared Know-How

Units often benefit from sharing knowledge or skills. They may, for example, improve their results by pooling their insights into a particular process, function, or geographic area. The know-how they share may be written in manuals or in policy-and-procedure statements, but very often it exists tacitly, without formal documentation. Value can be created simply by exposing one set of people to another who have a different way of getting things done. The emphasis that many companies place on leveraging core competencies and sharing best practices reflects the importance attributed to shared know-how.

Shared Tangible Resources

Units can sometimes save a lot of money by sharing physical assets or resources. By using a common manufacturing facility or research laboratory, for example, they may gain economies of scale and avoid duplicated effort. Companies often justify acquisitions of related businesses by pointing to the synergies to be gained from sharing resources.

Pooled Negotiating Power

By combining their purchases, different units can gain greater leverage over suppliers, reducing the cost or even improving the quality of the goods they buy. Companies can also gain similar benefits by negotiating jointly with other stakeholders, such as customers, governments, or universities. The gains from pooled negotiating power can be dramatic.

Coordinated Strategies

It sometimes works to a company's advantage to align the strategies of two or more of its businesses. Divvying up markets among units may, for instance, reduce interunit competition. And coordinating responses to shared competitors may be a powerful and effective way to counter competitive threats. Although coordinated strategies can in principle be an important source of synergy, they're tough to achieve. Striking the right balance between corporate intervention and business-unit autonomy is not easy.

Vertical Integration

Coordinating the flow of products or services from one unit to another can reduce inventory costs, speed product development, increase capacity utilization, and improve market access. In process industries such as petrochemicals and forest products, well-managed vertical integration can yield particularly large benefits.

Combined Business Creation

The creation of new businesses can be facilitated by combining know-how from different units, by extracting discrete activities from various units and combining them in a new unit, or by establishing internal joint ventures or alliances. As a result of the business world's increased concern for corporate regeneration and growth, several companies have placed added emphasis on this type of synergy.

---

turing. Consumers balked at buying the reformulated products.

Rather than encouraging interunit cooperation, the initiatives ended up discouraging it. As the failures mounted, the management teams in each country became more convinced than ever that their local markets were unique, requiring different products and marketing programs. After a year of largely fruitless efforts, with few tangible benefits and a significant deterioration in the relationship between the corporate center and the units, the chief executive began to retreat, curtailing the synergy initiatives.

A similar problem arose in a professional services firm. Created through a series of acquisitions, this firm had three consulting practices—organization development, employee benefits, and corporate strategy—as well as an executive search business. The chief executive believed that in order to justify the acquisitions, he needed to impose a "one-firm" policy on the four units. The centerpiece of this policy was the adoption of a coordinated approach to key accounts. A client-service manager was assigned to each major client and given responsibility for managing the overall relationship and for cross-selling the firm's various services.

The approach proved disastrous. The chief executive's enthusiasm for the one-firm policy blinded him to the realities of the marketplace. Most of the big clients resented the imposition of a gatekeeper between themselves and the actual providers of the specialist services they were buying. Indeed, many of them began to turn to the firm's competitors. Far from creating value, the synergy effort damaged the firm's profitability, not to mention some of its most important client relationships. Faced with an uproar from the consulting staff, the CEO was forced to eliminate the client-manager positions.

For both these chief executives, synergy had become an emotional imperative rather than a rational one. Spurred by a desire to find and express the logic that held their portfolio of businesses together, they simply assumed that synergies did exist and could be achieved. Like wanderers in a desert who see oases where there is only sand, they became so entranced by the idea of synergy that they led their companies to pursue mirages.

If business-unit managers choose not to cooperate in a synergy initiative, they usually have good reasons.

Parenting Bias. Corporate managers afflicted with the synergy bias are prone to other biases as well. If they believe that opportunities for synergy exist, they feel compelled to get involved themselves. They assume that the unit managers, overly focused on their own businesses and overly protective of their own authority, disregard or undervalue opportunities to collaborate with one another. As one exasperated CEO told us, "There's the I'm-too-busy syndrome, the not-invented-here syndrome, and the don't-interfere-you-don't-understand-my-business syndrome. If I didn't continually bang their heads together, I believe they would never talk to one another."

Assuming that unit managers are naturally resistant to cooperation, executives conclude that synergy can be achieved only through the intervention of the parent. (The parent, in our terminology, can be a holding company, a corporate center, a division, or any other body that oversees more than one business unit.) In most cases, however, both the assumption and the conclusion are wrong. Business managers have every reason to forge links with other units when those links will make their own business more successful. After all, they regularly team up with outside organizations—suppliers, customers, or joint venture partners—and they'll even cooperate with direct competitors if it's in their interest. In the music industry, to take just one example, the four leading companies will often share the same CD-manufacturing plant in countries with insufficient sales to support four separate plants.

If business-unit managers choose not to cooperate, they usually have good reasons. Either they don't believe there are any benefits to be gained or they believe the costs, including the opportunity costs, outweigh the benefits. The fact that unit managers do not always share their bosses' enthusiasm for a proposed linkage is not evidence that they suffer from the not-invented-here syndrome or some other attitudinal ailment. It may simply be they've concluded that no real gains will come of the effort.

At Worldwide Foods, for example, one of the corporate category managers attempted to create an advertising campaign that could be used throughout Europe. The single campaign seemed logical: It would promote a unified brand and would be cheaper to produce than a series of country-specific campaigns. And, because the campaign would be funded at the corporate level, the category manager presumed it would be attractive to the local managers, who would not have to dip into their own budgets. But several local managers resoundingly rejected the corporate advertisements, in many cases choosing to produce their own ads with their own money. The category manager, regarding the rejection as evidence of local-manager intransigence, asked the chief executive to impose the corporate advertising as a matter of policy. "How parochial can you get?" he complained. "They're even willing to pay out good money for their own ads rather than go along with the ones produced by my department."

But discussions with the local managers revealed that their rejection of the corporate campaign was neither reactionary nor irrational. They believed that the corporate campaign ignored real differences in local markets, cultures, and customs. The pan-European advertising campaign would simply not have worked in countries such as Germany, Sweden, and Denmark. "I'd have been delighted to get my advertising for free from corporate," stated the German product manager. "But I'd have paid much more heavily in terms of lost market share if I'd used their campaign. We had to go our own way because the corporate campaign wasn't appropriate for our distribution channels or target customers."

Because the parenting bias encourages corporate executives to discount unit managers' objections, it often leads them to interfere excessively, doing more harm than good. If, for example, unit managers believe that the opportunity costs of a synergy program outweigh its benefits, forcing them to cooperate will make them even more skeptical of synergy. If two unit managers have a bad working relationship, pushing ahead with a coordination committee will simply waste everyone's time. Although headquarters sometimes needs to push units to cooperate—when, for instance, some units are unaware of promising technical or operational innovations in another unit—it should consider intervention a last resort, not a first priority.

Skills Bias. Corporate executives who believe they should intervene are also likely to assume that they have the skills to intervene effectively. All too often, however, they don't. The members of the management team may lack the operating knowledge, personal relationships, or facilitative skills required to achieve meaningful collaboration, or they may simply lack the patience and force of character needed to follow through. In combination with the parenting bias, the skills bias dooms many synergy programs.

In one large retailing group, the chief executive was convinced, rightly, that there were big benefits to be had from improving and sharing logistics skills across the company. Knowing that competitors were gaining advantages from faster, cheaper distribution, he felt, again rightly, that his businesses were not giving this function sufficient attention. He therefore set up a cross-business team to develop, as he put it, "a core corporate competence in logistics." As there was no obvious corporate candidate to lead the team, the chief executive decided to appoint the supply chain manager from the company's biggest business unit, in the belief that he would grow into the role. As it turned out, the manager's lack of state-of-the-art logistics know-how, combined with his poor communication skills, undermined the team's efforts. The whole initiative quickly fell apart. The skills bias is a natural corollary to the parenting bias. If you are convinced that you need to intervene to make synergies happen, you are likely to overlook skills gaps—or at least assume that they can be filled when necessary. Professional pride, moreover, can make it difficult for senior managers to recognize that they and their colleagues lack certain capabilities. But a lack of the right skills can fatally undermine the implementation of any synergy initiative, however big the opportunity. What's more, learning new skills is not easy, especially for senior managers with ingrained ways of doing things. If new and unfamiliar skills are called for, it's a serious error to

underestimate the difficulty of building them. It may be better to pass the opportunity by than to embark on an intervention that can't be successfully implemented.

Upside Bias. Whether or not the intended benefits of a synergy initiative materialize, the initiative can have other, often unforeseen consequences—what we call *knock-on effects*. Knock-on effects can be either beneficial or harmful, and they can take many forms. A corporate-led synergy program may, for example, help or harm an effort to instill employees with greater personal accountability for business performance. It may reinforce or impede an organizational change. It may increase or reduce employee motivation and innovation. Or it may alter the way unit managers think about their businesses and their roles, for better or for worse.

> *The downsides of synergy are every bit as real as the upsides; they are just not seen as clearly.*

In evaluating the potential for synergy, corporate executives tend to focus too much on positive knock-on effects while overlooking the downsides. In large part, this upside bias is a natural accompaniment to the synergy bias: if parent managers are inclined to think the best of synergy, they will look for evidence that backs up their position while avoiding evidence to the contrary. The upside bias is also reinforced by the general belief that cooperation, sharing, and teamwork are intrinsically good for organizations.

In fact, collaboration is not always good for organizations. Sometimes, it's downright bad. In one consulting company, for example, two business units decided to form a joint team to market and deliver a new service for a client. One of the business units did information technology consulting, the other did strategy consulting. One evening, when the team was working late, the strategy consultants suggested that they order in some pizza and charge it to the client. The IT consultants were surprised, since their terms of employment did not allow them to charge such items to client accounts. The conversation then turned to terms and conditions more generally, and soon the IT consultants discovered that the strategy consultants were being paid as much as 50% more and had better fringe benefits. Yet here they were working together doing similar kinds of tasks.

The discovery of the different billing and compensation practices—what became known in the firm as the "pizza problem"—caused dissatisfaction among the IT consultants and friction between the two businesses. An attempt to resolve the problem by moving some IT consultants into the strategy business only made matters worse. Few of the IT consultants achieved high ratings under the strategy unit's evaluation criteria; consequently, many of the firm's best IT consultants ended up quitting.

> *Clarifying the objectives and benefits of a potential synergy initiative is the first and most important discipline in making sound decisions on synergy.*

As the pizza problem shows, viewing cooperation as an unalloyed good often blinds corporate executives to the negative knock-on effects that may arise from synergy programs. They rush to promote cooperative efforts as examples to be emulated throughout the company. Rarely, though, do they kill an otherwise promising initiative for fear that it might erode a unit's morale or distort its culture. Synergy's downsides are every bit as real as its upsides; they're just not seen as clearly.

The best antidotes for these four biases, as for all biases, are awareness and discipline. Simply by acknowledging the tendency to overstate the benefits and feasibility of synergy, executives can better spot distortions in their thinking. They can then put their ideas to the test, posing hard questions to themselves and to their colleagues: What exactly are we trying to achieve, and how big is the benefit? Is there anything to be gained by intervening at the corporate level? What are the possible downsides? The answers to these questions tell them whether and how to act.

Sizing the Prize

The goals of synergy programs tend to be expressed in broad, vague terms: "sharing best practices," "coordinating customer relationships," "cross-fertilizing ideas." In addition to cutting off debate—who, after all, wants to argue against sharing?—such fuzzy language obscures rather than clarifies the real costs and benefits of the

programs. It also tends to undermine implementation, leading to scattershot, unfocused efforts as different parties impose their own views about what needs to be done to reach the imprecisely stated goals.

Clarifying the real objectives and benefits of a potential synergy initiative—"sizing the prize," as we term it—is the first and most important discipline in making sound decisions on synergy. Executives should strive to be as precise as possible about both the type of synergy being sought and its ultimate payoff for the company. Overarching goals should be disaggregated into discrete, well-defined benefits, and then each benefit should be subjected to hard-nosed financial analysis.

At Worldwide Foods, for example, one of the newly appointed category managers found that her initial efforts were being frustrated by the imprecision of the CEO's goal. "Leveraging international brands" covered such a wide range of possible objectives, from standardizing brand positioning, to sharing marketing programs, to coordinating product rollouts, that she found it difficult to reach agreement about tasks and priorities with the various local managers.

During a visit to the company's Argentinean subsidiary, for example, she tried to persuade the local product manager to use a marketing campaign that had been successful in other countries. Dismissing the idea, he tried to shift the discussion. "That campaign wouldn't work in Argentina," he said. "What I would like is advice on new-product-development processes.

"I don't think you understand," the category manager countered. "I'm trying to create an international brand, and that means standardizing marketing across countries."

"No," said the local manager. "If we want to leverage our brands, we need to focus on product development."

Everywhere she went, the category manager found herself mired in similarly fruitless debates. All the local managers defined "leveraging international brands" to mean what they wanted it to mean. There was no common ground on which to build.

Finally, the category manager stepped back and tried to think more clearly about the synergy opportunities. She saw that the broad goal—leveraging international brands—could be broken down into three separate components: making the brand recognizable across borders, reducing duplicated effort, and increasing the flow of market-

Disaggregating a Synergy Program

All too often, executives set overly broad goals for their synergy programs – goals that make good slogans but provide little guidance to managers in the field. By disaggregating a broad goal into more precisely defined objectives, managers will be better able to evaluate costs and benefits and, when appropriate, create concrete implementation plans. Here we see how one broad and ill-defined goal – "leveraging international brands" – was systematically broken down into meaningful components that could be addressed individually.

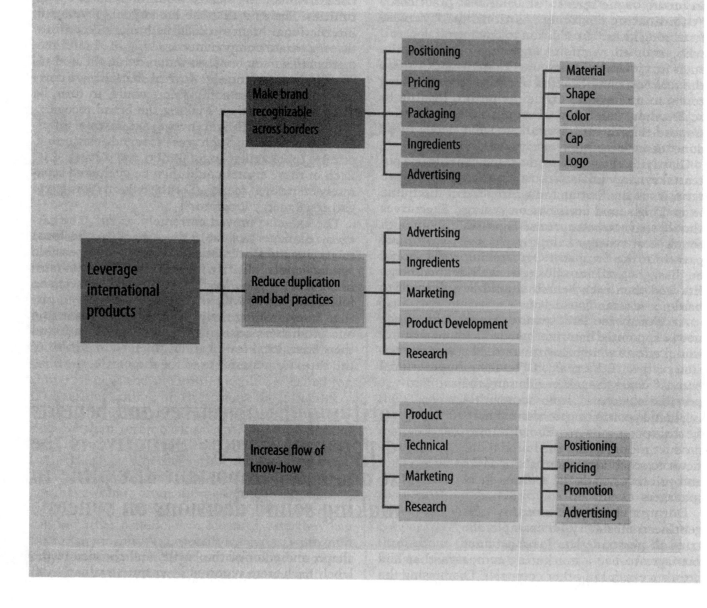

ing know-how. Each of these components could, in turn, be disaggregated further. Making the brand recognizable, for instance, might involve a number of different efforts affecting such areas as brand positioning, pricing, packaging, ingredients, and advertising. Each of these efforts could then be evaluated separately on its own merits. (See the exhibit "Disaggregating a Synergy Program.")

The exercise proved extremely useful. The category manager was able to go back to the local managers and systematically discuss each possible synergy effort, identifying in precise terms its ramifications for each local unit. In some cases, she found she had to take the disaggregation even further. In examining the possibility of standardizing one product's packaging, for example, she found there were local issues about the type and color of the cap; the material used for the bottle; the size, shape, and color of the bottle; and the size of the label. Each item required a separate evaluation of costs and benefits. The type of cap, for example, had a big impact on manufacturing costs—and thus was an attractive candidate for standardization—but some local managers argued that changes in cap design could hinder their marketing efforts. Customers in different countries preferred different cap mechanisms. By carefully balancing the cost savings from economies of scale in manufacturing against the possible loss of sales, the category manager and the local managers were able to reach a consensus on how much to reduce cap variety.

By disaggregating the objectives, the category manager was also able to gain a better understanding of how each effort should be implemented. Standardizing bottle shapes across countries, for example, would require a corporate policy. Otherwise, many of the local managers would go their own way, and economies of scale would be lost. Increasing the flow of technical know-how, by contrast, would be best achieved simply by creating better lines of communication among the technicians in each country. More heavy-handed, top-down initiatives would risk making technical managers resentful and could end up dampening rather than promoting efforts to share expertise.

Once the overall synergy goal has been broken down into its main components, the next step should be to estimate the size of the net benefit in each area. Uncertainties about both the costs and the benefits, however, often lead executives to avoid this obvious task. But without some concrete sense of the payoff, the decision maker will be forced to act on instinct rather than reason. That does not mean that an exhaustive financial analysis has to be performed before anything gets done. In most cases, order-of-magnitude estimates will do. Is the program likely to deliver $1 million, $10 million, or $100 million in added profits? Is the impact on return on sales likely to be half a percentage point, or one percentage point, or five? This is back-of-the-envelope stuff, but we have found that even such rough estimates promote the kind of objective thinking that counters the biases.

The estimated financial benefits don't always tell the whole story, though. They rarely take into full account the opportunity costs of a synergy program, particularly the costs that result from not focusing management's time and effort elsewhere. The difficulty lies in knowing when the opportunity costs are likely to be greater than the benefits. At one consumer-products company, for example, the corporate center was spearheading an initiative to take a product that had been successful in one country and roll it out in a number of other countries. The local managers resisted the idea. They argued that the program would incur considerable opportunity costs, forcing them to divert marketing funds and management time from other local brands. The key to resolving the dispute lay in determining the strategic importance of the planned rollout.

If the rollout was strategically important, either to the units involved or to the overall corporation, then the benefits would likely outweigh the opportunity costs. But if some other more strategically important initiative was likely to be delayed in order to implement the rollout, then the opportunity costs would be greater. After some soul-searching by the units and by corporate marketing, it was agreed that the rollout had low strategic importance, except in three units. Headquarters scaled back the initiative. It would give advice and support to those units that wanted to go ahead with the product launch, but it would not impose a rollout on the other units.

Sizing the prize provides a counterweight to the synergy bias, forcing corporate managers to substantiate their assumptions that the synergy initiatives they propose will create big net benefits. It also helps counter the parenting bias, as the careful analysis of opportunity costs can help corporate managers better understand the source of any unit manager's resistance. And, by leading to the disaggregation of broad initiatives into discrete, well-defined programs, sizing the prize can set the stage for a focused, successful implementation.

Pinpointing the Parenting Opportunity

Even when a synergy prize is found to be sizable, corporate executives should not necessarily rush in. We would in general urge a cautious approach unless the need for corporate intervention is clear and compelling. Corporate executives should start with the assumption that when it makes good commercial sense, the business-unit managers will usually cooperate without the need for corporate involvement.

When is intervention by the corporate parent justified? Only when corporate executives can, first, point to a specific problem that is preventing the unit managers from working together; second, show why their involvement would solve the problem; and third, confirm that they have the skills required to get the job done. In those circumstances, there is what we call a *parenting opportunity*. We have found that genuine parenting opportunities tend to take four forms:

Perception opportunities arise when businesses are unaware of the potential benefits of synergy. The oversight may be caused by a lack of interest, a lack of information, or a lack of personal contacts. The parent can help fill the perception gap by, for example, disseminating important information or by introducing aggressive performance targets that encourage units to look to other units for better ways to operate.

In general, the greater the number of business units in a company, the more likely it is that perception opportunities will arise. ABB, for example, has 5,000 profit centers organized into a number of business areas. In its power transformer area alone, there are more than 30 units. It is clearly impractical for every unit head to know what is going on in each of the other 29 units. The cost of scanning is too high. The area head, therefore, plays an important role in facilitating the information flow, passing on best-practice ideas and introducing managers to one another. In addition, the area head regularly publishes financial and operating information about each business, enabling cross-unit comparisons and helping each business identify units from which it can learn useful lessons.

Evaluation opportunities arise when the businesses fail to assess correctly the costs and benefits of a potential synergy. The businesses' judgments may be biased by previous experiences with similar initiatives, distorted by shortcomings in the processes or methods they use to assess cost-benefit trade-offs, or skewed by their own strategic priorities. In such cases, the parent should play a role in correcting the units' thinking.

The German subsidiary of one multinational company, for example, was fiercely protective of a new product it had developed. It was not only reluctant to help other units develop similar products, it even refused visits from unit and corporate-center technicians. The reason? The German managers did not trust their French and Italian colleagues to price the new product appropriately. They feared those units would not position it as a premium product and, as a result, would undermine price levels throughout Europe, reducing the exceptional profits being generated in the German market. The Germans' fear of the possible downsides clouded their view of the very real upsides. The standoff was resolved only when corporate executives walked the German managers through the cost-benefit calculations step by

step and guaranteed that prices would be kept above a certain minimum in all countries.

Motivation opportunities, which derive from a simple lack of enthusiasm by one or more units, can stop collaboration dead in its tracks. Disincentives come in a number of forms. Unit managers may, for example, believe that the personal costs of cooperating are too high—that their personal empires or bonuses may be put at risk. Or transfer-pricing mechanisms may, in effect, penalize one unit for cooperating with another. Or two unit managers may simply dislike each other, preventing them from working together constructively. Identifying and removing motivational roadblocks, whether they reside in measurement and reward systems or in interpersonal relations, can be one of the toughest, but most valuable, roles for the corporate executive.

In one company, the CEO tried for five years to get the managers responsible for North American and European operations to cooperate. The North American business was run by a headstrong young woman with a strong belief in an open management style. Europe was run by a reserved, traditional Englishman who preferred to operate through formal, hierarchical structures. Both managers privately aspired to run the entire global business, but publicly they argued that there were few overlaps between their businesses that would merit collaboration. After a series of failed attempts to get the businesses to work together, each of which ended in bitter rows and recriminations, the CEO finally lost patience and fired both managers. In their places, he appointed more compatible managers who were able to work together with a great deal of success.

Implementation opportunities open up when unit managers understand and commit to a synergy program but, through a lack of skills, people, or other resources, can't make it happen. The business heads of a European chemical company, for example, agreed that it would be valuable to pool their resources when setting up an Asia-Pacific office in Singapore. Their aim was to improve the effectiveness of their sales efforts in markets that were unfamiliar to all of them. The initiative failed because none of the businesses had a suitable candidate to head the office; the individual appointed was not well connected in the region and lacked the skills needed to open new accounts. If the parent had intervened, by providing a suitable manager from its central staff or training and by coaching the man appointed, the chances of success would have increased greatly.

Thinking through the nature of the parenting opportunity, and hence the role that the parent needs to play, helps corporate executives pinpoint which type of intervention, if any, makes sense. But any decision to intervene should also take account of the skills of the managers involved. Appointing a purchasing specialist to advise the businesses on gaining leverage by pooling their purchases may be an excellent idea, but if the parent does not have the right person to do the job, the new appointment will end up irritating and alienating the businesses. A lack of the right skills can thwart even the best of intentions.

The discipline of pinpointing the parenting opportunity is probably the most valuable contribution that we have to offer to corporate executives in search of synergy. Thinking clearly about why parental intervention is needed can help managers avoid mirages and select suitable interventions. Unless a parenting opportunity can be pinpointed, our advice is not to intervene at all.

Bringing Downsides to Light

The synergy is attractive; the parenting opportunity is clear; the skills are in place. Is it time to act? Not necessarily. A final discipline is in order: looking carefully for any collateral damage that may occur from the synergy program. Because the pursuit of synergy affects the relationship among business units and the relationship between the units and the corporate center—two of the most sensitive relationships in any big company—it can have far-reaching consequences for a company's organization and strategy. If corporate executives overlook the negative knock-on effects, they risk great harm.

Some synergy efforts send the wrong signals to line managers and employees, clouding their understanding of corporate priorities and damaging the credibility of headquarters. When one company set up a coordination committee to seek marketing synergies among its businesses, the unit managers thought the CEO was abandoning his much-communicated goal of promoting stronger accountability at the individual unit level. They saw the corporate committee as a sign of a return to more centralized control. In fact, the shift of accountability to the units remained a core strategic thrust—the synergy initiative was simply a tactical effort intended to save money. In another company, an initiative to coordinate back-office functions distracted employees from the corporation's fundamental strategic goal of becoming more focused on the customer. They began looking inward rather than outward.

Top-down synergy efforts can also undermine employee motivation and innovation. One consumer-goods company, for example, launched an effort to coordinate research and development across its European units. Although the effort appeared to be highly attractive, offering substantial productivity gains, it backfired. A key source of innovation in the company had been the internal competition between the U.K. and the Continental businesses. By establishing a combined research unit, headquarters ended the competition—and the creativity. The effort succeeded in eliminating duplicated effort and achieving economies of scale, but these gains were overshadowed by the unanticipated downsides.

In other cases, cooperation can distort the way unit managers think about their business, leading to wrongheaded decisions. Consider the experience of a diversified retailing company that tried to encourage greater cooperation between its two appliance-retailing businesses. One of the businesses, which focused on selling top-quality appliances at premium prices, was highly profitable. The other, which pursued a pile-it-high, sell-it-cheap strategy, was barely breaking even. The group CEO recognized the differences between the businesses, but he felt certain that synergy could be achieved, particularly in purchasing. To encourage greater cooperation, he put the head of the profitable business in charge of both operations.

The new leader of the two business units initially looked for areas where purchases could be pooled to gain greater leverage over suppliers. But although some small cost reductions were quickly realized, the program soon ran into difficulty: the two businesses were buying different kinds of products, with different price points and different proportions of store-branded items. It was clear that big savings could only be achieved if the two businesses bought identical products. The managers of the struggling unit initially resisted this course, but as they learned more about the product and pricing strategies of their more successful partner, their thinking began to change. Entranced by the wide margins available from selling premium goods, they began shifting their strategy. They bought better-quality products, boosted service levels, and raised prices.

The result was calamitous. The unit's traditional, price-conscious customers went elsewhere for their bargains, while upmarket purchasers stuck with their traditional suppliers. In emulating its sister company, the unit had undermined its business. It had tried to take its product mix upscale without taking account of its competitive positioning. The new strategy was soon reversed, but it took more than a year to remove the inappropriate prod-

A Disciplined Approach to Synergy

By taking a more disciplined approach to achieving synergy, an executive can gain its rewards while avoiding its frustrations. The first step is to evaluate the costs and benefits – to "size the prize." If the net benefit is unclear, more exploration is needed. If it appears to be small, the executive should not pursue the synergy unless the risks of corporate intervention are low. If it seems large, the executive should determine whether an intervention by the corporate parent makes sense. If the parenting opportunity is unclear, the intervention should be restricted to facilitating further exploration. If no parenting opportunity exists, the executive should resist any urge to intervene. If a clear parenting opportunity exists, the executive should tailor the intervention to fit the opportunity while minimizing any downside risks.

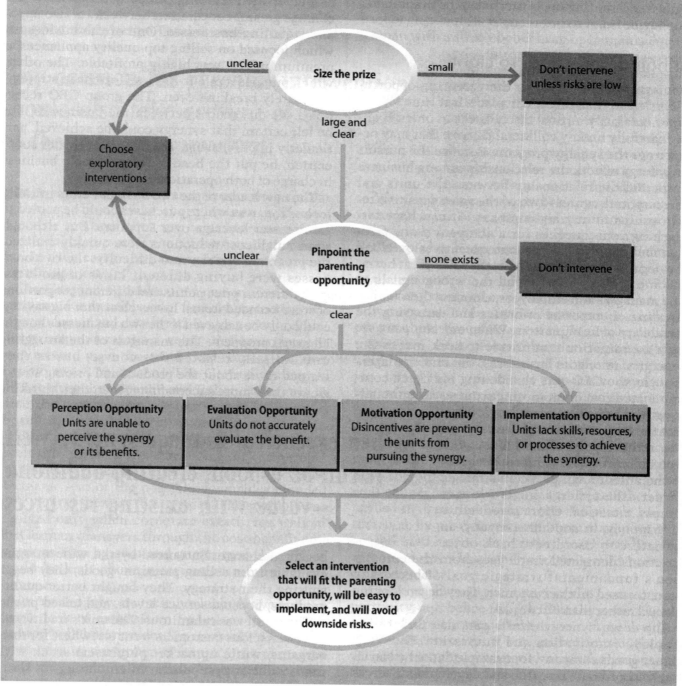

ucts from the supply chain. The unit suffered big losses and major write-offs.

It is never possible to predict all the unintended consequences that can flow from a synergy initiative (or, for that matter, from any management action). But by simply being aware that business-unit collaboration can have big downsides, managers will be able to take a more objective, rigorous view of potential synergy efforts. In some cases, they will be able to structure the effort to avoid many of the potential downsides. In other cases, they will be able to kill proposals that would have created more problems than they solved.

First, Do No Harm

Managers have sometimes accused us of being too skeptical about synergy. They argue that the disciplined approach we recommend—clarifying the real benefits to be gained, examining the potential for parental involvement, taking into account the possible downsides—will mean that fewer initiatives will be launched. And they are right. We believe that corporate managers should be more selective in their synergy interventions. In all too many companies, synergy programs are considered no-brainers. Cooperation and sharing are viewed as ideals that are beyond debate. As we've seen, such assumptions often lead to failed initiatives that waste time and money and, sometimes, severely damage businesses. Real synergy opportunities exist in most large companies, but they are rarely as plentiful as executives assume. The challenge is to distinguish the valid opportunities from the mirages. (See the exhibit "A Disciplined Approach to Synergy.")

In some cases, the analysis of synergy opportunities will raise questions that will be hard to answer. The size of the prize may be uncertain: Will a joint Internet marketing group help or hinder our businesses as they move into electronic commerce? The parenting opportunity may be unclear: Is the German product manager resisting the corporate marketing campaign out of chauvinistic stubbornness, or is the German market really different? The needed skills may be unproven: Will our technical manager be able to lead a coordination committee on production planning? The risks may be hard to pin down: Will a cross-Asian product-development group undermine innovation?

When uncertainty is high, we recommend that corporate executives proceed cautiously. Rather than intervene decisively, they should encourage further exploration. The mechanisms for exploration may be similar to those for implementation—pilot projects, fact-finding visits, temporary assignments and task forces, forums for sharing ideas—but they are very different in intent. An exploratory mechanism is designed simply to collect facts. The end result is a better-informed decision maker. In implementation mode, by contrast, the intention is to change the way managers are working or thinking.

Sometimes, the best course will be to do nothing. The opportunity may be too small to justify the expenditure of management time, there may be no clear reason for the parent to intervene, or the risks may be too high. The thought of doing nothing will, of course, make many executives distinctly uncomfortable. After all, it goes against the grain of the most basic managerial instincts: to take action, to get things done, to create a whole greater than the sum of the parts. Yet executives who are not prepared to countenance a do-nothing outcome should ask themselves whether they are in the throes of biased thinking.

If convinced that the benefit is sizable and the parenting opportunity real, executives can then search for the best kind of corporate intervention. There are usually several possible choices, all with different advantages and drawbacks. Synergies from combined purchasing power, for example, might be achieved by centralizing purchasing, by setting up a purchasing coordination committee, by establishing a corporate advisory center, by creating a cross-unit database on purchases, or by setting corporate standards for terms and conditions. The decision on how to intervene should depend on the nature of the benefit and the parenting opportunity. But it should also take into account the available skills in the organization and the ease with which implementation is likely to take place. And it should seek to minimize the downside risks. Carefully selected interventions are the best way to release truly valuable synergy.

When synergy is well managed, it can be a boon, creating additional value with existing resources. But when it's poorly managed, it can undermine an organization's confidence and erode the trust among business units as well as between the units and the corporate center. Synergy's upsides are real, but so are its downsides. And the only way for managers to avoid the downsides is to rid themselves of the biases that cloud their thinking. When it comes to synergy, executives would be wise to heed the physicians' creed: First, do no harm.

Index

A

achievement, in the knowledge economy, 68–75
adaptability, of organizational goals, 106, 107
advanced infrastructure, 142–143
African spirit hierarchy, 189–192
Albuquerque, New Mexico, clique analysis of mental health services in, 79–84
alignment, with organizational goals, 106, 107
Altman, Robert, 22
Amazon.com, 20, 23, 141–142, 144
ambition, of leaders, 106–108
America OnLine (AOL), 91, 92
ARCO, 185, 187, 188
artificial intelligence, 23
Asian Americans, discrimination and, 27
Asians, leadership style of, versus Caucasians, 195–203
At Home in the Universe (Kaufman), 18
AT&T, 89, 90, 92, 95
autonomy, of teams, 126–127, 130–131

B

Barnes & Noble, 20, 23, 142, 144
Baron, D. P., 88, 94–95
Baytos, Larry, 55–56, 58
BE&K Inc., 185, 186, 188
biotechnology, 148–158
birthrates, 146
bottom-line orientation, 186
Bowlin, Mike R., 185, 187, 188
Boyer, Herbert, 150
Brailsford, Lynn, 57
Brown, Tina, 108
Burke, Edmund, 44
business learning process, 92

C

California, telework program in, 169
capitalism, global, 45–47
careers: parallel, 75; second, 74
categorization, of the disabled, 50–51
Caucasians, leadership style of, versus Asians, 195–203
CEO. *See* chief executive officers
chaebol, 143
change, chaos theory and, 8, 10
chaos theory, and organizational theory, 8–18
characteristic function games, 115
chief administrative officers (CAOs), as political leaders, 109–113
chief executive officers (CEOs), 184–188. *See also* leadership; managers
Chrysler Corporation, 141, 143
citadel mentality, of self-contained organizations, 142–143, 144
clique analysis, 78–87
coalitions, in negotiations, 114–125
cold war, cultural identity and, 44–45
collaboration, 213–224
collectivists, 193–203

communication models, 98
communication, telework and, 169–171
communications industry, as an organizational hybrid, 156
commuting. *See* telework
compassion, of human resource professionals, 188
compatible interests, and coalitions, 116, 120–121, 122, 123
compensation, 155
competition: chaos theory and, 10; managers and, 19–25
competitive advantage, 173–183
complexity theory, 8–18
Confucian work ethic, 65
convergence model, of communication, 98–99
coordinated strategies, and synergy, 215
core competency, 144
core values: of organizations, 57; chaos theory and, 15
creativity, chaos theory and, 13–14
credibility, of gossip, 99, 102
culture: diversity and, 40–47; globalization and, 24; of work groups, 193–203, 212

D

Dandaro, 191
Dante's Dilemma: MBAs From Hell! (Baytos), 55
democracy, global capitalism and, 46–47
demographics, and the future of business, 146, 188
DePrees, Max, 106
destabilization, managers and, 16
destructive spirit, of management, 191
developed world, future of, 146–147
disability, in the workplace, 48–51; telework and, 164, 166
discrimination, in the workplace, 48–51
diversity, 188; chaos theory and, 14; disabled and, 48–54; history and, 40–47
downsizing, 31, 34

E

e-commerce, 22–23
economic context, of stakeholder mapping, 88–89
economic development, geography and, 12
economy, global, 146–147
Eisenhower, Dwight, 70
Eisner, Michael, 16
e-mail protocols, 208, 209–210
employees. *See* workers
employers, immigrant workers and, 26–27
empowerment, leadership and, 107
end-user adopters, 93, 94
Enron, 90
entitlement cues, and coalitions, 115–116, 121–122
entrepreneurs, social, 75
Ernst & Young, 18

ethical issues, 55–58. *See also* values
evolution, of a new organizational form, 148–158
executives. *See* chief executive officers; leadership; managers

F

family spirit, of management, 191
feedback analysis, and personal strengths, 69
feedback loops, chaos theory and, 10–11
flexibility, 23
Ford Motor Company, 142–143, 144
functional organizations, 140, 142
"future shock," 16

G

Galvin, Bob, 13
Gandhi, 106, 107
genealogical processes, 148–158
Genentech, 150
geography, economic development and, 12
Gerstner, Louis, 24
Geuss, Arie De, 14
global teams, 206–210
Global Work: Bridging Distance, Culture and Time (Johansen), 207
globalization, 12; capitalism and, 45–47; chaos theory and, 9–10; competition and, 20–22; e-commerce and, 23
Goodrich, T. Michael, 185, 186, 188
gossip, in the workplace, 98–105
grapevine, versus gossip, 98, 99
grieving, public, and stress, 36

H

Hawking, Stephen, 23
Hays, Dennis, 109–113
health and human service networks, clique analysis of, 78–87
health care industry, as an organizational hybrid, 156
HeartMath, 36–37
Hewlett-Packard, 13, 36
Hispanics, discrimination and, 27
history, cultural diversity and, 40–47
Hock, Dee, 11, 12, 15
hollow organizations, 141, 142, 144
home-based telecommuting, 160, 163–167
human capital, and knowledge organizations, 152–155
human resources management, 152–155; chief executive officers and, 184–188
human rights, global capitalism and, 46
humility, and progress, 61
humor, in the workplace, 212

I

IBM, 24
ICMA Retirement Corp., 185, 186, 187

strengths, personal, and the knowledge economy, 68–69
stress: productivity and, 211–212; on toxic managers, 32–33
stress training, 36–37
structural change, 140–145
Sturken, Craig, 185, 186, 188
surplus capacity, 143
synergy, 213–224

task type, and team performance, 126–137
teams, 152; adaptability and alignment of, 107; chaos theory and, 14, 18; disabled workers and, 51; globalization and, 206–210; organizational renewal and, 60; structure and performance of, 126–137; virtual, 162
technological context, of stakeholder mapping, 91–94
technological revolution, managers and, 21, 22–23
technology, chaos theory and, 9
technology competitors, 88–89, 93–94
technology complementors, 88–89, 94
telecities, 171
telecommuting. *See* telework

teleconferencing, 207, 209–210
TeleService Resources (TSR), 163
telework, 9, 159–172
temporary employment, 144
Third Way, global capitalism and, 46–47
3-Com, 208–209
"3G" model, 14
3M, 14, 15
Tocqueville, Alexis de, 40
Toffler, Alvin, 16
toxic handlers, managers as, 28–37
training programs, 16
transactional leadership, 193–203
transformational leadership, 193–203
transition, managers and, 15
Trojan horse strategy, 92
Truman, Harry, 70
truth spirit, of management, 191
Tucson, Arizona, clique analysis of mental health services in, 79–84
two-party negotiation, 115

underpopulation, 146
unions: immigrants and, 26; telecommuting and, 164
universities, and knowledge firms, 149–157

V

value net framework, for mapping, 88
values, 71–72; chaos theory and, 15; of organizations, 55–58, 72
variable-sum games
vertical integration, and synergy, 215
virtual global teams, 162, 168, 206
virtual organizational design, 140–145
Visa, 11, 12, 13
Volkswagen, 143

W

Wells, Frank, 17
Wheatley, Margaret, 12
women, as leaders, 107–108
work ethic, 64–65
workers: chaos theory and, 15; communication and, 51; disabled, 48–54; gossip and, 98–105; immigrant, 26–27; and the information age, 9; organizational renewal and, 62; resilience of, 15–16; telework and, 159–172; work ethic of, 64–65
work-family balance, telecommuting and, 165–166, 167
work-relatedness, of gossip, 100, 102
WorldCom Corporation, 95

Test Your Knowledge Form

We encourage you to photocopy and use this page as a tool to assess how the articles in **Annual Editions** expand on the information in your textbook. By reflecting on the articles you will gain enhanced text information. You can also access this useful form on a product's book support Web site at **http://www.dushkin.com/online/.**

NAME: _____   DATE: _____

TITLE AND NUMBER OF ARTICLE:
_____

BRIEFLY STATE THE MAIN IDEA OF THIS ARTICLE:
_____

LIST THREE IMPORTANT FACTS THAT THE AUTHOR USES TO SUPPORT THE MAIN IDEA:

_____

WHAT INFORMATION OR IDEAS DISCUSSED IN THIS ARTICLE ARE ALSO DISCUSSED IN YOUR TEXTBOOK OR OTHER READINGS THAT YOU HAVE DONE? LIST THE TEXTBOOK CHAPTERS AND PAGE NUMBERS:

_____

LIST ANY EXAMPLES OF BIAS OR FAULTY REASONING THAT YOU FOUND IN THE ARTICLE:

_____

LIST ANY NEW TERMS/CONCEPTS THAT WERE DISCUSSED IN THE ARTICLE, AND WRITE A SHORT DEFINITION:

_____

ANNUAL EDITIONS revisions depend on two major opinion sources: one is our Advisory Board, listed in the front of this volume, which works with us in scanning the thousands of articles published in the public press each year; the other is you—the person actually using the book. Please help us and the users of the next edition by completing the prepaid article rating form on this page and returning it to us. Thank you for your help!

ANNUAL EDITIONS: Organizational Behavior 01/02

ARTICLE RATING FORM

Here is an opportunity for you to have direct input into the next revision of this volume. We would like you to rate each of the 29 articles listed below, using the following scale:

1. **Excellent: should definitely be retained**
2. **Above average: should probably be retained**
3. **Below average: should probably be deleted**
4. **Poor: should definitely be deleted**

Your ratings will play a vital part in the next revision. So please mail this prepaid form to us just as soon as you complete it. Thanks for your help!

RATING

ARTICLE

1. Shifting Paradigms: From Newton to Chaos
2. The New Frontier: Transformation of Management for the New Millennium
3. Employer Sanctions Against Immigrant Workers
4. The Toxic Handler: Organizational Hero—and Casualty
5. Cultural Diversity and the Dynamism of History
6. Individual and Organizational Accountabilities: Reducing Stereotypes and Prejudice Within the Workplace
7. Walking the Tightrope, Balancing Risks and Gains
8. The Beauty of the Organizational Beast
9. Motivation: The Value of a Work Ethic
10. Guide Lines
11. Managing Oneself
12. Networks Within Networks: Service Link Overlap, Organizational Cliques, and Network Effectiveness
13. Identifying Who Matters: Mapping Key Players in Multiple Environments
14. Passing the Word: Toward a Model of Gossip and Power in the Workplace
15. Leadership A to Z
16. The Manager as Political Leader: A Challenge to Professionalism?

RATING

ARTICLE

17. Interest Alignment and Coalitions in Multiparty Negotiations
18. Team Structure and Performance: Assessing the Mediating Role of Intrateam Process and the Moderating Role of Task Type
19. Structure-Driven Strategy and Virtual Organization Design
20. The Future That Has Already Happened
21. Creating a Hybrid Organizational Form From Parental Blueprints: The Emergence and Evolution of Knowledge Firms
22. Telework: The Advantages and Challenges of Working Here, There, Anywhere, and Anytime
23. Knowledge Transfer: A Basis for Competitive Advantage in Firms
24. What Do CEO's Want From HR?
25. Managing Social Capital
26. Effects of Leadership Style and Followers' Cultural Orientation on Performance in Group and Individual Task Condition
27. Building Teams Across Borders
28. Less Stress, More Productivity
29. Desperately Seeking Synergy

(Continued on next page)

ABOUT YOU

Name _____ Date _____

Are you a teacher? ☐ A student? ☐

Your school's name _____

Department _____

Address _____ City _____ State _____ Zip _____

School telephone # _____

YOUR COMMENTS ARE IMPORTANT TO US !

Please fill in the following information:
For which course did you use this book?
_____

Did you use a text with this *ANNUAL EDITION*? ☐ yes ☐ no
What was the title of the text?
_____

What are your general reactions to the *Annual Editions* concept?
_____

Have you read any particular articles recently that you think should be included in the next edition?
_____

Are there any articles you feel should be replaced in the next edition? Why?
_____

Are there any World Wide Web sites you feel should be included in the next edition? Please annotate.
_____

May we contact you for editorial input? ☐ yes ☐ no
May we quote your comments? ☐ yes ☐ no